UNIFYING EFFECTIVE PSYCHOTHERAPIES

UNIFYING EFFECTIVE PSYCHOTHERAPIES

Tracing the Process of Change

J. SCOTT FRASER

American Psychological Association
Washington, DC

The opinions and statements published are the responsibility of the authors, and such opinions and statements do not necessarily represent the policies of the American Psychological Association.

Published by
American Psychological Association
750 First Street, NE
Washington, DC 20002
www.apa.org

APA Order Department
P.O. Box 92984
Washington, DC 20090-2984
Phone: (800) 374-2721; Direct: (202) 336-5510
Fax: (202) 336-5502; TDD/TTY: (202) 336-6123
Online: http://www.apa.org/pubs/books
E-mail: order@apa.org

In the U.K., Europe, Africa, and the Middle East, copies may be ordered from
Eurospan Group
c/o Turpin Distribution
Pegasus Drive
Stratton Business Park
Biggleswade
Bedfordshire
SG18 8TQ
United Kingdom
Phone: +44 (0) 1767 604972
Fax: +44 (0) 1767 601640
Online: https://www.eurospanbookstore.com/apa
E-mail: eurospan@turpin-distribution.com

Typeset in Goudy by Circle Graphics, Inc., Columbia, MD

Printer: Sheridan Books, Chelsea, MI
Cover Designer: Beth Schlenoff Design, Bethesda, MD

Library of Congress Cataloging-in-Publication Data

Names: Fraser, J. Scott, author. | American Psychological Association, issuing body.
Title: Unifying effective psychotherapies : tracing the process of change / J. Scott Fraser.
Description: Washington, DC : American Psychological Association, [2018] | Includes bibliographical references and index.
Identifiers: LCCN 2017038851 | ISBN 9781433828676 | ISBN 1433828677
Subjects: | MESH: Psychotherapeutic Processes | Treatment Outcome | Evidence-Based Practice
Classification: LCC RC480 | NLM WM 420 | DDC 616.89/14—dc23 LC record available at https://lccn.loc.gov/2017038851

British Library Cataloguing-in-Publication Data
A CIP record is available from the British Library.

Printed in the United States of America
First Edition

http://dx.doi.org/10.1037/0000078-000

10 9 8 7 6 5 4 3 2 1

CONTENTS

ACKNOWLEDGMENTS

I dedicate this work to my wife, Beth, whose love, support, and companionship have always sustained me. This work would also not have been possible without the collaboration of my colleague and close friend, Andy Solovey. His discussions, reading, and editing of Part I of this work were invaluable. I continue to prize his clinical wisdom, clear thinking, and his fondness of laughter. Finally, I want to express my gratitude to Susan Reynolds of APA Books, whose faith and patience in my work have made this book possible, and to Beth Hatch and the editorial staff of APA Books, who helped make this book better.

PROLOGUE

The ancient Celtic spirals on the cover of this book were chosen deliberately. They symbolize the process of change in psychotherapy. Like the concentric patterns in a spiral, our behaviors are cyclical: We tend to respond to a problem in the same way over and over again, whether or not the outcome is what we desire. Our problems may "spiral" out of control! The process of change in psychotherapy involves helping clients change their solution patterns from one cycle of behavior (an unhelpful one) to another (a helpful one). Thus, the spirals represent both the vicious (unhelpful) and virtuous (helpful) cycles of problem formation and resolution.

At the same time, the spirals represent the multiple yet similar effective psychotherapy treatments for the same problem. Often, different treatments with different (even contradictory) theoretical assumptions are known to effectively treat the same problem; yet, like the Celtic spirals, all effective psychotherapies are interconnected, or unified. They share a common process of change. The spirals represent the unification of effective psychotherapies through a process perspective—a time-honored point of view whose time has likely come. This book invites you to trace the process view to discover the connections among effective psychotherapies and a paradigm that fits them all.

UNIFYING EFFECTIVE PSYCHOTHERAPIES

INTRODUCTION

Over the past several decades, there has been a surge of interest in psychotherapy, specifically in the question of whether it actually works and, if so, how it works. As a result of more recent research, there is now little dispute over the fact that psychotherapy works (see Chapter 1); however, there remains intense interest in the question of *how* it works. This book is about unifying effective approaches to psychotherapy—that is, finding the common process underlying all therapeutic change.

The task of unifying effective approaches to different psychological problems would be straightforward if there were clear agreement on the question of "what is effective" in psychotherapy. All effective treatments would link with each other in some basic ways, both theoretically and practically. One treatment approach would have been found most effective for each problem. We would simply note which "active ingredients" to apply to each problem. It would be like arranging the medications in our medicine cabinet.

http://dx.doi.org/10.1037/0000078-001
Unifying Effective Psychotherapies: Tracing the Process of Change, by J. S. Fraser

One medication might be best for headaches, another for body aches, still another for stomach upset, another for itching, and so on.

However, rather than finding one approach that works best for each different psychological problem, we have gradually found that there are many equally effective approaches for a wide range of problems. Furthermore, many of these equally effective treatments grow out of very different premises or theories explaining the nature of problems and their resolution. How can this be? This question has launched an intense debate in the psychotherapy literature. One camp advocates that the specific ingredients of each effective treatment are the key to their effectiveness—and they present strong data to back up their claims. Another group that is just as intense in its positions advocates for common factors present in all effective psychotherapy as the keys to effective treatment—and they present equally compelling research to back up their claims.

Although this debate has raged on, governmental agencies, third-party payers, community agencies, and practice groups have converged in supporting the idea of evidence-supported psychotherapy. Who can argue with the idea that practitioners should offer only those treatments that work for the problems at hand? However, practitioners have found themselves overwhelmed by the growing number of evidence-supported approaches available. How can they learn them all? Furthermore, they have often found many of these approaches not to be a good fit with their own training or personal qualities, expertise, or approach to treatment. What's more, how can practitioners integrate different effective treatments that are often based in such different premises on the nature of problems and their resolution? Things might be different if there were one common definition of problems and their resolution that linked with therapeutic rationales and related procedures for effective treatment. At present, this is simply not the case. Furthermore, the debate rages on over what works in psychotherapy and how to integrate treatments that work, both conceptually and practically. This book aims to address this debate and offer a process for resolution. It argues that the key to unifying effective psychotherapies is tracing the process of change.

The recent intense debates in the literature and in practice are reminiscent of what Thomas Kuhn (1976) termed a *paradigm shift*. Paradigms represent the premises and related practices of fundamental points of view on how to describe, investigate, and practice within a chosen area of interest. For example, we are all immersed in a so-called positivist paradigm, which assumes that we discover the truth from interacting with our experienced world. This view has always tended to work for us. We learn not to bump into walls and to go through doors instead. This positivist paradigm has also fueled our work across sciences, particularly in medical fields, where rational–empirical methods and clinical trials comparing alternate treatments prevail.

The area of psychotherapy has adopted this positivist paradigm and its medical model and clinical trials methods as it has perused answers to what works in psychotherapy. As we have seen, this has recently led to confusion and intense conflict, both in the literature and in practice. However, alternate paradigms commonly coexist. When researchers find increasing examples of data that don't fit the current paradigm's predictions, then confusion and conflict prevail until an alternate point of view emerges that fits the data as well or better. This is the current state of psychotherapy.

The purpose of this book is to uncover a unifying perspective that explains the nature of client problems and their resolution and integrates psychotherapies that work for these problems. My goal is to find out what they all share. Along this journey, I consider an alternative paradigm that has a long history. The alternative paradigm is that of process. I refer to it as a *process of change perspective* because its basic premise is that everything we experience in our lives is in the process of change. As I discuss at length, change often creates distress for our clients, and change is what they seek in therapy. Change is also our goal as practitioners. Therefore, if change is at the heart of clients' problems and the target of effective treatment, then it makes sense to adopt a perspective with change at its core. The thesis of this book is that following the process of change will help integrate effective psychotherapies.

The book comprises three parts. In Part I, I track the journey taken so far by researchers addressing what works in psychotherapy. I look at progress made in research addressing evidence-supported psychotherapy and travel through intense debates to some recent suggestions for resolution (Chapter 1). These suggestions encourage using flexibility and fit in matching the best treatments to problems, clients, and therapists. I then look closer at how to find the "truth" about what works, and I describe alternative views on the nature of human interaction (Chapter 2). I also present a long-standing alternate paradigm, termed a *process view*, that has existed in parallel to the prevailing positivist perspective for centuries. I suggest that this alternate paradigm, which incorporates the nature of change (Chapter 3), the idea of process-based systems (Chapter 4), and the influence of context (Chapter 5), explains the common process underlying all effective psychotherapies.

With this alternate process view in hand, chapters in Part II examine the therapies that work for a range of different psychological and interpersonal problems to see whether the predictions of the process of change view hold up as a "golden thread" running through and connecting them all. I address evidence-supported treatments for anxiety (Chapter 6), depression (Chapter 7), posttraumatic stress disorder (Chapter 8), and the interpersonal problems between couples (Chapter 9) and among family members (Chapter 10). If the predictions of the process of change paradigm fit the data on all of these evidence-supported approaches across all of these problem areas, then a strong case will emerge for using it in the future to unify effective psychotherapies.

Part III translates this process view into clinical practice. Consisting of one final chapter (Chapter 11), this part offers a practical way to apply the process view to clinical practice, and it illustrates this application using a case example through an initial session. It recounts a live demonstration video from the APA Psychotherapy Video series (see *The Process of Change in Integrative Psychotherapy*; http://www.apa.org/pubs/videos/4310979.aspx). In the video, I conduct a consultation session, during which I build a strong working alliance and apply numerous evidence-supported interventions.

This example and these models are just that—only models extrapolated from the process view.[1] It will remain for the field, and for you as a reader, to see whether this alternative view will fit the task of integrating psychotherapies that work.

[1]For this book, several identifying aspects of the cases have been altered to preserve confidentiality.

I

SEARCHING FOR WHAT WORKS IN PSYCHOTHERAPY

1

THE EVOLUTION FROM EMPIRICALLY SUPPORTED THERAPIES TO EVIDENCE-BASED PRACTICES

Various parties are invested in the question of "what works" in psychotherapy. Behavioral health funding agencies, insurance companies, and universities that conduct research and train future therapists all want to know about and endorse the delivery of only the proven best practices for consumers. And who can deny their good intentions? Who among us would want our family physician to choose an unproven treatment over one shown to have evidence of effectiveness? Knowing what is effective is a responsibility not only for therapists but also for agencies and larger entities supporting behavioral health practice. Moreover, certainly we want our universities to research what is most effective and teach future practitioners the best practices available.

This endeavor to find out exactly what is effective in delivering mental health treatment is an important enterprise. It constitutes a journey that psychology has traveled for at least the past 50 years and philosophy and

http://dx.doi.org/10.1037/0000078-002
Unifying Effective Psychotherapies: Tracing the Process of Change, by J. S. Fraser

science for centuries. Every journey needs a map and compass. It also needs a related set of ideas or premises on the nature of the world and our place in it. As behavioral health has forged its place in academia, psychology and related disciplines have adopted the medical model and scientific method as the map and compass to find direction to discover what works. It is important for us to examine this map and compass to see where they have taken us on the journey to discovering what works in psychotherapy. It is also important to look for alternative maps that might get us to our destination even better.

In this chapter, we follow researchers' journeys to discover what works and to find those best practices and evidence-supported treatments advocated by mental health funding agencies and academic training programs. We will run into a number of muddles and puzzles along the way, along with polemic debates about *specific factors* versus *common factors* as the most important contributors to effective treatment. The thesis of this book is that the answer to that debate lies in the middle path between common and specific factors. It is not either–or, but both–and. Moreover, there is a perspective that not only supports this conclusion but also explains both the generation of problems and their resolution. As we will see as we follow this journey to recent trends, researchers are beginning to converge on the same conclusions. Nevertheless, a coherent new paradigm or point of view to explain that middle path is lacking. In this and the next few chapters, I pursue that alternative and unifying point of view. First, however, let us turn to a quick overview of the journey so far to find out "what works."

THE MEDICAL MODEL AND FINDING WHAT WORKS

Psychology and behavioral health disciplines have turned to the biological sciences and the scientific method used in medicine for authentication. As such, this holds behavioral health practitioners to similar practice standards as physicians and other medical practitioners. We expect our physicians to be up to date on the newest and most effective medical procedures. Moreover, we expect them to use only those procedures and medications approved as safe and effective by such regulatory agencies as the U.S. Food and Drug Administration (FDA). We assume that methods and medications have been subjected to randomized clinical trials (RCTs) that have tested their specific effects against both placebos and alternative methods. Given the soundness of this reasoning, it only makes sense to hold behavioral health practitioners to the same standard.

Although these assumptions seem both self-evident and long-standing to us today, they have actually emerged relatively recently in the medical field and even more recently in psychology. It was not until 2001 that the

Institute of Medicine in the United States adopted a definition of *evidence-based medicine* similar to that of the United Kingdom and Canada. The definition urged physicians to base their practice on reviews of evidence. Yet even more recently in 2006, the American Psychological Association (APA) confirmed a definition of evidence-based practice (EBP) in clinical psychology that closely follows the definition of the U.S. Institute of Medicine. Thus, the time-honored practice of basing our clinical work on scientifically collected evidence is actually a relatively new phenomenon. Because psychology and related behavioral health fields have come to adopt guidelines from medicine on EBP, it will be important to know what those guidelines have to say about the evidence they find credible. This logically seems to be the right course for us to follow in determining "what works."

HISTORY OF THE MEDICAL MODEL

Over the past century, the medical model gradually evolved its position on what was effective by determining, through research, what specific medication or practice components worked for specific diagnoses. In the early 1900s, following a philosophy of science that emphasized objectivism, medicine began to emphasize observable results (mainly in the organismic, biological, or materialistic sphere of observations). It looked for *specific effects* to prove that the treatment or medication was more effective than placebos and to fit with the supposed mechanism of change. Again, this seems quite logical. This medical model designated *a target disorder or diagnosis*, with a *specified cause or explanation*, leading to a predicted *mechanism of change*, and then researchers applied a *specific treatment* compared with no treatment or an alternative treatment to see whether that treatment was effective in the predicted way. This approach had wide-ranging positive effects, resulting in vaccines or cures for illnesses that had previously been devastating, such as polio and bacterial infections. It is therefore little wonder that, at the turn of the previous century, behavioral health turned to the medical model and eventually converged with the FDA standards to gather evidence that supported the effectiveness of psychotherapy. Most recently, the criterion for effectiveness used by the FDA to identify an evidence-based drug or intervention as being effective was that at least two studies show a specific treatment to be superior to placebo. This also required strict control of any extraneous factors or variability and demonstration that the effects were due in large part to the specific treatment tested. To most informed readers, this process will be clear and self-evident. Such scientific methods are taught in both undergraduate and graduate studies in related sciences.

Challenges of This Model

In structuring psychotherapy research to fit the medical model, there have been a few significant challenges. The first was to be sure that all participants, both subjects and therapists, were *blind* to the treatments or control or comparison conditions. The second was to be sure that all subjects *had the same diagnosis* with a minimum of confounding problems or alternative diagnoses so the treatment for the specified disorder could be measured against the exact disorder. The third was to be sure that therapists remained as *neutral* as possible to the treatment and performed the treatment exactly as it was to be done. This led to the development of treatment manuals and measures of *fidelity*, or compliance with the treatment manual. Only the specific treatments and not the personality of or other factors associated with the practitioner were the focus of the trial or experiment. Manuals and strict controls around selection for inclusion in studies have been helpful in many ways. Nonetheless, even if therapists are blinded in a study (i.e., are not informed whether they have been assigned the control or experimental treatment), it is nearly impossible for therapists not to know whether they are providing a control versus experimental treatment because most traditional control therapy options have differed significantly from the experimental treatments either in format or in training and supervision practices during the research. For example, control treatments often referred to as *supportive counseling* have usually included no treatment rationale and have prevented therapists from doing things in treatment that they usually do. In addition, therapists in experimental groups usually receive extensive training and supervision during clinical trials, whereas control treatment therapists rarely receive either. Similarly, patients and medical practitioners often figure out that a medication is a placebo because it has no side effects or the patients notice that the practitioner is less enthusiastic or hopeful in administering it. Consequently, there are few or no double-blind conditions in psychotherapy research. Furthermore, it has been more than a little challenging to find and include subjects in these studies who do not have other co-occurring problems that might compromise the purity of the targeted disorder studied. These challenges for psychology and related mental health researchers have bedeviled their work, although their progress has still been commendable.

Yes, but Does Psychotherapy Actually Work?

The first point for us to visit because of this thrust into empiricism and examining what works in psychotherapy is the major question of whether it works at all. Can any psychotherapies meet the challenging scientific standards just outlined? Despite the problems with blinds and co-occurring conditions, the answer is a resounding yes. A visit to the website for the APA's Society of Clinical Psychology (http://www.div12.org/PsychologicalTreatments/faq.html), established in 2008, finds a list of 80 current evidence-supported treatments (ESTs) for a variety of disorders. Since the website's inception, there have been continual updates because of the growing number of treatments added to the list. This is impressive, to say the least. As a result, a number of websites and other listings of specific treatments judged to have varying degrees of empirical support for a range of particular disorders have emerged in recent years (cf. Chambless & Hollon, 1998; the aforementioned Society of Clinical Psychology website; the U.K. National Institute for Health and Care Excellence website, http://www.nice.org.uk; the National Registry of Evidence-Based Programs and Practices website through the Substance Abuse and Mental Health Administration, http://www.nrepp.samhsa.gov).

Furthermore, there is a strong literature backing up these ESTs. An all-time classic text reviewing research on psychotherapy, *Bergin and Garfield's Handbook of Psychotherapy and Behavior Change* (Lambert, 2013), is in its fifth edition (now including qualitative methods in addition to RCTs). Nathan and Gorman's (2015) book on ESTs, *A Guide to Treatments That Work*, is now in its fourth edition, and covers a wide range of ESTs, and is one of Oxford Press's best sellers. Building on this trend, Oxford Press is now publishing an extensive set of treatment manuals and workbooks on specific ESTs for specific disorders in their Treatments That Work series. Finally, David Barlow has now published the fifth edition of the best seller, *Clinical Handbook of Psychological Disorders: A Step-by-Step Treatment Manual* (Barlow, 2014), which offers research and clinical examples of applications of EST approaches to a similarly wide range of specific disorders. (I revisit all of these texts and others in many of the central chapters of this book.) This growing literature has made these ESTs more accessible to practitioners and fueled the movement toward disseminating them into everyday clinical practice.

Given the groundswell of support for different treatments, the proliferation of ESTs, and the success of collections explaining these methods, one wonders whether we have just discovered the map and compass for our journey toward practicing effective psychotherapy. All that seems to remain is for those treatments to be disseminated and taught to community practitioners, while researchers stay busy developing new treatments for the remainder of the disorders commonly encountered in clinical practice. However, this is not the whole story. As it turns out, more challenges to the medical model have arisen. Consequently, a growing parallel perspective fueled by related research has threatened to upset the EST bandwagon.

Growing Challenges

Over the past decade, however, a number of added challenges have arisen for the medical model's philosophy, methods, and results, which we will presently visit. Some of these include the following:

- Some practitioners are finding it difficult if not impossible to keep up with learning and practicing the growing proliferation of evidence-supported approaches.
- Furthermore, those who have tried have often found erosion of competence and subsequent drift away from the protocols learned.
- Because the vast majority of current ESTs have aligned with cognitive behavioral therapy (CBT) methods, many practitioners who have been trained in alternate theoretical and practice methods have found the CBT approach difficult to fit into their own therapeutic style.
- CBT approaches have lent themselves quite well to RCT research methods. Consequently, a large number of academic researchers have strong allegiance to the CBT approach. However, it is important to remember that just because an approach to psychotherapy has not yet been researched for effectiveness does not mean that it is not or will not be found to be effective (American Psychological Association, 2006).
- Advocates for approaches to psychotherapy other than CBT have suggested that the research methods of RCTs do not fit alternative approaches with time-honored traditions such as psychodynamically and humanistic/existential approaches.
- Others have complained that the medical model's focus on specific treatments for specific disorders may not be the right path for studying more complex, human problems.
- Furthermore, medical model research has relegated the client's and the practitioner's contributions to treatment to mere nuisance factors in studying specific treatment effects. Most practitioners are quite aware that characteristics of both therapists and clients and their interaction are often crucial to success or failure.
- A final and possibly even stronger challenge has come from the review and meta-analysis of much of the RCT research from which the ESTs have arisen. Not only is there growing evidence of the equivalence of numerous alternative treatment approaches, there is equally compelling evidence that common

therapeutic factors, shared by all treatment approaches, account for larger contributions to the success of psychotherapy than specific ingredients measured in RCTs.

BURSTING THE EST BUBBLE

The problem with hitching our wagons to the medical model is that, on closer analysis, the promise of finding the right psychotherapy treatments for specific diagnoses has been more of an illusion than reality. A now famous and widely used phrase coined by Sol Rosenzweig back in 1936 has come to fruition in the light of more recent analyses of psychotherapy research. Reviewing what he referred to as some implicit common factors in diverse methods of psychotherapy, Rosenzweig used a quote from the children's story, *Alice's Adventures in Wonderland:* "At last the Dodo said, 'Everybody has won and all must have prizes.'" He suggested that "all methods of therapy when competently used are equally successful" (Rosenzweig, 1936, p. 143). This has come to be referred to as "the dodo bird effect" and refers to the observation that the most likely reason that most bona fide approaches to psychotherapy have been found to be effective is that they share a set of common factors. As opposed to the supposed specific effects of treatment approaches, such as cognitive restructuring in CBT, common factors have more to do with qualities of the relationship between clients and therapists in treatment. More specifically, common factors refer to the *therapeutic alliance*, *agreement on goals and tasks of treatments*, and related agreements on *explanations of client problems* and *treatment rationales*. A widely referenced summary by Michael Lambert (1992) summarized his overview of the research data to that date. His nonstatistical review of the literature suggested that the largest influence on client improvement (40%) came from what he termed *extratherapeutic change*, such as client strengths, fortuitous events, and social support that help in recovery despite psychotherapy. The next most influential (30%) was likely common factors, including such things as empathy, warmth, acceptance, encouragement of risk taking, and so on. Finally, he estimated the influence of *therapeutic techniques* unique to specific therapies to be about 15%, which was about equal to the influence of *expectancy* or *placebo* effects (15%) relating to the hope generated by being in treatment and a belief in the treatment rationale and related procedures.[1] Nine years later, upon concluding his review

[1]Lambert's analysis was criticized because it was based on his observations and so was not empirical. Wampold used meta-analytic techniques to put Lambert's analysis to the test. Lambert's analysis is noted here because he explicated what Wampold listed as general effects.

of the literature based on multiple meta-analyses, Wampold (2001) offered an even more dramatic reading of the amount of variance accounted for by specific and general effects. He noted that the influence of specific effects (read specific therapeutic techniques and protocols) was at most 8%. The second edition of this book (Wampold & Imel, 2015a) found little change in those estimations. These are powerful challenges to our assumptions about ESTs. They have also fueled intense debates between specific versus common factor advocates.

The Move From ESTs to EBPs

The challenge to the RCT approach noted earlier and its resulting lists of best practices has, as one might expect, ignited a heated and ongoing debate between the so-called specific factor camp of ESTs and the common factor camp. Although the debate remains unresolved, there is growing acknowledgment of the limitations of a pure focus on treatment methods and specific effects. Consequently, the field is moving toward broader definitions of effective psychotherapy practices, or "what works." These newer definitions now include both elements of the practitioner as well as the client as they interact with specific treatment procedures. Although still within the medical model, behavioral science researchers are becoming mindful of EST criticisms and are moving toward including more of the elements obviously present in any psychotherapy situation. In so doing, however, they continue to take a major page from medicine's playbook. For example, the Institute of Medicine (2001) defined evidence-based medicine as "the integration of best research evidence with clinical expertise and patient values" (p. 147). This definition introduced both the patient and practitioner into the medical procedures and thus took a great step forward toward recognizing the input and influence of both sets of participants in the healing enterprise. The APA (2006) Presidential Task Force on Evidence-Based Practice made a similar positive step when it paralleled this advance in medicine and defined EBP in psychology as "the integration of the best available research with clinical expertise in the context of patient characteristics, culture, and preferences" (p. 273). Recognizing that research will not always address the real-world needs of the practitioner, the Task Force declared:

> Major issues in integrating research in day-to-day practice include (a) the relative weight to place on different research methods; (b) the representativeness of research samples; (c) whether research results should guide practice at the level of principles of change, intervention strategies, or specific protocols; (d) the generalizability and transportability of treatments supported in controlled research to clinical practice settings; (e) the extent to which judgments can be made about treatments of

choice when the number and duration of treatments tested has been limited; (f) the degree to which the results of efficacy and effectiveness research can be generalized from primarily White samples to minority and marginalized populations. (p. 274)

This APA Task Force also took pains to identify a wide range of appropriate sources of research methods in addition to RCTs, including clinical observation, qualitative research, systematic case studies, single-case experimental designs, public health and ethnographic research, process–outcome studies, effectiveness research in naturalistic settings, and RCTs and meta-analyses. This broadened both the definition of what combines to yield effective treatment and what constitutes good clinical evidence. It opened consideration for examining the effects of participants in therapy—both clients and therapists (including expertise, values, and diversity variables, among other elements). These three factors in the EBP definition—best available research, clinical expertise, and patient characteristics/culture/preferences—have come to be referred to as the three pillars or the three legs of the therapeutic stool.

The central intersection of all three of these elements characterizes the area of EBP decision-making. This represents an impressive advance from the EST approach, which focuses on only one element (research on the specific factors of a treatment). However, much of the research to date still focuses on the specific treatment element of this definition. What constitutes the best available research is still mainly defined by RCTs, with funding sources for research continuing to stipulate RCTs as the gold standard of good research. Thus, although the new definition of EBP is broader, there is room for a more inclusive definition. The evolution toward a more inclusive definition is still new and proceeding relatively slowly.

The Emergence of Common Factors as an Alternative Force

Building on the growing research evidence emphasizing the influence of so-called common factors, as indicated by Lambert (1992) and Wampold (2001; Wampold & Imel, 2015a), there has emerged an equally strong and competing voice calling attention to the influence of factors common across the entire spectrum of psychotherapy. This competing voice might be termed *evidence-supported relationships*. On the basis of the collected efforts of the APA's Division of Psychotherapy, an overview of the research evidence supporting common factors in psychotherapy was published. Now in its second edition, *Psychotherapy Relationships That Work: Evidence-Based Responsiveness* (Norcross, 2011) offers an accessible overview of research supporting the influence of the *therapeutic alliance*, *empathy*, *goal consensus*, *collaboration*, *client state of change*, and a range of other factors found to be quite powerful in accounting for client success in psychotherapy. Another influential edited book emphasizing the power of common factors in psychotherapy is *The Heart and Soul of Change: What Works in Therapy*, now also in its second edition (Duncan, Miller, Wampold, & Hubble, 2010; Hubble, Duncan, & Miller, 1999). As with the Norcross text, this easily accessible work reviews the empirical case for common factors, the place of client factors in outcome, the influence of the relationship, the influence of hope, the contributions of therapeutic models, and the influence of gaining feedback, among other general factors influencing success in psychotherapy.

The Place of Theory and Rationale

Within the couple and family therapy area, another relatively recent and popular book, *Common Factors in Couple and Family Therapy: The Overlooked Foundation for Effective Practice* (Sprenkle, Davis, & Lebow, 2009), added another dimension to the common versus specific factors debate. Here, the authors indicated that extreme common factor arguments wrongly suggest that methods and techniques are unnecessary to therapy outcomes. Instead, the authors put forth a moderated common factors approach to treatment. Arguing that all common factors occur within the context of a given, agreed-on therapeutic rationale or approach, their review of research in systemic treatment opts for a middle path that combines common factors and treatment rationales.

Moreover, in following the framework of Jerome Frank, there is a growing agreement that common factors cannot stand alone (cf. Fraser, Grove, Lee, Greene, & Solovey, 2014; Fraser, Solovey, Grove, Lee, & Greene, 2012; Laska, Gurman, & Wampold, 2014; Laska & Wampold, 2014; Sprenkle, Davis, & Lebow, 2009; Wampold et al., 2010; Wampold & Imel, 2015a). They are always embedded within and facilitated by a given agreed-on therapeutic rationale. Therapy without an explanation is not sufficient. Laska and Wampold (2014) reiterated this point: "One of the aspects of all treatments is that the patients are provided an explanation for their disorder and that there are treatment actions consistent with that explanation" (p. 520). The particular theoretical explanation or rationale used is most likely to emerge from a best fit between the perspectives of the client and therapist. Agreement on tasks and goals of therapy is highly correlated with successful treatment facilitated by agreement on a therapeutic rationale to explain the nature of the client problem and imply a direction to move toward resolution. In fact, these elements align with what C. R. Snyder, Michael, and Cheavens (1999) defined as *hope*. That is, the provision of a therapeutic rationale that is accepted by both therapist and client to explain the nature of the problem, imply a direction in which to go, and enlist client motivation to take action in that direction. Readers familiar with Jerome Frank's work may recall his suggestion that the idea of *renormalization* or *instilling hope* in clients is a core outcome in all successful psychotherapy. If hope is a core outcome, it makes sense that there are multiple equally useful therapeutic rationales for practitioners to use. This is because a criterion for success is whether the client takes the rationale as hopeful versus correct. This helps to explain what we have seen in the literature on equivalence of approaches, or the dodo bird effect. Whether CBT, interpersonal therapy, emotion focused therapy, or another rationale works best is less dependent on the "truth" of the approach and its assumptions on the mechanisms of change than the *fit* of the rationale as judged by participants in the treatment. As we have noted, there is growing agreement that most effective treatment includes *flexibility* to adapt the treatment to the characteristics of the patient (Beutler & Clarkin, 2014; Beutler, Harwood, Kimpara, Verdirame, & Blau, 2011; Beutler, Harwood, Michelson, Song, & Holman, 2011a, 2011b). This call for flexibility and fit is even more relevant as we consider that most of the evidence-based research, until recently, has been conducted in the United States with largely homogeneous Caucasian populations. There is a considerable literature noting the struggle in disseminating ESTs to diverse populations and to other cultures, with the general conclusion that there is poor fit (Benish, Quintana, & Wampold, 2011; Huey, Tilley, Jones, & Smith, 2014). As Laska and Wampold concluded,

> Given the substantial amount of evidence on the importance of therapist and patient factors on outcome (Baldwin & Imel, 2013; Bohart & Wade, 2013; Lambert, 2013), and the emphasis of the APA's (2006) Presidential Task Force on Evidence-Based Practice (2006) has placed on these factors, one conclusion that results from the CF [common factors] approach is a greater emphasis on ideographic methods and individualized evidence-based practice. (p. 522)

In a similar vein, the role of theory and treatment rationale in guiding therapy remains crucial in effective psychotherapy. A coherent rationale builds strong working alliances. Clear agreement on goals and tasks of treatment engages clients and therapists in productive actions toward successful problem resolution and increased quality of life. Given this, therapists might choose their theory based on what they find comfortable and appealing and *what fits* with their worldview. Nevertheless, therapists would do well to learn a range of treatment alternatives to *become flexible* and *adaptive* to the needs of clients. Following the perspective of Jerome Frank (Frank & Frank, 1991), a clinician's theory need not be "true" in a strict scientific sense. Instead, it should be *coherent* and *believable* for both therapist and clients, resulting in energetic commitment of both to the treatment endeavor. All of these recommendations, along with others from the common factors domain, have impressive research support.

In addition, in a special section of the January 2014 issue of the journal *Psychotherapy*, a set of points and counterpoint position papers appeared that staked claims to positions on the nature of effective therapy. This time, the lead article was titled "Expanding the Lens of Evidence-Based Practice in Psychotherapy: A Common Factors Perspective" (Laska, Gurman, & Wampold, 2014). This work does not argue against disseminating ESTs. What the authors urged is the inclusion of patient characteristics and therapist expertise, therapist variables, and client preference in the formula for what constitutes effective psychotherapy. To this end, they saw what they termed the common factors approach as consistent with the definition of EBP discussed earlier. Their common factors approach suggests that "(a) most therapists achieve commendable and desirable outcomes, (b) improvement will follow from managing outcomes, (c) *any* variable shown to influence outcome is scientifically important, and therefore (d) data-gathering efforts should focus on changing any therapist behaviors that influence outcome" (Laska et al., 2014, p. 468). Although different ESTs are often based on different theories and mechanisms of change, they saw the trend toward more *unified treatment protocols* and *transdiagnostic treatment approaches* as nice developments (cf. Barlow, Allen, & Choate, 2016; Moses & Barlow, 2006, for mood disorders, including anxiety and depression). Following the lead of Jerome Frank's classic work (Frank & Frank, 1991), they viewed all therapy as a *socially constructed and mediated healing practice*. They followed this by describing the common factor model's factors that are both necessary and sufficient for change as follows:

> (a) an emotionally charged bond between the therapist and patient, (b) a confiding healing setting in which therapy takes place, (c) a therapist who provides a psychologically derived and culturally embedded explanation for emotional distress, (d) an explanation that is adaptive (i.e., provides viable and believable options for overcoming specific difficulties) and is accepted by the patient, and (e) a set of procedures or rituals engaged by the patient and therapist that leads the patient to enact something that is positive, helpful, or adaptive. (Laska et al., 2014, p. 469)

This definition of psychotherapy is built on Frank's views. Supported by the current literature, it is another step broader than the APA definition of EBP. It allows considerably more flexibility in practice while constraining and defining that practice within the boundaries of what has been termed bona fide psychological treatment. The authors suggested that both common factor and specific factor approaches need integration. In fact, they ended their article as follows: "Rather than argue about which perspective is more or less scientific, we issue the following challenge: How can we integrate the two models of empirical inquiry in a way that the field can more forward?" (Laska et al., 2014, p. 476). (Yet the reason why agreement on problem definition and treatment rationale, goals, and procedures is so important remains unclear. As we will soon see, the process of change perspective goes a long way toward doing this.)

However, despite movement toward a common ground, there is still much space between proponents of both camps. Norcross, Beutler, and Levant (2006) put out another well-framed debate among advocates of opposing sides of the battle, *Evidence-Based Practices in Mental Health: Debate and Dialogue on the Fundamental Questions*. They invited authors to contribute position papers on each side of a range of critical questions and then offer rejoinders to their counterpart. This offered another nice window into the state of the debate. Beginning with the question of what qualifies as evidence of effective practice, the chapter by Kihlstrom (2006) makes the traditional argument that RCTs should remain the gold standard for psychotherapy research. However, a chapter by Reed (2006) brings in the argument that clinical expertise needs to be acknowledged in the formula. He referred to the definition of clinical expertise by Goodheart (2004), who emphasized that expert therapists have the ability to integrate knowledge of the literature with their experience, their skills in relationship building, decision-making, critical thinking, and personal self-assessment all within a fluid, often ambiguous, and changing situation. According to Reed,

> Given that other factors are likely to be more important in determining outcome—that is, the patient, the clinician, the culture and context, the therapeutic relationship, and the match between patient and treatment—a practice that is truly evidence-based has to consider all of them. (p. 21)

This is a tall order, but it brings in a compelling and realistic reflection of what most experienced therapists understand. It also parallels the APA definition of EBP noted earlier. Messer (2006) went on in his position paper to refine this argument by emphasizing the importance of patient values and preferences. Noting that the best current research and discussion does not support cookbook, one-size-fits-all approaches, he stated that it is often more important to know what kind of client has the problem than what kind of disorder the patient has. From this view, fitting treatment rationales and procedures to patients' beliefs, values, and expectations of therapy is critical to finding the best fit for patients and key to building strong therapeutic working alliances.

Yet the battle continues. In their position papers opposing these arguments on common factors and fit, Addis and Cardemil (2006) made a strong argument for how psychotherapy manuals can improve outcomes by standardizing what has been found to work and enabling practitioners to learn and apply that knowledge. This follows the points noted earlier related to RCTs and ESTs. However, in their related counterpoint position paper, Duncan and Miller (2006) pointed out that while manuals can aid in effectively training practitioners in a given approach, there is compelling research showing that there is often no improvement in treatment outcome from the use of a manual. Additionally, there is often a negative correlation between strict manual adherence and outcome. Consequently, they argued, as did Wampold earlier, that therapist flexibility and fit to client values and expectations frequently defines the core of effective treatment. They went on to emphasize an approach they termed *practice-based evidence* (a nice turn from evidence-based practice). Here, clinicians and researchers pay closer attention to feedback on client progress and adjust their approach as needed to maintain client success (for more details, see the special issue of *Psychotherapy*, "Progress Monitoring and Feedback," 2015 [volume 52, issue 4]). Furthermore, identifying clinicians who tend to be generally successful across client problems, or with particular types of clients, and studying them, may hold as much or more promise in learning what works best in effective treatment.

Taking the extreme pole of the debate, Wampold (2006) put forward a position arguing that there is "not a scintilla of evidence to support empirically supported treatments as more effective than other treatments" (p. 299). Updating the research reviews of his 2001 analysis, he deconstructed the research methods used to support ESTs and turned the argument toward other largely ignored elements of effective treatments, such as therapist effects. (See Castonguay & Hill, 2017, for an outstanding edited volume on how and why some therapists are better than others.)

Turning to Principles of Therapeutic Change

As you can see, all of this debate has turned the discussion in various directions. Even the arguments for the importance of relationship and other related common factors may have inadvertently done no more than feed into the already polemic debates of either–or positions on what works in psychotherapy. In essence, the either–or position of the debate between specific factor ESTs and common factor camps is conceptually flawed and empirically untenable. Castonguay and Beutler (2006a) stated,

> Despite the best intention of its proponents, we also believe that by delineating separate lists of "empirically supported treatments" (EST; Chambless & Ollendick, 2001; Nathan & Gorman, 2002) and "empirically supported therapeutic relationships" (ESTR; Norcross, 2002), past APA Task Forces may have inadvertently fueled this controversy. (p. 353)

These two authors sought to bridge this gap by tasking a number of experts from each camp to collaborate in searching the literature and synthesizing what they termed *common and unique principles of therapeutic change*. Representing the work of a Task Force jointly sponsored by the APA's Division 12 (Society for Clinical Psychology) and the North American Society for Psychotherapy Research, they edited a work titled *Principles of Therapeutic Change That Work* (Castonguay & Beutler, 2006b). The details of their analysis are far beyond what may be covered here, but they concluded that the Task Force identified 61 principles of therapeutic change, with several overlapping, and 26 derived from treatment of at least two of the four problem areas analyzed. The editors suggested that it is not appropriate to refer to these principles as empirically supported, but rather they are best thought of as being "empirically derived" from the literature and inspection of research on supported treatment manuals. This is still quite a list of principles for practitioners to understand and use; nonetheless, the authors saw this as a step in the right direction. They suggested that

> successful implementation of effective techniques is based on, or facilitated by, a collaborative process, well-established relationship, or empathic and genuine attitude of the therapist [and] those principles related to these three domains are in a constant flux of interaction and interdependence. (Castonguay & Beutler, 2006b, p. 368)

They concluded that none of these three sets of therapeutic factors, or pillars of EBP, is sufficient on its own. This is quite an evolution from the recent polarities of the specific factors–common factors debates! Broader definitions of "what works" in psychotherapy are emerging.

The Current State of "What Works"

This discussion of "what works" in psychotherapy would not be complete without looking further at the term *what*. Stiles, Honos-Webb, and Surko (1998) introduced the concept of *responsiveness* to address this question. They defined responsiveness as the interaction between clients and therapists as they actively try to find a solution to the problem at hand. This includes concepts of bidirectional causation and feedback loops that I address in future chapters. From this perspective, therapy is always a flexible process from moment to moment in a session as well as across sessions and treatment as a whole. Rather than being preplanned, content and process in treatment emerge as sessions advance. They suggested that all effective treatments include responsiveness to the context of client and therapist age, gender, ethnicity socioeconomic status, and the nature of the problem as well as fitting and choosing treatment approaches and interventions. They pointed out that, contrary to the supposed rigidity of most treatment manuals, most manuals demand skill and clinical judgment about when and how to apply the specified techniques. They recommended close attention to the way clients respond to interventions and to the developing context of therapy, and they suggested different tactics based on clients' emerging requirements (e.g., Beck, Rush, Shaw, & Emery, 1979; Greenberg, Rice, & Elliott, 1993; Klerman, Weissman, Rounsaville, & Chevron, 1984). Terms such as *trial and error, adapting to patients' personal style and typical coping techniques, adapting to clients' level of problem urgency and severity*, and *finding an approach "that really fits"* are all included in Beck et al.'s (1979) manual under "selection of targets and techniques." In their more recent review of research on responsiveness since the early introduction of the concept, Kramer and Stiles (2015) concluded that

> a psychotherapeutic intervention (the "what") is not a coherent entity but a fluid, adaptive process that stands in the way of the straightforward answers everyone would like. Responsiveness appears in the present review as an underlying principle of human interaction that characterizes all psychotherapy approaches. (p. 289)

Therefore, the "what" of the question "what works?" refers most appropriately to an ongoing flow of adaptive process than to a specific or fixed approach at any given time. This fits with what I will presently describe as a *process perspective*.

With all of the positions on the debate about what works in psychotherapy in mind, what conclusions may we draw? The overall conclusion remains that psychotherapy is resoundingly effective. In a brief article summarizing findings from the second edition of *The Great Psychotherapy Debate*, Wampold and Imel (2015a) offered a set of conclusions, which they said "we know for sure" or are relatively sure about regarding the effects of psychotherapy. They concluded the following:

- Psychotherapy is remarkably effective. The effects of psychotherapy are greater than the effects of many medical practices, including flu vaccines, most interventions in cardiology, and treatments for asthma, some of which are very expensive and have significant side effects. Psychotherapy is as effective as medication for most mental disorders, without the side effects. As well, psychotherapy is longer lasting than medications (i.e., lower relapse rates after treatment is discontinued) and is less resistant to additional courses of treatment.
- Therapists in practice achieve outcomes comparable to those achieved in RCTs. Indeed, they seem to achieve the same benefits, in fewer sessions, than in clinical trials.

- Factors, such as the working alliance, empathy, expectations, psychoeducation about the disorder, and other so-called "common factors" are robustly related to outcome. Moreover, and importantly, those therapists who can form an alliance with a range of patients, have a sophisticated set of facilitative interpersonal skills, worry about their effectiveness, and make deliberate efforts to improve are the therapists who achieve better outcomes.
- Providing information about client progress to the therapist and the client improves the quality of psychotherapy, primarily by reducing the likelihood of treatment failures for clients not making expected progress. Monitoring client progress to improve the quality of services, which is often called practice-based evidence, is becoming more widely used.
- Adherence to a treatment protocol is not related to outcome. That is, therapists who adhere to what is expected in a treatment do not get better outcomes than therapists who deviate from the manual. Actually, it appears that therapists who, regardless of how the client responds, sticks to the treatment have poorer outcomes. It is those therapists who flexibly provide a treatment who achieve the best outcomes.
- It appears that "treatments" with no structure are less effective than treatments that have deliberate actions focused on the client's problems. Therapists delivering non-structured treatments are not able to provide the client an explanation for his or her distress nor explain how the work the client does in therapy will help the client with his or problems, two aspects of therapy that seem to be important for producing benefits. (Wampold & Imel, 2015b)

There is now no doubt that psychotherapy can and does work, but exactly how the process comes together is still evolving. Evidence supports a growing number of approaches to treatment, such as CBT, interpersonal therapy, emotion-focused therapy, behavioral activation, prolonged exposure, and mindfulness-based therapy. Yet the field is moving toward agreement that effective treatment is not all about techniques or one theoretical rationale. It must include considerations such as the qualities and expertise of the therapist; the qualities, values, cultures, and preferences of clients; and consideration of the best evidence we have on what has been found to work with different problems. To this end, the field is moving toward addressing context and clarifying the nature of change, theories of change, and identifying principles of change. Although there is optimism that the future will allow us to identify these unifying concepts and practices, the outcome remains to be seen.

Addressing the context of the patient, including culture, language, values, and other factors, as well as that of the therapist, is emerging as crucial to designing and delivering effective treatment. This leads us to a growing conclusion that converges on something similar to the three pillars (or Venn diagram of three intersecting circles) of EBP that address the best available research intersecting with clinical expertise and patient characteristics. Above all, researchers and theoreticians are calling for greater clarity on ideas about mechanisms of change that may help to unify psychotherapies that work. This, again, is the focus of this book.

2

CHANGING PARADIGMS: WHAT'S IN A POINT OF VIEW?

What we have learned in our answer to the question of "what works" in psychotherapy is that we need to expand our views. At the most fundamental level, we need to reexamine our view on the nature of humankind, on the nature of change, and on how to approach knowledge of our world and our relationships within it. Most of our recent approach to gaining knowledge in the area of psychotherapy and related mental health areas has been based on a rational–empirical or positivist perspective of the scientific method—the basis of the medical model. We have gained much by looking through the lens of the scientific method, with its quantitative methods and structural assumptions. However, as Chapter 1 described, this lens also comes with a set of blinders that can restrict our field of vision.

Questions remain, such as how it is that so many different treatments, with different assumptions on the cause of problems, are equally effective. What, if anything, do they share in common? Another key question remains

http://dx.doi.org/10.1037/0000078-003
Unifying Effective Psychotherapies: Tracing the Process of Change, by J. S. Fraser

as to whether specific factors or common factors contribute most to effective psychotherapies. How and why do they come together? The data present such conflicts on this issue. Are these conflicts the hallmarks of paradigm clash? How can these questions be resolved?

Because of the limitations of the medical model, the field of psychotherapy is in need of a new paradigm or compass and map for understanding how psychotherapy works. This alternate viewpoint comes in the form of a metatheory, referred to as a *process view*. This chapter takes this view as its focus. I first visit the process view historically and then in the way I am referring to it now. Next, I place it in context with its long-term rival, rational empiricism. I then consider the work of Kuhn (1976) regarding paradigms and apply it to the need for paradigm shift in psychotherapy. In concluding, I return to some of our original questions on how and why there are so many effective psychotherapies for depression, as a case in point.

ORIGINS OF THE PROCESS VIEW

There appears to be a growing chorus in professional journals and publications calling for a new paradigm. At the same time, a case for a new paradigm has not been established. However, such a paradigm on the nature of the way things are and the philosophy of science already exists and has a long, proud tradition. Furthermore, this alternative view promises some practical, down-to-earth guidance for both theoreticians and clinicians on psychotherapy research and practice. This alternate viewpoint comes in the form of a metatheory that we refer to as the process view.

In early 1924, 63-year-old Alfred North Whitehead (1861–1947) received an invitation to join the faculty of philosophy at Harvard University. He continued to teach at Harvard until age 76, retiring in June 1937. Whitehead was one of the most prominent developers and proponents of an alternate process philosophy. Thus, it is interesting to note that Whitehead achieved this level of professional success—joining the faculty at Harvard—at roughly the same time that Charles Peirce and William James were developing the pragmatic and radically empirical perspective. Whereas Whitehead's process view suggested that reality was constantly changing and that truth was variable and an equal product of the observer's questions and methods, the empirical model proposed a more stable version of reality, a reality verifiable by careful experimentation and agreed upon methods. As Mesle (2008), a major and interpreter of Whitehead's process relational philosophy, wrote, "Unfortunately, Whitehead was developing his profoundly new vision of the world just as Anglo-American philosophers were throwing out the metaphysical baby with the bath water" (p. 4).

The empirical perspective is essentially what we have all been taught as the scientific method of experimentation and verifiable fact-finding. Such empirical models were widely accepted and successful across most other domains of science. The pragmatic and empirical perspective thus carried much more sway in affirming psychology as a verified scientific discipline that was to proliferate across universities and faculty across the nation and then around the world. The developing process view was just an interesting broad philosophical view at best, and at worst, vague metaphysics.

Of course, positivism, logical positivist, and empirical perspectives have served psychology and sociology well. Simply speaking, empiricism represents the scientific method of discovering verifiable facts about the outside world. Truth is based on observation in positivism. Logical positivism includes the role of deductive logic and language. It seeks the truth in the external world through verifiable experimentation. These approaches have helped the social sciences uncover truths. So why consider a process perspective? How could one ever determine truth in social sciences based on such a shifting definition of the subject? The answer to this question is the focus of this chapter. First, however, a basic overview of the process perspective is in order.

BASIC OVERVIEW OF THE PROCESS PERSPECTIVE

Nicholas Rescher (1996) said about a process perspective that "the guiding idea of this approach is that natural existence consists in and is best understood in terms of *processes* rather than *things*—of modes of change rather than fixed stabilities" (p. 7, emphasis added). This idea is not new. In ancient Greece, Heraclitus launched this approach in his dictum "everything flows." Later, Leibniz (1646–1717) became a proponent of process theory in modern philosophy, suggesting that all things are mere phenomena and not unified substances at all. Hegel (1770–1831), through his dialectic view of the interaction of opposites, argued that whatever exists in the world of things or ideas is never stable but always in the process of evolving and changing. Nonetheless, although this recent history includes other key figures, Alfred North Whitehead, through his seminal work *Process and Reality* (Whitehead, 1978), has become synonymous with the process view in recent times.

Rescher (1996) suggested the following:

- Process philosophy "is really less of a theory than a point of view taking the line that one must prioritize processes over things and activities over substances. . . . Process philosophy thus prioritizes change and development in all of its aspects over fixity and persistence" (p. 35).

- Process in this view represents, "a coordinated group of changes in the complexion of reality, an organized family of occurrences that are systematically linked to one another either causally or functionally. . . . Processes are correlated with occurrences or events: Processes always involve various events, and events exist only in and through processes" (p. 39).
- Processes may also evolve over time and can encompass changes without themselves changing.[1] In this sense, "things" should always be viewed as processes. Therefore, a "thing" such as a river becomes an enduring entity while still flowing and changing.
- "Heraclitus was only half right: We indeed do not step twice into the same *waters*, but we can certainly step twice into the same *river*" (pp. 52–53).

Practically speaking, a client may experience panic attacks in different situations and with different intensity, yet he or she remains the same client with the same repeating panic attack process. Thus, the emphasis in a process view is on constant change within systems, and these systems are dependent in their definition on the observer.

What we view as observers and describers within our worlds depends on the nature of our language, constructs, our culture, and the focus of our interests and attention. Furthermore, our concepts and related actions develop through an ongoing process of interaction with our world. This is a cocreative process. From this process view, the universe is a set of relationships between relationships, all of which change over time, and none of these relationships is ever static. In the process view, process is primary, and what we call substance is merely a temporary pattern produced by that process. The appearance of enduring substances is thus merely a product of our limited point of view. The description of static reality as simply the product of our limited perspective of ongoing pattern at a given time has also led us to the postmodern views of socially constructed realities, and cultural and cross-cultural diversity in perspectives. Thus, the frames we use to construct our world constrain the process of interactions, and those interactions further refine and evolve our frames.

The same is true for the therapeutic rationales we use to guide different approaches to psychotherapy. They each become both enlightening and

[1]This concept is one I will visit in depth presently through the constructs of first- and second-order change, or changes that occur within a designated entity, process, or relationship, yet do not change that entity, versus those changes that actually change the group process itself. Whitehead and Russell (1912) developed this perspective on change through their application of set theory and the theory of logical types.

self-confirming. As we will see, in open social systems, a given problem may have a range of different causes or starting points, and from the same starting point a wide range of eventual states may evolve. What is viewed as a problem and expressed in one way within one culture may not be expressed in the same way or even be seen as a problem within another culture. Something that may seem to be an outrageous, paradoxical, or counterintuitive solution to a given problem may be just the right resolution. Understandably, this process view may seem vague and abstract at this time. However, when winnowed down, it offers a way of thinking that solves some of the current challenges, muddles, and controversies facing the idea of effective treatments in psychotherapy.

KEY PRINCIPLES OF A PROCESS VIEW

The three core elements of a process view as I put them forward are *context*, *process*, and *change*. These are the focus of the next three chapters. Those chapters wrap these intersecting ideas into an understandable and practical process of change perspective. The process is circular. It flows like the river of Heraclitus and Lao Tzu that I will presently discuss. The following represent some key principles of a process view.

- *Context defines the process*. Clients define what they decide is a problem and what needs to be done to resolve it. Therapists conceptualize those problems from their own theoretical view and offer rationales and treatment plans to help redirect the process of those problems. All of this occurs within broader cultural contexts of language, norms, and traditions that gradually shape the process.
- *The process of change shapes the context just as that context cocreates the process*. As clients and therapists agree on how they define the problem and plan their course of treatment, their definitions and actions combine to shift the flow of their interactions and help redirect and resolve the process of the clients' problems.
- *Change is constant*. Stability is an illusion, or better said, an often-desired description we use as participants in and observers of our lives. Clients are struggling with the process of change. From the process view, as clients struggle to reestablish desired stability, their solutions often exacerbate the problem in escalating spirals. Therapists intervene to change the way clients are attempting to change. This allows clients to move forward in the process of their lives.

- *Cycles and spirals make up the flow of constant change.* Whether we define those cycles and spirals as vicious or virtuous cycles is merely a product of the observer's values as they stand on the metaphorical riverbank. A Western therapist may define a Native American tribal tradition of not repeating the name of loved ones who have died as denial. The tribal tradition, on the other hand, lends comfort to its members. Another tribal tradition of relating with the spirits of the dead may spiral into a problem for some members as they struggle with those spirits. Context, language, and culture define problems and the need for and subsequent nature of their resolution. Therapists are not immune from the context of their culture, language, and traditions as they define problems and offer therapeutic rationales. All must fit to initiate change in problem cycles.
- *Change may occur slowly or suddenly.* As with riverbanks and river bottoms, change may be gradual. Change may also be sudden, as in the sudden shifts in flow of rivers from smooth points, to spiraling whirlpools, to the turbulence of repeating spirals, as we shall see in the chapter on process. Contrary to the gradualist Darwinian-like tradition of slow, linear change, sudden changes are more common than we have assumed, for example, the abrupt fall of the Berlin Wall or the quick resolution of a client's problem.

A BRIEF HISTORY OF STABILITY AND CHANGE

While much more can be said of the rational–empirical viewpoint, suffice it to say that it has provided such a strong lens for examining the effectiveness of psychotherapy that we are often "like fish in water," not realizing the medium in which we swim. We study what works using a logical empirical method. It is important to realize that our travels and directions have remained a function of this point of view. However, this does not exclude other viewpoints that might work better in certain circumstances. The rational–empirical perspective, which has been dominant in the modern study of psychotherapy, represents a sociopolitical choice made in the fields of psychology and sociology. The choice was made long ago to help gain standing in academia as a respected discipline of scientific investigation. At the same time, alternative views on the nature of "the way things are" in our world and us within it may easily be traced back to Greece and China. Interestingly, in both places there were philosophers who were putting forth strikingly different perspectives on the issue of stability and change.

Stability and Change in Greece

In Greece, we might turn to Aristotle and Heraclitus as early examples of rational–empirical and process thinkers, respectively.

Aristotle's (384–322 BCE) philosophy emphasized a world of substance and permanence with change occurring only occasionally and then returning to stable order with linear cause and effect. Reality is out there to discover and is defined by stable structures with inherent properties. (This should sound familiar and "make sense" to most of us who have adopted this view in Western culture.)

Heraclitus (535–475 BCE), on the other hand, suggested that everything flows and nothing stands still. Reality is defined by change, and stable structures are but a momentary description of process in dynamic flux. This is embodied by his most famous quote, "No man ever steps into the same river twice." The river changes as we step into it, and so do we. Rather than stable things to be discovered out there, the world is composed of events and processes. (So, if Aristotle's position "made sense" to most of us, then Heraclitus' position likely sounds like "double talk" and makes us shake our heads in confusion.)

Stability and Process in China

There were similar counterparts in the Chinese philosophers Confucius and Lao Tzu. Confucius stressed stable order, whereas Lao Tzu believed that all is change and flow.

A quote from Confucius (ca. 500 BCE) is "This equilibrium is the great root from which grow all the human acting in the world, and this harmony is the universal path which they all should pursue" (Confucius, *Doctrine of the Mean*). Preserving social order and stability was a core concern. Laws and rules preserved the stable good. Stability was the norm. Change only occasionally threatened the stable norm.

For Lao Tzu, change is the constant, sometimes slow and other times rapid, but always flowing and changing in interaction within context. Lao Tzu (ca. 500 BCE) suggested that "the more that laws and regulations are given prominence, the more thieves and robbers there will be." "Everything flows" (Lao Tzu, *Tao Te Ching*). His "watercourse way" included opposites in constant change similar to Heraclitus.

Why Does This Matter?

As you can see, the argument about whether things are fixed or constantly changing has gone on a long time. How does this apply to psychotherapy?

If "things" are fixed, then psychological concerns are entities or nouns. Depression is a never-wavering state of being and doesn't change. Yet we know this is not the case. Depression comes and goes. It is notorious for going into remission on its own, even without treatment. Treatments for depression, such as cognitive behavioral therapy and interpersonal therapy, focus interventions on either internal or external interactional processes. While these therapeutic methods are just two examples, psychotherapy treatments are and have always been process based. The problem in research occurs when trying to put treatments into a static mold or paradigm that doesn't fit.

PARADIGM SHIFTS

Calling for a shift to a process view may seem audacious. For some, thinking from a process point of view may seem alien and possibly even disturbing. The reader might ask, why now? The answer is that the need for paradigm shifts is common in all areas of scientific inquiry. It is the nature of science that a philosophy or theory takes a particular line of inquiry to a certain point. The line of inquiry gets stuck, and then to further knowledge, a radical shift in thinking needs to occur. To this end, Thomas Kuhn has studied how paradigm shifts occur.

Points of View

In 1962, the American physicist Thomas Kuhn published a book that became so influential that it outsold copies of the Bible the subsequent year. This book, *The Structure of Scientific Revolutions* (Kuhn, 1976, 2nd edition), introduced the notion of paradigms and paradigm shift as an explanation of how all mature domains of scientific inquiry evolve and advance. The *Merriam-Webster Dictionary* (http://www.merriam-webster.com) defines *paradigm* as "a philosophical and theoretical framework of a scientific school or discipline within which theories, laws, and generalizations and the experiments performed in support of them are formulated; broadly: a philosophical or theoretical framework of any kind." Kuhn used the term in two ways. The first was to point to what the members of a scientific community have in common in terms of viewpoints, approaches, assumptions, and values. The second referred more specifically to a paradigm as a particular set of assumptions, premises, and rules of investigation defining a coherent tradition of investigation. Kuhn places unique emphasis on the set of humans involved, as scientists in the process of deciding how to follow a particular paradigm. The process of choosing a paradigm is as important as the nature of the paradigm itself. By his reckoning, the community of practitioners and investigators within a domain of science hold particular sway over what paradigm is adopted and sustained at any given time. The investigators and the paradigm are in some ways inseparable. This is essentially a consensus model of truth.

While shifts in paradigm typically make watershed differences in the way a given discipline views its subject and interacts with it, Kuhn made it clear that the process of change is typically long and fraught with conflict. Kuhn suggested that paradigm shifts follow a characteristic set of phases.

- First, the predominant paradigm begins accumulating a growing set of anomalies not well explained or not predicted within that paradigm. This may sound familiar in the domain of psychotherapy.
- Once the set of anomalies near a critical number of unaccounted for problems, the discipline is thrown into a crisis where alternate ideas or perspectives are tried, some of which may have existed all along.
- Eventually, camps of followers of new perspectives form and begin to clash with those holding to the old paradigm, and often vicious attacks and debates follow for years (sometimes ending only as the old guard dies out). One might suggest that the intense arguments between the so-called specific factor advocates versus the common factor camp in explaining the effects of psychotherapy, or between quantitative versus qualitative methods of research (cf. Gergen, 2015b; Jackson, 2015a, 2015b; Landrum & Garza, 2015a, 2015b; Madill, 2015), represent just such a debate. This long battle stands in contrast with some popular ideas of "paradigm shift" happening in the blink of an eye.

For example, Darwinian evolutionary theory has had generations of anthropologists and paleontologists looking for elusive "missing links" in the supposed smooth evolutionary chain while overlooking the possibility of sudden evolutionary shifts. The idea of a massive meteoroid hitting earth, causing mass extinctions and paving the way for marginal mammals such as humans to become dominant, was hard to imagine. Gould (1977), in his first book of essays that sold more than a quarter of a million copies, *Ever Since Darwin: Reflections in Natural History*, noted that even Darwin likely revised and overlooked data that contradicted his gradual evolution theory in the face of sociopolitical pressures of his day. Changing paradigms is not only an intellectual exercise, one that presents strikingly different and often paradoxical differences, it is almost always a sociopolitical struggle, if not an outright battle!

Following the Process

Turning to the example of depression, let us examine three very different, yet strongly evidence-supported, psychological treatments, summarized in Table 2.1. Such a diverse array of effective approaches presents a challenge for a medical model. The medical model would assume a specific cause or origin of depression that would best be treated or cured by a specific treatment. The medical model struggles with the existence of multiple effective approaches, each of which assumes a different cause and applies different treatment procedures.

However, what if it is not the root cause of depression that creates the problem, but instead the current pattern of interaction of the system, or in this case, the way a person is struggling to rid herself of depression, that is the problem? Because the way individuals are struggling to recover "makes sense" to them, altering the pattern of their current solutions for being depressed is hard for them to conceive. Such alternatives may not make sense or may even feel somehow uncomfortable. They need someone who understands their plight and who feels supportive of their goal to feel better. They need an explanation for their situation that makes sense or fits in some ways with their way they view themselves and their world. Yet they also need a rationale that makes sense of how and why they should take action on their depression in a new way that may actually help them recover. Finally, they need a compassionate, supportive, and skilled guide to help them through that journey to change. Each of the originally described evidence-supported approaches in question represents a different yet equally plausible description of the reasons a person may have become depressed and offers a reasonable path toward change. The extent to which each approach makes sense or fits with the client and the therapist as they negotiate an alliance is the extent to which each approach is likely to be effective.

CONVERGING ON THIS CERTAIN "SOMETHING"

The title of this chapter is "Changing Paradigms." We are witnessing a convergence on a certain "something" that most all recent theoreticians and researchers are referring to as a paradigm shift, as we will see in the next several chapters. However, a prospective view of some more recent developments may help to put such efforts in context.

The influence of social constructionism, to be discussed in Chapter 5 (Gergen, 1985; 2014; Gergen, Josselson, & Freeman, 2015), cannot be overstated in its calls for paradigm shift. Turning to the potential of a process approach, Gergen (2014) suggested, "In my view, the serious pursuit of a

TABLE 2.1
Premises and Procedures for Three Strongly Supported Treatments for Depression

Therapy	Basic premise	Essence of therapy
Cognitive therapy for depression	Aaron T. Beck's cognitive theory of depression proposes that persons susceptible to depression develop inaccurate and unhelpful core beliefs about themselves, others, and the world as a result of their learning histories. These beliefs can be dormant for extended periods of time and are activated by life events that carry specific meaning for that person. Core beliefs that render someone susceptible to depression are broadly categorized into beliefs about being unlovable, worthless, helpless, and incompetent. Cognitive theory also focuses on information processing deficits, selective attention, and memory biases toward the negative.	In cognitive therapy, clients are taught cognitive and behavioral skills so they can develop more accurate and helpful beliefs and eventually become their own therapists.
Interpersonal therapy for depression (IPT)	Depression often follows changes in one's interpersonal environment (e.g., struggle with a significant other, loss of a loved one). Once depressed, symptoms can lead to compromised interpersonal functioning, which can precipitate continued stressful events. The goal in therapy is to address both the stressful life events and improved social support.	IPT focuses on improving problematic interpersonal relationships or circumstances that are directly related to the current depressive episode.
Behavioral activation (BA) therapy for depression	When people get depressed, they may increasingly disengage from their routines and withdraw from their environment. Over time, this avoidance exacerbates depressed mood, as individuals lose opportunities to be positively reinforced through pleasant experiences, social activity, or experiences of mastery.	BA seeks to increase the patient's contact with sources of reward by helping them get more active and, in so doing, improve one's life context. One version of BA therapy for depression is briefer, focusing specifically on identifying values that will guide the selection of activities. In addition to a focus on increasing activities, the second version of BA also works on identifying processes that inhibit activation and encourage avoidance and teaching problem-solving skills.

Note. Data from American Psychological Association, Society of Clinical Psychology (2016a).

process perspective could deeply enrich the potentials of (our) field. . . . In a more fully processual account; there would be no 'things' in themselves. There would only be processual change" (p. 198). Regarding system views, Gelo and Salvatore (2016) also called for a paradigm shift based on a dynamic systems approach to psychotherapy (discussed in Chapter 4, this volume).

Sprenkle, Davis, and Lebow (2009) called for a paradigm change from the polemic conflicts of specific versus common factor positions. Saying that common therapeutic factors such as the therapeutic alliance never occur in a vacuum, they stressed that a coherently structured therapeutic rationale in which a practitioner is invested and good at is always joined with common factors in effective treatment.

Moving beyond insulated separate protocols for myriad problems, Barlow and his team have developed and studied what they termed a *unified protocol for transdiagnostic treatment of emotional disorders* (cf. Barlow et al., 2010), as discussed in Part II on mood disorders. They described this as a step toward a new paradigm.

In their edited volume *Principles of Therapeutic Change That Work*, Castonguay and Beutler (2006b) addressed principles of change to move toward unified treatment across perspectives. The developers of context-responsive psychotherapy foresaw a paradigm shift in evidence-based training and practice (Constantino, Boswell, Bernecker, & Castonguay, 2013; Constantino, Overtree, & Bernecker, 2014) that offers a melding of common and specific factors approaches.

Wampold (2001; Wampold & Imel, 2015a) has advocated for a contextual model of therapy applicable to all bona fide therapies. This is another move toward a unified model of psychotherapy grounded in the research literature. Laska, Gurman, and Wampold, (2014) suggested that whether one or another rationale works best is less dependent on the "truth" of the approach and its assumptions on the mechanisms of change than the fit of the rationale as judged by participants in the treatment. There is growing agreement that the most effective treatment includes flexibility to adapt to the characteristics of the patient, as embedded in the process perspective yet not yet articulated in the current literature on psychotherapy.

Beutler, Norcross, and colleagues (cf. Beutler & Clarkin, 1990; Beutler & Harwood, 2000; Norcross, 2011; Norcross & Beutler, 2014) have developed a *systematic treatment selection* approach combining research on therapeutic relationships that work with what they called "patient-treatment fits that work." The relationship factors include the alliance, empathy, collecting client feedback, goal consensus, collaboration, and affirmation/positive regard. On a broader level, Henriques (2003, 2008) proposed a grand "tree of knowledge" approach to achieve a theoretical unification of psychology, integrating seemingly contradictory theories.

Finally, Tryon (2016) proposed psychotherapy integration via theoretical unification, advocating an applied psychological science approach based in neural network models. Similarly, Melchert (2016) also called for leaving behind what he said is professional psychology's "preparadigmatic" past and moving toward a "unified clinical science," shifting also toward neuroscience and behavioral science research and methods. (Yet, arguing that these two approaches are simply a retreat to biological reductionism, see also the strong rebuttals on metatheory and paradigm shifts by Henriques [2017], Joseph [2017], Tryon [2017], and Jackson [2017]). The paradigm debates continue.

All are moving toward a similar goal: to identify a certain something that might serve as a basis for unifying effective psychotherapies across diagnoses and treatment rationales. However, while all of these excellent approaches are calling for a paradigm shift, none has converged on one to unify their efforts. Reviewing alternate paradigms contrasting the positivist, rational–empirical paradigm underlying the medical model with that of the process view, a process of change perspective may offer a better fit.

THE NEW–OLD PARADIGM

A process view offers a way of understanding change that can guide us to a better understanding and use of varying approaches to psychotherapy. If the business of psychotherapy is all about change, then change needs to occupy a central place in all of our discussions of theories and practices of psychotherapy. Currently it still does not.

Although the literature on effective psychotherapy is moving toward context, fit, and flexibility, it still has no base or ground on which to stand. These concepts are reflected in the emergent literature on effective psychotherapy, but they do not fit the prevailing paradigm of the medical model and rational empiricism. Findings such as the importance of considering context (including culture, client, and therapist factors), and flexibility of the therapy rationale to fit with clients and therapists should emerge from a set of premises embedded in a paradigm. They currently appear as compelling outliers to the prevailing view. Furthermore, it is still unclear as to what all effective interventions converge on as they achieve success. Despite his outstanding work in synthesizing research on psychotherapy, Wampold (2001; Wampold & Imel, 2015a), when explaining the outcome of all therapies from his contextual model, offered only a vague set of phrases. He suggested that

> the Contextual Model posits that the specific ingredients in all therapies induce the client to do something that is salubrious. That is, the client engages in some action that is health promoting in that the activity

> results in an increase in something healthy or a decrease in something unhealthy. (Wampold & Imel, 2015a, p. 60)

The process of change paradigm is much clearer and more explicit on this. *The outcome of all effective psychotherapies is pattern shift or second-order change*, as discussed in a future chapter.

The rational–empirical paradigm retains stability as opposed to change as the implicit norm. It assumes linear over circular causality and expects gradual over rapid change. It still privileges the individual over their context. All of this points to the need for a new paradigm to fit human interaction, problems, and their resolution that is better than the prevailing one. History points to an alternate paradigm, as we have seen in this chapter. It moves us toward a process perspective. The process point of view is an alternative to the medical model. It does not replace it but subsumes it in the same way the Gould's theory of *punctuated equilibrium* subsumed Darwin's theory of evolution. Adopting a process view does not mean clinicians should throw away their *DSM–5* or ICD–10. It does mean that we should be aware of their limitations. As stated earlier, although the process view is an alternate paradigm, it has been there all along. What remains is for us is to fill in the point of view by considering what we mean by context and change in a process of change paradigm.

Now, all of this may seem rather speculative, and the terms may seem relatively vague or unfamiliar. However, as we move forward through the next several chapters, this point of view on problems and their resolution should become clearer. It is a process perspective. It is about change. The next chapters turn to the idea that everything is in the process of change. For simplicity's sake, I call this a *systems view of process and change*. The intersecting spirals of the Celtic symbol appearing on the cover of this book represent the ever-flowing influences of context, process, and change in the process perspective. Yet first, we need to address what we mean by the concept of change. That is the focus of the next chapter.

3

CHANGE

The question is, why have we built a perspective on problems and their resolution based on a premise of stability, when the essence of all effective psychotherapy is change? Up to now, the dominant assumptions of psychotherapy (i.e., the medical model) have been steeped in a positivist view of the world, with its related rational empiricist models of finding truth in the world "out there." The process view assumes that change, not stability, is constant. Seemingly stable objects or states are simply the product of an observer's description of ongoing processes at a given time and place. This may sound like "high-flying" and abstract theory (which it definitely is at some levels), yet it is critically important to understand as the basis for a process view to unify psychotherapies that work.

This chapter moves from theory to application. First, I visit the relationship between stability and change and introduce the ideas of first- and second-order change. Next, turning to the theoretical roots of this view of

http://dx.doi.org/10.1037/0000078-004
Unifying Effective Psychotherapies: Tracing the Process of Change, by J. S. Fraser

change, I explore group theory and logical types. A practical illustration of these ideas using the "children's finger trap" offers a down-to-earth idea of these concepts. The following section addresses problem formation, discussing "solution-generated problems." The final section discusses problem resolution from a process of change view, including clinical examples, premises and corollaries, operationalizing second-order change, relationships as change agents, and finally the place of change and contingency.

STABILITY AND CHANGE

The terms *stability* and *change* can be misleading. We generally think of these terms from a linear perspective. Consequently, stability is viewed as structural, like a well-built, sturdy table. Change would then involve a change in some element of the structure, like adding a leaf to make the table longer. From a process view, however, we are addressing change from a systems perspective that is nonlinear. Thinking in terms of systems, circular causation and constant change is inherently challenging for us. Regarding systemic causation, Lakoff (2014) wrote the following in his discussion of language, frames, and metaphors:

> Every language in the world has in its grammar a way to express direct causation. No language in the world has in its grammar a way to express systemic causation. . . . We learn direct causation automatically as children because that's what we experience on a daily basis. Direct causation, and the control over our immediate environment that understanding it allows, is crucial in the life of every child. That's why it shows up in the grammar of every language. . . . Systemic causation cannot be experienced directly. It has to be learned, its cases have to be studied, and repeated communication is necessary before it can be widely understood. (p. 36)

From the systems view, change is always occurring, especially with interactional systems. While change is constant, there are different levels of change or types. Stability refers to a pattern of changes that result in redundancy of a pattern, whereas change refers to an interruption of redundancy, which in turn initiates a different pattern. Take for example, the difficulty of the problem solver lost in the woods. He has been walking for hours and is remaining lost. After a while, he begins to notice a familiarity to various aspects of the woods and is struck by a revelation: He is walking in a circle over and again. Moving to the top of a hill, he looks down to see his circular folly and alternate paths out. From a process perspective, walking in circles over and again is stability. Change means breaking out of the circle and walking in a direction that leads out of the woods. Moving to a metalevel outside the problem offers perspective and new directions to resolution.

THE NATURE OF CHANGE

If you as a reader have been following our discussions so far, you have been reading the term *process of change* over and again. While I have driven home the idea of process as an alternative to the traditionally static and structural paradigm dominating the field, I have said less about the key concept of change. Of course, change is the central feature of Lao Tzu's watercourse way, of Heraclitus's river, and of recent views on chaos and turbulence, as I discuss in the next chapter. However, there is so much more to be addressed on this central concept. After all, change is what all clients struggle with when dealing with psychological and interpersonal problems; it is what they come to psychotherapy to achieve; and it is the central goal of all psychotherapies and psychotherapists alike, no matter what school of thought or model they follow. It's about pattern shift in ongoing process.

The process of change perspective potentially unites all effective psychotherapies. Critical to understanding how this may be is a more careful look at the *nature of change*. To this end, I devote special attention to the concepts of first- and second-order change. By way of definition:

- *First-order change* is defined as a class of solutions that *do not change a problem* or else *make a problem worse*. A woman suffering from insomnia may try to "will herself to sleep," or a man who is unable to achieve an erection may attempt to "will sexual arousal." In both of these examples, the person finds that the "solution" only exacerbates the problem.
- In contrast, *second-order change* is a change of those first-order solutions, which results in *problem resolution*. When a child visits their bedroom closet to discover there is no "monster" hiding there, they solve their fear by reversing their initial solution of hiding under the covers.
- First-order change is related to *stability*; second-order change is related to *transformation*. As we will see, reversing classic avoidance solutions in panic attacks through exposure resolves, or re-solves, the panic attacks.
- First-order change is a change that occurs in a system that itself remains the same. These changes of intensity, frequency, duration, and so on are solutions taken according to the existing

assumptions and tacit rules of a system. Not only do they not change the system, they affirm the system by repeating its assumptions, rules, and patterns. They stay within the prevailing frame or metaphor of the system. Running in a dream keeps the dreamer trapped in his or her dilemma.

- When first-order change turns problematic, it invariably becomes a *vicious cycle*. First-order change may be seen in the frustrated folly of the client who attempts to force herself to sleep or in the man who tries to will himself to become passionately aroused for lovemaking. In these and most other human dilemmas, the solutions become the problem. They create vicious cycles.
- Second-order change offers solutions that are often viewed as counterintuitive or paradoxical from the original perspective. Sleep or sexual arousal occurs spontaneously as we allow ourselves to become immersed in the situation. This is the essence of much sex therapy and sleep hygiene. As we may know, the answer to falling asleep or becoming aroused is to stop trying to will it to be so. The only way to escape a nightmare is to wake up. Yet such a shift for the person caught in these dilemmas will typically not make sense, at least without some further frame or rationale. As we shall see in our discussion of the theory of logical types, such frames and rationales, offer a way to "wake up," so to speak, and have a metaperspective on the first-order dilemmas, whether they are our nightmares or our real-life problems. These kinds of shifts are examples of second-order change.

All may agree that change is at the heart of psychotherapy, but many are eager to say they possess the royal road to change. Little agreement in the field exists, however, on precisely what is important to change. Behavioral therapies, for instance, emphasize extinguishing maladaptive behaviors and shaping new skills. The now popular cognitive approaches stress challenging dysfunctional thought patterns and replacing them with more adaptive constructs. The psychodynamic tradition affirms the importance of a corrective emotional experience and replacing neurotic relationship patterns with less problematic ones. The humanistic and existential school suggests that learning to become and experience one's authentic self in the moment is what change is all about. These are but a few broad statements on the nature of effective therapeutic change. Each is different and compelling in its own way, yet all seem to compete and each seems mutually exclusive of the others. Each definition of change remains within their own frames, premises and assumptions. How might we get outside of these specific views to a metalevel, and observe change from a broader and more unifying perspective?

STABILITY AND CHANGE REVISITED

If agreement cannot be reached about the nature of change at the theoretical level, then at the least, it is reasonable to concede that stability is the opposite of change. Yet on examination, even this turns out to be far from the case. Stability, in fact, is maintained by change. Stability and change are not found on opposite sides of the coin; they are closely related, entangled in surprising and sometimes complex ways.

A closer look at constancy or stability shows that continual change supports stability. For example, a tightrope walker makes constant adjustments, both large and small, to maintain balance or stability on the rope. Most have had the experience, moreover, of riding a bicycle where many changes in direction, weight distribution, and speed must be made to maintain stability and direction. Relationships, too, require continual adjustments and renegotiation to remain viable. As can be seen, each example reveals a singular connection between change and stability.

Sometimes efforts designed to maintain stability produce an unwanted effect, actually destabilizing the situation. This is observed with the tightrope walker who overcorrects while attempting to maintain balance. When handling a bike, if the rider holds the handlebars too rigidly and does not make needed corrections in direction (or undercorrects), the bicycle will inevitably tip over. Overcorrection or undercorrection can induce a loss of balance and a tragic fall. The possibilities of over- and undercorrection further complicate the relationship between change and stability. As we will see in the next chapter on process, when we discuss Gregory Bateson's (1979) alternating ladder of change, negative feedback attempts at regaining stability are linked with positive feedback loops of escalation to the next attempt at stability. The entire spiral is actually an example of the *vicious cycle of first-order change* within a given system or group. All changes are according to the rules and within the existing system's frame.

A moment's reflection on the preceding examples suggests that effective change often entails a paradoxical kind of effort. This kind of change, counterintuitive as it may first appear, is the process of change found in all effective therapies and is the subject of this book. However, before proceeding to the examination of change that makes things better, we must further understand the sort of change that makes things worse. This class of change creates and perpetuates problems and brings people to therapy in the first place. It's the essence of Bateson's evolutionary spiral. Turning to the basic theories behind these concepts may help.

> *Only Heraclitus, it appears, envisaged change in a different perspective. In addition to his well-known dictum about the impossibility of stepping into the same river twice, he asserts in another fragment: "All change is contradictory; therefore contradiction is the very essence of reality."*
>
> —From *Change* (Watzlawick, Weakland, & Fisch, 1974, p. 10)

The implications of this view on change are extraordinary for the practice of psychotherapy. It suggests that change operates on a principle other than what has been described in the major theoretical frameworks that comprise the behavioral health field. Yet what is the basis for the operant principle that is at the heart of change? Struggling with how to address the relationship between stability and change, Whitehead and Russell (1912) turned to group theory and theory of logical types in their opus magnus, *Principia Mathematica*. This seems like an unlikely place to look for a path to understanding change in psychotherapy, yet our understanding has grown through this resource. When the terms first- and second-order change were first defined in the book *Change: Principles of Problem Formation and Problem Resolution* (Watzlawick et al., 1974), the authors used *set theory*, or the *theory of groups*, as the explanation for first-order change, and the *theory of logical types* as the rationale for second-order change. Although these theories serve as a sound foundation for understanding how change occurs, they are highly complex, rather abstract, and often confusing to follow. Because of the conceptual challenge of these theories, most people familiar with the work have overlooked or forgotten them. They are, nevertheless, firm foundations for understanding change, and they deserve attention.

Group Theory

> *You can never solve a problem on the level on which it was created.*
>
> —*Albert Einstein*

There are aspects of group theory and the theory of logical types that are important to the case for the process view. For the purpose of our current discussion, I describe these two theories very simply. Turning first to group theory, a group may be any kind of like members, from people to ideas. The theory of groups suggests that once a group is set, all interactions within the group, according to the assumptions and rules of the group, will maintain the group's identity. Thus, once set, all interactions preserve and perpetuate the identity of the group. There can be many changes in the interactions of the group, yet no change of the group will result. A group may not change itself from within. This is the case of the man who tries repeatedly to will sexual arousal by forcing it to occur, to little avail, or the woman with insomnia trying to consciously force herself to go to sleep. They are trapped in their own solutions, and those solutions define and are defined by the rules of their worldview or frames on how to solve such problems.

Groups are defined and bounded by their group definitions and related interaction rules. These are the *frames, rationales, and metaphors* discussed further in Chapter 5 on context. In applying this mathematical analogy to human dilemmas, it does not mean that if the group contains people, that people cannot change the group. It does mean that change cannot be initiated with the same assumptions and interactions that have created the problem. This is impossible from the perspective of group theory and formal logic. Thus, the goal of psychotherapy, whether it is group therapy or individual therapy, is to be the outside force that disrupts the group (i.e., client's) rules/assumptions.

In other words, human psychological problems are rooted in how interactions with self and others are understood. Understandings of problems are shaped by premises and assumptions on the way things are. This will be the essence of our discussion of frames and metaphors. They provide context. Once problem-solving constructs have been set, escape is difficult if not impossible. This simple definition may seem so obvious as to be confusing. Suffice it to say that the theory of groups underlies what has thus far been described and exemplified as first-order change, with all of its vicious cycles of solution-generated problems. As with most mathematical theory, the basic ideas are rather broad reaching and universal.

The Theory of Logical Types

All generalizations are false, including this one.

—*Albert Einstein*

Second-order change is based upon the theory of logical types, which is closely related to group theory. It was used by Whitehead and Russell (1912) to solve the problem of self-reference, or the famous liar's dilemma (i.e., the Greek citizen from Crete who said, "All Cretans are liars!"). If the statement is true, then it is false because it is made by a person from Crete! It turns back on itself unless one steps out of the frame to reflect on its dilemmas. Once trapped in a self-referential system, interactions and statements become problematic and even contradictory like the statement of the man from Crete or like the statement "This statement is false" or a sign stating, "Ignore this sign." If the statement is true, then it is false. If you obey the sign, you shouldn't obey the sign, and so on. Once clients are trapped in their worldviews, their cultures, their languages, and their definitions of a problem and therefore what to do about it—they are trapped in the logic and consequent vicious cycles of their world.

As previously stated, group theory demonstrates the futility of attempting to initiate change using the same set of constructs that initiated the problem. It's self-referential. It's a vicious cycle that turns back on itself. It's a paradox. The theory of logical types shows how constructs from outside a group can be incorporated into a group, resulting in a change in the original group's identity. To make such a foundational change in any group, the very assumptions that define the group and its interactions must be changed. To accomplish this, one must move to a higher level or class of assumptions and definitions that subsume the original ones and describe and explain them as well or better. Such a shift moves us to a higher level to enable us to reflect on the processes and dilemmas of the lower level. It is like the person, lost and going in circles in the woods, who climbs the hill to see his circular folly and then notices alternate paths out. This kind of change is a basic shift in premise or mental set. From a dialectical perspective, this is the "synthesis" that integrates apparently opposing positions. It solves the paradox. To get out of the trap of the signs mentioned earlier, you need to be able to step to a higher level and comment on them as being crazy or contradictory. When we do this, we move to the next level of logical type. Joining a therapeutic alliance with a therapist does the same thing for clients in psychotherapy because they can reflect on the folly of their former solutions. (We should also remember, however, that such transformations may also happen by chance.)

Importantly, this shift to a higher level of logic or metaperspective is the essence of therapeutic agreements on the nature of clients' problems and the therapeutic rationales implying further steps toward resolution. This is second-order change in psychotherapy. As shown in Part II of this book, this shift in logical levels, this second-order change, is the common golden thread that weaves its way through all psychotherapies that work.

THE FINGER TRAP

One of the simplest examples of first- and second-order change is the "finger-trap" toy that so many children have had fun with over the ages (see Figure 3.1). The finger trap is a small cylinder made of woven hemp strips. The cylinder is not firm but flexible. One child asks another to put the index finger of each hand into each end and then try to escape these "handcuffs" by pulling his fingers out. As you might remember, simply pulling your fingers out only causes the fibers of the finger trap to bind more closely to your fingers. The more you pull, the tighter the finger trap becomes. It is only by giving up the logical solution of pulling out, and instead pushing in, that the trap finally releases and your fingers may be gently removed. Pushing in to get out is a second-order change. Getting to that illogical solution is what often creates the fun.

Figure 3.1. "Finger-trap" toy.

A question can be raised about the logic that drives problem-solvers to try pulling out of the trap as a first-order solution. The instinct to pull out is universal; virtually all children initially try to solve the puzzle in this manner. Most children then get stuck in the cycle of trying this method over and over again. More careful consideration may shed some light on the hidden complexities of the finger trap and of second-order change.

In the process of development, children learn many fundamental lessons about life. An important lesson involves solving certain challenges in daily living by "pulling out" of them. If a child places her hand on an object that is too hot or cold, she instinctively pulls her hand away. She learns to pull her feet out of her socks; the same procedure is used for taking off her shoes. If she steps in a mud puddle and her foot becomes stuck in the mud, she pulls out her stuck foot. When she grows older, she learns more complex variations on the same theme: To find your way after getting lost, you retrace your steps. In other words, you find your way out of a challenging situation by going in the opposite direction from the way that you entered it. A child's mind thoroughly understands this rule. Upon seeing the finger trap for the first time, the child's mind immediately reads the problem, determines the problem-solving level, and goes into action. This process occurs so fast that it is almost instantaneous. There is only one problem. The finger trap represents an exception to the rule of pulling out. It cannot be solved that way.

This is an elementary example of first- and second-order change. The logical solutions of pulling one's fingers directly out only further trap the fingers. The harder one pulls, the tighter the trap becomes. More of the same solution breeds more of the same results. This is the now familiar vicious cycle. The solution makes sense to the child, but it makes the problem worse. The resolution is a classic second-order change. The resolution is a *reversal* of the first-order solution. Pushing the fingers together releases the trap and allows the child to gently slide free. This resolution is based on viewing the dilemma differently. It is a product of using a different level of logic. The child solves the problem by doing less of the same instead of more of the same. The resolution is paradoxical and counterintuitive to most children. It usually results in cascades of laughter after discovering the "trick" of the trap.

A similar classic example is the old nine-dot problem wherein the problem-solver is tasked to connect all nine dots (arranged as a box of three dots in each of three rows) with four straight lines. The solution is, of course, to go outside the imagined "box." (More on this example can be found in Fraser & Solovey, 2007, pp. 46–48.)

These elements are also typical of second-order change. First-order change appears logical to those trapped in the problem cycle, and thus second-order change seems ironic, illogical, or even funny when viewed from the original position on the problem. (This, by the way, is the same principle that makes the Bobby McFerrin song "Don't Worry, Be Happy"—sometimes referred to as the psychotherapist's national anthem—and the Bob Newhart therapy skit, "Stop It," where he tells his client to simply stop it, so funny to us [cf. https://www.youtube.com/watch?v=d-diB65scQU; and https://www.youtube.com/watch?v=Ow0lr63y4Mw]. Viewed from outside the system, they are so ironic as to be funny.) The finger-trap puzzle, although simple in form, has many profound ramifications. As mentioned earlier, avoidance or pulling away is a common mistake that sets up many complex human problems. Depression, anxiety disorders, chronic pain, and many other clinical conditions share this same fundamental error in logic.

PROBLEM FORMATION

There is always an easy solution to every human problem—neat, plausible, and wrong.

—H. L. Mencken, 1917

Analogically, clients' problems often resemble the predicaments of tightrope walkers maintaining stability by changing their balance poles and of pilots-in-training who must learn to pull out of a "death spiral" drawing them down by pushing the control stick down instead of pulling back. In particular, the "natural" steps clients take to maintain a pleasant stable situation or to change a problematic one often make the situation worse. Their efforts to create stability or initiate change for the better often cause or aggravate problems and make them more persistent and impervious to change. Clients often indicate this when they say, "The more I try to get control of my anxiety, the more anxious I get" or "The more I try to move on from my grief, the more I find myself breaking down in tears."

An inescapable dilemma attends problems and problem formation. Most of the time and for most people, the difficulties encountered in daily living are readily resolved with good old common sense. Yet on occasion, the very same commonsense assumptions become the driving force in the development of serious problems. From this perspective, all humans, including therapists, share the vulnerability of falling into a first-order trap.

The Quest for Stability

Naturally wanting predictability, stability, and control, people first filter challenges when they occur through their beliefs and premises about how the world works. The goal is to make sense of the challenge: to define it, establish its significance, and parameters. The beliefs used derive from experience, precedent, tradition, culture, folk wisdom, or the conventions of the time. As well-conceived or ill-conceived as the premises may be, they are preconceived. They are what people bring to the table when a challenge is laid before them.

At its core, importantly, a premise is a basic assumption on the way of the world. It is a proposition, or better said, a set of presuppositions, from which conclusions are drawn and future actions are decided. In a person's psychological economy, they perform an organizing function. As such, they are conservative, even protective, and surprisingly resilient.

"Triggers"

The precursor to any problem is a stressor or adaptive challenge. Yet these occur all the time for everyone, and not everyone develops problems. As the late John Weakland, celebrated therapist and coauthor of *Change: Problem Formulation and Problem Resolution* (Watzlawick et al., 1974) put it, "Life is one damn thing after another, but it's the only game in town" (personal communication, 1990). Problems are not due to stressors or challenges but to how people experience them. Context, as we will soon see, shapes what clients see as problems. Following the assessment of the stressor or challenge, people then choose an action or solution for management. They select a solution from the known universe of alternatives suggested by their beliefs and premises. They might decide to do nothing. They might decide to manage the challenge by changing it or themselves in some way. Perhaps they decide to contend with the difficulty by actively avoiding it. If the action or solution works, life goes on until the next, inevitable "damn thing" presents itself.

Recalling Piaget (1950), people often resolve life difficulties by assimilating or accommodating them into their familiar repertoire. Such frames and actions work much of the time. For example, parents often use rewards to help children directly achieve developmental goals (e.g., toilet training).

Later, as they face other developmental stages, they return to the strategies that served them and the family well before.

Fine and good so far, yet what happens if the solution does not work? For the stressor or adaptive challenge to devolve into a problem and not remain one of life's many annoyances, two conditions need to be satisfied. First, we select the same solution or type of solution as before. Second, we apply the solution or type of solution repeatedly. Should this occur, a vicious cycle rapidly sets in motion. This is what Albert Einstein meant in a popular saying attributed to him: "Insanity: Doing the same thing over and over again and expecting different results." Similarly, Weakland said that once a vicious or problem cycle takes hold, life changes from one damn thing after another to the same damn thing over and again.

Downward Spirals—Solution-Generated Problems

Failed solutions, it bears emphasizing, will be repeated until interrupted. It is as though they have a life of their own. In addition, repeating failed solutions almost always results in a downward spiral, like the pilot's death spiral. It is the inevitable and terrible logic of the vicious cycle. Instead of creating improvement, the attempted and failed solution makes the problem worse. As the situation deteriorates, more of the same attempted solution is applied, exacerbating the problem and then provoking varying escalations of the solution. From this vantage point, the solution actually becomes a bigger problem than the original problem it was meant to solve. The term *downward spirals* is repeated prominently in a later chapter on depression in Part II.

We might even call this vicious cycle a *solution-generated problem*. Over time, the problem will probably manifest little resemblance to the original difficulty. Such patterns are classic and occur in diverse contexts and at different levels of interpersonal commerce.

Willing Arousal

Getting trapped in vicious cycles is easier than it might seem. All that is required is for the problem-solver to misinterpret oscillations in the pattern of stability. To illustrate, almost within minutes of turning on the television, the viewer is bombarded with ads for medications for erectile problems. Apparently, the pharmaceutical industry would have the public believe that erectile problems in men (i.e., attaining and maintaining erections) are epidemic, sponsored by rampaging vascular difficulties, which do occur. For all that, years ago, the renowned sex therapists Masters and Johnson (1970, 1976) demonstrated that many erectile problems are related to a vicious cycle—a solution-generated problem. The more a man feels anxious about whether he will have or keep an erection, the more his attention is riveted on the second-to-second performance of his sex organs. Hardly stimulating, to pun a phrase.

All men, for sundry reasons (e.g., fatigue, too much alcohol or tobacco, stress, prolonged bicycle riding, lack of rapport with a partner), will face erectile inefficiency. If accepted as inevitable and temporary, it remains what it is: an irritation or passing inconvenience. On the other hand, what if the inefficiency takes on a different meaning? What if a man regards the incident as a sign of something more serious or sinister?

Maybe the man interprets the lack of an erection as a demonstration of inadequacy or lack of virility. He then might feel embarrassed or ashamed, humiliated before his partner. In this case, so the worst fears do not become true, the "failure" cannot be repeated. The erection, come hell or high water, must be achieved quickly, aggressively, and proudly. Fretting, the man's solution is somehow to make the erection happen. Use the right stimulation, the right position, the right mood, or the right atmosphere. The result is predictable: Instead of enjoying the satisfactions of the moment, the man becomes mired in failed attempts to achieve deliberately a state that best comes spontaneously.

The resolution became obvious to Masters and Johnson. Redirect the man's attention away from the erection to the sensuality of the total sexual encounter. By interrupting the man's solution (e.g., through sensate focus), calm returns and pleasure is felt. This allows nature to take its naturally arousing course. As in archery, the chance of hitting the bull's-eye increases when we are less anxious about hitting the target. Women who attempt to force themselves into an orgasm fall into a near identical trap. As with men, the joy of sex morphs into the job of sex. Again, the solution is not to work harder but to relinquish the solution.[1]

The following chapters discuss many more examples of problems. As they are presented, it helps to recall that a problem (either psychological or interpersonal) does not arise in the original stressor or challenge. Events that may precede problem formation are too numerous to categorize, and besides, people exhibit a wide variety of responses, many of which are adaptive and even growth-promoting. In this sense, stressors are not and never will be the cause of a problem. The actual "kick point" for a problem is the solution that falls flat on its face. Should a person relinquish an ineffective solution and move on to one that actually manages the stressor, a problem still does not exist. Once the person repeats the ineffective solution, then the problem is forming.

[1]See Fraser and Solovey (2004) for more examples of second-order change in sexual problems. A revised second edition of this work and our chapter should be available in 2018.

First- and Second-Order Change Redux

In sum, the misguided and repetitive attempt to accomplish a change for the better by whatever means is a first-order change. It is a change derived from the *first* (preexisting) set of premises a person uses for managing a challenge. In considering first-order change, moreover, remember that it does not always give rise to failure. This is an important caveat. Often enough, we choose first-order solutions because they worked in similar or past situations. They may very well resolve the current difficulty. If the solution works, no problem ensues.

On the other hand, if it fails or falters, then a change of a different order is needed. This type of change, called a second-order change, is derived from a *second* or altogether different set of premises that fit the situation as well or better than the first. The alternatives that arise in second-order change represent a completely new set. Because they do not reflect the person's current worldview, the individual or participants trapped in a vicious or first-order cycle experience them as strange, weird, out-of-the-blue, paradoxical—often contrary to common sense.

Although the language of solution-generated problems and first-order change presented in this chapter may be unfamiliar, the field has long been fascinated with vicious or problem cycles. We will turn our attention to the role they have played in several therapeutic systems as our journey enters the middle chapters of this book.

PROBLEM RESOLUTION

Context

Social constructivism and the process view—the context in time, place, and culture—have everything to do with what we decide are problems, how we express those problems, and what we think should be done about them, as Chapter 5 on context explores. We will learn that the way people express posttraumatic stress disorder in Sri Lanka is different from what occurs in Western cultures. We will learn how differently soldiers expressed their reactions to trauma in the Boer War versus the American Civil War, in World War I versus World War II, and so on. We will learn of the influence of Western cultural ideas on eating disorders as they traveled to the Eastern context of Hong Kong. However, we get ahead of ourselves here.

The context, including time and location, language, culture, norms, and traditions, powerfully shapes the metaphors we live by. Consequently, they should also match the theory and practices, or therapeutic rationales, we use to help clients resolve their problems. Although people cannot fully escape from the frames and metaphors they live by, as therapists, we can do our best to fit ours with those of our clients as we seek to help them. As discussed in the Chapter 5, therapists using a social constructionist view on truth will understand that there is not one truth, just as there is no one true or best psychotherapy. The proof of the pudding is in the eating, as the old saying goes. A contextually relevant version of the pragmatic model of truth suggests that what people find useful is what becomes real and true for them.

Jerome Frank (Frank & Frank, 1991) operated from such a contextual model or social constructionist view when he described the interpretations or therapeutic rationales used by therapists in Western cultures or healers from other cultures as convenient "myths." He emphasized that the rationales need not be "true" in an absolute sense or in the sense of being scientifically verified. Instead, the most important element is that the description, frame, or rationale makes sense to both the client and therapist as they join in a therapeutic alliance. It must fit so that the client gains hope. The fitting rationale thus offers a clear description that explains their problem and an associated set of procedures that will lead to resolution. This all makes sense from a process view.

Most critical, and true to the theory of logical types, the agreed-on metaview allows both therapists and clients to step out of the first-order vicious cycles, view them with new perspectives, and take new actions previously considered counterintuitive or paradoxical. It also fits with the social constructionist emphasis on context. Language and frames reciprocally shape the therapy process between therapists and clients.

Thus, a process perspective suggests that therapeutic frames and rationales that join clients and therapists in an alliance, with clear and agreed-on goals, is the cornerstone of effective treatment. It helps clients make sense of the counterintuitive paradox of negotiating second-order change from a new metalevel. Remember also that successful treatment is always about change, and most often about facilitating second-order change.

Fit

Given the discussion so far, you can see that effective psychotherapy is all about helping clients step outside of their problem-generating worlds with their solution-generated problems. Not only is this challenging for clients, but it may also be confusing, counterintuitive, paradoxical, and anxiety provoking, if not downright frightening. To make this pattern shift or reversal in the flow of their life and in the direction of their goals, clients need to have faith in their therapist. Therapists promote faith by showing they understand clients' problems. Therapists validate clients' distress because they understand the context for it. Finally, they inspire hope by offering a therapeutic rationale that makes sense. This helps the client to see the therapist as skilled and capable of successfully guiding them on their journey. A key element in this formula is fit.

A relevant meta-analysis showed that when clients received their preferred approach to treatment, they had better outcomes and experienced fewer premature terminations of therapy than did clients receiving treatments they did not prefer (Swift, Callahan, & Vollmer, 2011). Whereas the clinical trials approach demands treatment manuals and strict adherence to the protocol, or fidelity, such strict fidelity has often damaged the therapeutic alliance and led to premature dropouts. Furthermore, research has also shown little connection between adhering to a model and clinical outcome (Branson, Shafran, & Myles, 2015; Webb, DeRubeis, & Barber, 2010). Flexibility in approach is now emerging as a common recommendation (cf. Owen & Hilsenroth, 2014; and the American Psychological Association [2006] Presidential Task Force on Evidence-Based Practice). This flexibility includes, as the Task Force has suggested, such things as clients' culture, values, language, economic resources, social support, and a range of other contextual variables. Therapists also tend to do best when they have a strong allegiance to their approach, reflected in their enthusiasm and skill in the treatment and encouraging faith and trust in the approach and the therapist by the client. A coherent therapeutic approach that fits with both the understanding and investment of clients and therapists is emerging as one of the strong correlates of effective treatment. Wampold (Wampold & Imel, 2015a) summed up this set of observations by saying that coherence clearly beats adherence when it comes to doing effective psychotherapy.

Although therapeutic rationale forms the frames that shape and guide the flow of treatment, there must be a fit among the therapist, the client, and the approach. How might this best happen? This process is the same for therapists as it is for clients from the process of change view.

For the therapists, the treatment approach that best resonates with or fits their own worldview will be best. Therapists using approaches that resonate with their lived experiences of the world are most likely to be authentic and compelling when delivering a therapeutic perspective. The clinician can also be genuinely hopeful and enthusiastic about the effectiveness of their approach and consequently develop strong skills in delivering it. However, therapists must remain flexible, and that means gaining a point of view that allows flexibility.

A process perspective offers such a flexible point of view for therapists. At the same time, it is important that clinicians become familiar with several approaches to therapy while becoming aware of their own multiple identities. Additionally, it is crucial that clinicians honor client diversity by learning about clients' contexts and lived experiences. This is a tall order, yet it is the therapist's role to do this.

Furthermore, the therapist is responsible for the outcomes of treatment. A recent issue of the journal *Psychotherapy* ("Progress Monitoring and Feedback," 2015) is devoted entirely to approaches to routine client outcome monitoring. It makes it clear that when therapists use some routine approach to tracking and adjusting to client outcomes, therapy achieves better success. Yet there is a limit to the therapies that any therapist can or should offer. Some treatments have actually been shown to be harmful to clients. The idea of providing a bona fide approach to treatment articulated by Wampold and colleagues (1997), suggesting that treatment should have a reasonably defensible psychological basis. Turning back to the therapist's belief and investment in the treatment delivered, Wampold and Imel (2015a) suggested that "the therapist should be convinced that the treatment is a good fit for him or herself and a good fit to the client, is accepted by the client, and the client is responding to the treatment" (p. 275). As with the work on routine outcome measurement, if the client is not responding to treatment, it is up to the therapist to flex to an approach that is a better fit. There should be a continual feedback loop during treatment to allow for adjustments as the trajectory of the treatment moves toward pattern shifts in the vicious cycles of the problem pattern.

Countering the Paradox Through Frame and Rationale

The overriding goal from the process view is pattern shift, and second-order change in clients' solution-generated problems. Fit is crucial to this often anxiety-provoking and counterintuitive venture. A fitting metaframe for the problem helps both clients and therapists take the second-order step outside the first-order level of vicious cycles and adopt a rationale for solution. Recall that clients experience pattern shifts and reversals in their common solutions as paradoxical from the level of their struggle with their difficulties. Stepping out of their problem patterns into a therapeutic alliance with frames, rationales, and agreed-on goals helps clients "make sense" of those eventual paradoxical pattern reversals. It has to make sense to push your fingers into the child's finger trap rather than to continue trying to pull them out.

Also, remember that the theory and rationale that therapists adopt will help those same reversals make sense to the therapist. At the metalevel of the therapy alliance, neither client nor therapist should feel that the direction and procedures of treatment are "paradoxical" (cf. Fraser, 1984). *Paradox* is defined as "a logical contradiction following consistent deductions from correct premises" (Watzlawick, Beavin, & Jackson, 1967). If either a client or a therapist feels a technique, position, or solution is "paradoxical," then this implies it does not fit with their premises and assumptions about treatment or about problems and their resolution. Agreement on a theory or frame for problems and investing in agreed-on rationales and goals for therapy are crucial to making the paradox of solution pattern reversals make sense to both therapists and clients.

PSYCHOTHERAPY EXAMPLES

Consider the following list of interventions. Each describes an example of sound, evidence-based practice, yet each is relatively counterintuitive.

- A therapist, working with a client who has panic attacks, asks her client to bring on a panic attack during the session. Why is a client who is trying *not* to have panic attacks being told to have one?
- Another therapist, working with someone who has been recurrently depressed, teaches his client to allow depressing thoughts into mind and then let them pass through without needing to respond to those thoughts. However, isn't the client trying *not* to think of those depressing things?
- Still another therapist asks a quarreling couple to pick a fight with one another when they are not mad. Yet the couple came to treatment because they were fighting too much!
- A sex therapist prohibits a couple from having intercourse, their desired goal, despite prescribing arousing exercises. However, having intercourse is just what they have been trying to do. Why should they be told *not* to?
- Another client is told that there may be good reasons not to change. But this is just the opposite of what everyone else has been urging. Why would a therapist align with reasons *not* to change?
- A parent, needing to regain control of her child's behavior, is taught to take charge by not always taking charge. Yet this parent has always feared giving in. Why *discourage* taking charge?

Let us briefly review the therapy modalities, frames, and rationales that make each of these counterintuitive interventions seem like reasonable approaches.

From a cognitive-behavioral point of view on panic attacks, the first client has been attempting to master his panic by worrying about losing control. The client needs to be able to think differently about the sensations that may trigger panic, the thoughts that precede panic, and the situations in which panic tends to occur. Thus, he needs to go toward the anxiety and learn more about it to master it.

In the second example, the reader will recognize that this chronically depressed client is being trained in mindfulness, the 2,000-year-old practice that has recently become a trendy and effective new practice. She is being taught to avoid the vicious cycles of repeated depressive rumination by allowing those depressing ideas to appear and yet not acting on them. Letting them float by as clouds in the sky without judging them. This simply stops the vicious cycle before it begins.

The quarreling couple in the third example is being trained in one of the evidence-supported approaches to couple therapy; in this case, it might be the integrative couple therapy approach of Jacobson and Christensen (1996). The therapist is putting the partners into the paradoxical situation of learning from their inevitable quarrels rather than avoiding or catastrophizing over them.

The next couple is participating in a classic, Masters and Johnson (1976) sex therapy intervention. The therapist is helping the partners escape the vicious cycles of performance anxiety and allowing them to discover the spontaneous passion of intimacy. They had been trapped in the classic "be spontaneous" paradox of trying to will a response that will come naturally if they will only allow it.

When the client in the next example is told that there may be good reasons not to change, the therapist is most likely operating from the stage of change model common to the motivational interviewing approach of Miller and Rollnick (2012). The therapist is aligning with the client's view that he may not really have a problem, or if he does, that the risks of changing may far outweigh the benefits. This is really the ultimate of empathy with clients. They are the ones who will need to make the change if they decide to. From Miller and Rollnick's perspective, this makes sense.

The therapist who is cautioning the parent not to always forcefully take charge with her misbehaving child is pulling from the explosive child approach of Ross Greene (2001) and using the ABC baskets or the three plans to prioritize interventions with the child. If the parent "goes to the mat" or reacts strongly to everything her child does, she will continually invite meltdowns or escalating vicious cycles. Parents need to negotiate on some things and just let other things pass. Natural consequences will take care of much of this. Life is a good teacher. We all know this, as both parents and therapists!

As stated, each of these evidence-supported approaches offers what might be viewed as a counterintuitive approach to clients trapped in their problems. It seems like clients or problem solvers are being asked to do the opposite of what makes sense to them and, in fact, to most people. The objective of this chapter is to show that this shared irony points to a powerful unifying framework that is at the heart of all effective psychotherapies. The common goal of change runs through all treatments that work. This may seem trivial or self-evident, yet we consistently overlook the nature of change when discussing what unifies therapies that work.

PREMISES AND COROLLARIES

To provide effective therapies, clinicians need a theory of how problems are formed and maintained. The process view provides a metalevel explanation for common errors that initiate vicious cycles. This view subsumes varying rationales provided by specific treatment models. The following offer some variations on first-order solutions.

1. *Unnecessary actions are taken to solve a problem.* Unnecessary actions are actions that move the problem-solver in a direction that goes away from the problem or move in a direction that over-pursues the problem. Movement away from the problem includes avoidance or other means of escape that involve attempts to rationalize the problem away or disqualify it. Movements that go too close to the problem involve efforts that are designed to make the problem go away by force or make something happen that can only occur more naturally.
2. *Necessary actions are not taken.* This involves lack of action or failure to attend to situations that are becoming increasingly problematic. This is like the old saying about hiding ones' head in the sand or about the emperor, Nero, fiddling while Rome burned.
3. *Efforts to solve the problem occur at the wrong level.* This involves the way that the problem-solver understands the problem. Vicious cycles occur when problem-solvers read too much or not enough into the problem.

OPERATIONALIZING SECOND-ORDER CHANGE

On the basis of our discussion thus far, predictions can be made about the direction effective therapies will pursue in response to different types of vicious cycles. The phrase *something to do with* is used out of respect for the many ways that exist for bringing about second-order change. Because change is so complex, many of these elements may be observed in any given case.

1. If the first-order solution is to go away from the problem, the second-order solution will have something to do with going toward it.
2. If the first-order solution is to overpursue the problem, the second-order solution will have something to do with stopping and reversing the pursuit.
3. If the first-order solution is to not attend to the problem, the second-order solution will involve acknowledging the problem and taking necessary problem-solving action.
4. If the first-order solution involves making the problem overly complex, the second order solution will involve simplifying the problem and narrowing problem-solving efforts down to the problem at hand and clarifying the problem's parameters.
5. If the first-order solution is to overintervene with normal difficulties of daily living, second-order solutions will involve tolerating and accepting the amount of unpleasantness that is a natural part of the human condition.
6. If the first-order solution reads too little into the difficulty, or simplifies the problem so much as to trivialize it, the second-order solution will honor the complexity of the problem. To honor complexity entails both respecting and assisting the problem-solver with building an understanding that clarifies the problem and its parameters in a way that is understood by the problem-solver.

RELATIONSHIPS AS CHANGE AGENTS

The long-standing debate between common factors and specific factors has begun to resolve, yet only gradually, as discussed in Chapter 2 (see also Fraser & Solovey, 2007). Many still emphasize techniques within specific theories with only passing acknowledgment of the need for the right kind of relationship (cf. Nathan & Gorman, 2015). Others press the effects of relationship and common factors so strongly as to relegate the effects of specific techniques to minor roles in treatment (cf. Duncan, Miller, Wampold, & Hubble, 2010; Norcross, 2011; Wampold & Imel, 2015a). It is becoming clearer, however, that all therapists offer specific techniques within a trusting relationship. It is also gradually emerging that the nature of a therapist's relationship with clients is an intervention itself and not merely a precondition for the active ingredients of specific techniques (Frank & Frank, 1991; Fraser & Solovey, 2007). Furthermore, all interventions occur within the context of a given theory or therapeutic rationale, agreed on by both therapist and client (Fraser, Grove, Lee, Green, & Solovey, 2014; Fraser, Solovey, Grove, Lee, & Greene, 2012; Sprenkle, Davis, & Lebow, 2009). A quick look at how relationships connect with second-order change may clarify how they fit with the process of change view.

Recall from Chapter 2 that both Lambert (1992) and Wampold (Wampold & Imel, 2015a) affirmed that, aside from extratherapeutic factors (which I address subsequently), the next most influential factors in client improvement (30%) were likely common factors, including such things as empathy, warmth, acceptance, encouragement of risk-taking, and so on. Jerome Frank (Frank & Frank, 1991) made the strong case across all healing relationships that a validating and affirming relationship offered the opposite of what most clients expect from others when they share their sense of demoralization. He termed this effect *remoralization*, and it is the core of Rogerian and other person-centered humanistic approaches. This represents the classic pattern reversal of second-order change. However, how else do these elements of effective relationships influence pattern reversals from the process of change perspective?

In his text *Psychotherapy Relationships That Work: Evidence-Based Responsiveness*, Norcross (2011) addressed the range of effective elements of effective therapy relationships. He included chapters on the *alliance* in individual, child, couple, and group therapy; *cohesion* in groups and *empathy* in individual therapy; *goal consensus* and *collaboration*; positive *regard* and *affirmation*; and *congruence* and *genuineness*, among other elements I address later. Each of these elements becomes an intervention itself. Let's take a look at each of these in turn from the process view and how they contribute to effective pattern shift.

- The *alliance*, including bonds, goals, and related tasks, not only offers hope for problem resolution to clients but also offers clients an alternative context for their problem. This helps make the process of pattern shift or second-order change make sense. Frank would also say that such hope is a second-order change in itself in that it reverses most clients' pattern of hopeless demoralization. The process view also suggests that therapists must enter the "river" of the relationship to have influence to shift its process, as discussed in Chapter 4 on process.

- *Cohesion* and *empathy* offer consensual validation for the experience of the problem, validating and normalizing clients' experience and helping them build trust in their therapist for the journey ahead. From the process view, empathy allows the therapist to identify clients' worldview and the context of their experience. It also offers clients the experience of having their views and lived experiences validated. This is the first step outside the client's problem level as clients and therapists join in their journey of pattern shift. It is crucial that the client joins into a new metalevel group or therapeutic alliance to help make the therapeutic pattern reversals make sense.
- *Goal consensus* and *collaboration* both address elements of context from the process view, discussed in Chapter 5. Overlapping with alliance factors, clients need to agree with therapists on a rationale that helps to explain their problem patterns and to make sense of the related procedures and techniques that will often appear counterintuitive or paradoxical from their original viewpoint. Recall that all second-order change appears paradoxical from the viewpoint of first-order solutions.
- *Positive regard and affirmation* further reinforce Frank's emphasis on remoralization. Therapists offer clients a *reversal* of the hopelessness and lowered self-worth they often feel about themselves and expect from others. At times, these two elements alone become the major effective ingredients of the second-order change needed by clients. Receiving acceptance, affirmation, and positive regard when they expected rejection becomes a *pattern reversal in itself* for clients and may be all that is needed. At other times, they provide the first step into the metalevel relationship allowing clients to gain perspective on their failed solutions.
- *Congruence and genuineness* offered by therapists allows clients to believe that the qualities of this working relationship are valid and true. The process view and its social constructionist base allow therapists to genuinely offer as many approaches and relationships as are needed by clients without feeling somehow ungenuine or incongruent with themselves and their point of view as they change their positions and interventions.
- From the process of change perspective, all of these relationship elements converge on the goal of second-order change with clients.

CHANCE AND CONTINGENCY

A final note regarding the place of extratherapeutic factors as they relate to the process of change is in order. Recall from Chapter 2 that both Lambert (1992) and Wampold (2001; Wampold & Imel, 2015a) affirmed that the largest influence on client improvement (40%) came from what they termed *extratherapeutic change*, such as client strengths, fortuitous events, and social support that help in recovery aside from psychotherapy. The place of fortuitous events should not be underestimated when it comes to pattern shift and second-order change. The influence of the typical "therapy hour" can be grossly overestimated. Sometimes, at best, therapy may offer a frame for understanding and acting on fortuitous events outside therapy. Simply stated, numerous factors may either block or redirect clients' typical solution patterns and open the opportunity for new learning or patterns. Stephen Jay Gould (1990) made a major change to Darwinian evolutionary theory by pointing to chance and contingency in evolution. A chance meteoroid colliding with the earth, for example, created a cascading set of extinctions and opened space for the evolution of mammals. As we will see in the next chapter on process, in Heraclitus' stream, a chance encounter with a boulder in the stream can create cascading changes in directions and turbulence. So too can a couple's intimacy be rekindled by sleeping in a new bed on vacation that was pushed against the wall and required them to crawl over each other. It remains for therapists to reinforce these changes by fitting them into new frames and encouraging clients to own the new patterns as their own.

Several approaches incorporate chance and contingencies outside treatment into their treatment process. Some current approaches actively encourage clients to redirect their attention to what might be chance exceptions to the problem pattern. Approaches, such as solution-focused therapy, actively ask clients to attend to the exceptions to their usual vicious cycle patterns between sessions and build on those. Clients focus their attention on different events, ideas, and interactions than those usually part of their current vicious cycle pattern. As they attend to these new triggers for interaction, they break the former cycle and open the possibility of initiating an alternative virtuous cycle. This is a direct pattern interdiction aside from setting a formal new frame for the old vicious cycle. However, the client and therapist must at least implicitly agree that there are differences to look at, or times of strength in the face of adversity on which to build. Other approaches, such as mindfulness, seek to acknowledge chance triggers in everyday life but block common solutions, thus interdicting vicious cycles before they begin. The ancient practice of mindfulness is being taught to clients who then practice engaging with chance triggers without applying their usual solution patterns, such as judging or acting on them to either challenge or go away from them.

These interventions engineer new paths by redirecting attention or blocking vicious cycle patterns outside treatment. Both options facilitate pattern shifts in the process of change.

Chance and contingencies in the ongoing flow of life are at the heart of the process perspective. The process view embraces extratherapeutic factors and brings them into the context of treatment. Not all change is planned and engineered through therapy. If therapists embrace and incorporate change as expected and consistent elements of their clients' lives, they can anticipate and build on apparently random or chance shifts and ultimately accelerate desired changes for clients. Extratherapeutic factors become part of therapy within the process view. In fact, most good therapists already do this. Embracing the process view offers both context and meaning to those practices.

CYCLING BACK

This chapter has been all about change. Change is what our clients want from therapy. Desire to change unwanted difficulties is what has triggered their struggles to return to normal. Their struggle to change their identified problems is the real problem. The problem is not the trigger, as I discuss further in the next chapter on process. The client's response to that trigger creates the vicious cycle of first-order change. Therefore, from a process of change view, change is the problem, change is the goal, and change is the solution. As discussed, knowingly or not, second-order change is the target of all effective psychotherapies. This is a change in how clients are attempting to change their problem. To make this shift, clients need a fitting frame or rationale that takes them out of their current level of logical views and solutions (a metaview from the theory of logical types) and enables new and most often opposite solutions. All clients and therapists are seeking this second-order change. All effective treatments target and achieve this. It unifies them. Furthermore, all of this naturally flows from the process paradigm.

4

PROCESS AND SYSTEMS

Consider the case of John. John had gone to the outdoor rock concert with friends, not knowing they had brought along some brownies with marijuana baked into them. His date that day had also brought some sugar cubes with LSD in them. After eating the brownies and a sugar cube, John had to be taken to the concert infirmary. He thought he was going insane. His friends assured him that his reactions were to the drugs and apologized, but the terrible, frightening event continued to play out for John over the next year. Whenever he was in an uncertain situation or one requiring him to be clearheaded and articulate, he found himself having racing thoughts, a pounding heart, tingling in his hands, and a need to sit down before passing out from hyperventilation. Each time, the more he tried to calm himself, the

Select passages from this chapter first appeared in *Integrative Families and Systems Treatment (I-FAST): A Strengths-Based Common Factors Approach*, by J. S. Fraser, D. Grove, M. Y. Lee, G. J. Greene, and A. D. Solovey, 2014, New York, NY: Oxford University Press. Copyright 2014 by Oxford University Press. Adapted with permission.

http://dx.doi.org/10.1037/0000078-005
Unifying Effective Psychotherapies: Tracing the Process of Change, by J. S. Fraser

more out of control he seemed to become. It wasn't until John went to the university's health service and learned about the physical bases of a panic attack that his troubles went away.

Now consider Nick and Sandra. Nick couldn't get the image of his wife, Sandra, making love with another man out of his head after she had confided that she and a former boyfriend had actually had sex. Eventually, it became hard for Nick and Sandra to make love with each other. He had become insanely jealous of Sandra in social situations and when she went to work. Despite her protests and assurances that Nicolas was her one and only love, Nick couldn't get over being suspicious. Sandra confided her distress to her boss at work when he found her in tears one day. His compassion and understanding drew her closer to him, and now she worried that Nick would find out. Nick and Sandra eventually separated, and Sandra began dating her boss.

Now consider these events in November 1989. On November 8, 2014, on page A21 of the New York edition of *The New York Times*, an op-ed article appeared with the headline "How the Berlin Wall Really Fell." It recounted a set of events and interactions that led to the opening of the Berlin Wall on the night of November 9, 1989. As it turns out, the opening was not really planned but occurred as a sequence of interchanges that led to cascading sequences of events that no one might have ever predicted. Excerpts from this article present the picture this way:

> In truth, the opening of the Berlin Wall on the night of Nov. 9, 1989, was not planned. Well into that year, East Germany remained nearly inescapable: The last killing by a guard at the wall occurred in February 1989; the last shooting, a very near miss, in April; the last death during an escape attempt on the larger East German border, only 10 days earlier. . . . However, in response to some political climate changes, Politburo members in East Berlin decided to make minor changes to the state's draconian travel rules—but to retain their power to deny travel permission on a whim.
>
> The announcement of this pseudo-reform, at an international news conference televised on the night of Nov. 9, was botched. The bumbling Politburo member running the conference, Günter Schabowski, read the news release for the first time on air. Much of his reading was garbled, but a few phrases popped out: trips abroad would be "possible for every citizen," starting "right away, immediately." Shorn of their context, these phrases mistakenly gave journalists and TV viewers the impression that the wall was open. . . . And so, when tens of thousands of Berliners headed toward the wall in the minutes after the news conference, the entire system cracked.
>
> When one of the regime's most loyal subordinates, a Stasi officer named Harald Jäger who was working the Nov. 9 night shift at a crucial

checkpoint in the Berlin Wall, repeatedly phoned his superiors with accurate reports of swelling crowds, they did not trust or believe him. They called him a delusional coward. Insulted, furious and frightened, he decided to let the crowds out, starting a chain reaction that swept across all of the checkpoints that night.

What is the connection between these three rather different and seemingly unrelated instances? What, if anything, do they have in common? One is the case of an individual struggling with himself over panic attacks; the next is a couple anguishing with each other over jealousy; and the third is the amazing true story of how a set of accidental communications brought down the Berlin Wall. The answer is that they all offer examples of the process of change in human systems. Each is a patterned flow of interactions at successively more complex levels of systems. Each is the product of what might be seen as a purely accidental incident or trigger. Moreover, each evolved into a vicious cycle of something surely not intended. Each is an example of *process* and *change* within open social systems. This alternative perspective or paradigm relates to all levels of human interaction. It applies to societies, groups, individuals, to clients and therapists at moment-to-moment therapeutic interchanges. However, what do we mean by this, and how is it relevant to the idea of integrating psychotherapies that work?

EVOLVING A NEW PARADIGM

The Evolution of a Systems View of Change

A key element of the process point of view over centuries is the idea of ongoing flow of interactions in the process of change. Interactions do not occur willy-nilly but form systems of mutual influence similar to Heraclitus and the river. (This is also reflected in the concept of responsiveness in psychotherapy; Kramer & Stiles, 2015; Stiles, Honos-Webb, & Surko, 1998.) This turns our attention to what has been broadly termed *systems theory*. Systems theory is the interdisciplinary study of systems in general, with the goal of discovering patterns and principles that are applicable to all types of systems, at all nesting levels, in all fields of research. In many ways, systems theory shares the same roots as the process of change view discussed in the previous chapter. Differentiated from Western rationalist traditions of philosophy, system thinking links with the *I Ching* of Lao Tzu as a systems approach and shares a frame of reference similar to pre-Socratic philosophy and Heraclitus in Western thought. It charts the flow of the river of human interaction.

The systems view is based on several fundamental ideas:

1. All phenomena can be viewed as a web of relationships among elements, or a system.
2. All systems—whether electrical, biological, or social—have common patterns, behaviors, and properties.
3. Observers can analyze common patterns to develop insight into the behavior of complex phenomena. Such observations can move closer toward a unity of the sciences.

Basic Concepts of Systems Theory

A brief tutorial of the basic concepts may be helpful here, and then we will move forward to look at proposed differences in system levels and some of the newest applications across scientific domains. First, let us define some of the key ideas of a systemic view.

System

A system is a "set of units or component parts that together make up a whole arrangement or organization" (Goldenberg & Goldenberg, 2012, p. 472). A system has been defined as a regularly interacting or interdependent group of items forming a unified whole. In the most general sense, system means a configuration of parts connected and joined together by a web of relationships. A system is composed of parts in ongoing interaction, and yet the boundary of a system is a decision made by an observer, or a group of observers based upon their focus, interests, ideas, language, and traditions. Systems are goal directed, rule governed, and self-correcting. A primary goal of a system is to maintain itself as it interacts with its environment or to change itself as the environmental context of the system changes. Maintenance and change occur through a system of interaction, referred to in systems theory as positive and negative feedback loops. (Positive and negative feedback loops are discussed in more detail later in this chapter.)

Wholeness and Nonsummativity

It is said of systems that the whole is more than and different from the mere sum of its parts. This means that the ongoing patterned interaction among elements of a defined system is what defines it. A system cannot be defined by an explanation of any one or several items of the system on its own but only by their patterned process of interactions. Think about the sound of one hand clapping. The couple's relationship at the beginning of the chapter cannot be defined by looking at each one separately but only by addressing their patterns of interaction.

Open and Closed Systems

Any defined interacting set of items is said to have a boundary defined by observers and describers. The extent to which the system interactions occur only among elements within that system or to which those interactions are open to inputs from outside the defined boundaries defines their respective *closed* or *open* nature. A closed system might be the proverbial "house of cards" that has rigid equilibrium among the balanced cards and collapses at any introduction of outside breeze or touch. A semi-open system might be the human body, which depends upon the input of air, food, fluids, et cetera, and yet which must maintain certain homeostatic balances to maintain life. Open systems refer to the focus of most human interaction, from our student struggling with panic attacks, to the distressed couple, to the German citizens interacting around the eventual fall of the Berlin Wall.

Rules and Regularities

Systems are said to operate on set rules or regularities of interaction. These regularities may be set by the nature of the system, as they would be in a watch or a body. They may also vary according to the norms and beliefs of a culture, as they would in a system such as a marriage. Regularities also govern at macro levels, such as the sociopolitical system we saw around the fall of the Berlin Wall at the beginning of the chapter. The emergent patterns of flocks of birds are the results of only a few simple rules of how close to fly to the next bird and how to find safe landing places, for example.

Equifinality and Multifinality

This set of terms sound daunting and potentially confusing; however, they come down to a set of complementary principles of open systems. *Multifinality* is the idea that in open systems, you can get to a wide variety of *different ends* from the *same beginning point*. For example, imagine that you are sitting in a classroom, and someone comes in and starts insulting people at random. Some people may insult back, others may sit there and take it, others may leave the room, and yet another person may physically attack the guy. It's the same situation for everyone, but it leads to a set of different outcomes. This stands in contrast to sitting in a class and the fire alarm goes off. That's a case in which, with few exceptions, the same situation leads to the same outcome. Everyone gets up and leaves. *Equifinality* states that the *same end* may be reached from a widely *different set of beginning points*. An example of equifinality could be the many ways that people become depressed. The causes of depression are many, and they can be very, very different. Nevertheless, the intervening process from those different beginnings can lead to the same outcome: depression. The alternative is linear cause–effect: If you are infected with the influenza virus, you get the flu; the poliovirus, you get polio; and so on. The takeaway point is that it is not the beginning or end states in any open system that are important. Instead, the *intervening process* of evolving interaction among system elements makes the difference.

Circular Causality and Nonlinearity

Circularity in systems has been defined in this way: "The relationship of the progression of causes is such that the initial cause is also affected by the progression itself" (Simon, 1985, p. 212). This contrasts with *linearity*, in which "feedback processes are not involved . . . the cause–effect sequence does not lead back to the starting point" (Simon, 1985, p. 212). In effect, causality is a circle—or better said, a spiral as it moves forward. This leads us to the property of feedback.

Feedback

The term *feedback* describes the patterned nature of interactions within any system over time. The basic unit of operation of a feedback loop is change or difference. A detected difference from a set norm initiates a reaction on that difference. In linear cause–effect, Item A influences Item B, which then influences Item C in an A–B–C linear sequence. In contrast, systemic feedback is circular and it evolves. A influences B, which then feeds back to influence A^1 and in turn influences to B^1 and so on in a circular pattern. There are two main kinds of feedback loops:

1. *Negative feedback loops* are deviation reducing. They are circular processes of interaction among group members that seek to pull perceived differences from a desired norm or state back to the norm. If a child runs toward a busy street, parents call out warnings or act to stop them. In most instances, these negative feedback loops of interaction succeed in keeping the system well within its desired or normative patterns and rules.
2. *Positive feedback loops* are deviation amplifying. They are circular interaction processes among group members in which the resulting interaction increases the differences from the initial starting points. A well-known mechanical example of this is the screech heard from holding a microphone too close to a speaker. A small noise from the speaker is picked up by the microphone, amplified by the system, put out in its louder form through the speaker, and then picked up again by the microphone only to repeat the cycle of amplification. This produces a deafening screech until the microphone is moved away, and the feedback loop is broken.

Positive and negative feedback loops are the key sets of interactions we observe in the systemic process. One of the early adapters of systems theory applied to social systems was Gregory Bateson (1972, 1979). Bateson described the evolution of interaction in human systems as a kind of *alternating ladder*, as described in Chapter 3 of this volume on change. Attempts at stability (or negative feedback) at one level are followed by movement to another level of adjustment through positive feedback. This is followed by the next attempts at stability through negative feedback and so on. Attempts at stability often work, yet sometimes they create a *trigger* for escalation into a positive feedback cycle. For example, some attempts to get youth to come home on time do work. Other times the very attempt to correct a curfew violation is the kick point for an escalating fight, resulting in more curfew violations and a worse situation for all involved. Thus, positive and negative feedback link in an evolving positive cycle. Sometimes attempts to create stability succeed, and other times the attempt at stability is the very thing that destabilizes the system and moves it further from its desired form.

Physicists Briggs and Peat (1989), in describing dynamic systems, viewed the relationship between positive and negative feedback loops in a similar way as did Bateson. As they stated, "Negative feedback loops regulate, positive loops amplify. Myriads of loops are hooked together in such a way that the internal organization of an organism can continuously adjust to the demands of its environment" (153). In this sense, they refer to the *spiral* as an iconic representation of such evolution and process as it has existed over the millennia in human symbols all over the earth as reflected in the interconnected Celtic spirals used on the cover of this book. The vicious and virtuous cycles of our clients' lives and of the process of psychotherapy are both reflected in the work of Gregory Bateson and the more recent findings on dynamic systems.

Feedback and Value Judgments

There is one final note on the terms *positive* and *negative feedback*. Language can be confusing here. Negative feedback simply reduces deviation to return to a set state, whereas positive feedback simply increases perceived deviations. The terms *negative* and *positive* should not be confused with value judgments about good or bad. The term *positive feedback*, for example, says nothing about whether the escalating pattern is desired, good, or "positive." A positive feedback loop is simply one in which some deviation is amplified. The more of one thing that occurs is linked with the more of another thing happening. Positive feedback is escalation.

We have noted the microphone-speaker screech and the curfew escalation between parents and youth. These both have an implied negative value. We don't desire them. In this case, we would refer to these positive feedback loops as *vicious cycles*. The feedback escalated something not desired. The student's panic attacks and the couple's cycle of distrust and denial are both vicious cycles from their views.

However, there are as many or more examples of other positive feedback loops that increase desired results. A recent television commercial in the U.S. market shows people observing kind deeds done by another. Then the person who saw that kindness passes it on through another kind gesture for another. Someone sees that kindness done and does another kind deed for another, and so on. The message is to feed help and compassion forward, and our culture will improve for it.

In sum, when a positive feedback loop supports and amplifies something desired, valued, or viewed as "positive," we refer to it as a *virtuous cycle*. If what is being escalated or amplified is not desirable, we say it is a *vicious cycle*.[1] Whether a positive feedback cycle is labeled a vicious cycle or a virtuous cycle is the result of a *value judgment* on what is being escalated. This is the entrance point for *context*, which is discussed at length in the next chapter. The point being developed in this book is that in most effective treatment interventions, practitioners are noting, interrupting, and redirecting *vicious cycles*. At the same time, the goal of most effective interventions is to note, create, and then support *virtuous cycles*.

Levels of Systems

Before we get too far away from the basic theories of systems, one more important note needs to be made about the nature of the systems we are dealing with in psychotherapy. These systems are what we may all agree to be systems of *human interaction*, or *sociocultural systems*. Although the aspiration of the cybernetics and general systems theory movement has always been to unify approaches to systems across domains of science, and in many ways it has, the sociologist Walter Buckley (1967) made some important distinctions regarding the qualitatively different nature of three different levels of systems. Noting that the excitement over the new cybernetic systems theory had swept across sciences, including sociology, Buckley cautioned against the wholesale use of cybernetic and systems terms and concepts such as *equilibrium*, *homeostasis*, and so on, that are appropriate to some levels of systems and yet not to others, such as open social systems. Much of cybernetics and system theory was developed within the areas of mechanical, chemical, and biological systems and then imported for use with open social systems without examining its applicability. By way of example, Buckley called these levels the *mechanical/equilibrium*, *organismic/structural*, and *sociocultural/process-adaptive*.

[1]From Fraser, Grove, Lee, Greene, and Solovey (2014).

Most relevant to practitioners, the sociocultural/process-adaptive level in Buckley's scheme of levels represents the level within which we as psychotherapists are working. Outlining the most relevant properties of this process level for us as psychotherapists may help.

First, the elements of social systems are the interactions of *individuals* or *groups within social context*. Thus, the anxious college student interacted with his friends at the rock concert and then with himself as he escalated through successive panic attacks. The couple interacted with each other and others both currently and historically in the devolution of their marriage. The people of East Germany and their government and representatives interacted through information from news media and official communication pathways toward the stunning opening of the Berlin Wall.

Second, the interaction of social system elements is information exchange. These elements continually change and evolve through the process of information exchange and flow. In their classic work *Pragmatics of Human Communication*, Watzlawick, Beavin, and Jackson (1967) made clear that in human interaction, one cannot *not* communicate. Within context, all behaviors represent communication, no matter whether they are verbal or behavioral. Even the absence of action when it is expected is communication and offers information. (Not hearing from the German politicians that the gates should not be opened led to the opening of the Berlin Wall gates.)

Third, such social systems are fundamentally open. Buckley said the viability of these systems depends on variability. Although a couple might have a stable relationship, that relationship is constantly defined and redefined by the couple's interactions within a cultural context of observed rules and norms. This is not to say that fights and quarrels might not emerge through misunderstanding or perceived violations of expectations by the partners or that the relationship may dissolve as the result of those problems, as it did in the couple at the beginning of this chapter. The point is that all interactions within such systems are through information exchange within language and cultural contexts, rules, and norms.

As we shall see in more detail in the next chapter, these rules, norms concepts, and languages are themselves the products of coevolving interaction. Although they help shape, channel, and define the nature of interaction among individuals and groups, they are themselves shaped and evolved in a coevolutionary way as a product of feedback in these open social systems.

Similar to the process view, in systems theory, change is continual over time—sometimes more gradual and just as often rather rapid or sudden. None involved at that time might have ever predicted the sudden opening of the Berlin Wall, and yet it happened suddenly as a result of a cascading set of miscommunications.

Turning to the place of both negative and positive feedback in social systems, these systems alternate with both negative and positive feedback. This is similar to Gregory Bateson's (1972, 1979) alternating ladder mentioned earlier. An attempt to maintain stability (through negative feedback) at one point in time may be followed by an escalating positive feedback loop at the next, often the result of the prior solution's attempt to maintain balance. Thus, for example, the college student's attempt to calm down in the face of growing racing thoughts or rapid heart rate may escalate those very things because they point to his lack of control. The husband's attempt to remember to forget the image of his wife making love to a former boyfriend only served to affirm that image and make it even harder to forget. His wife's confiding in her boss only served to create another relationship to be denied. In the end, positive feedback cycles dominate sociocultural systems. They evolve over time through an emergent process of variation in response to both internal and external variations. The positive feedback cycle that led so rapidly to the fall of the Berlin Wall might be described as a vicious cycle, as it might have been through the eyes of the East German government members. However, it can also be described as a virtuous cycle, as it likely was in the eyes of the East German people wishing to leave. The labeling of the cycle is a product of the value given to that positive feedback cycle by observers of the pattern. Certainly most clinicians and patients would likely to describe the positive feedback cycles that repeatedly led to the college student's panic attacks as vicious cycles, as they also might have done when viewing the patterns of the couple's dissolving marriage.

This leads to the idea of *pattern*. The perceived sequence of interactions in an open social system like human relationships is pattern. Pattern in systems is an emergent quality of a system observed by a describer. The pattern of flocks of birds seems like a beautiful pattern to us when, from another perspective, the flock is simply flying according to a simple set of implicit rules of how the birds interact in flight. The rules may be "do not collide" and "find a good place to land." The pattern is a product of our description and not inherent in the system. However, such descriptions often serve us well as therapists as we observe the patterns of what may be called vicious cycles of client problems. These patterns may also emerge from research on a given problem within a dominant culture, like the vicious cycle of panic attacks or the approach–retreat cycle patterns in couples.

Newer Views of Systems and Change

Recent perspectives, however, blur the distinct levels of systems discussed thus far. Although these developments may modify system levels, they also reinforce the process view and reflect the complexities of change in psychotherapy.

Chaos

The study of complexity, nonlinear dynamics, and chaos in open systems has modified a wide range of perspectives on the nature of systems across many areas of study. James Gleick (1987) introduced the public to chaos theory in his best-selling book, *Chaos: The Making of a New Science*. In his preface, he resonated with a process view when he wrote, "To some physicists, chaos is a science of *process* rather than state, of *becoming* rather than being" (p. 5, emphasis added). However, John Briggs and F. David Peat (1989) made the best translation of this often complex and technical perspective through their book, *Turbulent Mirror: An Illustrated Guide to Chaos Theory and the Science of Wholeness*. In chaos theory, the levels of systems break down even further. Nevertheless, as they do so, chaos theory converges on the principles of Buckley's process level rather than those of the mechanical or organismic. Briggs and Peat echoed the influence of paradigmatic bias we discussed earlier as they noted, "We are used to picking out such shapes as parallel lines, circles, triangles, squares, and rectangles in nature of art . . . [when] . . . Regular, simple orders are in fact exceptions in nature rather than the rule" (p. 110).

The study of complexity, dynamical systems, turbulence, and chaos has arisen from studying phenomena that were never that easy to study using more static, structure dominated, and gradualist traditions. It seems ludicrous to group such seemingly unrelated things together to study as the formation of clouds and weather, the turbulence of a stream of tap water as it bursts into chaotic flow, the action of the stock market, or the fight-or-flight reactions of a dog. (This study of complexity and dynamic systems, however, is exactly the focus of study as we examine the complex interactions of clients and their problems and the complex flow of psychotherapy.)

The subject of turbulence interested great minds and scientists from the time of Leonardo da Vinci, who drew details of turbulence, through a number of prominent nineteenth-century scientists. Yet all of this remained on the sidelines until the development of superfast computers that allowed visual displays and simulations of these turbulent processes. What evolved was a cascade of new concepts and discoveries. Recall Heraclitus' famous example that we can never step into the same river twice. His river may serve as an example of some of the concepts of the newer perspective on process and change as adapted from Briggs and Peat (1989).

Consider Heraclitus' stream flowing through a meadow in the spring. The stream's banks channel or constrain its flow. At this point, the water in the stream flows at a relatively steady, smooth rate. The width of the banks, the incline of the stream bed, and the volume of water entering the stream also determine its rate. Occasional boulders, outcroppings, and fallen trees also shape its flow at any given time. Now, let us follow the flow of this little stream as the context changes by just one factor—that of the volume of water.

The current flow of the stream initially presents a smooth, stable, linear character with its flow, for example, always returning to the same point as it flows around a large boulder for long periods. This might reflect those smooth periods in our lives when change is orderly and predictable. We are attracted back to the same recurring patterns.

Now consider that spring rains begin to increase the volume of water in Heraclitus' stream. While all other constraints of the stream remain the same, the flow and speed of the river's flow increase. At some point, the pattern of water just beyond the boulder suddenly changes. From the original stable point of return as the water makes its way around the boulder, the water now forms a whirlpool or vortex that cycles it around before it makes its way forward. This whirlpool may stay in the same place for a long time as well, similar to the classic vicious cycles of the student with panic attacks or the distressed couple. It represents the draw of similar escalating, patterned solutions. It becomes a vortex. In human interactions, this vortex draws all involved into the attractor of solution-generated problems representing problem-generated systems.

Eventually, as warmer days of summer creep into the surrounding mountains, snow melts and adds more water to the stream. The increased volume of water increases the speed of its flow. Now, as the water makes its way to the other side of the boulder, another sudden shift occurs. The single whirlpool of the last phase begins to spin off duplicate whirlpools that make their way farther downstream from the rock and begin to resemble Leonardo's drawings of turbulence. Additionally, the choppy water undergoes much faster and irregular changes. This chaotic process resembles the escalating cycles and patterns in East Germany leading to the sudden fall of the Berlin Wall, or the spreading cycles of suspicion and denial in the couple, or the various situations in which the student tried to control his panic.

Finally, as the speed and volume of water in the stream continue to increase, the area behind the boulder seems to lose all of its order, and the rates of flow at different points vary widely. This descent into turbulent chaos seems to have lost all order. Yet has it?

Similar to Leonardo da Vinci's drawings of turbulence, the whirlpools tend to break down into similar and smaller vortices, which then break apart again and duplicate themselves. Thus, there is an apparent order in this chaos that is self-similar at larger and smaller levels or scales. This self-similarity has been given the term *fractal* in the literature and has gained popular fame in beautiful computer-generated illustrations of its multiple swirls and spirals in what is termed *phase-space*, or the graphic depiction of the system's movements across time and space. This idea of fractals and self-similar patterns is important because it suggests that patterns repeat at larger levels of systems and over time. A sample of three different quarrels is likely to generalize to the couple's classic advance–retreat cycles over time. Several examples of the student's struggle to master his panic are likely to generalize to his major pattern of mastering by avoiding and controlling over time.

Cascading Changes

Heraclitus's river offers an enlightening glimpse into the flow of interactions in our evolving universe. Profound insights emerge from the life of a simple stream. These same rapid changes resulting from relatively small shifts, amplifying results in the alternating cycles of positive and negative feedback, and self-similar patterns across scales from larger to smaller, have been found to occur similarly across a wide range of different systems, including human interactional systems.

In 1960, while computer simulating the development of weather systems over time, Edward Lorenz found by accident that changing one small initial condition at the start of a cycle had cascading effects over time. (This is the so-called butterfly effect, captured in the now famous phrase "The effect of a butterfly flapping its wings in Hong Kong can create a rainstorm in New York.") Similarly, from a process, or *dynamic self-organizing systems*, perspective relatively small yet strategic shifts in concept or related interaction may have cascading positive effects in psychotherapy.

Far from being new, however, such butterfly effects, or the cascading effects of seemingly small changes, have been recognized by most of us over time. For example, classic and popular movies such as the 1946 film *It's a Wonderful Life* and the 1985 film *Back to the Future* revolved around the effect of slight changes in the history of human relationships. In *It's a Wonderful Life*, the angel, Clarence, showed George where everyone's life would have ended up without him. Similarly, Marty McFly in *Back to the Future* learned that his own existence depended on just a few chance incidents. In fact, the process systems emphasis on the effects of change and contingency, of small changes cascading to large results, and of the repetition of similar patterns at larger and smaller scales parallels the points discussed earlier by Stephen Jay Gould about punctuated equilibrium as the major modification of Darwinian evolution. Within the ongoing contingencies and regularities of open systems, seemingly insignificant shifts may have cascading large results in the evolution of species or in the struggle of a couple around fidelity in their relationship. From a process view, effective psychotherapy across effective approaches is all about pattern shift from vicious to virtuous cycles of change.

Self-Similarity and Pattern Repetition

Benoit Mandelbrot (1982), the major investigator of what he termed *fractals*, made an early point by showing that the process of major recessions is similar to monthly and daily stock price fluctuations. He showed that the larger recession could be duplicated and predicted by much smaller daily stock price fluctuations such that the plots fooled the experts. By *self-similarity* or fractals, Mandelbrot meant the repetition of patterns at larger and smaller scales, a process that also occurs in the distribution of galaxies in the universe and the shape of the coastline of Great Britain. Our clients' problems are likely to represent repeated similar solution patterns at all levels of their lives regarding the problem issue and across time.

This finding has particular relevance to human interaction and our clinical domain. It should be clear now that a process view places our clients and their problems in dynamic, self-organizing systems of ongoing interactions. From this perspective, clients' problems emerge as vicious cycles of escalating yet repeating failed solution patterns. Knowing that those problem patterns repeat across the time and scale of our clients' lives gives us a matchless tool to track their problem patterns and design pattern shifts of effective psychotherapy.

Assessing Problem Patterns in Therapy

Fractals and self-similarity apply equally to the area of psychotherapy. Attractor patterns translate into the vicious cycles of first-order change in the problems clients bring to practitioners every day. The concept of fractals implies that there are repeating patterns in the flow of our daily interaction—repeated over time and at smaller and larger levels of our lives. This applies in particular to problem cycles. Vicious cycles in clients' lives repeat themselves over and again. Therefore, in dynamic systems like those of our clients, *clinicians need only gain a sample of those repeated patterns* to find the pattern of the problem and the likely target for pattern shift and second-order change. For example, John Gottman (1999) has shown that a 5-minute sample of a couple disagreeing predicts their separation with a high degree of accuracy. Adopting the process of change view makes it clearer that effective therapy is about assessing problem cycles and designing pattern shifts. Thus, fractal self-similarity becomes a powerful tool in that enterprise.

A Difference That Makes a Difference

However, not all small differences will set off a cascade of amplifying change. Although the ability of a system to escalate a small change is often the heart of both creativity and destruction in systems, not all small changes will do so. Briggs and Peat (1989) addressed this with examples as follows:

> Biological systems remain stable by dampening most small effects except in those areas of behavior where a high degree of flexibility and creativity is required. Here the system remains highly sensitive to influx, close

to a state of chaos. A single honeybee entering a hive of thousands of interacting colleagues can, by doing a little dance indicating the location of pollen-rich flowers, launch the entire hive into the air.

Systems are also highly sensitive near those places that are the crystallized "memory" of past bifurcations [critical splitting changes]. Nations have usually evolved through bifurcations involving intense conflict. Consequently, they are highly sensitive to certain kinds of information which recreate those bifurcations. A single headline in a newspaper can mobilize an entire nation to war. (p. 145)

Returning to our couple at the beginning of the chapter, the image of his wife making love to another uniquely triggered the husband's continual concern about her potential future infidelity. He was apparently particularly sensitive to or insecure about that from past instances or information. The fumbled message in that evening news conference in Berlin caught the attention of all of those East Germans listening that their fondest wish to leave was about to come true. Other minor changes or information within both the couple and the news in Berlin made little difference. In his 1972 collection of essays, *Steps to an Ecology of Mind: Collected Essays in Anthropology, Psychiatry, Evolution, and Epistemology*, Gregory Bateson described critical information as "a difference that makes a difference."

Not all information or perceived differences will result in actions within systems to balance and amplify around that difference. In each system, there are critical parameters that will set off reactions that are more significant. Context exerts a major influence in defining what is a problem and defining how to go about solving it. Many clients will pass by or easily assimilate many events, while other events may trigger devastating patterns of psychological and relationship problems. In essence, there are vulnerabilities. Similarly, in psychotherapy, some interchanges will have little effect, whereas others may represent a tipping point toward success.

FOLLOWING THE PROCESS

Given the twists and turns I have taken you on through our discussion of systems and process theories, a summary of key points might be helpful. Within relatively open, complex systems like social relationships:

- *Observers define systems*. There are no systems out there that exist separate from the concepts, focus, and interests of observers. Whitehead's (1978) process system view suggests that everything is process. The appearance of enduring substance or structures is only a product of our limited point of view or ideas on what we are observing. The universe is a set of relationships between relationships between relationships—all of which change over time. What we view as a system is merely an observation of events in the process of change in a given segment of time. A patient's panic attacks, a couple's struggles, or a nation's change are all products of our focus and definitions of those interactions.

- *Change is constant and can be rapid.* Stability and structure are products of an observer's description of ongoing process at a specific time and space in the life of a system. Yet, as in the succeeding phases in Heraclitus' stream, change can also be rapid as the system amplifies in intensity over time. This applies equally to the lives of our clients and to the life of the process of therapy.
- *Process is primary.* Because in open systems, you can get to any arbitrary end from a wide variety of beginnings and, conversely, the same beginning point may result in widely different arbitrary ends, contingencies and interacting processes are critical. Current process is the best definition and access point into any given system. History is always relevant but does not always predict the same end—such as a panic attack, a dissolved relationship, or the fall of a dividing wall.
- *The goal of psychotherapy is shifting patterns.* Patterns are a sample of a chosen process of interaction at a given point in time and space in the ongoing system. The interacting patterns of the couple at the beginning of this chapter leading to their eventual breakup are just one example. We might have chosen different samples and punctuated them in different ways, yet they would all reflect the couple's distress. Furthermore, *patterns repeat* in self-similar cycles across time and scope. This is especially true around the attractors or vicious cycles or clients' problems.
- *A small sample of current patterns may reflect much larger system patterns.* As in the fractal principle of self-similar patterns occurring at successively larger scales, a smaller sample of patterned process may suffice to surmise an overriding similar process over time. From this view, just a few examples or iterations of the college student's attempts to control his panic become emblematic of variations on the same patterned and escalating cycles over time. The successive spirals of fractal images are clear examples.
- *Small changes can have cascading large results.* The overriding effects of positive feedback loops within the regularities of an open social system will tend to amplify change over time. A misinterpreted message delivered on one night in Berlin led to

the cascading and dramatic opening of the monolithic Berlin Wall. A slight difference while plotting weather patterns led a researcher to the idea of the butterfly effect. Similarly, a key reframe in psychotherapy, or a random difference in a client's life outside of treatment, may quickly lead to problem resolution for our clients.

- *Not all small changes will initiate cascading change.* Each system has certain sensitive points of information that are more likely to create reaction. The same difference may be reacted to as a potential threat to the system, a potential opportunity, and so on. The point is that each system has parameters that will identify *a difference that may make a difference.* Some call these *vulnerabilities.* This is the influence of context. The college student's panic attacks were initiated by perceived situations that threatened to make him lose control. The husband's jealous rages were triggered by his view of contexts for infidelity for his wife. The fall of the Berlin Wall was triggered by a perceived opportunity for escape.
- *Positive and negative feedback loops are complementary.* In response to a perceived difference, attempts at balance through negative feedback at one level may have the successive results of creating a positive escalating feedback over time. Our college student's attempt to calm down in the face of potential panic may have only fed back into cycles of anxiety and growing panic. His solutions became the problem, as did the husband's jealous attempts to prevent his wife's potential attraction to another man.
- *Constancy/stability and change are interrelated.* As we saw in Heraclitus' river, the water in the river might change in multiple ways while the identity of the river remained the same. The banks of the river may erode more slowly, while the turbulence of the stream may increase and create sudden shifts, but the identity of the stream remains constant. Constancy and change exist at different levels, while both are in process of change, as we saw in the chapter on change. Clients' attempting the same solutions with more intensity and variations on the same theme perpetuate and escalate their problem. Their solutions become the problem and perpetuate its identity.
- *Rules, regularities, and constraints within open systems channel their ongoing interaction patterns.* In Heraclitus' river or our stream, the constraints of the riverbank, the steepness, or angle of the river bottom, and the placement of the boulder constrained and

channeled the flow of water. In human social systems, norms, social conventions, concepts, and expectations reflect the constraints of a given social system. The context of our client's lives, including their culture, language, and personal histories and identities, channels the flow of their lives, as I discuss presently. (The same applies to therapists.) Shifting frames and metaphors through therapy rationales and interventions may rechannel that flow. Similarly, rechanneling their behavior or interactions may alter their frames, metaphors, and context.

CYCLING BACK

If you have gotten lost as we launched into the elements of systems, levels of systems, and parameters of the new systems view of dynamical systems and chaos, you are most likely still wondering what all of this has to do with integrating psychotherapies that work. Let's think further about the dilemma of describing how therapy works from the perspective of the medical model. Given the constraints of the medical model, clinicians can explain how therapy works from their given theoretical perspective. At the same time, perspectives cannot go outside of themselves to explain how other therapies work. The clinician trained in eye movement desensitization and reprocessing (EMDR) can explain what she thinks she is doing from the EMDR perspective but cannot explain how present-centered therapy (PCT) works. The reverse is also the case for the PCT perspective. If both therapies are equally effective and operate on different premises, then the credibility of the premises that underlie each therapy is suspect. The best we can say is that both work for unknown reasons.

A unity emerges, as we understand psychotherapy from a process view. From this unity, practitioners of all theoretical persuasions note, interrupt, and redirect vicious cycles. At this metalevel, the goals of effective interventions are to note, create, and then support virtuous cycles. This may sound easier said than done, and it often is. However, this process is at the heart of all effective psychotherapies, as we will see.

So what does all of this have to do with integrating psychotherapies that work? The answer is that, from a process view, all problems are vicious cycle patterns rooted in context. The goal of all treatments that work from this process perspective is therefore pattern shift in those vicious cycles. From the process view, context and process combine to shape change. A shift in context or process around vicious cycles defines success across all treatments that work. Thus, when psychotherapies work, from the process view, they all achieve pattern shift in one way or another. This focus on pattern shift or change is lacking in all current approaches to integrating psychotherapies that work. The process perspective offers a platform that unifies all psychotherapies that work around these principles of *context*, *process*, and *change*. All of this emerges from the process paradigm.

The foregoing principles of the process and systems view will help in unifying effective psychotherapy transdiagnostically. Some practical applications for therapists thus emerge as follows:

- How problem patterns begin is less important than the current patterns or solutions clients are using as they wrestle with it here and now.
- A small sample of clients' current solutions should generalize to repeating patterns across time and situations.
- The dominant culture's research literature on typical or general problem patterns for the most common problems offers guidance on what a clinician might expect to see for any given client.
- The cultural and personal contexts of clients will then combine to form the unique constraints that shape the specific vicious cycles for each client.
- The dominant culture's research literature on effective treatments for various problems offers valuable frames, rationales, and tools that work to create successful vicious cycle pattern shifts for each general problem.
- Fitting these various treatment approaches to what "makes sense" for the client and therapist is the task of treatment planning.
- The result of a good fit is the working alliance, with positive bonds, goal consensus, and related treatment procedures targeting the ultimate goal of pattern shifts or change in the vicious cycle at hand.
- As clients gain trust and join in a metalevel alliance with their therapist or helpful other, they can gain perspective as they "look down" at the failed cyclical patterns of their problem-generating vicious cycles.
- Because all pattern reversals in vicious cycles are counterintuitive or paradoxical from the level of clients' problems, new explanations or *frames* for their problems and their related treatment rationales help clients "make sense" of formerly counterintuitive solutions.
- Ongoing feedback within and between sessions allows continuous adjustments maintaining the trajectory toward the ultimate outcome of pattern shift.

- As clients achieve the targeted pattern shifts, therapists support those changes and applaud clients' achievements as personal, positive, and pervasive.
- As clients resume the process of their lives, practitioners enhance resilience and instill relapse prevention by supporting flexibility, encouraging practice, predicting future challenges, and remaining open to future contact.

Even after these general applications of the process view to the course of effective psychotherapy, you may think that the notions of patterns and pattern interruptions are still too vague to be of much clinical use. This journey deserves further travel. As we examine how social system constraints or constructs are cocreated and evolve, whether for an individual, in a marriage, for a culture, or all of these, guidelines for unifying effective psychotherapy will emerge relevant to all therapies. In the next chapter, I turn to context that both shapes and is shaped by this process of change.

5

CONTEXT

Consider the following scenarios.

The day after Christmas of 2004, a devastating tsunami washed over Sri Lanka and drowned more than a quarter of a million people in the region. A team of Western experts in trauma and disaster intervention from Kiryat Shmona, Israel, flew to the country and immediately began training indigenous helpers like Buddhist monks and others to identify the typical responses to trauma and then to know how to intervene. Along with other Western experts, the public and local interveners were trained to recognize the three symptom clusters of avoidance, numbness, and hyperarousal. Speedy intervention and retelling or reworking the memories of trauma with trained professionals was the major protocol. The Red Cross models of "psychological first-aid" and "critical incident stress debriefing" were widely practiced.

Select passages from this chapter first appeared in *Integrative Families and Systems Treatment (I-FAST): A Strengths-Based Common Factors Approach*, by J. S. Fraser, D. Grove, M. Y. Lee, G. J. Greene and A. D. Solovey, 2014, New York, NY: Oxford University Press. Copyright 2014 by Oxford University Press. Adapted with permission.

http://dx.doi.org/10.1037/0000078-006
Unifying Effective Psychotherapies: Tracing the Process of Change, by J. S. Fraser

However, "clearly in denial" from the Western view, local adults and children only wished to go back to their families and schools. Failing in their efforts to resolve trauma in the face of Hindu beliefs in karma and Buddhist acceptance of pain and suffering as central to life, and the Sri Lankan people's remarkable and well-documented history of resilience in the face of hardship, the Israeli group returned home having learned more than they taught and hoping their interventions had not done more harm than good.[1]

At 1:00 p.m. on November 24, 1994, a 14-year-old girl in Hong Kong fell down and died in the street on the way home from school. She had died from the effects of self-starvation. Up to that point, the incidence of what we have come to call anorexia nervosa were extremely rare in Hong Kong (despite its being a very Westernized protectorate of Great Britain up to that time). In the few cases encountered each year, most patients explained their condition as caused by abdominal discomfort or tightness in the throat. There was no relationship between not eating and complaints about being fat or unsightly. Shortly after this 14-year-old girl's public death, the headlines in the Hong Kong newspapers all featured the story of her death, quoting Western experts on the growing threat of anorexia to capable young teenage girls. Although there was no evidence that anorexia was widespread in Hong Kong, within a year, there were calls for public education in the schools on the dangers of anorexia. Treatment clinics sprang up. Within a few years, several Hong Kong actors and singers were disclosing their struggles with anorexia and being compared with Western celebrities such as Princess Diana in England, who publicly disclosed her struggles with bulimia. Within the next 5 years, the incidence of anorexia in Hong Kong had grown exponentially. The causes given by patients now converged on the Western diagnostic manual symptoms of fear of being fat, distorted body image, and a striving for thinness as a sign of beauty in young, bright, and successful young women.[2]

In 1980, posttraumatic stress disorder (PTSD) was added to the third edition of the *Diagnostic and Statistical Manual of Mental Disorders* (*DSM–III*) of the American Psychiatric Association. By 2004, there were more than 20,000 articles, books, and papers indexed by the National Center for Post-Traumatic Stress Disorders, and the number continues to rise daily. The symptoms in the *DSM–III* are clear, but have they always been? It is clear that the diagnosis of PTSD can be true and real for a particular place and time yet not for all places and times. The more we look at differences in time and culture,

[1]As told to the author by the staff of the Community Stress Prevention Center (CSPC) in Kiryat Shmona, Israel, 2006.
[2]For a fuller account of this history and the cultural context surrounding it, along with other examples with other diagnoses, the reader is urged to refer to Ethan Watters's outstanding book, *Crazy Like Us: The Globalization of the American Psyche* (2010).

the more apparent it becomes that there is little about reactions to stress that are universal. Muscle weakness and joint pains were the common symptoms of traumatized British soldiers in the Boer Wars, whereas American Civil War soldiers complained of aching in the left chest, or withdrawal and apathy. "Shell shock" was the common term used in the World War I and included nervous tics, paralysis, and bizarre body movements. (See the classic 1930 film *All Quiet on the Western Front* for examples of shell shock in World War I; available online [https://www.youtube.com/watch?v=C4ERZoBipSM].) The impact of trauma in war is undeniable, yet the way it is expressed is a result of cultural beliefs at the time.

These interesting stories may appear to be unrelated to one another. They may seem disconnected from questions we have raised about the medical model, and psychotherapy outcome. However, they are quite related when understood through the lens of the process of change. More specifically these examples represent the effects of context.

Merriam-Webster's Collegiate Dictionary offers a simple definition of *context* as "the situation in which something happens: the group of conditions that exist where and when something happens" (http://www.merriam-webster.com/dictionary/context). The process and flow of all human interaction occurs within some form of context. Context helps define or explain the nature of all interaction. A smile may signify pleasure or happiness in one situation or be viewed as an evil leer in another. Context also helps channel the flow of interaction. For example, consider the simple social convention of greeting another on the street: The phrase "Hello. How are you?" is customarily met with the conventional reply "Fine, thank you. How are you?" Context also constrains many roles within our culture. As a man in Western culture, for example, my gender role often limits me from crying, or from wearing a skirt, or, as many would have it, from asking for directions. However, acknowledging my Scottish heritage at my daughter's wedding by wearing a kilt (or "skirt") was approved by all. Context shapes and channels the flow of all interaction in the process of change. It also defines for us what to expect and what to act on to correct or to see as a problem. It also suggests what appropriate solutions we should apply. If I belch at the dinner table in my own Western culture, I am expected to correct my poor table manners by saying, "Pardon me." However, in another culture, that same belch may be viewed as a compliment to the cook!

From the process view, context refers to factors that shape reciprocal interactions in which persons (individuals and groups) coconstruct their worldviews. Interactive factors include culture, language, gender, ethnicity, race, or other socializing influences and resulting norms. These factors channel or constrain interaction. Interaction within these constraints gradually shapes worldviews while in return, worldviews shape interactive factors or context. Returning to Heraclitus' river, we have referred to the banks of the river, for example, as context for the water. Those riverbanks both channel the water's flow and constrain it from overflowing its banks (unless torrential rains swell the flow of the waters to create a flood—the result of the broader context of the weather).

The term *context* is appearing more and more in the literature on psychotherapy. Jerome Frank (Frank & Frank, 1991) continually alluded to context in his cross-cultural examination of healing practices such as psychotherapy. Following Frank, Wampold (2001; Wampold & Imel, 2015a) has advocated a *contextual model* to unify psychotherapies around common factors. Constantino and colleagues (Constantino & Bernecker, 2014; Constantino, Boswell, Bernecker, & Castonguay, 2013; Constantino, Overtree, & Bernecker, 2014) have also applied the term *context* in explaining their approach to integrating psychotherapies. In broader terms, the recent emphasis in Western culture on *multiculturalism* and *diversity* emphasizes the influence of context as a foundation construct. The literature on psychotherapy now strongly emphasizes context. One might say that acknowledging context is the new context for psychotherapy!

The process view on context dovetails with Buckley's (1967) description of open social systems, discussed in Chapter 4 of this volume. From the process view, interactions are channeled by ideas; by constructs about the way things should be done; by explanations about the nature of experience; by understandings of what constitute appropriate gender roles; by the nature of the language used and words available in that language; by norms, metaphors, folkways, and morals within the system in question; and by what is considered a problem within a given system, and what we are typically supposed to do about it.

This chapter will shed more light on the ramifications of context as is related to clients and psychotherapy. I discuss the issue of *truth*, and models of truth. I argue that social constructionism offers a model of truth that is integral with the process of change view. Moreover, it offers clinicians a philosophical underpinning to integrate psychotherapy models whose premises may differ. I then expand the discussion to frames, metaframes, and therapeutic rationales and finally relate all of this to integrating psychotherapies that work.

TRUTH

> *We have to remember that what we observe is not nature in itself, but nature exposed to our method of questioning.*
>
> —*Werner Heisenberg*

Suggesting that our conceptual worlds are relative, such as in social constructionism, makes some fearful that we are advocating some form of solipsism. If reality is nothing more than a flow of constructs that change over time, then nothing is "true." If no true statements can be made, then no therapeutic rationales are valid. It follows that if treatment rationales are not valid, then clinicians cannot present them in a genuine way. Because genuineness is critical to delivering effective therapy, one might wonder how we could argue that social constructionism is a reasonable philosophical underpinning of the process of change perspective.

The preceding "realist"[3] concerns represent a misunderstanding of social constructionism (Gergen, 2015a). When understood in a proper context, social constructionism offers the opposite of realist fears. In other words, it offers an opportunity for clinicians to honor many perspectives and offer them in genuine ways that meet the unique needs of clients. Being able to resonate with multiple takes on reality increases compassion and empathy. To better understand the nature of social constructionism, I will place it in the context of other prevailing models of truth. The reader may be fascinated to learn, through our brief history, that just as there are many models of effective therapy, there are also many models of truth.

A BRIEF HISTORY OF TRUTH

Reality is merely an illusion, albeit a very persistent one.

—*Albert Einstein*

The Correspondence Model of Truth

Commonly, truth is viewed as the correspondence of language or thought to an independent reality. This is the *correspondence theory of truth*. This was the foundation of the Greek philosophers'—Socrates's, Plato's, and Aristotle's—views. Truth is determined by how it relates to "things" by accurately describing those "things." We check our hypotheses against the reality out there and find out what works. This is the basis of what I have discussed in previous chapters as a rational–empiricist perspective on finding truth, and it is a basis for medical models with their clinical trials. This model has its limitations, as discussed in previous chapters and as evidenced in

[3]Realism is similar to positivism and posits that there is an objective reality outside of the senses that can be discovered through scientific inquiry. This underlying philosophy does not work when there are multiple truths, as in the case of therapy models or conflicts between people's views.

some of the examples offered at the beginning of this one. The way trauma is usefully described and acted on in Western culture does not necessarily correspond to how it is experienced and effectively acted on in a culture like Sri Lanka.

The Consensus Model of Truth

Very simply, this perspective holds that truth is whatever is agreed on or might come to be agreed on by some specified group. At first glance, we might simply reject this position out of hand. It suggests that if a group agrees that Chicken Little was right that "the sky is falling," then it would most likely fall. Upon closer examination, it is apparent that the consensus theory of truth prevails in many aspects of our conceptual worlds. Consider that agreement among clinicians or of behavioral scientists, at a given time, generally defines what a discipline believes is true and subsequently dominates the directions and beliefs of that discipline. The *DSM–III* is a classic example. At one time, it was considered true that homosexuality is a disorder. We also saw this in our discussion of how Darwin's evolutionary theories dominated research and obscured alternative views of evolution. I also have previously suggested that this consensus model of truth can be found in the consensus reached long ago to follow the rational–empiricist or logical–positivist perspective in psychology. As we have discussed, this consensus has dominated research and theories in psychology, sociology, and related social science disciplines until recently.

Yet consensus does not always mean that there is not an alternative equally or more useful view. We see this in Gould's rather revolutionary punctuated equilibrium model of evolution, the removal of homosexuality as a disorder, or the process model I am discussing here.

The Coherence Model of Truth

In many ways, the coherence theory of truth dovetails with the correspondence and consensus models. It suggests that any related statement about the truth of something must generally fit within an overall perspective of what is considered a true perspective. Beyond logical consistency, this view demands that propositions within a theory generally support each other in a coherent model.

This is a characteristic of the logical–positivist theories of truth underpinning much theory building in the social sciences. Coupled with the correspondence theory and the consensus theory, however, coherence theory building has been challenged because logical conclusions do not always lead to a coherent model. For example, the fact that there are a number of quite different, yet equally effective, psychotherapies does not lead to a coherent theory about how psychotherapy works. This is evident despite the fact that all internal propositions within the different theories of psychotherapy are consistent and coherent within each theory, or true to the theory. If truth corresponded to reality, and there was consensus on that correspondence, a coherent, agreed-on set of propositions and related procedures would emerge. It would then follow that there would be one best and "true" approach to psychotherapy. As we have seen, this is not so.

The Pragmatic Model of Truth

As I noted in a Chapter 2, Charles Peirce, William James, and John Dewey introduced variations of the pragmatic model of truth around the turn of the 20th century. These are also some of the founding fathers of academic psychology as we have come to know it. Simply stated, the pragmatic model of truth says that truth is determined by its utility. Truth is verified by the results of putting one's concepts into practice. If I say that there is a door in that wall and there isn't, then when I bump my head as I try to walk through that "door," that confirms that I was wrong—"the door" in the wall was not a useful idea. It also did not correspond to the reality out there. This method of checking out our hypotheses against external reality through verifiable trials is also a basis for the empirical method at the heart of experimental methodology. How could this model of truth *not* be true?

The fact is that it *is* pragmatically useful in so many ways. However, by the model's own pragmatic standards, it is just not *always* useful! As we noted in Buckley's (1967) levels of systems, and in Heisenberg's uncertainty model of subatomic particles, with some systems, the very way we ask questions and the methods we use to find the answers strongly shape and determine what we find to be "true." As Heisenberg compellingly demonstrated, when a subatomic entity was measured as if it were a wave, so it was; yet when the same entity was measured as if it were a particle, it was a particle. Now, what does this have to do with our human interaction subjects at hand?

Especially in sociocultural level systems, our constructs, ideas, expectations, and cultural metaphors shape our interactions. These interactions in turn shape our ideas and beliefs. This occurs so often that it explains how the multiple "truths" that we commonly find in our experienced worlds emerge. As we shall see, this applies not only to the clients we see as they struggle with their own lives but also to us as psychotherapists as we study and apply the approaches we select to help our clients resolve their problems. Therefore, a pragmatic model of truth may be useful as long as we modify our expectations of finding *one truth*. There may be *many useful truths* given different contexts of interaction.

The Constructivist Model of Truth

The last few caveats imply that truth is a product of the process of discovering truth, and in turn, that successive process shapes the truth discovered in recursive loops. Jean Piaget (1997), the famous developmental psychologist who studied how children come to understand their world, first coined the term *constructivist epistemology*. (The term *epistemology* simply means the study of how one comes to gain knowledge of their world.) His study of children's abilities to interact with objects as if they were constant even though they were behind a screen was linked to their developmental abilities and their subsequent interactions with their world. George Kelly's (1955) seminal two volumes, *The Psychology of Personal Constructs*, put forward the view of humans as scientists testing hypotheses and evolving their own theories or personal constructs about their world. His fundamental proposition is that "a person's processes are psychologically channelized by the way in which he anticipates events" (p. 46).

In many ways, however, this is an individual view of how people come to construct their realities or find their own truth. It is a phenomenological position that emphasizes the separate experiences and worldviews generated by each of us. This is certainly a major position of person-centered therapists. It is also similar in other ways to the perspectives of the cognitive theory camp and the cognitive behavioral positions. These operate on the tacit and often explicit premise that our evolved ideas or constructs of our world are the major determinants of how we act and react to our environment. Therefore, the constructivist position focuses on the individual interacting with his or her external world. At times, their assumptions are useful; at others, they may be described as distortions, thinking errors, or dysfunctional cognitions. They do not match and do not work in the real world out there on which we all agree. This constructivist view is a step in the process direction, and yet it often retains correspondence, consensus, and pragmatic models of truth as implicit assumptions as it works to adjust distressed people's evolved cognitions to fit agreed-on external realities.

The Social Constructionist Model of Truth

About the difference between constructivism and social constructionism, Gergen (2015a) said,

> Where constructivism places the origin or knowledge in the head of the individual, social construction places the origin in social process. Constructivism is fiercely individualist; constructionism champions relationship . . . holding that we understand the world through mental categories, but we acquire those categories through social relationships. (p. 30)

This leads us to alternative views of truth that considers context.

From this view, the question of what is true is removed and replaced by what is accomplished. Although this sounds very much like the pragmatic model of truth, it does not ask which position or statement is true or right. Instead, it assumes there are multiple useful truths, and the best questions are how one or another *fits* with the values of a given context of time and place. One culture's truth is another culture's problem. Regarding this cultural context issue, Gergen (2015a) went on to say,

> when we are fully immersed in a given tradition or way of life, its constructions are no longer constructions. When we take our realities and values as essential and undeniable, we often trample on others' values and ways of life. (p. 28)

This is the essence of the first example in this chapter in which Western views of trauma and posttraumatic stress disorder (PTSD) and how to handle them were imposed on a culture in Sri Lanka, often causing more harm than relief. However, before getting ahead of ourselves, it might be useful to consider some of the core premises of the social constructionist view.

The current parameters of social constructionism likely took hold with Berger and Luckmann's (1966) book, *The Social Construction of Reality* (as we have seen in past chapters, an auspicious time for the ascendance of systemic, cybernetic, and process-based views as well). Social constructionism posits that people come to "know" the world, to "know reality" by interacting with it—the people, the organizations, and the institutions within society. Even language or the meaning of words is based on context. Ludwig Von Wittgenstein (1951) said the meaning of a word is how it is used. He based his linguistically based philosophy on "language games" in which meaning emerges as a product of social interaction and conventions of interactions through language.

In the end, although there are different "flavors" of constructivism and social constructionism, they all appear to have many things in common. These commonalities, as follows, may also serve as philosophical tenets that underlie a flexible approach to psychotherapy: (a) There is not an objective social reality standing outside individuals. Reality is not discovered but created by human observers. (b) There is no such thing as an objective observer. The very act of observing changes that which is observed. (c) People are active participants in developing their knowledge of the world rather than passive recipients of stimulus–response interaction with their environment. (d) Language and dialogue are integral to the social construction of reality. (e) Social interaction cocreates our understanding of reality. (f) The cultural context affects how people interpret and coconstruct reality.

The rational–empiricist search for the one true and right approach to treatment has run into the inevitable obstacle that there are many equally effective approaches to psychotherapy. This, in fact, matches with social constructivist premises. Thus, it is critically important to examine the values and premises imbedded in and implied by our scientific traditions. Social constructionism points toward an alternative view based on process rather than structure, flow rather than equilibrium, change rather than stability, and the cocreation of multiple useful realities rather than the search for one truth.

FRAMES, METAFRAMES, AND METAPHORS

Stepping back into Heraclitus's river, recall that the flow of water was channeled by the characteristics of the riverbanks, the incline of the riverbed, the obstructions such as rocks and boulders in the riverbed, and the volume of water flowing at a given time. It is important to remember as well that another way of viewing the course of the river is to go back in time and note how the water cut its way through the ground to gradually form the riverbed and banks. We can also chart the course of the river as we are observing it at this moment. The flow of water is shaped by, as it also shapes, the banks that channel its flow. This is similar to how our concepts, language, and frames shape our interactions with ourselves and others, while our interactions in turn shape our concepts, language, and frames over time. Such is the nature of language, ideas, and frames on the way things are in our world. Language shapes and channels our interactions with ourself and others and helps make meaning in our lives. From a social constructionist point of view, we typically refer to this as *cocreating*. So, from a process perspective, the flow of human interaction is channeled and yet cocreated as it evolves. Thus, we are well served by looking closer at what we might term our frames, metaframes, metaphors, and rationales to notice how they shape the worldviews and problems of our clients, as well as our own approaches to helping our clients.

Notice that we will usually refer to this as a *perspective* or a *point of view* on human interaction rather than as some new standard of truth. The social constructionist perspective is itself simply a point of view and equally subject to critique and deconstruction as were other perspectives. Similarly, we use this same convention when referring to the process paradigm as a *perspective* or *point of view*.

Frames

For simplicity's sake, a *frame* in language may be defined as a construct or set of constructs that describe and give meaning to interactional experiences. Like a picture frame, linguistic frames also create boundaries that direct further interaction. For example, upon observing Jacob, I might say that he follows directions inconsistently. Another way I might describe the same situation is that Jacob does not like to follow directions. Both frames will have different effects on further discussions about Jacob. Given the importance of frames, it is important to revisit the anthropologist Gregory Bateson, who provided seminal thinking on this subject. Recall his contributions to cybernetics and systems thinking discussed in Chapter 4, and his alternating ladder of positive and negative feedback over time. In close connection with this process view of human interaction, Bateson was one of the first to articulate the concept of framing in his classic book of 1972, *Steps to an Ecology of Mind*, in which defined a frame as "a spatial and temporal bonding of a set of interactive messages" (p. 197). In other words, the frames we use to describe and direct our interaction with our worlds help channel the process of how our lives evolve. Frames are said to be similar to a set of filters that people develop through biological and cultural influences. These filters subsequently serve as shorthand to help make sense of the world. They help reduce ambiguity and quickly put experience in a context of what we already know. Along with Bateson, the sociologist Erving Goffman (1974) is credited with articulating the concept of frames in his book *Frame Analysis: An Essay on the Organization of Experience*. Goffman described frames as a means of making meaning, organizing experiences, and guiding actions by helping us perceive, identify, and labelled events and occurrences. Once new events are identified and fit within a frame, appropriate actions can then be taken to assimilate or accommodate them into our world as we experience it.

In the introductory section of this chapter, I argued that context determines meaning or interpretation. Toward this end, framing plays a key role. Because communication can occur on more than one level at a time, *framing* helps explain how people communicate in ways that let others know at what level of abstraction a communication is to be taken, and thus interpreted (Bateson, 1972). For example, if I step on your toe and you view it as an accident, your reaction will be very different than if you frame my action as being done on purpose. We might understand a friend's winking their eye at us as the reaction to something irritating their eye; the signal that they are joking; or a flirtatious gesture inviting us into a different kind of relationship. Each frame will have cascading results and may lead in many directions depending on how closely the frame received matches on what was intended.

Lakoff and Johnson (2008) explained that frames are smaller narratives that make up the more complex narrative of a person's life story. The process of framing in social interaction involves focusing on one specific part of someone's reality and ignoring others, as in photography. For example, if one decides his toe was deliberately stepped on, a more charitable motive won't make sense and is likely to be ignored.

Framing is what we do when we classify and categorize our experiences as we go about everyday living (Bateson, 1955; Goffman, 1974). Frames help us make sense of the world and make it as predictable as possible (Borah, 2011, p. 248). Frames are socially influenced, cocreated, and play a large role in our experience of daily life. Here, we tend to pay attention primarily to those experiences that are consistent with our frames and ignore those that are not. Behavior confirmation plays an important part in this process.

Behavioral confirmation is

> a process in which one individual's preconceived *beliefs* and prior *expectations* about another person channel their interactions in such ways that these initial beliefs (even when they are based on erroneous stereotypes or hypotheses of dubious validity) come to be *confirmed* by the other person's *behavior.* (M. Snyder & Thomsen, 1988, p. 127)

When we meet someone for the first time, we tend to quickly form an opinion about him or her and then proceed to interact with and treat that person as if our first impression were true. Such is the case in classic studies in which randomly chosen schoolchildren whose teachers predicted they would do well in school that year did, in fact, do well compared with others. Frames exert powerful influences on our lives. They help us define problems, diagnose causes, make value judgments, and decide on remedies or solutions. They both shape our subsequent processes and are shaped in turn by the consequences of those processes over time and contexts.[4] As George Lakoff (2014) explained in his concept of *reflexivity*, "the word reflects our understandings through our actions, and our understandings reflect the world shaped by the frame-informed actions of ourselves and others" (p. 35).

However, this does not mean that once we have created our frames they never change. Through our social interactions with others, we continue to influence one another. In fact, people often change their behaviors and beliefs to conform to the expectations of others, a process referred to as *consensual validation.* The client's search for consensual validation plays a key role in how therapy works (Fraser & Solovey, 2007).

In sum, all actions are communication; we cannot *not* act; thus, we cannot *not* communicate, just as we cannot *not* frame our world and our communications and actions within it. At the clinical level, frames are important core elements that shape the worldviews and problems of our clients as they are stuck in vicious cycles. Changing frames plays a key role in shifting out of vicious cycles or becoming unstuck. Also, keep in mind that we as therapists are not immune to these same fundamental premises of the human

[4]Portions of this discussion also appear in Fraser, Grove, Lee, Greene, and Solovey (2014).

condition. We all use frames and metaphors to make sense of our worlds. We as psychotherapists do so within our personal interactions as well as in our use of major frames and rationales that direct our therapy with clients. We too can be caught in vicious cycles with our own frames and solution attempts.

Metaphors

Most of us remember learning that a metaphor is simply a comparison of two concepts or things without the use of the words *like* or *as*. It is a word or phrase for one thing that is used to refer to another thing to show or suggest that they are similar. However, contemporary study from cognitive science, linguistics, and the social sciences have moved metaphor into a central place in how we think and come to interact with our world. George Lakoff and Mark Johnson have been major proponents of metaphors as foundations of our conceptual system through cognitive linguistics. M. Johnson (2008) stated that "human thinking emerges from *patterns* of our ongoing engagement with environments that are at once physical, social, and cultural in character" (p. 151, emphasis added). Lakoff (1993) began his treatise on the contemporary theory of metaphor by stating that "metaphorical expressions are not in language, but in thought: They are general mappings across conceptual domains" (p. 1). As with frames, they are an implicit filter or shorthand (to use two metaphors here that are common yet implicit in our language) that enable us to quickly relate incidents to a core set of values and beliefs and thus respond to those incidents accordingly. Contemporary theory of metaphor is revolutionary. It not only defines how we understand language but is also the mechanism through which we comprehend abstract concepts and perform abstract reasoning. It allows us to understand unstructured or relatively abstract subject matter in more concrete terms (e.g., the *filter* or *shorthand* metaphor I just used). Metaphors offer conceptual mappings or image mappings across conceptual domains that enable us to respond with rather automatic responses with little noticeable effort. Again, like frames, they highlight related concepts and values and downplay or move alternative ideas into the background (to use another visual image of *foreground* and *background* as in a painting or a stage). For example, when we tell someone, "Don't think of an aardvark!" it is nearly impossible for them *not* to ask themselves if an aardvark is actually an anteater, and to imagine a furry, long-nosed creature, and so on. Lakoff asserted that framing and metaphors are the ways words and phrases become able to evoke not just ideas, but also a worldview. Therefore, metaphors and frames are not just words. Ideas and values are primary. Metaphors and frames carry and evoke our ideas as subsequent interactions reinforce our worldview.

The first example presented in this chapter offers some further insight into the impact of dominant metaphors. If we follow a benevolent parent metaphor for the way dominant cultures such as those of Western countries, like the United States, respond to tragedies across the globe, it makes perfect sense that professional helpers viewed Sri Lankans affected by the tsunami as victims in need of rescue. It would make further sense that the method of rescue would be teaching Western views on trauma and how it is to be resolved. Once we enter a metaphor, it rarely occurs to us that it is simply a point of view. Once the metaphor is set, then all language and images follow from it without conscious thought. This, of course, is useful because it allows us to make quick reactions to situations. However, when the metaphor so dominates our view that it shapes what we see as a problem and dictates what we need to do about it, it becomes a blinder on problem resolution (to use another metaphor).

You as a reader may be asking yourself: What does all of this theory about the search for truth, the social constructionist view, and the discussion of frames and metaphors have to do with psychotherapy or with integrating psychotherapies that work? The answer is *everything*.

From this process view, our clients and we as therapists are embedded within our language, frames, and metaphors about the way things are in our worlds. Our clients come to us with problems that have arisen through their view of the world, their personal histories, their language, culture, norms, frames, and metaphors that have shaped how they have identified dilemmas and evolved their solutions. Once more, we as therapists are subject to the same human condition. Our language, culture, norms, frames, and metaphors equally shape our views of our clients, the origin of their problems, and our subsequent approaches to helping them through psychotherapy. In the case of those frames and metaphors that shape the various evidence-based psychotherapies available, we must turn to the use of *psychotherapeutic rationales* to understand how they work.

Rationales for Psychotherapies that Work

A commonality across effective therapies is a *treatment rationale*. Treatment rationales explain what is wrong or the reason a client has a problem. In addition, the rationale provides a logical context for interventions. For example, the rationale of avoidance with anxiety conditions creates a logical context for interventions that involve exposure. Embedded in treatment rationales is validation for having the problem—that is, many people make the mistake of avoidance, which provides validation for change.

Rationales for treatment models are often presented from a perspective of objective truth or model superiority. The process of change perspective counters: There are multiple equally useful truths from this perspective, just as we are finding that there are multiple equally effective psychotherapies. The process view, along with a social constructionist perspective, allows clinicians to tailor rationales to meet the unique needs of clients.

It is important to note that Frank and Frank (1991) were clear that treatment rationales do not need to be scientifically valid to be effective. The key is that both the clinician and the client believe in them. This was borne out in Wampold's meta-analysis of psychotherapy outcome (Wampold, 2001; Wampold & Imel, 2015a). Jerome Frank (Frank & Frank, 1991) in his contextual model of treatment describes a two-step process that is crucial to intervening across all approaches to treatment where the practitioner first provides an explanation or rationale for the client's symptoms. The practitioner then offers a procedure designed to change the way that the client is trying to solve the problem. This coincides with the operational definition of hope offered by C. R. Snyder, Michael, and Cheavens (1999). These authors suggested that clients gain hope when offered an explanation or frame that makes sense of their problem, implies a direction toward resolution, offers procedures to follow toward resolution, and enlists client motivation to go that way.

Rationales Redux

Let's look at depression. Interestingly, there are three major schools of thought that form the basis of several major approaches to effective psychotherapy for depression. Each school of thought is quite different in its thinking about depression and treatments protocols offered. Yet each has been found to be equally effective. Interpersonal psychotherapy, with its positivist/realist basis, was found to be equally effective as cognitive behavioral therapy with its logical–positivist basis in the National Institute of Mental Health Treatment of Depression Collaborative Research Program (Elkin, 1994). Similarly, emotion-focused therapy (Greenberg, 2010; Greenberg & Watson, 2006), with its phenomenological base, has also shown clear effectiveness as an evidence-supported treatment for depression.

The process perspective, coupled with the social constructionist view, has little problem with this situation of similar outcomes from different points of view. Each view has its own frames and methods, and each one finds clear and reinforcing evidence for its approach. Creative clinicians can present any of these rationales on their own, find a way to mix and match, or invent one in a given client situation. The key is that the clinician believes the rationale is plausible and presents it in a genuine way, and that in turn the client believes in it. This is the case not only for depression; it is valid for all therapies, for all disorders across the *DSM–5* spectrum.

Following the Process of Change

In the previous chapter, I made a case for a process perspective in understanding human interaction. I liberally used the river metaphor from the ancient philosophical traditions of Lao Tzu's "watercourse way" for the flow of process, and Heraclitus' river that can never be stepped into twice. In this chapter, we have made a case for using a social constructionist viewpoint to guide our understanding of the constraints on process and flow.

Using the river metaphor, the riverbanks, river bottom, and objects in the river channel flow, as the flow of the river has, over time, cut and created the banks, bottoms, and objects in the river. From this perspective, we cannot step outside of the worldview that guides our actions. Likewise, we cannot separate ourselves from the actions that cocreate our worldview. In sum:

- Our clients come to us, having engaged in a world shaped by their culture, language, frames, and metaphors. The frames and metaphors they use will have shaped their interactions to either assimilate or accommodate perceived obstacles they have encountered along the way.
- This is an evolving spiral of alternating levels of attempted assimilation or negative feedback, and accommodation or positive feedback.
- As we judge this evolving process as good or agreeable, we call it a *virtuous cycle*. When we view it as a problem, we call it a *vicious cycle*.
- In other words, the kinds of problems clients bring to us have evolved from repeated attempts to solve problems, within their frames of reference, using variations on the same solutions tried over and again.
- Our goal as clinicians is to help clients break or redirect those vicious cycles. This amounts to helping clients change the way that they are attempting to change.
- To do this, we must enter the assumptive worlds of our clients' frames and metaphors to understand how they view and are struggling with their situations. We must also collaborate with them to help redirect their solutions. This journey is not easy for anyone.
- From within our worldviews, metaphors, and frames, the way we have identified problems and attempted to solve them makes such sense as to be implicit, automatic, and only reasonable. The problem is that the situation is usually worse, more distressing, and even more dangerous for our clients. To break from failed solutions at such a critical time appears to be a high-risk

proposition. If the spouse of a person who drinks alcoholically stops giving lectures and sermons on the perils of drinking, what will happen? Will the drinking spouse reconsider the need to stop, or take the lack of lectures as permission to drink more?

- For clients to take risks necessary for change, they need to know that their therapist understands and appreciates them, their views, and their distress and joins with them in their goals.
- This is where the theoretical rationales from those various effective treatments come in. The theory must *fit* well with the client, *be believed in* by the therapist, and *make sense* of the client's problem in context and *imply a direction for resolution*.

DIAGRAMING CONTEXT

We might depict the context of the psychotherapy contract from a process perspective by the Venn diagram in Figure 5.1. It represents three intersecting contexts of culture, clients, and therapists. The first sphere represents the general cultural context, including a sampling of cultural factors such as language, norms, frames, metaphors, and prevailing spirituality beliefs, along with what emerges as the general definition of a given problem within that broad culture. The second sphere represents the multiple, contextual identities of clients. As with therapists, these include such factors as gender, age, language, socioeconomic status, religion, ethnicity, disability, sexual orientation, important interpersonal relationships, and so on. These contextual factors converge to evolve clients' unique or personal approaches

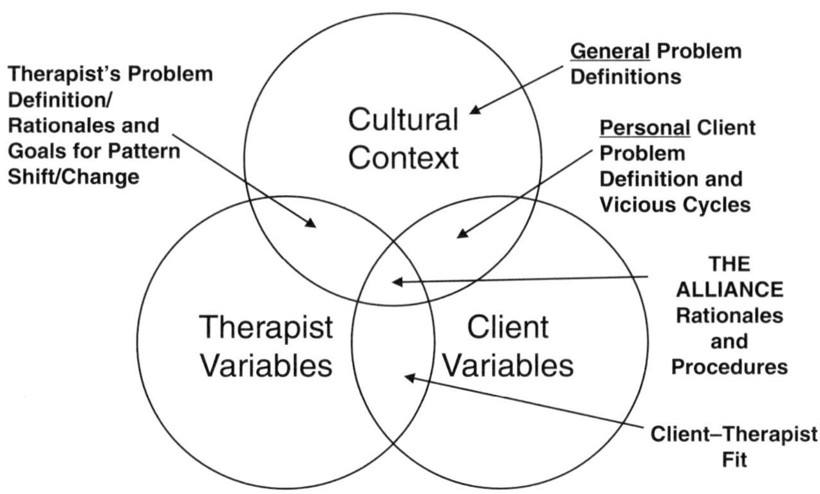

Figure 5.1. The process of change: Working diagram of the therapy contract.

to the problem as they define it and their consequent solution patterns—or the vicious cycles around the defined problem. The third sphere represents the therapist with his or her unique identities in context with the client. It also includes the therapist's approach to psychotherapy and his or her clinical expertise.

The full diagram is the intersection of all of the spheres—a working diagram of the psychotherapy contract. As such, it includes all of the elements of each of the preceding three spheres. The overlaps or *intersections* of the three deserve particular attention.

The overlap of client and culture spheres indicates how the client has both *generally* and *personally* defined her problem, her solutions, and subsequent vicious cycles of her solution-generated problem. The client's unique identities and circumstances help to add the specific spin to her problem cycles. Sometimes the patterns of her problem cycles match those generally prescribed by the culture. However, at other times, factors unique to the client(s) will alter the personal patterns of her problem.

The intersection of the therapist's sphere with the cultural context sphere points to how the therapist's unique multiple identities contribute to his view of the problem and the client through the lens of his particular model of psychotherapy and its related goals. It also implies his target goals for change.

The overlap of the client and therapist spheres indicates how closely the therapist and client's personal characteristics and worldviews match and/or require adaptation to create a good fit between them for a working alliance.

Finally, the central intersection of all three spheres represents the nexus of the alliance. This includes the typical agreement on a rationale to explain the problem and imply a direction and tasks toward resolution. It also includes the metaconstructs of *pattern shift* in the client's vicious cycle and the target of second-order change that we focus on in the next chapter on change.

CONTEXT AND PSYCHOTHERAPIES THAT WORK

Turning back to integrating psychotherapies that work, context has had much to say. From a process view, context shapes process and pattern, as those patterns coshape the context. Clients' culture, personal history and qualities, frames, and metaphors shape how they see problems and how to solve them. That context constrains the pattern of clients' problems. So too do the personal histories and theoretical rationales and expertise of therapists shape how they view clients' problem patterns and how to resolve them. Therapists' choice of therapy approach constrains their view of clients' problems and shapes the patterns of their treatment. Recalling principles of open dynamic systems from Chapter 4, there may be many paths to the same problem pattern. Similarly, there may be many equally effective paths to the same problem pattern shift or problem re-solution. This has multiple implications for the process of doing effective treatment across different approaches. We will see this in the chapters of Part II.

For now, however, some of the main implications of context for integrating psychotherapies that work from the process view are as follows:

- Context, frames, and metaphors shape clients' problem patterns.
- Client solution patterns "make sense" to clients within the frames and metaphors, or worldviews of their life.
- Solution pattern reversals and shifts will likely "not make sense" to clients from within their current worldviews. They usually seem counterintuitive or paradoxical.
- Thus, altering these frames, reframing, and using alternate metaphors is one potent path toward vicious cycle pattern shifts. These contextual changes, frames, reframes, and therapy rationales help "make sense" of the target pattern shifts needed for problem resolution.
- The closer the fit or match between clients' metaphors and frames and those chosen by the therapist, the stronger the eventual working alliance. Thus, treatment preferences and treatment selection among those approaches found to be effective is a critical ingredient to facilitating pattern shifts.
- Research within a dominant culture on the nature of general problem definitions and patterns is likely to offer therapists an idea of what patterns they will find for clients with the problem in focus. A classic example is patterns of *mastery by avoidance* in anxiety.
- Clients' personal histories and unique personal variables will modify those general patterns. Sometimes they will modify the general pattern little, but other times they will create a unique spin to the problem patterns. This also applies to how clients will tend to interact with therapists' unique variables of age, gender, ethnicity, authority, directiveness, and so on.
- Similarly, research in the dominant culture on which psychotherapy approaches are effective for the problem at hand also gives therapists a valuable range of options from which to choose.
- Fit with the client and their metaphors of the world and specific problem is important to this match. Equally important is the

therapist's knowledge of and expertise with each of the available approaches. Flexibility and fit come together here and can be a challenge for therapists.

- Adopting a process of change perspective on the nature of problems and their resolution is crucial for therapists. The process view helps therapists see that there are many useful ways to view the world, just as there are many useful ways to achieve vicious cycle pattern shifts with clients. No one way is "true." The "truth" of a given approach lies in its usefulness within context.

CYCLING BACK

From the examples at the beginning of the chapter, we learned that the belief systems of clients and clinicians are equally important. For therapy to be effective, clinicians must be flexible enough to accommodate to the worldview of their clients. To fail do so is at best ineffective, and at worst potentially harmful—even on a mass scale, as was the case with anorexia nervosa in Hong Kong. At the same time, this is not a trivial problem. A clinician's genuineness is also necessary for clients to feel understood and motivated to work with a clinician. The clinician's underlying philosophy about how reality is constructed makes a difference in this regard. If a clinician has an underlying rational–positivist belief system—eye movement desensitization and reprocessing (EMDR), for example, is the one and only truth—then accommodating the belief system of a client who does not fit the EMDR model will be ineffective. In contrast, a social constructionist perspective allows the clinician to alter his or her beliefs to meet the worldview of a client and remain genuine. We cannot say that a social constructionist view is the only way to develop and maintain clinical flexibility. However, a social constructionist perspective fits well with the current data, and there is ample evidence throughout the ages to support this perspective. Social constructionism fits with the process perspective that will guide our journey toward integrating psychotherapies that work.

II

APPLYING THE PROCESS PERSPECTIVE TO SPECIFIC CLIENT PROBLEMS

6

ANXIETY

Fear has big eyes!

—(*Russian Proverb*)

As we look at treating anxiety, consider the following cases.

Ann was an elementary school teacher. For Ann, the sensations she experienced were feelings of unreality, shortness of breath, and stomach upset. These would occur an average of three times per week, lasting from a few seconds to 10 minutes. Most of these sensations were expected, but occasionally they came from "out of the blue." They mainly occurred in public situations where she felt there was no escape, such as in cars if she wasn't driving, movies or plays, or in her classroom. Her internal triggers tended to revolve around stomach distress accompanied by thoughts of vomiting and never being able to control this again. She was concerned that maybe this was all physical in that she had chronic gallbladder problems, but she also feared vomiting in public, losing control mentally, and being humiliated. Her reactions to a panic attack invariably involved escaping from wherever she was, seeking help from therapists and a boyfriend, and being sure she had

http://dx.doi.org/10.1037/0000078-007
Unifying Effective Psychotherapies: Tracing the Process of Change, by J. S. Fraser

her medication bottle. She thus constantly avoided being out of control by likewise avoiding situations such as speaking in public, driving with others, or being at restaurants. She cognitively would count to 10, tell herself things would be OK, and generally distract herself from her sensations, and she would always know where her boyfriend was. As a result, her boyfriend was supportive yet increasingly frustrated with her, her parents had become more distant, she was becoming concerned about losing her teaching position, she had stopped performing as she had throughout college, and she was not going out with friends unless she was completely in control of the circumstances. Ann's mood had deteriorated to hopelessness, with frequent crying spells and greater isolation in her apartment. She was in a classic downward spiral when she reluctantly sought help from a therapist just one more time.

Sarah came to therapy "looking for more tools to defeat her anxiety and depression." She was a 40-year-old African American single parent of three, living in a large southeastern city in the United States. It seemed that the basic problem was her anxiety, in particular, her panic attacks. After these panic attacks and losing her temper with her children, the depression would set in, and it became hard to get out of bed. However, as a single parent with significant responsibilities, she had to get up. She worked as a nurse's assistant in a hospital and was taking college courses to finish her degree. Sarah had previously been in therapy for a few years and gained some skills from a trusted therapist, yet some things, such as relaxation exercises and guided imagery, just didn't fit for her. She didn't like the idea of medication and wanted to look into more "holistic psychological" options. One strength, however, was her newly renewed Christian faith.[1]

These cases, and others like them, including individuals with social anxiety, generalized anxiety, and agoraphobia, are all variations of one of the most common sets of problems seen in clinical practice: anxiety. I revisit these cases later in the chapter after addressing some key issues and models of anxiety and its effective treatment. Anxiety is the paradigm case of vicious cycles, as noted in the previous chapters. I draw on anxiety research and the perspectives of a variety of sources to detail the workings of these vicious cycles of anxiety. As already mentioned, anxiety comes down to mastery by avoidance, and resolution comes down to reversing people's solutions. I then describe the major empirically supported approaches to treating anxiety-related problems,

---

[1]This case is available on DVD in video format through the APA Psychotherapy Video Series (see *The Process of Change in Integrative Psychotherapy*: http://www.apa.org/pubs/videos/4310979.aspx). The DVD includes a consultation session with the author, along with discussion of the case and key video clip examples titled "The Process of Change in Integrative Psychotherapy," which may be helpful to the interested reader. This case is reviewed in some detail in the last chapter of this book. For this book, several identifying aspects of the case have been altered to preserve confidentiality.

including newer unified approaches. Finally, I discuss these approaches in light of the process of change.

THE PROCESS OF CHANGE IN A NUTSHELL

A chapter published on anxiety and second-order change (Fraser & Solovey, 2007, Chapter 6) discussed what were then the major evidence-supported approaches to anxiety-related problems and showed how they all focused on reversing clients' failed solutions. The main therapeutic rationales connecting all of these approaches were behavioral and cognitive behavioral. Today, there is further support for these approaches but also an increasing trend toward unifying treatments. After a brief review of the essence of the most effective current approaches to a range of anxiety disorders, I turn attention to unified approaches. This trend comes closest to the process-of-change view, yet limits its scope to mood disorders rather than applying the pattern shift perspective more broadly.

The Context and Process of Anxiety

> *[This is] the absolutely central problem in neurosis and therapy. Most simply formulated, it is a paradox—the paradox of behavior which is at one and the same time self-defeating!*
>
> —*(O. Hobart Mowrer, 1950, p. 486)*

Recall the three interacting components of the process-of-change viewpoint: context, process, and change. In this section, I address the broad context of the professional literature that defines anxiety-related conditions. Mainly on the basis of excellent empirical research, these data and descriptions form a broad context for what we have come to know as anxiety-related problems.

Because definitions from the *Diagnostic and Statistical Manual of Mental Disorders* (5th ed. *[DSM–5]*; American Psychiatric Association, 2013), certainly a medical model, have traditionally been used in behavioral health over the years in the United States, I typically refer to *DSM–5* definitions here. However, the *International Statistical Classification of Diseases and Related Health Problems* (10th rev. [ICD–10]; World Health Organization, 1993) is now being steadily adopted around the world, including in the United States where the *DSM* definitions have predominated. The ICD is also clearly steeped in the medical model. At this writing, an ICD–11 revision is about to be rolled out. For the sake of simplicity, *DSM* definitions are primarily used in this and subsequent chapters, but so-called crosswalks linking *DSM–5* with ICD–10 diagnoses are readily available (e.g., Azalea Health, 2017).

Remember, however, that the process of change subsumes such normative descriptions found in the *DSM* and ICD as simply one way of explaining and describing a given problem. What follows are descriptions from the sphere of context, which shapes our view of anxiety-related problems. Context also explains how, from clients' perspectives, solutions evolve into self-defeating vicious cycles.

Anxiety Defined

Anxiety in one or another of its forms is one of the most frequently encountered emotional problems in both medical and mental health practice. From 18% to 20% of the world's population suffers from anxiety-related disorders, according to a convergence of epidemiological surveys (Barlow, 2002; Barlow, Conklin, & Bentley, 2015; Craske & Barlow, 2014). Yet fear and anxiety alone are not necessarily problems. These two closely related emotions can offer great advantages. Whereas most sufferers would consider anxiety a burden they would gladly live without, most scientists and philosophers agree that "paradoxically, [anxiety] may well have been responsible for the survival of the species" (Barlow, 2002, p. 2).

Clinical Variations and Definitions: Context and Process

Before looking further at how anxiety becomes a problem, it will be useful to discuss how anxiety difficulties are defined clinically. *DSM–5* lists a range of anxiety-related disorders, as does ICD–10. In this chapter, I address four of the most common of these: panic disorder and agoraphobia, social anxiety, as well as generalized anxiety disorder (GAD) and its close relation, obsessive–compulsive disorder (OCD). As mentioned earlier, along with simple phobias, about one in four people will be affected by one of these anxiety-related disorders in their lifetime, and about 17% will experience some variant of these anxiety disorders in any 12-month period of time. There is also a greater prevalence of these disorders in women than men worldwide on a 2:1 ratio, most likely related to broad gender-role prescriptions about the appropriateness of showing or acting on fear and/or being allowed to avoid it (Kessler et al., 1994).

Vulnerability Factors

Context in the process-of-change approach also includes specific variables of what clients or problem solvers bring to the situation. These client factors help to explain why some problem solvers or clients respond to potentially anxiety-provoking situations with attempts to solve them, while others seem to take the same circumstances in stride. The literature has come to call these client characteristics *vulnerability factors*.

Turning to the potentially unique contributions of the individual sphere as we noted in the Venn diagram of culture, client, and therapist elements in Figure 5.1, there has been considerable convergence on a set of vulnerability factors in the sphere of the individual. In other words, some people may be more prone to respond to bodily distress with anxiety or panic because of factors that they uniquely "bring to the table." Craske and Barlow (2014) reviewed the contributions of genetics and temperament, anxiety sensitivity, history of medical illness and abuse, and interoceptive awareness. They described these potential vulnerabilities as follows:

- an increased potential to experience negative emotions in response to stressors as *a biological vulnerability* of some individuals;
- a potential for *anxiety sensitivity* as a fairly well documented tendency to respond with fear to physical symptoms of anxiety, viewing them as signals of harm or danger;
- *a history of medical illnesses* such as heart problems or asthma, for example, may generalize to future similar sensations as signs of pending illness; and
- *interoceptive awareness*, based on research supporting the tendency of some individuals to have a heightened awareness of or ability to detect bodily sensations of arousal.

Taken together, combinations of many of these predisposing vulnerabilities may increase some individuals' potential to respond with anxiety or panic to heightened body sensations. Nevertheless, the vicious cycle of escalation, once begun, remains remarkably similar. Recall from the principles of open systems that a vicious cycle may begin for a multiplicity of reasons. The best description of the cycle rests in its current repeated patterns. Interdicting that vicious cycle remains the goal across all anxiety treatments.

Definitions: Context in Dominant Western Culture

Panic Attacks

Turning first to *panic attacks* with related agoraphobia, Craske and Barlow (2014) stated that experimental, clinical, and longitudinal research supports the "conceptualization of panic disorder as an acquired fear of certain bodily sensations, and agoraphobia as a behavioral response to the anticipation of such bodily sensations or their crescendo into a full-blown panic attack" (p. 1). They further stated that panic attacks "are discrete episodes of intense fear or discomfort, accompanied by physical and cognitive symptoms, as listed in the *DSM–5* panic attack checklist" (p. 2). This list includes such physical and cognitive symptoms as palpitations, chest pain, sweating, trembling, shortness of breath, and numbness or tingling of extremities, along with such concerns as fear of dying, losing control, or "going crazy." Such attacks often seem unexpected from the client's perspective in that clients often are not able to identify a clear trigger for them. They tend to activate the autonomic fight-or-flight system. However, a significant number of people do experience isolated occurrences of panic without those instances growing into a pattern of panic disorder. What characterizes panic disorder is not the simple occurrence of panic on one or another occasion. Instead, it is distinguished by recurring anxiety that panic will reoccur and will have catastrophic consequences. *DSM–5* and ICD–10 require recurrent unexpected attacks that peak within 10 minutes and that are followed by 1 month or more of consistent worry about the consequences of the attack (e.g., fear of dying or going crazy) or of changed behavior because of the attacks (avoiding situations or taking specific precautions). People struggling with this difficulty thus either are or will become hypersensitive and aware of internal physical state changes. Barlow (2002) suggested that "the central problem of PDA [panic disorder and agoraphobia] is anxiety focused on the symptoms of panic; hence the well-known and commonly accepted characterization of agoraphobia as 'fear of fear'" (p. 329). The physiological sensations of arousal become the trigger for fear reactions that spiral into escalating vicious cycles of the classic panic attack.

Agoraphobia

The term *agoraphobia* refers to the tendency to avoid or endure with dread those situations in which escape might be difficult if panic sets in. This includes great concern over the potential embarrassment of losing control and fainting, vomiting, or losing bowel control, for example. Thus, having great difficulty traveling, needing to be accompanied outside the home, or always needing to have a quick escape route are common characteristics of agoraphobia. This was clearly the case for Ann, the first of the three cases at the beginning of this chapter. Although panic disorder may occur without such situational avoidance or dread, at least some mild agoraphobia is often present. Agoraphobia clearly fits the category of mastery by avoidance discussed earlier. In the case of agoraphobia, problem-solvers avoid the experience of confronting their fears (and the chance to learn new mastery options), which then becomes a self-reinforcing vicious cycle.

Social Anxiety

People with *social anxiety disorder* (SAD), according to *DSM–5* and ICD–10, are unusually concerned about a variety of social situations in which they fear being humiliated by being unable to perform adequately or by showing visible anxiety symptoms. Sometimes this fear is limited to only a few situations, such as speaking in public or performing, but more often there are general social interactions involved, such as dating, engaging in meetings or parties, or going on job interviews. Because people struggling with social anxiety are acutely concerned about the reactions of others, they tend to be hypervigilant for early indications of disapproval from others and of anything in their own actions that others might evaluate negatively. As might be guessed, the clinical and research literature has shown that this hypervigilance may lead to performance problems, which may then actually result in the feared disapproval of others, in the proverbial self-fulfilling prophecy. Turk, Heimberg, and Hope (2001) summarized this dilemma: "Negative predictions result in cognitive, behavioral, and physiological symptoms of anxiety, which eventually feed back into the negatively biased mental representation of the self and perpetuate the cycle of anxiety" (p. 123). Once again, the solutions become the problem in social anxiety disorders. Characteristically, people who struggle with this form of anxiety experience severe restrictions on their lives and often underachieve in both job and social arenas. Not surprisingly, epidemiological and clinical data suggest that a significant percentage of individuals with social anxiety abuse alcohol (Turk et al., 2001).

Generalized Anxiety Disorder

DSM–5 and ICD–10 define GAD by noting the key feature of excessive, uncontrollable worry about a range of life events or activities accompanied by at least three of six symptoms of negative emotion and tension. These symptoms include restlessness or feeling keyed up or on edge, being easily fatigued, difficulty concentrating or one's mind going blank, irritability, muscle tension, and sleep disturbance. Moreover, the individual perceives these worries as difficult to control; the worries lack any specific area of concern, and this consistent worry results in increasing impairment in job and/or social functioning. The process of excessive worry or "anxious apprehension" is the key feature of GAD. This seemingly uncontrollable repeated solution is defined as a future-oriented mood state in which one becomes ready or prepared to attempt to cope with upcoming negative events.

Borkovec (1994) provided one of the leading explanations of the function of such anxious apprehension or worry as a basic vicious cycle. He suggested that worry becomes negatively reinforcing because it is associated with escape from more distressing images or body sensations. Yet this distraction does not allow the individual to completely process the situation through effective problem-solving and resolution before the person diverts to another area of worry. Heightened states of tension and alert are thus maintained and rarely resolved by the worry that distracts the person from resolving the tension-filled situation. Worry also becomes self-reinforcing because it becomes associated with the nonoccurrence of negative outcomes, which usually are relatively unlikely to occur even without such worry or attention being paid to them (e.g., If I continue to worry about the sky falling and it hasn't done so yet, then maybe it is my worry that keeps the sky from falling).

Cognitively, people with generalized anxiety are said to overestimate the probability of negative events that are actually unlikely to occur. They are also found to make catastrophic judgments about situations that they view as intolerable, unmanageable, or beyond their ability to cope, without ever examining whether this is really so. Thus, the process of excessive rumination or worry becomes intensely self-reinforcing in another characteristic vicious cycle. The process of continual anxious apprehension or worry makes it a solution-generated problem. In all of these cases, clients find themselves trapped in a vicious cycle—a spiral of anxiety that needs interrupting.

Obsessive–Compulsive Disorder

Regarding OCD, *DSM–5* and ICD–10 note that the key signs of OCD are intrusive unwanted thoughts (obsessions) and repetitive behaviors (compulsions). Dougherty, Rauch, and Jenike (2015) stated that obsessions classically include preoccupation with contamination; doubting and uncertainly; violent, religious, or sexual themes; and the belief that something bad will happen if some ritual or checking process is not performed exactly right. Foa and McLean (2016) explained the cyclical mechanisms supporting OCD by noting that

> in addition to avoiding safe but feared situations, individuals with OCD develop compulsions or rituals that are designed to reduce anxiety or prevent expected harm from occurring. Like avoidance, the performance of rituals prevents individuals from disconfirming their belief that contact with feared but safe situations will be harmful, thus impending emotional processing. (p. 13)

Once again, variations of avoidance, compulsions, or rituals fuel the spiral of anxiety. For example, this was the situation for a client who was obsessed with the idea that she had put Vanish toilet bowl cleaner where it might harm others and was compelled to check places where she might have done so.

PROCESS AND THE SPIRAL OF ANXIETY

Recall that the idea of *process* in the process-of-change view relates to the subsequent and cocreating interactions that flow from the context. Context shapes process and process shapes context, as the banks of Heraclitus' river shaped, and were shaped in return by, the process or flow of the river.

Anxiety and its related variations offer a prime case in point to explain the process of vicious cycles of solution-generated problems. Recall that the essence of first-order change is identifying a potential difficulty or threat and taking appropriate action to resolve it. We might suggest that anxiety in the best of situations can alert us to a potential challenge or danger. Once we identify the source of danger, we may become afraid and take action to resolve the threat. However, if the source of potential danger remains vague and thus irresolvable, or if our solutions not only fail to resolve the perceived danger but actually maintain and perpetuate it, we become part of a vicious cycle. Our perceptions of danger and attempts to resolve it maintain anxiety and make it worse. Panic attacks, for example, are often initiated by some chance occurrence that causes us to react with symptoms of anxiety. The initial "kick point" or trigger for the first attack can be almost anything that causes us to feel wildly out of control, unsure if we can handle the situation, and worried that the situation is dangerous. (Recall the open system principle of *equifinality* from Chapter 4. In open process systems, one can get to the same end from a multiplicity of beginnings.) Innate fight-or-flight mechanisms set in. If we are aware of the cause of our physical discomfort, and the innate nature of these physiological responses, we may be able to categorize our reaction as unpleasant but natural. In so doing, we can often move beyond the incident. We might act directly on the situation that made us anxious. We might learn new skills to master it. We might decide that we misinterpreted the situation or find that our view was correct yet there was no cause for worry. In these instances, we will move beyond the incident with few, if any, residual effects.

On the other hand, we may become alarmed and worried about the panic attack itself. How did we get that out of control? What happened to us? Is there something physically wrong? Are we having heart problems? How can we avoid ever having that happen again? We get anxious about having gotten anxious. This can be the inception of a vicious cycle. Once panic attacks have occurred, they tend to be maintained by selective internal attention to bodily events, safety behaviors to bolster the person against the traumatic situation, and avoidance or escape (Barlow et al., 2015; Craske & Barlow, 2014). Our resulting solutions become the very things that produce the syndrome of escalating anxiety and ongoing recurrent panic attacks. Our solutions exacerbate the anxiety we seek to quell: Our solutions become the problem. This is a prime example of first-order change leading to a vicious cycle. Thus, in cases of panic, social anxiety, GAD, and OCD, the same processes of first-order changes are involved with each vicious cycle. All are solution-generated problem patterns. It is merely the process of how the anxiety progresses that differs.

If the thesis of this book holds true, then effective psychotherapy should involve some variations of second-order change. That is, generally, effective therapy should involve either a reversal of the first-order solution process or a shift in the assumptions or premises that underlie those first-order solutions, blocking or redirecting attention or actions to solve the problem, or some combination of several of these general interventions. A look at the literature on successful treatments for anxiety confirms this prediction.

CHANGE

In the interacting links of context, process, and change described in Part I, change refers to the ongoing patterns of a given system.

- *First-order change* may be ongoing acceptable processes or vicious cycles, depending on the describer's judgment or values. First-order changes may be changes in intensity, duration, location, and so on, but they always occur within a set of assumptions, premises, or point of view on the nature of the situation. They "make sense" within these assumptions or frames. Recall the children's finger trap. It makes sense to pull those fingers out rather than pushing in to escape. Because first-order solutions typically make sense, have usually worked, and are well practiced, they are remarkably resilient and resistant to change. They represent variations on the same solutions repeated over and again.
- *Second-order change* refers to a fundamental change in those first-order patterns. They typically represent reversals of first-order patterns, and they frequently are the result of quite different premises, assumptions, and frames on the problem and how it is to be resolved. They interdict vicious cycles in the various ways noted in Chapter 3 on change. However, because second-order change represents reversals of those first-order solutions that "make such sense," they appear counterintuitive, ironic, or paradoxical from the view of the client or problem-solver. Clients most often need a new frame or rationale to make sense of doing the opposite of their tried-and-true solutions. This is where therapeutic frames and rationales come in.
- *Paradox* is thus inherent in all pattern shift, or second-order change. It is also inherent in most all psychotherapy approaches. A simple definition of paradox is a perceived contradiction that follows correct reasoning from a set of premises (cf. Fraser, 1984; Watzlawick, Beavin, & Jackson, 1967). Therefore, all pattern reversals in treating anxiety are inherently paradoxical or

> counterintuitive to the client. Thus, all treatments for anxiety require reframing of clients' views of their anxiety and their solutions to stop, interdict, and or redirect their vicious cycle patterns. Paradox does not reside in any given intervention. It is not something a therapist "does to" a client. Rather, it is inherent in all therapy that targets second-order change. All second-order change requires a new frame or rationale.

Following the process of change, I have tracked the definition of anxiety in the dominant cultural context. I next tracked the general vicious cycle process expected to follow from that context and noted the implied targets for second-order change, or pattern shifts. I turn next to evidence-supported therapy options for the practitioner. The next section reviews the major evidence-supported options for a range of anxiety-related variations. In so doing, I address how each one first bonds with the client, validating their distress; then frames the problem in a new way, noting the vicious cycles; and finally offers a treatment rationale that makes sense for clients of doing the exact opposite solutions they once would have considered counterintuitive or paradoxical.

TREATING ANXIETY-RELATED PROBLEMS

This section on treatments that work for treating anxiety does not go into any real detail on each approach. I refer the interested reader to the primary sources of each approach for details. Instead, this chapter highlights the major rationale of each approach and shows its related procedures. At each step, I relate the rationale or intervention to how it facilitates the process of pattern shift or second-order change. I then follow by discussing the most recent approaches to treatment using unified protocols. Let's begin with the treatment of panic disorder.

Cognitive Behavioral Approaches to Panic Disorder: Context, Process, and Change

Recall that the solution-generated problem patterns in panic are triggered by alarm over bodily arousal in anxiety-provoking situations. The process of patterned responses amounts to escalating attempts to control anxiety along with mastery-by-avoidance strategies. This all "makes sense" to clients within their own frames and contexts. The pattern shift targets involve turning toward, rather than away from, anxiety-provoking sensations and situations. Mastery through exposure rather than avoidance is the key pattern reversal. Interventions thus include making sense of doing the opposite of client solutions and learning new skills for mastery. We will follow this process as we look at effective treatment for panic.

Craske and Barlow (2014) offered a succinct overview of a cognitive behavioral therapy (CBT) approach to panic disorder with agoraphobia. As with the other anxiety-related disorders, we will follow their approach through its major components.

Education: Reframing the Problem

According to Craske and Barlow (2014), "the treatment begins with education about the nature of panic disorder, the causes of panic and anxiety, and the ways panic and anxiety are perpetuated by feedback loops among physical, cognitive, and behavioral response systems" (p. 24). This includes telling clients about the adaptive nature of fight-or-flight responses, dispelling myths about losing control or going crazy, and conveying the idea that anxiety is preparing for future threat and panic as a response to a real or perceived threat. The treatment will help to sort out when there is a need to respond to true threat and when physical sensations of distress may simply be false alarms.

- Reframing the nature of the problem may itself have the result of easing panic and anxiety by normalizing the sensations and situations of fear and threat as something natural. The task becomes simply sorting out when it is appropriate and when it is not.
- This education also sets the stage for the following treatment. In effect, it helps to make sense of many of the treatment procedures that may look counterintuitive.

Self-Monitoring

This second step would seem paradoxical to most clients, except for their understanding of the educational rationale of the first step. It boils down to having clients move through their panic attacks and observe them to gain information and control. (Note that this is the exact opposite of their current avoidance strategies.) Therapists ask clients to complete a panic attack record closely after each panic attack to describe the cues, level of distress, symptoms, thoughts, and behaviors related to the attack. In addition, a daily mood record is completed at the end of each day noting average levels of anxiety. Once more, this intervention has three potential effects. The first, of course, is to give the client and therapist information on the pattern of the problem in some detail. This helps guide further intervention while offering more potential points of control for the client. Unique pattern variations and frames for each specific client will help practitioners fit their interventions appropriately. The second and more subtle effect is asking the client to *allow panic attacks to occur* for therapeutic reasons rather than continuing their attempts to control them—a paradox in itself. The third is to ask the client to step outside the moment-to-moment experience of the panic attack and observe it. This constitutes a pattern shift in that clients are disrupting the common experience of the attack, or defusing the attack from something overtaking them to something observed.

Breathing Training and Applied Relaxation

There is a long history of teaching clients to focus on deep, diaphragmatic breathing to counteract hyperventilation. Progressive muscle relaxation training also has a long history to counteract muscle tension. However, breathing retraining has the potential to become a new avoidance or safety ritual, and relaxation training has been found to have mixed results for panic attacks. The main effects of these interventions, according to Craske and Barlow (2014), are more likely to offer some distraction from the usual vicious cycle patterns and provide an increased sense of control. In each case, a major effect as noted is most likely pattern disruption. In addition, any increase in perceived self-control for clients who often feel wildly out of control is likely to offer a new perspective on whether they need to respond to bodily sensations with panic and further control efforts.

Cognitive Restructuring

The core intervention from a cognitive perspective is cognitive restructuring, which directly targets clients' assumptions, frames, and automatic thoughts about their situations and body sensations. Briefly, the approach follows an introduction to the role of thoughts in generating emotions, and the idea that those thoughts are hypotheses or guesses about the way things are rather than facts. This reframes the nature of panic as the result of a potentially unexamined "hypothesis" rather than "reality." This opens up the process of Socratic questioning, challenges, and experiments to check the accuracy of those appraisals, beliefs, and assumptions. These procedures follow in a sensible way from the assumption that clients and therapists simply need to check out the truth or correctness of the clients' hypotheses—or the result of accepting this new frame. The goal of this method is to counteract client overestimations of the risk of negative events or catastrophizing the meaning of events. Although its target is deconstructing prior client beliefs, this rarely occurs in the absence of "hypothesis testing" in the real world, "behavioral experiments," and "instructions" regarding exposure to the anxiety-provoking situations and feelings. From a process view, cognitive restructuring is likely to have the effect of gradually reframing clients' assumptions that underlie and drive their patterns of anxious apprehension and panicked responses. They also have the effect of offering another rationale for having clients doing the counterintuitive opposite to the vicious cycle patterns and deliberately exposing themselves or going toward instead of avoiding feared situations and feelings.

Exposure

Exposure is the ultimate paradox for clients. If a young woman's overriding solutions in anxiety are variations of mastery by avoidance, then gaining mastery by exposing herself to sensations and situations that have always signaled danger is clearly counterintuitive. However, exposure treatments appear to be the key active change mechanisms for panic disorder. Variations of exposure include *in vivo exposure*, which has its focus on agoraphobic situations. Of course, it is predicated on the idea that clients need to conduct experiments to see whether their assumptions about danger are unfounded, or variations on that theme. This is commonly done gradually by introducing less anxiety-provoking situations first and then progressing in intensity. *Interoceptive exposure* deliberately induces feared physical sensations over and again for periods of 30 seconds to 1 minute (in most cases), followed by discussing with the client what he or she learned about the physical sensations. These "experiments" can also include spinning in a chair, hopping, or running to increase heart rate; hyperventilating into a bag to induce other effects of panic; followed by discussions normalizing the experience. Of course, from the view of second-order change, exposure is the ultimate reversal of vicious cycles around panic and avoidant anxiety. Client compliance with such exposure, both in session and during homework, is the key to effectiveness. Therefore, a working alliance engendering trust, agreements on rationale, and goals is critical. When this occurs, exposure treatments and their variations are truly gold standards of effective therapy, as the process-of-change view would also predict.

Acceptance During Exposure

Newer approaches exploring acceptance and cognitive defusion, prominent in acceptance and commitment therapy (ACT; Hayes, Strosahl, & Wilson, 2012; Roemer & Orsillo, 2014), have their target as reversing what is termed *experiential avoidance*. In essence, therapeutic frames, rationales, and metaphors are used to explain how avoiding anxiety-producing sensations and situations thwarts clients from doing valued things in their lives. Mindfulness exercises in which clients are asked to imagine fear and anxiety-inducing situations without judging or reacting to them are a core of this approach. In addition, therapists frequently ask clients to actually perform and move through distressing sensations and situations in service of achieving valued goals.

From the process view, this is again counterintuitive for clients and requires strong frames, rationales, and metaphors. Yet it again represents complete reversal or second-order change of the vicious cycle or avoiding situations and not tolerating distressing sensations. What is meant by *defusing* is having clients take an observing view of their distress while experiencing it. This disengages the client from the experience of the distress while moving forward to do the opposite of the vicious cycle of avoidance.

Alternative Approaches to Panic Control Treatment

Lest the reader be left with the idea that all effective treatments for panic are based in CBT premises and techniques, there are a range of alternative approaches emerging as more research is conducted. In brief, such approaches as panic-focused psychodynamic therapy (Milrod, 1997), mindfulness-based cognitive therapy (Kim et al., 2009), ACT (Hayes et al., 2012), and even aerobic exercise have shown promising results. Although each has alternative premises and rationales for their interventions, all ultimately support exposure or reversal of client's major vicious cycle patterns around anxiety and panic. The many rationales and alternative "truths" of these varied approaches support the social constructionist base for the process view. All that matters are the coherence and fit of the rationale with the therapist and client to support ultimate pattern reversals.

In sum, each and all of these intervention components of panic and agoraphobic control treatment conform to the overriding process idea of pattern shifts and reversals. Combined, they have proven to be some of the most effective of the treatments that work for panic. Turning to effective treatments for other variations of anxiety, such as those for social anxiety, generalized anxiety, and OCD, the reader will find common themes.

Social Anxiety and Generalized Anxiety Disorder

Heimberg and Magee (2014) and Barlow, Conklin, and Bentley (2015) have offered excellent overviews of effective treatments for social anxiety. Social and generalized anxiety problems have proven challenging to treat effectively, yet several approaches have been shown to be relatively effective. A general review of the elements will prove useful in following the overall flow of the process-of-change perspective through these approaches.

Relationship Building

As we might expect in treatments for people anxious about potential problems with the negative judgment of themselves by others, and the potentially negative outcome of most events, a warm, positive, validating relationship with their therapist is crucial. In all approaches, this is a critical first step in offering clients an unexpectedly affirming audience and partnership in overcoming their struggles. Of course, this is directly reminiscent of Jerome Frank's admonition that all effective treatments are based in a remoralizing, hope-inducing, validating, and accepting relationship. In addition, this new affirming relationship offers the first reversal for clients expecting rejection and worse from others—a second-order change in itself.

Psychoeducation: Setting a New Frame

By now, and from here on, the initial step of offering clients education on the nature of their problem and the naturally related course of treatment should be no surprise. In all treatment approaches for SAD and GAD, clients are helped to see how normal physiological responses to distress and thoughts about them are normal, yet may spiral into vicious cycles of debilitating conditions. Therapists often validate and normalize clients' anxious apprehension and catastrophizing by putting them in normal contexts. Research increasingly supports the idea that some people have an innate tendency to be sensitive to physical distress, social criticism, coupled with social histories that reinforce the potential negative outcomes of many events. Treatments for both SAD and GAD describe the vicious cycles as including anxious rumination, distraction, and avoidance of experiences, along with the automatic negative thoughts about self, situations, and the future. All of this sets up the rationale for treatment as the quest to discover the "truth" about clients' current thoughts and patterns and enable them to more freely move forward in their lives. This sets the new rationale for the procedures that follow. As discussed in early chapters of Part I, all effective therapies offer some form of rationale, which gives an explanation of clients' problems, implies a direction and procedures for resolution, and enlists clients' motivations to go that way with the therapist. I noted this as the agreed-on definition of *hope*. Although these are cognitive and behavioral explanations, there is growing recognition that a range of alternative therapeutic rationales emphasizing emotions, or interpersonal relationships, for example, may also offer equally or more fitting treatment platforms for some therapists and clients. Such shifts in frame and understanding supply the critical groundwork for all treatments. They open clients to new directions for their ideas and solutions. They offer a crucial step toward pattern shifts and ultimately second-order change.

Cognitive Restructuring: The Rationale for Pattern Shifts

As with all CBT approaches, at least some emphasis is placed on the relationship between experiences (internal sensations, external situations), thoughts (cast not as facts but as "hypotheses" about the experience and predicted future similar experiences), and behaviors (subsequent responses to the appraisals of the experiences to respond to and manage future similar perceived distress or problems). Clients are then introduced to the process of collaborative empiricism and Socratic questioning that will gradually examine how accurate these thoughts or client appraisals and expectations might be. Although some approaches emphasize the critical nature of cognitive restructuring to successful treatment, others suggest that although it often contributes to outcome, it may have more effect by setting the stage for gradual exposure to the anxiety-provoking sensations, experiences, and situations while allowing the client to move forward in more valued directions.

In many ways, the practice of cognitive restructuring is directed toward deconstructing components of the client's rationale and frames that have made their solutions make sense to them. Although this is a gradual, collaborative, and validating process, it nevertheless offers one potent pathway toward pattern shift. All second-order change is paradoxical and counterintuitive to clients on at least some level. They must get a sense for how a new viewpoint and related actions may fit as well or better. Furthermore, more emphasis has recently been placed on the idea of examining thoughts as thoughts and not reality. This decenters them from appearing to be real instead of just simply ideas or hypotheses about the way things are. Clients are encouraged to take a perspective on their thoughts and experiences to examine them rather than fusing with them as "true." This represents another clear pattern shift and relates to the next common element of self-monitoring. (It also reflects the basic premise of a social constructionist view.)

Self-Monitoring

As explained earlier, most all treatments for SAD and GAD ask clients to do in-session and out-of-session monitoring of their thoughts, situations, sensations, and patterns of behavior around their problems. For both therapists and clients, this self-monitoring offers a clearer idea of the repeated patterns of the problem. It also gives clients permission to continue to engage in their "symptoms" or the vicious cycle while now observing it for a therapeutic purpose—again, a paradox in itself. In treating both SAD and GAD, clients are asked to notice how they respond to perceived distress, how their reactions offer perceived safety, and how the pattern perpetuates the cycle of the problem.

Once more, such self-monitoring in service of assessment is often an intervention in itself. It gives implicit permission to engage in the symptom, decenters the client from the thoughts and experiences, and offers information on the potential patterns and functions of the targeted vicious cycle. As Heimberg and Magee (2014) suggested, the result of this self-monitoring is "learning to disrupt this spiral of anxiety" (p. 128).

Exposure: The Ultimate Counterintuitive Pattern Reversal

In many ways, most all treatments for anxiety-related difficulties come down to exposure, or pattern reversals as we discuss this from the process model. The same is true for SAD and GAD. This is the ultimate in paradox and second-order pattern reversals. Once the therapeutic rationales are set, self-monitoring delineates the problem patterns, cognitive restructuring evolves, and then formal exposure to feared sensations and situations begins. As one might expect, engaging in feared social situations or in feared interactions of any kind will meet with resistance unless the therapeutic frames, goals, and related tasks are firmly set in an active and invested therapeutic alliance! In all treatment variations, graduated exposures occur first through discussion and images and then to in-session role-playing, and finally to real-life situations in safe, segmented steps. Common examples include having clients drink out of cups in the presence of confederates in session, stage public speaking behind a podium, directly observe others making mistakes, or even deliberately make minor mistakes in session and then in social settings. These are the ultimate in pattern reversals and second-order change.

Acceptance and Mindfulness

Roemer and Orsillo (2014) discussed an acceptance-based behavior therapy for GAD, and similar variations have been successfully applied to SAD. They listed three targets for clients with GAD as changing "(1) problematic ways of relating to internal experiences, (2) rigid strategies aimed at experiential avoidance, and (3) constriction or avoidance of meaningful actions" (p. 110). Their related goals thus become

> (1) to cultivate and *expanded* (as opposed to narrowed) awareness and a *compassionate* (as opposed to critical and judgmental), *decentered* (as opposed to entangled and fused) stance toward internal experiences; (2) to increase acceptance of/willingness to have internal experiences; and (3) to engage mindfully in personally meaningful behaviors. (p. 210)

Much of this approach coincides with the premises and procedures of acceptance and commitment therapy (ACT; Hayes et al., 2012). The interventions focus on *reversing* experiential avoidance of personal sensations and experiences. Therapists urge clients to accept and acknowledge such sensations and thoughts, while moving forward to do valued activities. Therapists teach clients mindfulness practices and have clients practice these as new skills outside of therapy as well. Not only do clients expose themselves to distress-inducing experiences and situations, they also embrace distress as expected, given their current and past histories and vulnerabilities, and then gradually do those things they formerly have not been able but want to do. From the process-of-change view, this is the ultimate in second-order change and pattern reversal.

This reversal is also predicated on clients buying into the new acceptance frame and rationales through the skillful use of new frames, exercises, and metaphors.

Obsessive–Compulsive Disorder

Edna Foa has been the ultimate champion of prolonged exposure-based and exposure and response prevention (EX/RP)–based treatments in the area of anxiety disorders, particularly for OCD and posttraumatic stress disorder (PTSD; for recent reviews, see Foa & McLean, 2016; Franklin & Foa, 2014). Early treatment approaches such as systematic desensitization, paradoxical intention, punishing obsessions and compulsions via thought stopping, aversion therapy, and covert sensitization all seemed promising yet ultimately proved ineffective. After exhaustive research, the most effective treatment to date comes down to EX/RP. The steps of EX/RP are as follows.

Education: Setting the New Frame

As in all the prior treatments, the first session starts with setting the frames and rationales for treatment. Therapists discuss the basic elements of how the OCD process and its vicious cycle begin and then are maintained through avoidance. This description of the problem sets the stage for the procedures of exposure and prevention of the OCD rituals. As is typical, this new frame is critical for clients to buy into. This is particularly important because the proposed exposure treatment without the safety mechanisms of rituals promises to be challenging and intensely distressing. Foa mentions rather high refusal and dropout rates. However, for those clients willing to invest in what often amounts to several hours a week of intense and prolonged exposure to the anxiety-provoking triggers in the absence of their common rituals, this has become a gold standard of effective treatments for OCD. Once more, the beginning and consistently reinforced reframe for OCD and its treatment rationale becomes the key to this paradigm case of second-order change pattern reversals.

Ritual Prevention: Blocking

Therapists make it clear that abstinence from rituals during treatment is essential to success. Both explicit rituals and implicit, or more subtle, rituals are identified and discussed, and alternative actions suggested. (These represent the unique elements and patterns in the client sphere of the Venn diagram of the therapy contract in Chapter 5. They contribute to fitting the specific procedures to each different client.) Because this is one of the linchpins of successful exposure treatment, the clients must embrace the reasons for preventing rituals.

In some ways, this stance of ritual prevention, although clearly a second-order pattern shift allowing for direct exposure, amounts to simply convincing clients to stop what they are doing to allow them to do the opposite. When this is successful, one can clearly imagine the following step of prolonged exposure to be successful.

Imaginal Exposure: The Ultimate Pattern Reversal

Gradual exposure to the distress-inducing sensations and situations is a common next component. Starting with imagery allows certain potential negative outcomes to be managed and allows for multiple settings and circumstances to be created and recreated in imagination. Clients begin with what they can just barely tolerate and then proceed to increasingly intense situations. The most important component of the exposure, in addition to sustaining the exposure with no negative results, is said to be processing the client's experiences during and after the exposure. Processing is done to modify or reframe the client's erroneous cognitions in light of disconfirming information from the exposure. This amounts to reinforcing a new and disconfirming frame for clients' experience to channel their new reactions and behaviors. Once again, this is the ultimate in reversing mastery by avoidance and replacing it by the originally counterintuitive action of mastery by exposure. This is the ultimate paradoxical second-order change.

By now, it should be abundantly clear that all available evidence-supported treatments are variations of pattern reversals, based on crucial reframes and rationales. This simplifies the options for practitioners. After defining the problem, its general patterns, and targets for intervention, all available treatment options emerge as variations of exposure. What remains is to fit the approach to the unique variations offered by each client and their problem pattern. This general unification across approaches to anxiety has not been lost on researchers and theoreticians. As we shall see in the final section, attention is now turning more toward unifying approaches.

UNIFIED PROTOCOLS FOR ANXIETY

If the proceeding section covering major treatments for anxiety-related problems seemed to take on a repetitive nature of variations on a theme, you are not alone in that observation. Most recently, several researchers and clinicians have begun to develop what they are calling *unified approaches*. For example, Barlow and Kennedy (2016), reflecting the new *DSM–5* treatment of anxiety, noted that what were originally 10 anxiety disorders have now been divided into a new total of 23 disorders with a proliferation of manuals developing for each. Commenting on the proliferation of treatment manuals, they said, "by the 2000's as many as 20 or more of these published interventions existed for each of the numerous narrowly defined disorders with little to choose among them creating great confusion for clinicians and patients alike" (p. 9). This is quite a statement for Barlow to make, as a champion of evidence-based treatments and randomized clinical trials using treatment manuals. Noticing the similarities among anxiety disorders and their effective treatment approaches, Barlow and Kennedy wrote, "For instance a patient with social anxiety (SOC) as the most severe presenting diagnosis might also meet criteria for several other anxiety or mood disorders at, perhaps, a somewhat less severe level" (p. 9). They, along with others, have begun to consider that treatments designed for a single diagnosis might target some "core" underlying features of all emotional disorders in some ways. Echoing our discussion in Part I of the need for alternate paradigms, Barlow and Kennedy remarked, "it seems that we are in the midst of yet another paradigm shift" (p. 11). In response to these observations, Barlow and his colleagues have set out to develop and test what they have called a *unified protocol for transdiagnostic treatment of emotional disorders* (UP; e.g., Barlow, Allen, & Choate, 2016).

Building a case for a set of core underlying features of all emotional disorders, Barlow and Kennedy (2016) began with research supporting an overriding and potentially inherited characteristic of what they termed *neuroticism*. They pointed to research supporting the observations that individuals with emotional disorders tend to react with distress to their own emotional experience, have greater difficulty accepting their own emotions, and are more intolerant of their negative emotions. They referred to this as a *neurotic temperament vulnerability*. They pointed to the tendency to react to an emotional trigger through an escalating vicious cycle as more important than the particular trigger or the resulting panic attack itself. This is exactly the point made by the properties of open systems we covered in Chapter 4. Recall the principles of multifinality and equifinality, which state that one can get to the same end point from a multiplicity of beginnings and, conversely, to a widely different set of end points from the same beginning. The intervening process of positive feedback is the best explanation for the pattern of the problem! The unique vulnerabilities or propensities of the problem-solver shape whether they will react by initiating that cycle. Explaining the essence of these resulting vicious cycles across anxiety disorders, Barlow and Kennedy went on to say:

> Differences among emotional disorders (i.e., different presenting symptoms in PDA, OCD, and SOC) may be determined by specific early learning experiences (Barlow, Ellard, et al., 2014); however, the core psychopathological mechanism or functional relationship in emotional disorders consists of intense negative emotional reactions and subsequent efforts to down-regulate emotional experiences. (p. 10)

Summarizing this concept of transdiagnostic elements underlying the development and maintenance of emotional disorders, the UP model suggests that people who develop them have a "propensity to find emotional experiences negative." The model suggests that such clients are anxiety sensitive, tend to respond with experiential avoidance, have deficits in mindfulness, make overly negative appraisals, and view the world as uncontrollable. (These variables represent the specific factors of the client sphere of the Venn diagram of the therapy contract from Chapter 5.) Therefore, for example, the unified approach suggests that research supports that people with major depression, GAD, OCD, and PTSD show high levels of emotion suppression. Rumination about past events and worry about future events are related to vicious cycles reinforced by the negative reinforcement of temporary distress reduction followed by more worry about worrying or ruminating. The unified approach views this as a common pattern across problems. The concept of anxiety sensitivity refers to the tendency to think that symptoms of anxiety will have negative consequences. Although this is particularly related to panic disorder, it is now viewed as cutting across most anxiety and related depressive disorders. The resulting transdiagnostic protocol suggested to apply to all emotional disorders consists of components, usually done in a group format with a mixture of emotional difficulties. Barlow and Kennedy (2016) stated that "the goal of this treatment is to help patients understand and recognize their emotions, and respond to their uncomfortable negative emotions in more adaptive ways" (p. 14). The protocol consists of five core treatment modules and three additional ones delivered over 12 to 18 weeks. They consist of the following:

- *Motivational enhancement for treatment engagement*—focusing on meeting clients at their own stage of change. This represents a pattern reversal for those therapists who have assumed all clients to be motivated to change and thus compliant with directions and interventions.
- *Psychoeducation and tracking of emotional experiences*—explaining the function of anxiety and tracking different emotions. This sets up the new frame to help make sense for clients who will be asked to the opposite of their common solutions.
- *Emotional awareness training*—linking thoughts, feelings, and behaviors (further framing).
- *Cognitive appraisal and reappraisal*, focusing on more flexible thinking (framing and practice).
- *Emotional avoidance and emotion-driven behaviors*—explaining cognitive, behavioral, and safety-seeking avoidance strategies that become problems. This describes the vicious cycle involved, and sets the rationale for reversals.

- *Awareness and tolerance of physical sensations*—creating somatic sensations of distress to show they are safe (This introduces counterintuitive pattern reversals.)
- *Interoceptive and situation-based emotion exposure*—inside- and outside-session practice engaging in emotion triggering behaviors; extinction inducing. This represents the core pattern reversals of exposure, both in and outside therapy.
- *Relapse prevention*—attention to booster information useful for the future. This represents efforts to support and sustain pattern shifts once they have begun.

As can be seen, most all of these components overlap with the treatments reviewed earlier, with the exception of motivational enhancement to increase client engagement and reduce dropout, which has been a problem. As discussed earlier, treatment rationale is critical to the education components. Tracking emotions and identifying triggers for problem cycles also reframes and decenters clients' experiences. Then paradoxical tasks exposing and engaging clients in feared experiences finish the process. This parallels the six-step process-of-change procedure laid out in Chapter 11. However, it fails to extend this process beyond mood disorders to such problems as couple, family, and other common psychological and interpersonal problems in clinical practice.

Resonating with the need for broader, more transdiagnostic approaches to emotional disorders like anxiety and depression, Clark (Clark, 2009; Clark & Taylor, 2009) stated that "common features of emotional disorders account for more variance than disorder-specific characteristics" (Clark & Taylor, 2009, p. 61). Recall that exposure is clearly pattern reversal, or second-order change in anxiety problems. Referring to specifically cognitive approaches, or the "C" in CBT, Clark and Taylor (2009) noted,

> Findings from comparative outcome studies and component analyses of CBT for anxiety and depression suggest that cognitive therapy is no more effective than 'purely' behavioral interventions, and specific cognitive interventions like cognitive restructuring or empirical hypothesis-testing do not provide incremental clinical effectiveness when compared to behavioral interventions like graded in vivo exposure or behavioral activation. (p. 61)

Regarding anxiety, they went on to relate that "the disorder-specific theories appear to differ primarily in content rather than in process. For example, selective attention to threat cues is a common feature of all anxiety disorders, but the type of threat attended to may differ across disorders" (p. 62). They also pointed to looking at shared variables across problems to determine how they feed into eventual vicious cycles of the problems that evolve. Clark

(2009) viewed Barlow's unified protocol as based in three change principles: (a) altering emotion-based misappraisals of critical life events (triggers or kick points for vicious cycles); (b) education about emotional disturbances (reframing the nature of problems and setting fitting treatment rationales); and (c) modifying emotion-driven behaviors (implementing pattern shifts and reversals in the solution-generated problem patterns of clients). This, in fact, fits nearly exactly with the process-of-change perspective.

Summing up this convergence on a process perspective, Steven Hayes (2016), in a newsletter feature titled "ACT and Process-Based Therapy," made a statement that resonates strongly with the process view put forward in this work:

> Evidence-based therapies, and Cognitive Behavioral Therapy (CBT) in particular, will soon be thought of more as comprising evidence-based processes and procedures for solving problems and for promoting human prosperity, than as named packages of therapeutic techniques linked to syndromes and the elimination of symptoms. (para. 2)

Following this course, Hayes, Pistorello, and Levin (2012) put forward ACT as a unified model of behavior change. Quoting from the planning committee for *DSM–5* (Kupfer, First, & Regier, 2008), they noted that "*DSM*-defined syndromes may never be successful in uncovering their underlying etiologies. For that to happen, an as yet unknown paradigm shift may need to occur" (p. xix). Following the arguments of Part I of this book, a prime alternative paradigm is the process-of-change perspective. As we follow the flow of this perspective through this and the following chapters on some of the more common problems seen in practice, you will likely see this emerge as well. In this chapter, we have traced the path of treatments that work for anxiety-related problems only to find that recent approaches converge on unification. The next chapter looks at the closely related mood disorder of depression to see whether the path of the process of change will continue. Yet before we finish, we need to return to the two cases that began the chapter.

REVISITING THE INITIAL CASES

Recall that the first case was the panicked schoolteacher. The second was a single mother who wanted new tools to master her anxiety and depression.

The Panicked Schoolteacher

The Context

This was a classic case of panic with agoraphobia. Ann was exceptionally bright and highly motivated. However, she had been in psychotherapy for years with different therapists using many different approaches and rationales, including "codependency" analysis, interpersonal relationship approaches, discussions of childhood abandonment and potential for abuse, CBT interventions, and extensive personal reading on panic and agoraphobia. Her unique personal experience included lifelong stomach problems and a recent gallbladder operation. She wondered if her problem was simply a result of her chronic gastrointestinal difficulties. We saw Ann in the context of her family physician's office in an integrated primary care setting.

The Process

The pattern of Ann's problem was her consistent attempts to control her catastrophic fear of fainting or vomiting in public by avoiding and/or escaping. She had even added good habits like putting marbles in a jar each time she mastered a fear. She also developed the habit of telling herself that her feelings were only temporary and would soon pass. However, she always succumbed to panic, she always plotted escape options, and she would not go out or would leave at the first sign of distress—even leaving her classroom.

The Change

The clear pattern reversal, based on the literature and on Ann's solution-generated problem patterns, came down to exposure without safety options or escape. The challenge was to help this make sense to her. The resolution resided in adopting Ann's hypothesis that "this all comes down to nausea." The question became whether her panic was a result of escalating catastrophic thinking and escape or was simply triggered by a physical sensation that would soon pass. She had noticed that when she had caffeine at breakfast, she was more likely to have a panic incident. Therefore, we gave her homework, with her physician's approval. Ann was to alternate her days of caffeine intake: One day she would drink several cups of coffee (supported by her physician as part of the team) and then observe her physical reactions in the classroom (yet stay in class through any distress). The next day she would go to class without caffeine and practice worrying and catastrophizing about potentially having a panic attack, observe her reactions, yet stay in class no matter what. Ann agreed.

The Outcome

Ann was a good student and did her homework faithfully. After a week, she noticed a pattern. After 6 weeks, she had resolved her panic attacks, with no recurrences, and she was staying in class and going out with friends. She decided "it was really all about nausea" and she simply needed to move through any physical distress and continue forward with her life. Ann's breakthrough was a product of the therapy team's accepting her viewpoint on her problem, then enlisting it as a vehicle for exposure without escape. This combined the literature on general patterns associated with panic and agoraphobia (exposure and escape prevention) with Ann's unique strengths and beliefs. The result was a second-order change or reversal in Ann's long-standing solution-generated problem cycles.

The Overwhelmed Single Mother

The Context

Finally, recall Sarah, who came to therapy "looking for more tools to defeat her anxiety and depression." She was a 40-year-old African American single parent of three, living in a large city in the southeastern part of the United States. It seemed that the basic problem was her anxiety—primarily her panic attacks. After these panic attacks and losing her temper with her children, the depression would set in, and it became hard to get out of bed. Sarah also worked as a nurse's aide in a local hospital and was finishing courses for her college degree. Determined to overcome her fits of rage, panic, and subsequent depressed episodes, she had sought treatment over several years with some results. However, in the face of overwhelming stresses, she repeatedly tried to control her anger and anxiety; upon failing, she sunk into deep periods of being depressed. The literature reveals a high co-occurrence of anxiety and depression, and Sarah is a prime example. In general, Sarah needed to break her cycle of control, panic and anger, and inertia. Calm acceptance of her circumstances and tasks, and deliberate action to take them on seemed a global target. However, what "tools" might help her do this?

The Process

Although Sarah had benefited by a long-standing positive relationship with a trusted therapist, her anxiety and depression continued. The tools she found somewhat helpful had been breathing exercises and support. However, relaxation tapes and techniques never felt comfortable, and she rejected several courses of medication. Sarah said she sought "a more holistic approach." She was determined to defeat these problems and get on with her life. Her one recent comfort lay in her faith. She had returned to the Christian church a few years ago and now "truly embraced the Lord" in her life. This was a strong personal strength.

The Change

In many ways, Sarah's dogged determination to defeat her anxiety and depression lay at the heart of her problems. Denying the obvious life stresses she faced daily, she saw her anxiety, panic, and rages as signs of her inevitable failures and subsequently sunk into depressed phases. The tool offered promised something completely different and completely paradoxical to her way of fighting. The therapist introduced Sarah to mindfulness through several stories and metaphors, followed by tapping into her faith in an in-session exercise. The children's finger trap solution of pushing in to get out was followed by the metaphor of using both hands to keep a lid on her anxiety and having no hands to live her life. The *Star Wars* story of Luke putting away his light saber and thus defeating the "Dark Lord" was met with Sarah saying, "And that Dark Lord was the Devil." Sarah said that prayer and reflection brought calm and the Lord into her life, and so she agreed to do that in session in a present and mindful way. She then brought successive thoughts of her unpaid bills and lack of money into her mind without judging or acting on them, just allowing them to pass on as if they were clouds.

The Outcome

After several minutes, Sarah was bidden to come back to her conversation with the therapist, and she did so with a big smile. She got it. She got the new tool and connected it tightly with her newfound faith. Agreeing to practice in coming weeks and do so with her chosen word, *calm*, she discussed how this would likely free at least one hand, if not both, to tackle what she now acknowledged as stressors that would overwhelm most anybody. She also agreed to relink with her trusted former therapist. The outcome was a complete reversal of her former patterns. She would defeat her problems by acknowledging them but not fighting with them directly. In some ways, this is clearly exposure and response prevention. It interdicted the vicious cycle before it began. This paradox, however, needed to make sense to Sarah. The stories and metaphors helped, yet linking with the personal strength of her faith served to drive home how this new tool would set her on a new path to do what she needed to do and peruse those things she most valued. Obviously, using mindfulness with Sarah matched well with the cascade of research supporting its use with both anxiety and depression.

7
DEPRESSION

There is nothing either good or bad, but thinking makes it so.
—William Shakespeare, *Hamlet*, Act II, Scene 2

To be or not to be: That is the question: Whether 'tis nobler in the mind to suffer the slings and arrows of outrageous fortune or to take arms against a sea of troubles, and by opposing end them . . .
—William Shakespeare, *Hamlet*, Act III, Scene 1

Consider the case of Shela. Shela was a 28-year-old single mother of four. She had gone through two divorces. Both men had left her and her kids. They had affairs during the marriages, as had Shela. Shela had come from a single-parent family herself. Her mother was drug addicted and never really in the home. Her father, who was abusive to her and always put her down, raised her. Shela's uncle and older cousin had sexually abused her as a child and adolescent, and she revealed to her therapist that she had always been sexually promiscuous. Now she realized that she had contracted genital herpes. Shela was having more crying spells lately, and many days she struggled to get out of bed to take care of her kids. She was anxious about her future.

Shela's therapist, Tasha, struggled with finding the best evidence-supported approach to use with Shela. Tasha felt that an approach focusing on Shela's history and interpersonal relationships fit best with her client's presentation and with Tasha's own training and way of approaching cases. However, Tasha, viewing cognitive behavioral therapy (CBT) as the best

http://dx.doi.org/10.1037/0000078-008
Unifying Effective Psychotherapies: Tracing the Process of Change, by J. S. Fraser

evidence-supported approach, was surprised to learn that other evidence-supported approaches existed, and some matched better with her own preferences. This offered a pleasantly surprising revelation. For example, recall the three evidence-supported approaches for depression presented in Chapter 2 (Table 2.1), as a sample of 12 research-supported psychological treatments for depression listed by Division 12 (Society of Clinical Psychology) of the American Psychological Association as of January 2016: cognitive therapy, interpersonal therapy (IPT), and behavioral activation (BA) therapy. Questions remain for practitioners as to what the common thread might be connecting these approaches and, more practically, which to use. As we have seen, this is a common dilemma for all practitioners across all problem areas. Our task once more is to take a step to a metalevel and see what most clients in the dominant culture share when they struggle with depression. Once determined, the related task is to step above the variety of therapies that work for depressed clients to see what they share in common as a class of effective interventions. Finally, we need to determine how to join with our clients to form a new therapeutic alliance that offers a fitting metalevel frame for their problem that makes sense to them and offers a rationale and new solutions to resolve, or re-solve their depression. This is the focus each of the chapters of this section of the book. Finally, I return to Shela's case at the end of this chapter and address how we might engage various effective treatment approaches for her and how one or another might offer the best fit. Before we step into our task, let's turn briefly to the two Shakespearian quotes that open this chapter.

The two quotes regarding William Shakespeare's famous "Melancholy Dane," Hamlet, embody the major themes of two of today's prominent evidence-supported treatments for depression. The first theme is that our thoughts or cognitions have a significant influence over our mood. Hamlet's thinking was pervaded by consistently dark thoughts about himself, his situation, and his future. The second theme is that interpersonal distress and relationship issues are the main causes of mood disorders such as depression and thoughts of suicide. Hamlet considered his own suicide in the face of his overwhelming grief over his father's death and the subsequent loss of his mother's attention to her new husband, who may have murdered Hamlet's father. As we might guess, the two leading treatments for depression, CBT and IPT, focus their treatment on each of these two factors supposed to underlie depression: cognitions and relationships, respectively. Another evidence-supported approach, BA therapy, focuses on turning Hamlet's downward spirals of withdrawal toward more active and rewarding paths. Yet another approach, emotion-focused therapy (EFT), turns Hamlet's attention toward resolving his basic emotional distress over his historically broken attachments to loved ones. But which is most effective? If they are all equally effective, how can this be so? These varied assumptions or premises for treating depression seem to be so different. Both dark thoughts and interpersonal tragedy were equally present in Hamlet's life. Hamlet had certainly become more inert and ruminative. Nothing in his life was rewarding or fulfilling. Finally, he had most definitely experienced broken attachments and perceived betrayals with those he most loved. What should be the focus? Is treatment choice a product of what the therapist chooses to focus on? Alternatively, is it what makes sense to the client? Is it changing the way the client struggles to overcome depression—or all of these? This chapter addresses these questions.

THE CONTEXT AND PROCESS OF DEPRESSION

We follow four major approaches to depression in this chapter to sort out their similarities. They conveniently represent four of the main theoretical approaches: cognitive, interpersonal–dynamic, behavioral, and humanistic–existential. We follow the path of each of these four as they describe the process of depression and its related treatment. Our task as always is to find convergence and common patterns that will help group them into a class of psychotherapies that work for depression. First, we need to turn to the definition of depression in dominant Western culture through the fifth edition of the *Diagnostic and Statistical Manual of Mental Disorders* (*DSM–5*; American Psychiatric Association, 2013), and similar to the tenth revision of the *International Statistical Classification of Diseases* (ICD–10; World Health Organization [WHO], 1993).

Depression Defined

Together with anxiety, depression is one of the most commonly seen problems by physicians and mental health providers alike. Major depressive disorder is the most frequently diagnosed disorder in adults. In 2015, an estimated 16.1 million adults aged 18 or older in the United States had at least one major depressive episode in the previous year. This number represented 6.7% of all U.S. adults, and women had approximately twice the prevalence of men (National Institute of Mental Health [NIMH], 2015). Gender differences also hold up across populations. A leading cause of disability, depression has enormous interpersonal and financial costs in both the cost of treatment and in lost productivity.

This chapter addresses two major categories of depression. These are major depressive disorder (MDD) and dysthymic disorder. Because definitions from the *DSM–5* (American Psychiatric Association, 2013), certainly a medical model, have become the standard for the Western mental health field, I typically refer to *DSM–5* definitions in this text. As stated in the previous chapter on anxiety, the ICD–10 (WHO, 1993) is another firmly medical model diagnostic manual used across the world. Although its coding is different for these two categories of depression, the criteria are largely the same. Remember, however, that the process view subsumes such normative descriptions as simply one way of explaining and describing a given problem. What follows are descriptions from the sphere of context, which shape our view of depression-related problems. Context also explains how, from clients' perspective, solutions evolve into self-defeating vicious cycles. The *DSM–5* and ICD–10 offer official criteria for each of these disorders. For MDD, the person must evidence marked distress or a decrease in her level of functioning. Furthermore, she must also experience a daily occurrence of dysphoric mood (tearful, sad, or empty) or lack of interest or pleasure in most activities. In addition, the person must also experience at least four of the following (three if both loss of interest in activities and depressed mood are present), with most occurring nearly daily: significant loss of weight or change in appetite, inability to get to sleep or sleeping too much, psychomotor agitation or retardation, loss of energy or fatigue, feelings of worthlessness or excessive or inappropriate guilt, decreased concentration or indecisiveness, or recurring thoughts of death.

MDD has been the major focus of most treatment research and the source of greatest treatment success. Dysthymic disorder, added to the *DSM* in 1980, continues to be refined as a disorder to distinguish it as a chronic disorder rather than a form of personality disorder. It affects approximately 3% of adults in the United States and may account for as much as 36% of the population of mental health clinics, with women 2 to 3 times more likely to have the diagnosis than men (Markowitz, 2004). The *DSM–5* and ICD–10 set out the criterion that the depressed mood is present for most of the day, for more days than not, for at least 2 years, with at least two or more of the list of six symptoms used for major depression present. The person must have never been without the symptoms for more than 2 months at a time over the previous 2 years, with no major depressive, manic, or psychotic episodes and no evidence of the depression having been the result of substance abuse, medication, or medical conditions. Overall, the symptoms must have caused clinically significant distress or impairment in social, occupational, or other important areas of functioning. Dysthymic disorder refers to a chronic depressed condition, and it has been much less successfully treated; even when treatment has appeared successful, there is a high incidence of relapse.

Competing Descriptions of Depression

Various perspectives describe the process of depression. However, in keeping with our look at those treatments designated as effective based on available research, I focus first on two major evidence-supported treatments.

The first of these is cognitive therapy for depression (designated as CBT for cognitive behavioral therapy), developed by Aaron T. Beck and his colleagues (Beck, Rush, Shaw, & Emery, 1979). The second is IPT developed by Gerald L. Klerman and his colleagues (Klerman, Weissman, Rounsaville, & Chevron, 1984). To be clear, I also discuss two more evidence-supported approaches for depression, BA and EFT, along with others based in mindfulness and acceptance. However, the first focus is on the CBT and IPT approaches to conceptualizing and intervening with depression. One reason for discussing these two alternative approaches is that they represent very different psychological and philosophical traditions. CBT follows cognitive, rational, empirical, and logical–positivist assumptions. IPT follows interpersonal, dynamic, and process assumptions. These separate assumptions generally lead therapists in very different directions in conceptualizing and treating depressed patients. The main reason for choosing to begin with these two, however, is the broad attention they gained by being selected for study in one of the largest and most carefully controlled studies to date on the effectiveness of different treatments for depression.

The NIMH Treatment of Depression Collaborative Research Program (Elkin et al., 1989) was the largest multicenter comparative clinical treatment trial in psychotherapy ever conducted to date. It compared medication and management with the drug imipramine with CBT, IPT, and placebo with clinical management. The study included 250 outpatient clients identified as suffering from MDD as measured by a number of widely accepted diagnostic scales. Each patient was randomly assigned to one of the four 16-week conditions just described. All treatments were standardized, and manuals were used to train and supervise therapists. Treatment adherence measures were carefully monitored to be sure that the standard treatment was being applied. Treatment was provided at several separate centers, and a broad range of measures was conducted throughout treatment. Although this massive study has been the subject of many subsequent analyses, the major finding that has received so much attention is that for those patients who completed the study, all three active treatments succeeded *equally* in reducing depression posttreatment. For example, the percentage of patients reducing their depression below the clinical level (Hamilton Rating Scale for Depression score of 6 or less) for each condition respectively was CBT (36%), IPT (43%), and imipramine hydrochloride plus clinical management (42%). This and other more refined results from the study provided a strong statement that psychotherapy was at least as effective as medication in treating depression. This was reason for rejoicing among psychotherapists, yet it raised some equally compelling questions. The main question among these was how such apparently different approaches to depression as CBT and IPT had such similar effectiveness in helping depressed clients feel better. I address some answers to this question presently, but first we need to look at how each approach describes depression. Therapists practicing each approach are guided by these assumptions about the condition that they are treating. The same will then be done using the assumptions of the BA, EFT, and mindfulness/acceptance approaches.

How CBT Explains Depression: Self-Fulfilling Prophecies

Aaron Beck's cognitive model (Beck et al., 1979) suggests three specific concepts to help explain depression. The combination of these three paints a picture of what becomes the self-fulfilling prophecy of depression for clients. The three areas are (a) the cognitive triad, (b) schemas, and (c) cognitive errors (i.e., faulty information processing). The *cognitive triad* is composed of three patterns that draw the person into viewing herself, her future, and her experiences in a unique way. First, the client develops a *negative view of herself*, assuming that because of her presumed deficits, she is undesirable and worthless. The second pattern is that the depressed person tends to *interpret her ongoing experiences in a negative way*, viewing situations as intolerable obstacles and confirmations of how bad things really are. The third component is that the individual has *negative views of the future*, anticipating that her current difficulties or suffering will continue indefinitely. The resulting symptoms of depression noted earlier are thus viewed as following from the combination of these three client "distortions" of her reality. When clients are listless and withdraw to avoid their life demands, these actions are viewed as a result of their pessimism and hopelessness given that they expect negative events and a negative outcome of their efforts. Clients become increasingly dependent on others because they view themselves as inept and helpless, and they overestimate how difficult normal tasks will be and assume their efforts alone will only turn out badly. Apathy and low energy are seen as logical results of the client seeing that he or she is doomed to failure.

Beck agrees that most depressive episodes are triggered by the wide range of life difficulties that we all encounter. These may particularly include real or perceived losses but may also include the numerous economic, health, and interpersonal distresses that may arise. Beck adapted the concept of *schemas* from the work of Piaget (1997) and others to explain how the depressed person comes to act on these as triggers to evolve what we have called *solution-generated problem patterns*. He has defined schemas as relatively stable cognitive patterns that serve as the basis for interpreting particular sets of situations. They help screen out, differentiate, and code stimuli into familiar, understandable, and predictable patterns that may then be responded to with an appropriate repertoire of reactions. Beck described people as evaluating experiences through a matrix of schemas that have generally been developed though early life events. These schemas are not particularly good or bad. As discussed earlier, the concept of schemas is another way of describing the normal and natural process we all use to help make our world a little more safe and predictable. They tend to be the set of premises and assumptions on the way things are in a given domain that forms the basis of what we have described as first-order change. Beck suggested that many of these schemas lie dormant until energized by specific environmental inputs (e.g., stressful situations). A person's idiosyncratic schemas may or may not match those of most others for a given situation, but they will match that person's personal history and serve as a filter for him to arrange and react to it. In the case of depression, these schemas are described as particularly negative, distorted, and dysfunctional. However, the more those schemas are used, the more they drive the self-fulfilling negative prophecy, and the more widely they are evoked and applied. Eventually, these schema-driven patterns are said to take on a life of their own, becoming autonomous. The depressed person becomes less and less able to entertain the idea that her negative interpretations may be erroneous. She may eventually become preoccupied with pervasive negative thoughts about herself, her world, and her future, with all of the related symptoms of depression present.

Cognitive errors or *faulty information processing* is the final leg of the three-legged stool. These are a series of logical errors characteristic of depressive thinking that serve to maintain the person's belief in the validity of his negative concepts. Beck (Beck et al., 1979) has described these errors as nondimensional and global ("I am fearful"), absolutistic and moralistic ("I am a despicable coward"), invariant ("I always have been and always will be a coward"), *character diagnosis* ("I have a defect in my character"), and irreversible ("Since I am basically weak, there's nothing that can be done about it"). These qualities are compared with more functional thinking, which is characterized as multidimensional, relativistic, and nonjudgmental, variable, reversible, and leads to *behavioral diagnoses*. Beck's list of thinking errors includes (a) *arbitrary inference*, when a conclusion is drawn in the absence of evidence or in the face of evidence to the contrary; (b) *selective abstraction*, when a detail is taken out of context to characterize a whole experience, ignoring other salient features of the situation; (c) *overgeneralization*, when one or more isolated incidents are used to draw a general rule or conclusion and apply it across broadly related and unrelated situations; (d) *magnification and minimization*, when perceived negative events or qualities are inflated and positive ones depreciated; (e) *personalization*, in which a person relates external events to oneself when there is no basis for making such a connection; and (f) *absolutistic, dichotomous thinking*, in which all experiences are cast into one of two opposite categories. As might be imagined, each of these errors and their combination tends to initiate and perpetuate their own vicious cycle of problems that characterize the depressed person's experience.

Beck has noted that the person who is depressed tends to have enough of an effect on his environment and those around him to actually create situations that match his expectations. Although he may isolate himself from others, others may withdraw from him because he is not enjoyable to be with, and so on. This can create an interpersonal self-fulfilling prophecy in which what the person expects from his world eventually shapes his interactions to match those beliefs. However, Beck et al. (1979) paid much more attention to what they described as "the primacy of cognitive factors in depression" (p. 18). They suggested that

> in taking a "cross section" of the symptomatology of depression, we have arrived at the position that we should look for the primary psychopathology in the peculiar way the individual views himself, his experiences, and his future (the "cognitive triad") and his idiosyncratic way of processing information (arbitrary inference, selective recall, overgeneralization, etc.). . . . If the diagnostician does not search for other pathology, he may miss the primary phenomenon in the chain of events, namely the thinking disorder. (p. 19)

Although the model does not address the ultimate etiology or cause of major depression, it does point to the way depressed people think of their self, their experiences, and their future as the primary factor that drives the self-fulfilling prophecies of their depression.

How IPT Explains Depression: Interpersonal Vicious Cycles

The IPT approach to depression follows a different tack to describe depression. This perspective locates the essence of depression in the interpersonal relationships of the person who is depressed. It is grounded firmly in the interpersonal dynamic views of Harry Stack Sullivan (1953) and in Bowlby's (1969) attachment theory. In their manual on the IPT approach, Klerman, Weissman, Rounsaville, and Chevron (1984) stated,

> The theoretical foundation of the interpersonal approach has been best summarized by Sullivan, who taught that psychiatry involves the scientific study of people and the processes between people, rather than focusing exclusively on the mind, society, or the brain. Hence the unit of clinical study is the patient's interpersonal relations at any one particular time. (p. 47)

Thus, this perspective views disturbances in *interpersonal relations* as antecedents to emotional distress like that of depression. In their IPT manual, Klerman and his collaborators went on to say that

> while we believe that past and ongoing interpersonal relationships are related to depression, we cannot always establish the direction of

> causation . . . although disruptions of interpersonal relationships are not in themselves "necessary and sufficient" to produce clinical depressions, interpersonal difficulties are usually associated with clinical depression. (p. 51)

Klerman et al. (1984) cited Bowlby (1977) as suggesting that psychotherapy should help the patient examine current interpersonal relationships and understand how they have developed from experiences with attachment figures in childhood, adolescence, and adulthood. This is an area that should sound vaguely similar to that of Beck as he described the development of schemas. However, the interpersonal approach makes much more of the reciprocal vicious cycles that evolve in the relationships of depressed people and those who interact with them than does the cognitive view. Markowitz (2004), in his IPT manual for treating dysthymic disorders, described this as follows:

> The fundamental concept of IPT is that depression does not occur in a vacuum, but rather in a social context. When bad things happen, you feel bad. Conversely, when you feel depressed, you tend to mishandle your social role, to interact ineffectively, and so bad things are likely to happen. This can result in a vicious cycle; bad events lead to worsening mood, which in turn leads to further bad events. (p. 44)

The interpersonal view emphasizes some very real reciprocal patterns that cocreate depressive patterns in the depressed person's partner relationships, family, work, and community activities. Klerman and colleagues (1984) cited the work of Coyne (1976), among others, who found that depressed people not only elicited unhelpful responses from others but also created mutual negativity and received depressed reactions from the people with whom they interacted. Recall that Beck and his colleagues remarked on the same. Klerman et al. noted that depressed people are depressing to have around; they are evaluated negatively and often avoided. Thus, a vicious cycle evolves in which the depressed person not only feels negative about herself, her experiences, and the future, but those appraisals come to match her situation through coevolving interactions with others. As Markowitz (2004) suggested, "Depressed patients tend to withdraw socially and retreat inwardly, frequently spending much of their time alone or even laying [*sic*] in bed. . . . The patient who lies in bed thinking, 'I'm useless, I'm not doing anything' is in some measure correct" (p. 52). A depressing personal and interpersonal reality is thus created and is quite real. At one level, this view is at odds with the cognitive perspective that assumes that the depressed person's cognitions represent errors or distortions of their reality. The interpersonal position suggests that the depressed person's appraisals of their situation may in some ways be correct. Yet those depressing situations and relationships may be equally correctable as the depressed person examines their options and takes actions to change them.

The interpersonal viewpoint notes that sadness and an occasional depressed mood are a normal part of the human condition, with disruptions in interpersonal relationships resulting in nearly universal feelings of sadness. However, when a particular instance of interpersonal distress matches an important area of historical distress for a person, such as a critical loss of a loved one, or the threat of loss, and so on, this triggers responses similar to those discussed from the cognitive approach as schema related. This might also be viewed as personal vulnerabilities, as discussed in the last chapter on anxiety. At times, our assumptions and related ways of interacting may easily assimilate our distress and/or help us adjust to it. Problems develop, however, when our initial solutions fail and some variation reapplied. This is an exact parallel to what we have discussed previously as first-order assumptions driving first-order solutions into the now familiar solution-generated problems.

A major set of constructs that guide the interpersonal description of depression is that there tend to be four main areas on interpersonal distress around which depression evolves (Klerman et al., 1984). These interpersonal domains include (a) *grief*, which focuses on the person's reaction to the actual death of a person or people either now or in the past; (b) *role disputes*, which involve analyzing interpersonal disputes with friends, family, partners, or coworkers; (c) *transitions*, which involve role change resulting from life events such as marrying, taking a new job, becoming a student, or becoming a parent and the like; and (d) *interpersonal deficits*, which relate mainly to interpersonal isolation and the related poor quality and quantity of the depressed person's interpersonal relationships. The key element here is that the depressed person responds to each of these areas of interpersonal distress in a way that sets up a characteristic vicious cycle that eventually takes on a life of its own. The cycle eventually becomes an actual syndrome called clinical depression. One critical aspect of treatment, as we shall see, is educating the depressed client about depression and letting them know that it is no more their fault than having diabetes or a broken leg would be. The interpersonal view suggests that the depressed symptoms are a natural result of failing to look at options to resolve critical areas of interpersonal distress and then take action to resolve them.

Commonality Between CBT and IPT: Solution-Generated Problems

Both approaches to depression view it as evolving from reactions to distressing yet common life events. In their chapter on cognitive therapy for depression, Young, Weinberger, and Beck (2001) emphasized the following:

> Research dealing with the onset of particular episodes of adult depression has concluded that the majority are provoked by life events or ongoing

> difficulties; the role of events has emerged as clearly the more important of the two. . . . Studies have suggested that about 66%–90% of depressed episodes have a severe event occurring within six months of onset. . . . The majority of these events involve some element of loss. (p. 265)

Similarly, in Beck et al.'s (1979) now classic manual for doing cognitive therapy for depression, they stated, "The precipitants of depression revolve around a perceived or actual loss" (p. 24). In his manual for doing IPT for depression, Markowitz (2004) stated, "The fundamental concept of IPT is that depression does not occur in a vacuum but rather in a social context. When bad things happen you feel bad" (p. 43). In the original IPT manual for treating depression, Klerman et al. (1984) stated, "Clinical depression and related affective disorders involve an accentuation in the intensity or duration of otherwise normal emotions" (p. 29). Just as with most problems, however, it is not the event that creates the problem but instead the way the event is handled or responded to that creates the pattern of the problem. Those people who develop the classic symptoms of depression have tended to take themselves and their emotions out of context. Thus, as they attempt to solve their distress, they focus on themselves and initiate a downward spiral that becomes a self-fulfilling prophecy. Furthermore, because feeling depressed is such a common emotion, Klerman and his colleagues also noted "family and friends tend to minimize the severity of the patient's difficulties because the manifestations seem to be normal responses to life situations" (p. 30). This feeds the cycle of disconfirmation and alienation for the person feeling depressed, further locking in the downward spiral. Describing this problem pattern of depression, Markowitz went on to say that

> when you feel depressed, you tend to mishandle your social role, to interact ineffectively, and so bad things are likely to happen. This can result in a vicious cycle; bad events lead to worsening mood, which in turn leads to further bad events. (p. 44)

Beck et al. (1979) echoed this analysis in suggesting that

> A person slipping into depression may withdraw from significant other people. Thus alienated, the "significant others" may respond with rejections or criticisms, which in turn, activate or aggravate the person's own self-rejection and self-criticism. . . . Thus the vicious cycle can continue until the patient is so depressed that he may be impervious to attempts by others to help him and show him love and affection. (p. 17)

Looking at a similar process, Young and colleagues (2001) stated, "The severely depressed patient is caught in a vicious cycle in which a reduced activity level leads to a negative self-label, which in turn results in even further discouragement and consequent inactivity" (p. 281).

Both of these two major approaches thus describe depression in terms of what we have called solution-generated problems. Our past experiences shape our premises and assumptions, which in turn direct our actions or solutions, which in turn shape the pattern of our interactions. Once again, the problem is not the distressing event, change, or perceived difficulty. Instead, the pattern of how clients view or respond to the perceived difficulty and try to solve it becomes the problem. Change is constant and inevitable. The process of how we negotiate change inevitably becomes the focus of our assessments and interventions. Our task as therapists is to help clients to change how they are negotiating change. That is, to help clients negotiate a second-order change—in this case, of their depressive cycle. Both CBT and IPT take this goal as their task in treating depression. Turning our attention to two more evidence-supported approaches will reinforce these conclusions, albeit operating in two other domains of focus. The first approach emphasizes behavior; the second stresses emotions. Finally, I briefly address a few more promising approaches that use mindfulness and acceptance, always with the goal of tracking pattern similarities shared across all of these approaches.

How BA Therapy Explains Depression: Downward Spirals

An often-cited classic study by the late Neil Jacobson and his colleagues (Jacobson et al., 1996) asked what the necessary and sufficient components for change were in the cognitive therapy approach. One would clearly assume that a critical component of cognitive treatment would be modifying dysfunctional schemas and automatic thoughts. To test this, Jacobson and colleagues broke down the key elements of CBT into a BA component, a component for dealing with depressing events and concurrent automatic thoughts, and a component for modifying depressive schemas. Then they dismantled treatment into three treatment approaches. The first treatment focused only on activating patient behavior. The second included that activation element and a treatment related to coping skills associated with automatic thoughts. The third was a complete package including BA, coping skills, and identifying and modifying dysfunctional core schemas. Surprisingly, all groups were equally effective at both termination and follow-up. This casts doubt on the necessity of including the cognitive components of the cognitive approach. Certainly, the IPT approach did not include explicit procedures to challenge automatic thoughts or to draw direct connections between thinking, emotions, and depression, yet it was also equally or more effective than the CBT approach in the NIMH multisite depression study. Klein and Ross (1993) reported another related and surprising finding from the results of this massive study. The Beck Depression Inventory (BDI), heavily influenced by questions on cognitive distortions, was given as one of the outcome measures. One would expect that Beck's cognitive approach would produce superior results on this, his own cognitive scale. However, IPT was superior to CBT on the BDI among all clients completing treatment. This adds even more doubt and confusion on the mechanisms of change. How can an approach focusing on improving interpersonal relationships produce better results on a cognitively saturated measure of depression like the BDI than the cognitive approach of the scale's creator? Returning to the effectiveness of simply activating behavior, the Jacobson et al. (1996) study lent credibility and subsequent focus on a more behavioral approach to depression that emphasized one of the study's components, activating patients' behavior or BA.

Lewinsohn (see Lewinsohn & Gotlib, 1995, for an overview) was one of the first to develop a targeted program for depression, based on the views of Skinner (1953) and Ferster (1973). This approach was closely complemented by the self-control therapy of Rehm (1977), among others. Behavioral approaches in their various forms share the common assumption that MDD is related to a decrease of positive reinforcing behaviors. Consequently, they focus on increasing positive daily activities, improving communication and social skills, increasing assertiveness skills, decreasing negative life experiences, and increasing positive reinforcement contingencies for new adaptive behaviors. This behavioral approach has had equally impressive results in treating depression as those of the cognitive and interpersonal approaches. For example, in a well-designed and controlled study (see Gortner, Gollan, Dobson, & Jacobson, 1998), a therapy including only BA elements was found to be equally effective (at the end of 20 sessions and at the 6-month follow-up) as one including BA and modification of automatic dysfunctional thoughts and a third treatment including the full CBT package. In another study, an approach focusing on the consequences of client's behavior and teaching social problem-solving to resolve interpersonal difficulties (BA) was found to be equally effective as was an antidepressant medication (nefazodone); the combination of the medication plus the behavioral activation therapy was more effective than either treatment alone (Keller et al., 2000; McCullough, 2000).

Developers of the BA approach (see, e.g., Dimidjian, Martell, Addis, Herman-Dunn, & Hubley, 2014; Martell, Dimidjian, & Herman-Dunn, 2013) trace much of their approach to the behavioral theories of Ferster (1973) and Lewinsohn (1974). Ferster suggested that depressed people might not engage in reinforcing behaviors frequently enough and that depressed clients suffer decreases in reinforcing behaviors because they actively escape and avoid actions and situations they view as aversive. This produced a downward spiral, similar to that inherent in the process paradigm. Lewinsohn built on this downward cycle. He suggested a three-phase process described by Dimidjian et al. (2014) as follows:

> First, when people's efforts do not result in reward, they often become more focused on responding to their own internal state than to potential sources of positive reinforcement in the external environment. This is classic "turning inward" that is often seen in depression, and that makes sense from a behavioral perspective . . . second . . . was a narrowing of individuals' repertoire of adaptive behaviors. This makes logical sense as well because fewer and fewer behaviors are being maintained by positive reinforcement. . . . Finally . . . increases in aversive consequences following behavior typically lead depressed individuals to become preoccupied with escape and avoidance. In effect, more energy is expended attempting to avoid or escape from anticipated aversive consequences than attempting to contact potential positive reinforcers in the environment. (p. 354)

Social avoidance was a core element of Lewinsohn's (1974) model of depression. The BA view of depression assumes that contextual events in people's lives may result in lower levels of reinforcement or positive experiences, and heightened aversive experiences. Less rewarding lives can lead to feelings of sadness and depressed mood, causing them to disrupt routines and pull away from their world in various ways. This downward spiral not only maintains but also exacerbates depression in the positive feedback pattern core to what occurs in the process-based open systems discussed in Chapter 4. The more depressed people pull away from and avoid their perceived aversive and unrewarding environment, the less reward they receive. The less they engage, the less skilled they become at engaging in what they truly value and desire. Turning inward and ruminating becomes a fundamentally avoidant technique or solution pattern that turns back on itself, exacerbating the very process the depressed person is trying to overcome. Thus, reversing this pattern of inward-turning avoidance becomes the key element of the BA approach. Client acceptance of this problem frame and rationale is critical because clients will need to comply with homework and activities in the face of depression-activating triggers and situations. Regarding client buy-in, Dimidjian et al. (2014) said:

> It is essential that the therapist obtain "buy-in" from the client with the basic elements of the treatment model. Therapy works best if the client accepts and buys into the rationale for treatment and the case conceptualization (Addis & Carpenter, 2000). (p. 358)

As an example, they offered an excellent quote from a therapist who is offering the frame and rationale of BA:

> THERAPIST: It makes total sense that you would pull away when you are feeling so down. The problem with pulling away like this is that it tends to keep people stuck. In feeling depressed, and the pulling away can

> become a problem in its own right. So that is the arrow that links what you do and how you feel in a kind of downward spiral. The more you pull away or the more you are caught in your thoughts, the worse you actually feel, the less energy you have. (p. 371)

Commenting on the case, the authors wrote, "Treatment sought to reverse the downward spirals of depression by scheduling and structuring activities" (Dimidjian et al., 2014, p. 370). By now, the reader will recognize the vicious cycles of solution-generated problems as first-order change, and the counterintuitive or paradoxical nature of this intervention as a hallmark of second-order change and pattern reversal. We shall see other convergences between this behavioral-based approach and the cognitive and interpersonal approaches to depression as we turn to treatment. However, one more promising evidence-supported approach deserves our attention. Representing the humanistic–existential perspective is EFT.

How EFT Explains Depression: Emotional Vicious Cycles

Just as the developers of the BA approach saw their work as revitalizing long-overlooked behavioral factors, so too did Less Greenberg, who developed EFT, seek to revive and validate the equally long-overlooked humanistic–existential perspective. Greenberg (2002; Greenberg & Watson, 2006) described EFT as based in the person-centered views of Carl Rogers (1961), the experiential focusing approach of Gendlin (1962), the Gestalt therapy of Perls (Perls, Hefferline, & Goodman, 1951), and existential therapy (see, e.g., May, 1967; Yalom, 1980). If we view the three preceding approaches to depression as focused on cognitions, relationships, and behavior, respectively, the clear contextual focus of this view is on emotion.

Following the humanistic–existential premise that humankind's basic emotions are positive life forces, EFT suggests that client problems evolve from disconnecting with those basic emotions. As Greenberg (2015) explained,

> A central EFT assumption is that dysfunction results from avoidance or disclaiming of primary experience and the resulting inability to integrate certain experiences into existing self-organizations. . . . So people need to reown their primary adaptive emotional responses and reprocess disclaimed or painful emotions. . . . Dysfunction arises from the disowning of healthy growth-oriented resources and needs, the suppression of unacceptable aspects of experience, and the avoidance of painful emotions. (pp. 54–55)

Although emotions have always seemed to be both self-evident and somehow ill-defined, EFT has spent considerable effort anchoring them in physiology. EFT theory includes extensive detail on the physiological bases of emotion (see Greenberg & Watson, 2006, pp. 21–35). Emotional responses are viewed as primary, preconscious, automatic, physiological reactions to environmental triggers. The felt emotion is then translated into conscious experience and then into behavioral expression. As Greenberg (2015) stated, "A key principle of EFT is that emotions provide access to needs, or goals and the action tendencies associated with them" (p. 37). In this view, our history of interacting with our environment eventually creates adaptive links between environmental stimuli and emotional responses. These "*emotional memories* and organizations of lived emotional experience [are then] formed into *emotional schemes*" (p. 38, emphasis in the original).

Scheme activation occurs without awareness. Only after one experiences this preconscious emotional activation does it then influence conscious processing. As Greenberg (2015) noted, "Schemes are elicited by cues that match the input features of the scheme and produce experience and action as their output" (p. 38). Returning to physiological bases, these emotional schemes are described as neural networks representing the basic history of our lived experience. Using fear as an example, when we see a frown or hear a raised voice, a fear scheme may be activated. As Greenberg (2015) explained,

> Each scheme includes its basic components of affect, action tendency, need, and cognition structured in a wordless narrative; the person experiences the other as a threat, the body tenses and prepares for escape, and negative beliefs about self become primed. With attention the activated scheme or schemes in turn may be symbolized in language giving rise to conscious emotion, the concern or desire, an action tendency and thought, and then combine, in the case of fear activation, to influence behavioral avoidance. (p. 41)

Contrary to cognitive approaches, which assume cognitions produce emotions, EFT assumes emotions come first and are then interpreted through cognitions. Emotions thus function to rapidly process complex situations, offer us feedback on our reaction, and prepare us to take effective action. Fear cues us to act to avoid or reduce danger, shame signals that we may have acted inappropriately and motivates us to correct or hide our actions in social context. Thus, EFT views primary emotions as adaptive in that they aid our effective functioning. They only become maladaptive when they interfere with effective functioning. It describes such maladaptive emotional responses as overlearned reactions to repeated or intense emotional experiences, such as trauma, shame, rejection, humiliation, and so on. Secondary reactive emotions are emotional reactions to primary adaptive emotions and largely replace them. Thus, people may feel ashamed of being afraid, or guilty about their anger, or sad about being anxious, or ashamed over their sadness. Once these emotional schemes are set, they repeat over time to help guide our lives.

Greenberg and Watson (2006) stressed, however, that clients need to agree on the frame, tasks, and goals for therapy for treatment to be effective:

> Clients need to agree that they are having difficulty processing their emotional experience either because it is too overwhelming or because they have difficulty attending to it. If the client does not agree with the therapist's formulation, then the therapist needs to readjust his or her framework and conceptualization to fit better with the client's perspective. (p. 167)

Turning to emotional disorders, Greenberg (2015) said, "Many disorders stem from the same basic underlying processes of affect avoidance and problems in affect regulation and core maladaptive emotion schemes" (p. 102). He went on to say,

> Depression and anxiety are clearly affectively based. The negative views of self, world, and future and the behavioral withdrawal that one finds in them are reactions to and results of the avoidance of painful core maladaptive emotions often of fear, shame, lonely abandonment, or anger as well as the result of maladaptive ways of trying to cope with the events that evoke these painful emotions. . . . Instead of experiencing themselves as strong, vital, and joyful, people who are depressed experience themselves as vulnerable, damaged, and blameworthy and react to setbacks and disappointments with a significant loss or self-esteem. The self is organized as hopeless, incompetent, and worthless because of the activation of emotion schematic memories of crucial losses, failures, humiliation, or entrapment. (p. 103)

Thus, depressed clients have developed emotion-schematic responses shaped by their developmental history to protect themselves from further fear or shame. Describing clients in their studies who responded to EFT, Greenberg and Watson (2006) explained the downward vicious cycles of depression as follows:

> Once negative affect was evoked in relation to current circumstance or painful memories, these clients' responses to the painful affect were more harmful than helpful. They deadened to stop feeling, withdrew from others, become overwhelmed by a cascade of self-recrimination, or become outer directed and blamed others. None of these methods of coping with the original feelings of vulnerability, sadness, shame, or fear were adaptive; these attempts to cope led to more depressive experience, rather than less. (p. 10)

Returning once again to the physiology of how schematic memories are developed, the authors referred to research on memory development that notes that after an initial period of flux, memories become set and resistant to change (Greenberg & Watson, 2006). Thus, the depressive schemes that fuel and feed these depressive vicious cycles become relatively fixed and firm over time. However, citing recent research, they also note that upon reexperiencing such distressing emotions, they again become open to flux in interpretation and to potential change. Herein lies the key to the EFT approach.

Through the paradox of re-experiencing the problem-generating emotions rather than avoiding them, new and more flexible and adaptive emotions and responses can be initiated, understood, solidified, and supported. As Greenberg (2015) wrote,

> Paradoxically, one of the most effective ways of helping clients contain emotion may actually be helping them to become aware of it, express it, and decide what to do about it as soon as it arises. This is because suppressing an emotion and doing nothing about it tend to generate more unwanted emotional intrusions, making it more overwhelming or frightening. (p. 72)

Again, relating to the paradox of therapy, he noted,

> It is only through experience of emotion that emotional distress can be cured. One cannot leave these feelings of worthlessness or insecurity until one has arrived at them. What is curative is first the ability to symbolize these feelings of worthlessness or weakness and then to access alternate adaptive emotion-based self-schemes. (Greenberg, 2015, p. 83)

Thus, once again, the described pattern of the problem is resolved (or re-solved) by doing the counterintuitive thing and experiencing what the client least wants to do. In the case of EFT, it is experiencing the emotions that the client has avoided. In BA, it is taking opposite action in the face of patterns of withdrawal, rumination, and inertia. As we have seen, the same goes for the cognitive and interpersonal approaches as they reverse cognitive and behavioral cycles. Two more intervention approaches deserve attention before we apply them to the case at the start of this chapter. The first is variations of acceptance and mindfulness, and the second revisits Barlow's (Barlow, Allen, & Choate, 2016) unified protocol noted in the previous chapter on anxiety.

How Acceptance and Mindfulness Approaches Explain Depression: Vicious and Ruminative Depressive Cycles

The BA authors make a point of noting the similarities between their approach and that of Linehan's (1993) *dialectical behavioral therapy*, and Hayes, Strosahl, and Wilson's (2012) ACT. Both focus on reversing the spiral of avoidance in the process of depression. Linehan's use of the technique of *opposite action* supports the paradox of having clients note triggers for depressing inaction and avoidance and use them to do the opposite by engaging in action counter to the downward depressive cycle. The ACT approach emphasizes the role of "experiential avoidance" in depression along with many other disorders. ACT teaches mindfulness and attention to triggers and ruminative depressing thoughts while either not reacting to them or acting in accordance with a client's values despite the wish to withdraw or ruminate. Both of these approaches emphasize the *downward vicious cycles of depression* and intervene with *counterintuitive* support for either not acting in the typical patterns of falling into inertia and withdrawal or acting despite old habits and wishes to avoid and withdraw. This is clearly the paradox of second-order change at the core of the process of change view.

Similarly, Segal, Williams, and Teasdale (2002) applied mindfulness in their evidence-supported approach to preventing relapse, called *mindfulness-based cognitive therapy for depression*. They developed an approach for people with three or more previous relapses or episodes of depression that nearly cut in half the relapse and reoccurrence rates over the follow-up period compared with treatment as usual. So what did they do, and how did they come to this intervention? In studying clients who tended to have recurrences of depressed episodes, they noticed that these people were becoming more and more easily triggered into a characteristic vicious and ruminative depressive cycle in response to new situations that may have made them feel sad or distressed. There was evidence not only that characteristic depressive thought patterns could produce depressed moods, but conversely, that sad or depressed moods could also trigger familiar depressive thinking patterns. It is interesting that Segal and his colleagues described the person who relapses as being caught in the classic *solution-generated problem cycle*. A person who was formerly depressed might experience a sad or distressing mood from which she wants to escape. Her solution is to try to think her way out of her distress, which in itself perpetuates the distress through rumination—the classic first-order change of reapplying the same solutions and expecting a different result. Segal et al. suggested that

> he or she may remain upset, not so much because of the original situation, but because his or her mind goes round and round trying to work out why he or she got so upset in the first place . . . people dig themselves deeper into the very hole from which they are trying to escape. . . . [Thus] attempts to solve problems by endlessly thinking about them can serve merely to keep individuals locked into the state from which they are trying to escape. (p. 69)

This is the classic paradox that is the hallmark of a first-order vicious cycle in which the solutions have become the problem. It is interesting that the heart of Segal and colleagues' (2002) intervention approach constitutes the kind of pattern reversal that is also the very hallmark of second-order change. What they teach these clients is techniques of waking meditation, or mindfulness, to practice and use as they move themselves purposely toward depressing moods or situations or as they encounter such distressing moods and situations in their daily lives. The idea is for clients to actively experience formerly distressing situations and essentially notice them pass without the need to act on them. This is the ultimate acceptance strategy. Clients learn to accept a perceived change or potentially distressing circumstance without triggering the actions or solutions that formerly created the vicious cycle of the solution-generated problem of their depression. This is a reversal of going toward the distressing situation and not doing the logical solution to resolve it. This is like pushing in rather than pulling out to escape from the child's finger trap, illustrated in Chapter 3. It is by definition a second-order change—a hallmark of the process paradigm.

A Unified Protocol Revisited

As we discussed in Chapter 6 on anxiety, Barlow and colleagues (Barlow et al., 2010; Barlow & Kennedy, 2016; Payne, Ellard, Farchione, Fairholme, & Barlow, 2014) have developed what they called a unified protocol (UP) for the treatment of emotional disorders, including anxiety and depression. Summarizing this concept of transdiagnostic elements underlying the development and maintenance of emotional disorders, the UP model suggests that people who develop them have a propensity to find emotional experiences negative. The model suggests that such clients are emotion sensitive, tend to respond with experiential avoidance, have deficits in mindfulness, make overly negative appraisals, and view the world as uncontrollable. (These variables represent the specific factors of the client sphere of the Venn diagram of the therapy contract in Chapter 5.) Therefore, for example, according to the unified approach, research supports that people with MDD show high levels of emotion suppression. Rumination about past events and worry about future events are related to vicious cycles reinforced by the negative reinforcement of temporary distress reduction followed by more worry about worrying or ruminating. The unified approach views this as a common pattern across problems. The resulting transdiagnostic protocol suggested to apply to all emotional disorders consists of components, usually done in a group format with a mixture of emotional difficulties. Barlow and Kennedy (2016) suggested that "the goal of this treatment is to help patients understand and recognize their emotions, and respond to their uncomfortable negative emotions in more adaptive ways" (p. 14). The core elements of this approach (following linking and educating clients on an emotional avoidance frame) involve having clients identify and *bring on distressing emotional states* and then practice *moving toward them* while opening flexible new options of reacting and engaging with these formerly distressing triggers. Once again, the core of this approach rests on pattern reversals or second-order change in the former solution-generating problem cycles—an intervention theme that the reader will by now have heard over and again across these effective treatment approaches.

PROCESS AND CHANGE IN DEPRESSION

Remember that the process perspective views all problems as vicious cycles of clients' often well-meaning solutions (or first-order changes) within the context of the way they explain their circumstances and what "makes sense" to do to resolve their dilemma. Group theory suggests that such problems cannot be resolved from within the premises, rules, and patterns of the group. Clients must step out of their problem-generated system to a metalevel (or make a second-order change) to reflect on their assumptions and solution patterns and consider alternative courses. Each of the reviewed approaches does just this. Most often, the new solution patterns will appear counterintuitive or paradoxical from the original group level and are rarely considered. Each of these reviewed approaches offers a new frame for the client's problem, and a related rationale to make sense of formerly counterintuitive solutions. In many ways, all treatments seek to initiate some form of problem pattern disruption or difference, but that difference must be a difference that makes a difference. First-order change within the current rules and patterns of a client's problem simply reaffirm the problem and are more of the same. Second-order change changes the system itself. Clients must effectively join a metalevel group with therapists to form a working alliance to resolve their problems. Joining in this working alliance is the first step in the second-order change process. Each of these effective approaches first allies with clients and then offers frames and rationales to make sense of formerly paradoxical pathways toward resolution.

Therapists' empathy, warmth, genuineness, and validation of the client's struggle and pain offer the first step into this alliance. This is the first element of the second-order change process. Each of the preceding approaches reviewed here emphasizes such empathic joining as at least a precondition for change—and sometimes as a major change itself for the client who feels flawed and unlovable.

The next step involves agreeing on a frame that helps "make sense" of the problem and its patterns for the client in new ways. This new frame enables the client and therapist to agree on a related rationale for treatment. This rationale will help formerly unconsidered or counterintuitive options "make sense" for the client. Most therapeutic interventions make sense within a given frame for a problem and its related treatment rationale, yet they are inherently paradoxical from the level of the client's initial understanding and related solution patterns. CBT offers a cognitive frame to explain depressive self-fulfilling prophesies and encourages new actions to check out a client's negative assumptions about herself, her situation, and her future. IPT offers an interpersonal frame to validate the client's depression and make sense of taking action on new solutions to those interpersonal issues. BA explains the downward cycle of withdrawal from anticipated negative situations and feelings and helps clients make sense of taking opposite-actions from their current avoidant solutions. EFT offers an emotion-based frame for the recurrent avoidant patterns of clients' depressive cycle and explains that reexperiencing these intense emotions is the pathway toward resolving them. Acceptance and mindfulness–based approaches explain the vicious cycles of clients' depressive patterns and then teach them to go toward depressive thoughts and triggering situations while not judging them or becoming caught into their former vicious cycles. Each effective treatment offers clients a compelling new frame to reconceptualize their cycles of depression that make new sense of interdicting former downward cycles by taking new opposite action to re-solve them. Finally, the treatment alliance with the therapist supports, amplifies, and generalizes the new pattern shifts once they begin to evolve a new virtuous cycle. Each of these effective approaches echoes the premises of a process paradigm described in the chapters of Part I.

If the process view holds true, although frames and foci may be different, the process of problem pattern reversal should hold constant. If there is general agreement that depressed clients tend to react to distressing perceived losses and life changes by withdrawing, avoiding, and ruminating in a downward spiral, then effective interventions will reverse these patterns in some way. Applying these effective treatment strategies to the case of Shela may help bring this to life.

REVISITING THE INITIAL CASE

Recall from the beginning of this chapter that Shela's therapist, Tasha, became confused as she struggled to apply an evidence-supported treatment for her client. Tasha was most comfortable with linking Shela's past relationship conflicts, losses, and betrayals with her current depression. She would then build Shela's sense of self-respect, self-confidence, and initiative by validating her depression as understandable, given her history, and affirming that much of the abuse and betrayal was not her fault. The task now would be to take action to solve her current dilemmas and triumph over them by following her own valued goals. However, Tasha's initial understanding was that only CBT was the "best practice" for depression. Finding out that there were several evidence-supported approaches, some of which were similar to her own ideas, was both puzzling and a pleasant surprise. How could each of them apply to Shela's case, and which might be best to choose? In partial answer, let us take a hypothetical look at how each of these effective approaches might work with Shela. Let's first assume that Tasha was familiar with the CBT approach, as was her supervisor.

CBT for Depression

Using CBT, Tasha is likely to see Shela's tragic history and current situation—her losses, her history of abuse and betrayal—as triggers for her current depression. They most likely contributed to Shela's view of herself as worthless and damaged, her appraisal of her current life situation as overwhelmingly discouraging, and her future as holding more of the same. She would have developed a negative schema, driving her automatic thoughts in the same depressing themes, feeding frequent depressive rumination. She may well assume that everything confirms to her negative view of herself, without examining the evidence. Magnifying negative events and overlooking positive ones, she would assume that her whole world is bleak. In addition, taking her misfortunes out of context and personalizing them as her own fault, she would take all of her troubles on herself as her own failures. As her therapist, Tasha will thus draw Shela's attention to these cognitive distortions and thinking errors, collaboratively examine their validity, and develop new functional views and action plans for her future.

As with all approaches, Tasha will begin by listening to Shela's story, empathizing with her, and validating her pain. During the first two sessions, she will explain the relationship between thoughts and feelings, using examples and taking advantage of Shela's own emotions to show the connection with her thoughts. Tasha will describe the natural course of depression and its symptoms and relate that course to common ways clients have learned to think of themselves and their world. She will note how these ways of thinking then become automatic habits that go unexamined and often become disconnected from what may actually be true about herself, her situation, and the future. Shela will be offered hope as she learns that these common thinking patterns have been found to underlie depression and that a collaborative process of learning about these thinking patterns, examining their truth and usefulness, and taking action to alter her thinking and situations has been found to be successful in relieving depression. Importantly, Tasha will also discuss the cognitive triad described earlier as the rationale for understanding depression and make the link with the collaboratively empirical approach that Shela and Tasha will take to examine the evidence supporting or disconfirming Shela's depressive assumptions.

As a team, Tasha and Shela will first seek out the nature of Shela's automatic thoughts and schemas and then take them on in the same way that scientists address questions, treating each thought and schema as a hypothesis to be tested and gathering evidence that will either support or refute each hypothesis. To do this, Shela will need to actively gather data and examine evidence. In this way, she may discover the illogic or inconsistency of her thinking on their own, rather than having Tasha confront or persuade her of this. Rather than avoiding those circumstances that provoke anger, sadness, hopelessness, anxiety, guilt, and other emotions related to depression, Tasha will ask Shela to attend to them in session and at home to learn more about them. Tasha may also ask Shela to evoke these emotions in session by asking her to picture these emotion-evoking situations. She may also role-play interpersonal situations with Shela to actively evoke emotions and reveal her related automatic thoughts. To develop a record of the situations that trigger Shela's emotions and automatic thoughts, Tasha will also ask her to make careful observations of her daily activities rather than simply move automatically through her day. As Shela gradually shares the patterns of her thoughts, emotions, and reactions to life situations, she will engage with Tasha in examining the evidence. The variety of procedures used will likely include logical discourse and Socratic questioning, role-playing, use of imagery and image restructuring, behavioral experiments and examining the evidence, and direct problem-solving of dilemmas. As she discovers her automatic thoughts and schemas, Shela will then be asked to list evidence from her own experiences for and against her depressive assumptions. Tasha and Shela may also design experiments to test these hypotheses. When the results of the experiment contradict Shela's predictions, then her automatic thoughts will need to be revised.

Tasha will also design direct reversals of Shela's withdrawal and inactivity to help her use her time more adaptively and become involved in more constructive activity. Scheduled activities might include mastery and pleasure exercises; role-playing, modeling, and coaching to rehearse new and more assertive behaviors; self-reliance training that helps Shela take increased control of routine tasks such as bathing, cleaning, cooking, or shopping; and diversion techniques that redirect negative thinking through physical activity, play, work, social contacts, and so on.

In summary, the first phase of therapy will concentrate on induction into the rationale for and process of treatment and on symptom reduction and will include all of the elements just described. This phase will likely achieve direct reductions in depressive symptoms through keeping thought records, identifying and challenging dysfunctional thoughts through questioning and experiments, and constructing and following agendas and activity schedules until Shela's depression is lifted. Tasha will then design the second phase as relapse prevention, focusing more on Shela's schemas. Long-standing fears such as fears of abandonment, fears of inadequacy, problems in entitlement or self-control, needing to subjugate to others or self-sacrifice, or being overly self-punitive, inhibited, and negative toward herself are but a few of the most common schemas rooted in Shela's childhood, family and social history that may be covered. Tasha and Shela will then collaborate in evaluating the evidence for these historical beliefs by examining the evidence, then designing and carrying out experiments. Shela will be encouraged to modify long-term interaction patterns that have reinforced their schemas throughout her life and ultimately act against the dictates of her beliefs. To prevent relapse, Tasha will encourage Shela to understand her own schemas and their origin and to learn how they will be triggered, reinforced, and maintained in the future unless she continues to be vigilant and use the tools she will have learned in treatment to counteract these vicious cycles of self-fulfilling prophecies.

Although this treatment plan appears sound and makes sense, it may not fit with the client or the therapist. Such a logical cognitive frame and rationale may simply not make sense to Shela. Nor may it fit with the training and personal preferences of Tasha, as we mentioned earlier. In this case, Tasha may be equally confident using a more interpersonal approach, such as IPT.

IPT for Depression

Using IPT, Tasha is again likely to see Shela's tragic history and current situation—her losses and her history of abuse and betrayal—as triggers for her current depression. However, she will now validate Shela's depression as a reasonable response to her rather overwhelming history. In contrast to the cognitive approach, Tasha will cast Shela as having quite reasonable emotional reactions to unreasonable circumstances, rather than responding to dysfunctional thoughts about potentially reasonable situations. The two early tasks in IPT are establishing a collaborative working alliance and identifying the interpersonal focus that best represents the reasons for Shela's depression. Similar to CBT, Shela will be reassured that she is depressed and that depression is a highly treatable condition. A common disorder, it responds well to treatment. The outlook for recovery is excellent. Most people recover promptly with treatment, and the prognosis is quite good. Tasha will continue by validating Shela's distress as real and painful and then explaining the nature of vicious cycles and self-fulfilling interpersonal prophecies that are in fact very distressing and can commonly take on a life of their own and develop into the syndrome of clinical depression. Importantly, Tasha will tell Shela that she has the clinical disorder of depression. Having an "illness" like depression, which takes on a life of its own, is no more her fault than having diabetes or high blood pressure would be. Hence Shela will not need to fix her symptoms as a personal flaw. They are actually commonly occurring results of chronically unresolved interpersonal difficulties that need addressing. Her responsibility is simply to cooperate with treatment to get better. In the IPT approach, this entails identifying the current interpersonal challenges confronting Shela, evaluating options to address them, and then taking action to change those relationship challenges in some way. Tasha will thus set the frame and rationale for Shela's problem as one of resolving interpersonal dilemmas. Their task is to sort out what those dilemmas are and then design an action plan to resolve them.

Turning to treatment, Tasha will explain that treatment will have a here-and-now focus. Shela will need to address current concerns and review current interpersonal relations, evaluate options and needs for action, and initiate action to change things. They will then prioritize the main interpersonal areas of distress, including grief, interpersonal disputes, role transitions, and interpersonal deficits in Shela's life. Regarding her grief, Tasha will directly encourage Shela to engage with the process of her painful and unresolved losses. Tasha will encourage her to master and integrate her grief by "remembering to remember" and experiencing the sadness and pain, rather than "remembering to forget." Turning to Shela's interpersonal disputes, the nature and pattern of their current vicious cycles will be analyzed and evaluated, and a new course of action will be planned. They will determine the stage of the dispute and decide if there is a renegotiation needed, if there is an impasse, or if the relationship needs dissolving. Shela's expectations and assumptions fueling her solution-generated problem patterns will be evaluated and other options discussed and put to the test through role plays and actions in her life. Turning to her role transitions to parenthood, single parenting, and setting a new independent course for herself, Tasha will facilitate Shela's mourning the loss of her old roles; begin viewing her new roles more positively, and acknowledging her anxiety and developing mastery in her new roles. Tasha and Shela will evaluate the escalating problematic patterns around the role transition, validate the emotions related to the change, and then plot a course of action to move out of the vicious cycles around the transition and integrate the changes into Shela's life. Finally, Shela is most likely reasonably depressed because she currently and historically has few social relationships and is socially isolated. Tasha will use her own relationship with Shela as a starting point for building closeness and new social skills and then move her toward reducing isolation through encouraging new social relationships. The key to success in this area, as in all others, is to encourage Shela to consider her depression as a reasonable reaction to recent and past life situations, to examine her expectations and interactions that tend to fuel her impasses, and then to take new and often very different actions to resolve those difficulties. Tasha will reemphasize that depression is not Shela's fault; it is a reasonable response to unreasonable situations. It will resolve by Shela acting on new options.

Yet Tasha, realizing through her graduate training that activation appears to be a common element associated with effective treatment for depression, might decide to apply BA instead. After all, both CBT and IPT seem to encourage deliberate action to counteract clients' low-functioning levels, avoidance, and the downward spirals of self-recrimination. Maybe a pure BA approach would be most efficient.

BA for Depression

Applying BA, Tasha will begin treatment as in all other approaches: by listening to Shela's story and her pain and viewing her tragic history and current situation—her losses and her history of abuse and betrayal—as triggers for her current depression. However, Tasha will pay close attention to the behavioral sequence of Shela's past and current patterns of behavior. Tasha's assessment will be highly individualized to Shela's history and patterns. Her goal will be to increase rewarding experiences for Shela by increasing activation and engagement in her life. It will be important to learn her unique depressive patterns. They appear to be passive patterns such as sleeping excessively, watching television, and not going out to dull her negative feelings. (However, they could have involved active things, while engaging in such constant vicious cycles of ruminative thinking that she would have gained little pleasure from her activities.) It will be important to find both what is most personally rewarding and in line with what Shela values, as well as how she is avoiding what is aversive and painful for her in the downward vicious cycle.

Tasha will begin by telling Shela that their work together will be both collaborative and structured, as the form and agenda for each session. This will help them keep on task to make the best use of their time. Tasha will give Shela a small booklet that frames depression as a pulling away from things most rewarding and offering the rationale that becoming more active in pursuing those things will resolve that downward spiral. Shela's buy-in to the frame and rationale for treatment is crucial because she will need to comply with outside homework assignments and agree to try on new active behavior patterns in the face of old triggers for depression. Tasha will explain that there are often things that happen in people's life that are not only painful but that also make it hard to do the things that make them feel good. With Shela's drug-addicted mother never home, her abusive father putting her down, and her uncle and cousin sexually abusing her, along with both Shela's husbands leaving her, Shela's life experience had resulted in more than enough pain to get in her way. Tasha will then use a three-circle diagram that they will fill in together, with the first circle representing the context, the second how that context makes her feel, and the third indicating what she does or doesn't do. The diagram also includes circular arrows showing primary feedback and secondary downward cycles that keep Shela stuck. Together Shela and Tasha put all of Shela's stressors in the first circle; her fatigue, low energy, and bad feelings about herself as normal responses in the second; and the way she pulls away from her life by staying in bed, calling in sick to work, not going out with friends, and turning her thoughts over and over in her head in the third circle. Tasha will then explain that it makes sense to pull away when feeling down, yet pulling away becomes a problem in itself and keeps her stuck. The second downward spiral from her solution of pulling away makes things even worse as her boss is getting frustrated and her friends are stopping calling her. Reversing these vicious downward spirals is the goal. Once Shela agrees to this, Tasha will move to the next steps in treatment.

Tasha will use the BA model to track the antecedents, consequences, and actions of distressing interactions Shela brings in throughout treatment. She will also have Shela complete weekly activity records to document her activity at least 3 to 4 hours each day and rate her associated mood. Tasha will then review these activity records in detail to begin identifying patterns that may be maintaining or exacerbating Shela's depression. She will question what Shela might be doing instead if she were not depressed, how life contexts affect her mood, how her withdrawal is keeping things the same or making them worse, and what Shela is missing and what she has lost through her coping skills. A key task for Tasha is to help Shela learn that her moods are linked to what she does or doesn't do, where she is doing (or not doing) it, and what the outcome is for her. The major work will then occur between sessions. Scheduling graded activities and monitoring their outcome will then be used throughout treatment. Shela will learn to work from the "outside in" rather than the "inside out" as she learns to take action on what she values despite the feelings of inertia and the triggers that typically make her feel like pulling away.

Tasha will teach Shela to use the acronym TRAP to recognize the *trigger* in the environment that produces the *response* or emotional reaction and the resulting *avoidance pattern* to cope with the emotions. Shela will learn to remove herself from the trap of depressing triggers and get back on track by experimenting with alternative behaviors.

Tasha will also teach Shela the ACTION acronym to help her *assess* whether the behavior is approach or avoidance, making her feel better or worse; *choose* to continue a behavior that makes her feel worse or try a new behavior; *try* the chosen behavior; *integrate* any new behavior into her routine to give it a fair chance; *observe the results* to see the effects of a new behavior; and finally, *never give up*, remembering that making changes always requires diligent and repeated attempts. As an added variation of her BA approach, and if Shela is open to it, Tasha might also teach her mindfulness skills to allow her to experience old triggering traps and stay centered as she resists the temptation to respond. As Shela begins trying new actions, she and Tasha will troubleshoot difficulties as they arise. As Shela is successful in doing more things to feel better, they will broaden and generalize those activities. Finally, they will both work on relapse prevention by identifying and preparing for high-risk situations to inoculate her against falling back into old traps. Therapist and client will keep the door open to booster and maintenance sessions.

Ultimately, however, Tasha may realize that each of these approaches seems to have skirted around the truly intense emotions Shela has experienced and how she is currently defending herself from reexperiencing them and getting back in touch with her authentic self. Tasha may also feel that the in-session work of most of the other approaches seems stale compared with the intensity of Shela's past and current experiences. She may also find that she is personally comfortable doing intense emotionally focused work in sessions with Shela. In this case, she might turn to EFT.

Emotion-Focused Therapy for Depression

Applying EFT, Tasha will pay close attention to Shela's story and validate her experiences in warm and supportive ways by listening to Shela's story and her pain and viewing her tragic history and current situation—her losses and her history of abuse and betrayal—as triggers for her current depression. However, Tasha will invest herself intensively in this process in a truly I–Thou relationship of shared, authentic experience, likely going beyond the other approaches. Tasha will first attend to bonding and awareness by empathizing with Shela's feelings and her sense of herself, providing a rationale for working with her emotions, making her aware of her internal experiences, and establishing a collaborative focus. It is critical that Shela agree that she is having difficulty processing her emotional experience, either because it is too overwhelming or because she has difficulty attending to it. Once this problem frame is set, the rationale for treatment can move forward. Tasha will learn how Shela is handling her emotion by paying attention to her history but also by remaining exquisitely attuned to how Shela expresses herself on a moment-by-moment basis in session. Is she overwhelmed by her emotion, or is she having trouble identifying and attending to it? Tasha will process Shela's early attachment difficulties and the trauma of her multiple betrayals from her parents and family. In so doing, she will learn the interpersonal and intrapersonal issues contributing to Shela's pain and share this understanding with Shela. Rather than avoid or deflect these emotions, she must agree to move toward them and experience them intensely before she can free herself to take new and more positive action in her life.

Tasha will then move forward by evoking and exploring Shela's emotions, offering support for the experience, arousing problematic feelings in Shela, undoing interruptions of emotion, and helping Shela access her primary emotions or core maladaptive schemes. Once more, the guide for Tasha's interventions will come from markers of Shela's in-session actions around emotional issues. Such varied in-session markers may lead Tasha to evoke vivid reexperiencing of Shela's emotions, empathetically validating her vulnerability, putting words to her felt bodily senses, or initiating a two-chair enactment. For example, Tasha may have Shela engage in a two-chair dialogue with each of her parents or her perpetrators to sort through her emotions and find new words and meanings to allow her anger and ability to move forward. She must experience the emotions she avoids to release new emotions and empower new action. In other words, Shela must go backward to move forward. Through these experiences, Tasha will generate new emotions to transform maladaptive schemas and help create new meanings with Shela by promoting reflection to make sense of her new experience, validating her new feelings and her emerging sense of herself. Shela's path to resolution is likely to lead her to express her adaptive grief or hurt over her early traumas and betrayals, allow her to feel anger or learn to self-sooth, and thus empower self-acceptance and personal agency. As treatment succeeds in getting Shela back in touch with her primary emotions, action will replace resignation, and motivated desire will replace her hopelessness. In closing, Tasha and Shela will review where she was when they started, validate where she is now, and envision her future. As they do this, they will anticipate setbacks and new hurdles and discuss how Shela will resist being drawn back to old patterns of avoiding her experience and remaining open to her own vital self.

Summary

The story of Tasha's choice of treatment for Shela's depression is one of flexibility and fit. The flexibility is on Tasha's part as therapist. She must first be aware of, comfortable with, and skilled at each of these effective approaches. This is quite a challenge for any therapist. She must then judge how each frame and treatment rationale might also best fit Shela. Not every treatment theory and related rationale will make sense to all clients. Some will make more sense than others. Therefore, how is a serious therapist interested in doing the most effective treatment to proceed? The process paradigm holds some promise.

Recall that the process view suggests we are self-organizing, dynamic systems within ever-changing contexts. We meet change with assimilation into or accommodation of the ongoing patterns and assumptions of our current world as experienced. Some change is easily handled and the flow moves on within our lives. Problems emerge as we reapply failed solutions over and again according to the current assumptions and patterns of our life. These evolve into the classic vicious cycles that clients bring to treatment.

Resolution almost always involves not only interdicting these failed vicious cycle solutions but also reversing them. In depression, it involves reversing from inward withdrawal to outward new action, from avoidance of painful experiences and emotions to engaging in and overcoming them, from assuming failure and futility to instead taking new empowered action.

According to group and logical type theories, these new solutions will appear counterintuitive until our clients are able to move to a metalevel and see the rules and patterns of their lives and problem cycles in a new way. Once clients take this metalevel step, then new frames for their problems become available with new rationales for solution. This metalevel step or second-order change thus enables problem-solvers to make sense of formerly paradoxical solutions and proceed to engage them. This second-order shift is the key to all treatments that work for depression. Once therapists understand this perspective on problems and their resolution, they free themselves to choose the best fitting approach for themselves and to flexibly match that approach with their clients.

CYCLING BACK

Depression is defined in the context of Western culture as patterns of decreased functioning; lack of interest or pleasure in most activities, and associated symptoms of sleep disturbance, weight loss, agitation, or lethargy; feelings of worthlessness or excessive guilt; problems concentrating; loss of energy; and often recurring thoughts of death. All effective treatments reviewed in this chapter refer to these patterns as self-fulfilling prophecies, vicious cycles, and downward spirals, with client solutions becoming the problem. Each approach lays out a process for joining with clients in a new treatment alliance. Each offers clients a different frame to describe and make sense of their depression, along with a related treatment rationale. These new frames and rationales enable clients to engage in new solution patterns formerly seen as paradoxical or counterintuitive but that now make sense in the new frame and rationale. Once pattern reversal begins, clients' trusted and supportive alliance with their therapist helps make sense of and supports the new process. If depression comes down to avoidance and withdrawal from painful experience, and it is exacerbated by clients' solutions, then the "re-solution" lies in the once counterintuitive active engagement in life. Flexibility and fit between therapists and clients are both key to the approach that will help clients best make sense of this change, amplifying it in a new virtuous cycle of re-solution.

8

POSTTRAUMATIC STRESS DISORDER

Consider the following.

The 11-year-old boy settled into bed in his new home. It was 1958, and his "Uncle Bob," or Bobbie as he had become known, had married his mother, and they had moved to his home in a new state. The boy loved his new dad, because Bobbie had been close friends with the boy's own father in Scotland, where they had both grown up. Bobbie was much older now. He had served with the Ninth Royal Scotts as a teenager in the first expeditionary force to go into battle in 1914 through 1918 during the First World War. It was now 40 years later. The boy had learned that Bobbie had fought in kilts in the trenches for years. He was one of a handful of survivors of the first German gas attack, yet he had also been part of the first Christmas when both German and British soldiers sang "Silent Night" in the dark across no-man's-land between their trenches. He had received a near mortal head wound when a bomb exploded in front of him yet, after recovering back home in Edinburgh, he returned to the trenches of France. He witnessed

http://dx.doi.org/10.1037/0000078-009
Unifying Effective Psychotherapies: Tracing the Process of Change, by J. S. Fraser

his friend's head explode from a sniper's bullet, but he was also awarded the Military Cross for bravery by King George and Princess Mary. All of that was long ago, and he had built a wonderful new life in America. Tragically, years later, his only son, Ian, or Schotchie as he was called, perished as a navy pilot in a crash over the ocean. Now, Bobbie was beginning a new chapter—with a new wife and a new son. Therefore, the young boy was frightened and puzzled that night and others when his new dad would wake, yelling out in the middle of the night.

Now consider this case:

Susan came to the mental health center after being hospitalized for a suicide attempt. She had dropped out of college after a year, and she was now living on her own. She had a strained relationship with her single mother and an ambivalent relationship with her older brother. Recently, a man she met online attacked and sexually assaulted her in her own apartment after a date. Lately, Susan had been hearing voices mocking her and saying she was no good, and she was losing sleep fighting back with them through the night. She had been increasingly reluctant to leave her apartment the past month, and had finally decided life was not worth living. After taking pills, she had second thoughts and called the hospital. That's what brought here following discharge. Reluctantly, Susan shared that her older brother had sexually abused her for years when she was growing up, yet she loved and admired him while still feeling terrible about the abuse. She confided the sexual abuse several times to her mother, only to have her mother not believe her initially, and then blame her when she came to her again. Now, she feared more flashbacks of those assaults, and the persecuting voices were returning.

Finally, consider a third case:

Isaac was a devout Orthodox Jewish father of three living in Tel Aviv, Israel. There had been a number of terrorist bombings of public gathering places in the city recently. Isaac had joined a group of men from his temple committed to gathering the remains of the dead for proper Orthodox burial, but these bombings proved more challenging. After explosions, body parts were often scattered and difficult to find and match with the person's original body. Last year, there was a bombing at a nightclub where young people gathered. Isaac had diligently gone to the scene to collect the bodies of the dead, yet once more the body parts were scattered so widely as to make the task impossible. He now could not get the image of that evening out of his mind—particularly the image of that young woman's severed head he retrieved from under a bench. She was about his eldest daughter's age. He recovered somewhat until he received notice there had been another bombing, this time of a bus that he knew his eldest daughter took to work. Rushing to the scene, he was relieved she was not on the bus, but his symptoms—including flashbacks, ruminating, panic and exaggerated startle reactions—had gotten much worse since then.

As you may guess, all of these cases fit the profile of what we have come to call *posttraumatic distress disorder,* or PTSD. I return to these cases at the end of the chapter to address their treatment. We first need to define what we are working with, however. Throughout history, humankind has experienced overwhelming traumatic events from wars, natural disasters, tragic accidents, and sexual assaults, to name but a few examples. Such unimaginable experiences overturn our ordered sense of safety and predictability in ways that call for us to either assimilate or accommodate them into our experience. For some of us, and at some times, this process seems to happen relatively naturally, allowing us to move forward with few real effects; for others, the experience leaves the lasting scars that we have come to call PTSD. Recall from Chapter 5 on context that trauma is experienced in a wide range of ways across cultures, and there are an equally wide range of ways that survivors have come to express their reactions to such trauma. Recall the differences in cultural response to the trauma of the tsunami in Sri Lanka and its lack of fit with Western disaster workers' ideas of helping heal the PTSD discussed in Chapter 5. Also recall the different ways soldiers responded to the trauma of war from the Boer War, through World Wars I and II, and beyond. Trauma is trauma, yet different individuals, in different contexts and at different times, experience it differently. So how are we to understand PTSD, its symptoms, and its treatment, given these contextual differences?

THE CONTEXT AND PROCESS OF POSTTRAUMATIC STRESS

We have already cautioned about attending to the cultural and temporal contexts for clients before assuming a particular response pattern or assuming what constitutes a trauma and in varying contexts. Generally, we will find rather common response patterns similar to the mastery-by-avoidance cycles seen with anxiety. Another paradox comes when survivors attempt to "remember to forget" the event and its trauma, and are trapped in the same dilemma of one told "don't think of an elephant": the very attempt to put it out of mind is the thing that brings it back up, often at times least expected. However, there will be some important variations and some equally important caveats on intervention. As in past chapters, I look at how PTSD is generally defined in dominant Western culture, what typical problem cycles have been found, and what major theories exist to explain it. I describe the vicious cycle patterns, then move on to available evidence-supported treatments. Finally, I return to the cases described at the start of the chapter and address treatment applications from a process perspective.

PTSD Defined

As in past chapters with other disorders, I begin here by accessing definitions of PTSD from the dominant Western culture source, the fifth edition of the *Diagnostic and Statistical Manual of Mental Disorders* (*DSM–5*; American Psychiatric Association, 2013). Significantly, whereas in previous *DSM* editions, PTSD was classified as an anxiety disorder, the *DSM–5* describes it as a trauma- and stressor-related problem, accounting for the common range of emotions beyond anxiety, such as anger, sadness, guilt, or horror, and alternations in thoughts and mood. The *International Statistical Classification of Diseases* (10th revision; World Health Organization, 1993) mirrors this shift but includes three variations: posttraumatic stress disorder, unspecified, acute, and chronic.

The first major criterion for PTSD requires the person to have experienced, witnessed, or otherwise faced an event or events involving *actual or threatened death, serious injury, or sexual violence* from which the person does not recover. Symptoms cluster into categories of *reexperiencing, avoiding, negative alterations in cognition and mood* (e.g., memory difficulties, feeling detached, persistent negative beliefs) and *hyperarousal. Re-experiencing* may include memories of the trauma coming up without warning, vivid flashbacks of intense reexperiencing the trauma, nightmares of the event, or experiencing intense terror, disgust, sadness, rapid breathing, or heart rate triggered by cues similar to the traumatic event. *Avoidance symptoms* include avoiding thoughts and feelings about the trauma, situations, and events similar to the trauma, and related intense feelings associated with them. Paradoxically, temporary relief from decreasing painful emotions typically increases avoidance patterns in the classic vicious cycles we have seen so far in anxiety and depression. *Negative alterations in cognitions and mood* often include detachment or numbing to reduce painful feelings from intrusive memories, although some survivors experience the opposite, having continuous intense emotions such as anger or shame. This category also includes cognitive symptoms including self-blame, the idea that they will never be normal again, or that nowhere is safe. *Hyperarousal* is similar to the person being in a constant fight-or-flight state as they may have been during the traumatic event. This may include constant scanning for danger cues and constant states of tension eventually resulting in sleep disturbances, irritability, overreactions, and decreased concentration.

Because many, if not most, of these symptoms, are present for most people who have experienced intense traumatic events, several criteria must be met for PTSD to be diagnosed. First, the symptoms must have been experienced for at least a month after the event. At least one intrusion example must be present, such as recurrent dreams, distressing memories, and physiological responses to trauma cues, and so on. Avoidance of either internal or external reminders of the traumatic event is also required. Furthermore, the person must be experiencing at least two of the following symptoms: forgetting important parts of the traumatic event; exaggerated negative thoughts about oneself, others, or the world; distorted blame of self or others; detachment or estrangement from others; inability to experience positive emotions; lack of interest in activities; or globally negative experiences of fear, horror, anger, guilt, or shame.

PTSD is relatively prevalent. Except for specific phobias and social phobia, it exceeds all other anxiety disorders in prevalence (Kessler et al., 2005). In a national civilian prevalence study, Kessler et al. (1994) found that after trauma experiences, 20.4% of women and 8.2% of men were likely to develop PTSD. Rape was identified as most likely to lead to PTSD in both men and women. After rape, for men, the PTSD probability for other events were 39% for those exposed in combat, 24% from childhood neglect, and 22% for those who experienced physical abuse in childhood. For women, the prevalence of PTSD from traumatic events other than rape were 49% from childhood physical abuse, 33% from threat with a weapon, 27% from sexual molestation, and 21% from physical attack. Accidents and natural disasters showed much less likelihood of producing PTSD.

PTSD Models

Four major models have been put forward over the years to explain the process of PTSD, including representatives from learning theory, information processing theory, cognitive theories, and constructivist theories. After considering each in turn, I look at vicious cycles in the context of PTSD.

Learning Theory

Early on, learning theory views of PTSD were based on Mowrer's (1950, 1960) two-factor theory, combining classical and operational conditioning. Intense distress from a traumatic event was said to be associated with stimuli related to the traumatic event and setting. Then, when the conditioned memory or other related cues of the event elicit fear and other intense emotions, people's escape and avoidance responses reduce intense emotions and become operationally reinforced to occur again with greater frequency. This prevents the trauma cues from being extinguished despite the absence of the original danger. The vicious cycle becomes self-perpetuating. However, this learning theory had trouble explaining the occurrence of repetitive intrusive traumatic memories and nightmares.

Information-Processing Theory

Lang (1977) proposed that a fear network develops in memory that triggers escape and avoidance. The fear network includes stimuli, response, and meaning components composing a schema, or fear structure elicited by anything associated with the traumatic event. This fear structure is proposed to be reactivated relatively frequently in people experiencing PTSD. When activated, the full package of the fear network reenters consciousness, causing intrusive memories and flashbacks. Subsequent attempts to avoid this reactivation account for the avoidance symptoms of PTSD. The solution-generated process evolves.

Cognitive Theories

Similar to information-processing theory, cognitive theories turn their focus to the survivor's belief system, addressing how the person adjusts their prior beliefs and expectations to the traumatic event. Without being fully integrated into existing beliefs and expectations, memories and trauma-associated stimuli retain their ability to trigger intrusive and avoidant reactions. In some ways, this is similar to the Piagetian concepts of assimilation and accommodation to novel events. A dynamic tension is thought to arise, creating swings between the need to integrate the experience on the one hand and the need to avoid the emotional pain arising from intrusive thoughts and trauma-related stimuli on the other. This vacillating cycle sustains and amplifies the PTSD. Ehlers and Clark (2000) proposed that people with PTSD are unable to see the event as time-limited and thus generalize it to the future. Assuming that normal events are more dangerous than they are, they overestimate the probability that the traumatic event will recur. They see false alarms as true alarms or see their symptoms as signs that they cannot cope with similar threats in the future. Still others have proposed alternate two-stage theories (Brewin, Dalgleish, & Joseph, 1996), proposing that memories consist of those that are nonconscious and not easily accessed and those that are verbally accessible and may be called up voluntarily. The first may be triggered by cues similar to the trauma or deliberate thoughts of the trauma and result in intense, intrusive sensory images or flashbacks and intense physiological arousal. The second consists of cognitive appraisals of the event. The first produces conditioned emotions of fear and anger. The second yields secondary emotions that add guilt, shame, and sadness. The first memories are said to be best treated by exposure therapy, whereas the second are suggested to be best treated by cognitive therapy. However, no matter which approach is used, the intervention reverses the pattern of avoidance.

Constructivist Theories

Turning to the content of cognitions around the traumatic event, constructivist views address how the traumatic event shatters survivors' basic assumptions about a safe world. Their prior beliefs about safety, trust, predictability, control, esteem, and intimacy, to name a few, are violated by the traumatic event. Resick, Monson, and Chard (2007) used the *just world myth* to explain how traumatic events destroy the human wish for a predictable and controllable world. Survivors' natural avoidance of intense emotions and the uncontrollability and unpredictability created by memories and trauma-related stimuli thus inhibit the event from being fully assimilated into their beliefs and expectations. From a constructivist perspective, however, survivors' prior beliefs and appraisals will also shape their reactions to the perceived threat of the trauma. Fearing that reexperiencing emotion may overwhelm them, many will avoid thoughts about the event and stay busy as much as they can. Others may feel they need to make sense of the event and ruminate about how it happened and how to prevent it. Still others may become immobilized and have trouble making decisions, feeling that the event was punishment for something they did. This view postulates alternate response patterns for alternate points of view. Recall the Venn diagram of the process model in Chapter 5 of this volume (Figure 5.1). These individual differences reflect unique elements from the client sphere, creating "unique spin" or variations in the resulting vicious cycles. Nevertheless, the solution once more creates and perpetuates the problem.

Vicious Cycles of PTSD

Recall the process of change paradigm of open, dynamic, self-organizing systems discussed in Part I. The first premise is that systems are ever changing and constantly evolving in an alternating spiral of negative and positive feedback processes. Those processes are constrained by the context of the system (as in the riverbanks and river bottom of Heraclitus' river). As in Gregory Bateson's (1979) evolutionary spiral, attempts at stability at one level (or negative feedback) will spiral into positive feedback to the next level, where increased stabilizing efforts will likely feed into the next escalation, and so on. Following the social constructionist view described in Chapter 5, if the system neither assimilates nor accommodates new input needing attention, then the new input is likely to serve as a trigger for escalating vicious cycles. Regarding context, and following the work of Bateson, not all differences or new inputs into a system will trigger a response. For Bateson, the input must be "a difference that makes a difference" in the context of the system. For some individuals and in some cultures, a given event may be experienced as normal, expected, or as more of the same, and the system takes little note. For others, the same event or change may draw intense attention and response. The process perspective on change suggests that all such failures at assimilation or accommodation will fit the pattern of escalating cycles of positive feedback, or vicious cycles. People's attempts to assimilate or accommodate the experienced traumatic event while dealing with its accompanying intense emotions often succeed following an interval of adjustment. Some individuals may not even experience the same event as traumatic within their own worldview or personal or cultural context. However, failed attempts to assimilate or accommodate such intense and traumatic events such as actual, witnessed, or threatened death; serious injury; or sexual violence will likely trigger escalating vicious cycles fitting the symptoms of PTSD.

As we can see in the preceding theories of PTSD, all suggest that the survivors of trauma find themselves trapped in vicious cycles similar to the mastery-by-avoidance patterns seen with anxiety and depression. Another trap is survivors' attempts to "remember to forget" the trauma and its emotions, resulting in the event and its emotions surfacing at unexpected times and places or in dreams. As usual, the theories each have different bases for their explanation. Recall as well, the six points operationalizing second-order change laid out toward the end of Chapter 3 on change (see the section Relationships as Change Agents). The first point states that if the first-order solution is *to go away from the problem*, the second-order solution will have something to do with *going toward it*. As we will soon find out, most evidence-supported approaches to treatment target mastery by avoidance and remembering to forget patterns, and their interventions do just that—that is, they have the survivor *reverse and go toward* the distressing experience and habituate, assimilate, or accommodate it in one way or another. (This echoes the now-familiar counterintuitive paradox of second-order change as clients get out of the child's finger trap, so to speak, by pushing in and going toward their dilemma rather than pulling away. They must go toward the trauma rather than away to move beyond it. They must remember to remember to escape the paradox of their past solutions.)

However, recall as well the second and third points from those points operationalizing second-order change from Chapter 3. The second point suggests that if the first-order solution is to overpursue the problem, the second-order solution will have something to do with stopping and reversing the pursuit. Point 3 suggests that if the first-order solution is not to attend to the problem, the second-order solution will involve acknowledging the problem and taking necessary problem-solving action. A perspective on the solution patterns of trauma survivors experiencing PTSD is that they remain overly engaged with the event while overlooking its impact and not taking new and different directions to move forward. As we will also see, some newer, present centered approaches to PTSD have been found equally effective as those that focus on variations of exposure. These alternative, present-centered approaches likely fit Points 2 and 3. These present-centered approaches help clients acknowledge the traumatic event and its distress, then, through collaboration, redirect the survivor's efforts to present and future solutions. This intervention essentially blocks and redirects prior vicious cycles, reorienting clients toward present and future directions. This is an alternative to, and a second-order pattern reversal of, exposure treatments. Furthermore, present-centered approaches have the added benefit of engaging many PTSD clients in treatment who simply cannot face the paradoxical solution of reexperiencing their trauma and its intense emotions through exposure-based approaches.

As we have seen, from the process view, the bottom lines in all psychotherapies that work are helping clients interdict and reverse their problem-generating solution patterns, or the vicious cycles of their problem. To do this, all approaches engender felt validation and trust in their clients to step out of the level of their current solution-generated problems and enter into a metalevel working alliance with their therapist. From this metalevel, they can view the failed solution patterns surrounding their problem, accept a new and fitting frame for their problem, and buy into a related treatment rationale that helps make sense of new and formerly counterintuitive solutions. Next, as we shall see, this same pattern recurs across all evidence-supported approaches to PTSD.

CHANGE: TREATMENTS THAT WORK FOR PTSD

Turning to treatments that work for PTSD, the first stop might be the website for research-supported psychological treatments for PTSD compiled by the American Psychological Association (APA; 2016b), Division 12, the Society of Clinical Psychology. Seven treatments are listed—five as strongly supported, one with modest research support, and one with no support and potentially harmful (psychological debriefing). Of those five strongly supported treatments, three are considered exposure-based treatments and two as present-centered or combination approaches. The strongly supported exposure-based approaches include prolonged exposure (PE), cognitive processing therapy (CPT), and eye movement desensitization and reprocessing (EMDR). The two present-based approaches are present-centered therapy (PCT), with strong support, and stress inoculation training, with modest support. For the purposes of this chapter, the approaches with strong support are discussed.

Exposure-Based Approaches

As noted, given the vicious cycles of mastery by avoidance evident in the descriptions of PTSD, the logical intervention involves reversing those patterns and exposing clients to their traumatic experiences and emotions.

This paradoxical—from the perspective of survivors—intervention requires not only a trusting and supportive treatment alliance with therapists but also problem frames and treatment rationales that help clients "make sense" of doing the opposite of what seems logical to them. As with depression, several of these approaches use different premises and problem frames to help clients with this. PE has a behavioral base, CPT has an obviously cognitive base, and EMDR is based on the effect of rapid eye movement. I briefly review each of these before commenting on them and turning to PCT.

Prolonged Exposure

As we reviewed in the chapter on anxiety (Chapter 6), PE has a long and successful history in treating both anxiety disorders and PTSD. Edna Foa has been the ultimate champion of PE-based and exposure and response prevention–based treatments in the area of anxiety disorders, obsessive–compulsive disorders (OCD), and (for recent reviews, see Foa & McLean, 2016, and Franklin & Foa, 2014). This typically 9- to 12-week 90-minute session approach first gathers information, explains the nature of PTSD, and offers a treatment rationale in the first two sessions. Therapists discuss the basic elements of how the PTSD process and its vicious cycle begins, and then maintains itself through avoidance. Once accepted, this description of the problem sets the stage for exposure. As is typical in psychotherapy, it is critical for clients to buy into this new frame. This is particularly important because the proposed exposure treatment is generally challenging and intensely distressing for clients. Foa described rather high refusal and dropout rates.

As the APA (2016b) Division 12 website summarizes, the basic premise of PE is that repeated exposure to trauma-related thoughts, feelings, and situations can help reduce their power to cause distress. This is viewed to happen through a combination of habituation to the trauma stimuli and discussion of the experience of exposure immediately during and after each sequential experience. It explains the essence of therapy as consisting of exposures through imagery, which involve recounting the traumatic memory and processing the experience, as well as in vivo exposures in which the client repeatedly confronts trauma-related stimuli that were safe but previously avoided.

The exposure protocol proceeds similarly to that described in Chapter 6 on anxiety and OCD. Gradual exposure to the distress-inducing sensations and situations, starting with imagery, allows certain potential negative outcomes to be managed and multiple settings and circumstances to be created and recreated in imagination. Clients begin with what they can just barely tolerate and then proceed to increasingly intense situations. The most important component of the exposure, in addition to sustaining it with no negative results, is processing the client's experiences during and after the exposure.

Processing is done to modify or reframe the client's erroneous cognitions in light of disconfirming information from the exposure. This amounts to reinforcing a new and disconfirming frame for clients' experience to channel their new reactions and behaviors. Once again, this is the ultimate in reversing mastery by avoidance and replacing it with the originally counterintuitive action of mastery by exposure. This is the ultimate paradox of second-order change.

Craske, Treanor, Conway, Zbozinek, and Vervliet (2014) presented strong research-supported recommendations for maximizing the results of exposure therapy: "Habituation models posit that fear reduction during an exposure trial is a necessary precursor to subsequent, longer lasting cognitive changes in the perceived harm associated with phobic stimulus" (p. 4). Translated to trauma, the stimuli will be trauma-associated. As opposed to pure habituation reducing fear to trauma-related stimuli, or the standard "belief disconfirmation" approach of CBT, Craske et al. described their research supporting an inhibitory learning model of extinction. They noted that successfully extinguished fears spontaneously recover in the absence of repeated exposure after treatment. In addition, relapse is likely to occur when clients encounter the feared stimuli in contexts different from those used in treatment. Aversive experiences after successful extinction are also likely to cause relapse of previous traumatic responses. Finally, fears that have subsided may quickly and easily reoccur with retraumatization, as may happen in combat and other dangerous settings.

Craske et al.'s (2014) approach has clients focus on how imaginal and in vivo exposure without the feared results disconfirms their original expectations of danger, as opposed to simply repeating exposure until fear reduces, habituates, or extinguishes. Rather than have clients cognitively reduce their expectation of danger before exposure, they wait until after exposure and then discuss how the results disconfirmed what they typically expect. As with PE, clients also reduce or eliminate "safety behaviors," such as needing to be with others or carry objects, to maximize exposure. Exposure trials should include a wide variety of cues of varying length and intensity to resemble real life more closely, and clients simply label their emotions as they experience them to create inhibition of emotional reactions; this is in contrast to the traditional CBT method of having clients change the content or nature of their appraisals. Thus, with a woman experiencing PTSD after a sexual assault, Craske et al. recommended beginning with the typical frame and rationale: the nature of associative learning and how avoidance and safety behaviors perpetuate it. A hierarchy of trauma-invoking stimuli is then gradually introduced, in imagination and in vivo, with emphasis on how the experience contradicts clients' expectations of negative results.

Craske and colleagues (2014) reported that this inhibitory learning approach to exposure treatment has proven successful despite the fact that "it avoided inclusion of cognitive restructuring prior to, or during exposure, and employed exposure and extinction processes rather than cognitive interventions, to target additional conditional reactions such as shame" (p. 15). Although exposure treatments will likely be further refined in the future, these strict behavioral approaches have become the gold standard for PTSD treatment and have been widely disseminated within the U.S. Department of Veterans Affairs and other settings. Strict solution pattern reversal has shown powerful effects, in line with the process view. Once again, however, strong therapeutic alliances and strong buy-in from clients of the problem frame and rationales for treatment are crucial to clients' accepting in-session exposure—and particularly to clients' complying with homework involving similar exposure work between sessions. Even with such efforts, somewhat large dropout rates are described, as might be expected with clients whose major solution is to reduce or avoid their traumatic reactions. Pattern reversals are not only counterintuitive, they may also be intensely aversive and emotional. Without support and buy-in to a fitting rationale, clients will often leave treatment.

Cognitive Processing Therapy

Turning to the cognitive realm, Monson, Resick, and Rizvi (2014) described CPT as "trauma focused and constructivist, focusing on the particular meanings that the traumatic event(s) has for the client and how those interpretations of the event contradict or seemingly confirm previously held beliefs about self and others" (p. 75). Developed initially to treat PTSD symptoms in survivors of sexual assault, the approach suggests that *distorted assumptions* about the event may maintain the posttraumatic process. These beliefs focus on the belief that *the world is just and predictable* and that *we have control* of ourselves and the world around us. Randomness does not fit these two related belief systems. Assuming that one should have been able to stop an event from happening tends to create shame, guilt, and lower self-esteem for having been unable to prevent or control it.

The major frame of this approach is similar to our discussion of the constructivist concepts of *assimilation* and *accommodation* around a traumatic event. The client is assumed to have either distorted the event by assimilating it into her prior belief in a "just world" ("It's my fault the rape happened. I should have been able to stop or avoid it") or is assumed to have overaccommodated her beliefs about herself and others in an attempt to regain her sense of control or safety ("So I really cannot trust others at all any more. I just need to remain vigilant."). Karlin et al. (2010) adapted CPT into a veteran/military version and offered a manual laying out a general protocol. Farmer, Mitchell, Parker-Guilbert, and Galovski (2017) noted that, according to the manual, there are four key elements of CPT: "(a) the use of Socratic questions; (b) prioritizing the challenging of assimilated beliefs before overaccommodated beliefs; (c) emphasis on out-of-session practice work (i.e., homework); (d) the promotion of the expression of natural affect" (p. 2).

Described as predominantly cognitive therapy, CPT is delivered to either individuals or in groups over 12 structured sessions. As is typical, treatment begins by presenting the frame for the clients' PTSD symptoms and the rationale for therapy. Therapists encourage faith and trust as they validate their clients' distress. Clients are asked to write an Impact Statement, tracking how their most distressing traumatic event has affected their lives. Reviewing this with clients, therapists ask them to address any self-blame they feel about the event and the effects it has had on their views of themselves and others. Therapists use this statement and discussion to understand how the client may have distorted what caused the event or overgeneralized its meaning. As is typical with CBT approaches, clients are also taught to label their emotions and recognize the cognitive connections among events, thoughts, and feelings. The client is then asked to write a detailed account of the traumatic event on index cards and read them to herself daily. Homework compliance has been found to be critical to success, so client buy-in is again important. In each session, clients then read the cards to the therapist, who encourages them to feel their emotions about the event. Emotional expression is considered important to recovery. Clients also complete worksheets on "stuck points" they encounter around reexperiencing the trauma. Therapists then use Socratic questioning to challenge problematic thinking, and after rereading the account a second time, the therapist teaches clients to challenge their thoughts and assumptions themselves by using a series of worksheets. Assumed assimilated stuck points about why the trauma occurred are addressed first before attending to overaccommodated stuck points about others and the world in general as an unsafe place. As they review the event with this Socratic tool, therapists then ask their clients to generate more balanced, alternative thoughts about the event and their overgeneralized views of their self and the world. In a recent study by Farmer and colleagues (2017) analyzing 533-taped CPT sessions from 68 clients, the most significant improvements in PTSD symptoms were associated with therapists' competence in Socratic questioning and their skill in prioritizing assimilated stuck points before overaccommodated stuck points.

The APA (2016b) Division 12 website lists CPT as having strong evidence of effectiveness. Like its strictly behavioral counterpart PE, the strongly cognitively based CPT approach has been found to be equally effective. The VA is now disseminating both approaches to VA treatment centers throughout its system. Both reverse avoidance patterns through exposure yet use different frames, rationales, and procedures. However, there is one more approach that has generated extensive controversy yet has been found equally effective: EMDR.

Eye Movement Desensitization and Reprocessing

Francine Shapiro (1989; Shapiro & Forrest, 2001) has been the main force behind EMDR. She proposed an adaptive information processing (AIP) model. According to Shapiro and Maxfield (2002),

> The AIP model suggests that if the information related to a distressing or traumatic experience is not processed fully, the initial perceptions will be stored essentially, as they were input, along with any distorted thoughts or perceptions experienced at the time of the event. A central tenet is that if distressing memories remain unprocessed, they become the basis of current dysfunctional reactions. (p. 935)

Regarding the effects of lateral eye movements on the retrieval and modification of such traumatic responses, they posited the following:

> It is hypothesized that the eye movements and other dual-attention stimuli enhance information processing . . . eye movements decrease the vividness of memory images and related affect. This effect may enhance processing through desensitization by decreasing distress and related avoidance. It is hypothesized that as the image becomes less salient, clients are better able to access and attend to more adaptive information, forging new connections within the memory network. (p. 935)

There are eight phases to EMDR, flexibly applied over fewer or longer periods depending on the extent, intensity, and complexity of the traumatic response.

- Phases 1 and 2 entail the therapist forming a trusting relationship with the client, setting expectations, explaining the AIP frame to explain the client's PTSD symptoms, and the related eye movement treatment rationale and procedures. Once client buy-in has been achieved, the therapist takes a history of the traumatic event, including targets for EMDR (e.g., disturbing memories), current and historical distressing situations, and imaginal templates to fit the treatment plan. The therapist teaches the client relaxation, and they develop "safe place" images to use early and throughout the treatment.
- In Phase 3, the client identifies the most vivid and compelling visual image associated with the traumatic event. The client is also asked to identify the most compelling current irrational negative belief about him- or herself (e.g., "I'm a failure," "I'm

unlovable"), and another positive desired belief (e.g., "I can succeed," "I'm loveable") and rate each on a 7-point scale from most to least believed, with 7 being *most believed true*. Then the client combines the visual image with the negative belief, often activating strong emotions, and rates their response on a 10-point scale, with 10 being *most distressing*, locates the body sensations evoked by the image, and separates these from cognitive impressions.

- Phase 4 begins the eye movement portion, in which the client focuses on the visual image, negative belief, and body sensations and "lets whatever happens, happen," while focusing on the therapist's fingers moving side to side for 15 or more seconds. The therapist then asks the client, "What do you get now?" and that image becomes the focus of the next set of eye movements; this sequence repeats several times. Client and therapist then focus on more adaptive associations that either emerge or are supplied by the therapist. As the negative imagery, beliefs, and emotions become less vivid and intense, the therapist looks for more positive ones to become stronger and more salient, concluding when the client reports zero distress for the original image.
- Phases 5 and 6 begin when the original image no longer elicits distress. The client consolidates and reviews his or her insights, which may include greater self-acceptance. These new positive cognitions are then paired with the original image with accompanied lateral eye movements, repeated until the client reports a strong belief rating of 6 or 7.
- Phase 7 then focuses on repeating the positive associations with the image until the client reports no disturbing body sensations.
- The final phase, Phase 8, represents a reevaluation of the memory links to determine their positive strength with new beliefs and sensations. Clients keep journals to track the effects and generalization of their progress, and additional treatment is initiated to complete and consolidate the results.

As noted earlier, EMDR has been established as a strongly effective treatment through multiple meta-analyses and is recommended as a first-line treatment, along with PE and CPT. However, the evidence supporting lateral eye movements as a crucial treatment ingredient is still mixed and uncertain after several dismantling studies yielded mixed results. Nevertheless, on a broader level, it takes its place among other strongly supported exposure treatments for PTSD. From the process of change perspective, this represents the perfect second-order change and pattern reversal, as we have seen with anxiety and depression approaches. This would seem to wrap up the case for resolving PTSD by reversing avoidance patterns, but this is not the case. As noted earlier, PCT, or present-centered therapy, is equally effective but *actively avoids exposure to the past trauma.* The next section looks at the research on this approach, provides a brief overview, and then sees how it fits with the process view.

Present-Centered Therapy

Given how much sense it makes to have survivors who actively avoid trauma reverse their solution pattern and go toward the experience to master it, it seems to make little sense to do anything else. However, researchers have found PCT to be equally effective. An interesting point is that this result came almost by accident. Attempting to devise more bona fide yet nonspecific treatments to use in clinical trials testing the specific effects of different therapy approaches to PTSD, a present-focused alternative was designed that avoided exposure to the past trauma (cf. Classen et al., 2011; McDonagh et al., 2005; Pukay-Martin, Torbit, Landy, Macdonald, & Monson, 2017; Schnurr et al., 2003). Schnurr et al. (2007) said that PCT was simply designed to present a credible alternative to control for nonspecific effects compared with PE treatment. Summarizing the surprising results of these studies, Frost, Laska, and Wampold (2014), reporting on their review of five clinical trials and their own meta-analysis of PCT compared with exposure treatment, wrote,

> In three of the five trials, PCT performed as well as the evidence-based comparisons. In the other two trials, the evidence-based treatment was superior to PCT on some measures. However, across the five trials, the meta-analysis showed no significant differences between PCT and the comparison evidence-based treatment on either targeted measures or secondary measures, as well, across the trials, PCT had significantly fewer dropouts. (p. 6)

How can this be? What was this treatment? McDonagh et al. (2005) described PCT as

> a collaborative therapeutic intervention in which the therapist's information and expertise are used to assist the client to recognize the impact of her trauma history on her present coping style and by teaching her a systematic approach to problem solving to enhance coping. The main elements of PCT are psychoeducation about the diagnosis of PTSD and the common aftereffects of childhood trauma, training in problem solving, and journal writing. . . . PCT was specifically designed to omit the hypothesized active ingredients of CBT (breathing retraining, PE, in

> vivo exposure, and CR). Although the role of trauma was acknowledged in assessing current difficulties, the trauma itself was never the focus of the treatment. (p. 518)

Describing PCGT, Schnurr et al. (2003) noted,

> In PCGT, sessions 1 through 4 focused on initiation of rapport, education about PTSD symptoms and associated features, and the connection between PTSD symptoms and difficulties in relationships and problem solving, sessions 5 through 24 focused on identification and clarification of individual members' specific issues and the development of plans for dealing with these issues, relying heavily on interaction of group members for input and feedback. (p. 483)

Classen et al. (2011) described their present-focused group therapy (PFGT) for survivors of childhood sexual abuse as

> illuminating in the here-and-now maladaptive expectations and behaviors that emerge in the group process, and learning more adaptive ways of interacting with others as well as better affect-regulation strategies. The aim of PFGT is to identify and modify maladaptive patterns of relating and restructuring views of self and others. (p. 86)

None of these present-centered approaches used exposure. In fact, they assiduously avoided it at all costs. However, they have all been found comparable enough to current strongly effective approaches to PTSD to be included in the APA (2016b) Division 12 lists of evidence-supported treatments. How does this fit with the process of change view? As stated earlier, present-centered approaches acknowledge the traumatic event and its distress, then, through collaboration, redirect the survivor's efforts to present and future solutions. This intervention essentially blocks and redirects prior vicious cycles, reorienting clients toward present and future directions. This is an alternative second-order pattern reversal to that of exposure treatments. Instead of clients being overly engaged in struggling with or avoiding past traumatic events, their attention is reversed and redirected to present and future effective problem-solving and interpersonal effectiveness. This pattern redirection from former vicious cycles makes perfect sense as a re-solution to former solution-generated patterns of overinvolvement with the past and the trauma. Furthermore, these present-centered approaches have the added benefit of engaging in treatment many PTSD clients who simply cannot face the paradoxical solution of reexperiencing their trauma and its intense emotions through exposure-based approaches.

Imel, Laska, Jakupcak, and Simpson (2013) conducted a meta-analysis of dropout in treatments for PTSD and found little difference in dropout rates across most active treatments with the exception of PCT, which tended to have lower dropout rates. Across three large trials, including 695 patients in total, dropout rate was lower in PCT compared with trauma-specific treatments. They concluded their meta-analysis as follows:

> If future research replicates this pattern of comparative efficacy and a lower rate of dropout relative to other treatment modalities, it would seem appropriate to consider PCT a first line treatment, especially for patients who do not prefer a trauma-focused treatment. (p. 402)

Relating to dropout rates from PTSD treatments, Benish, Imel, and Wampold (2008) concluded that because

> about one-quarter of patients drop out of psychotherapy treatment for PTSD (Hembree et al., 2003) and dropout appears to be related to symptom change (Bradley et al., 2005), keeping patients in treatment would appear to be more important in achieving desired outcomes than would prescribing a particular type of psychotherapy. Having several psychotherapies to choose from may enable a better match of patients to type of psychotherapy that fits the patient's worldview and is more tolerable to that particular patient. (pp. 755–756)

These conclusions match those from the psychotherapy literature reviewed in Chapter 1 recommending flexibility on the part of therapists and fitting approaches to client preferences rather than prescribing a one-size-fits-all approach. This may be especially true when working with clients with PTSD, who may understandably be very reluctant to go toward or reexperience their trauma. Clearly, many clients develop the kind of trust in their therapist and belief in the frame for their problem and its related treatment rationale that they are able to devote themselves to the paradoxical task of immersing themselves in the trauma they have struggled so long to avoid. However, as we can now see in the PCT alternative, others can be helped equally well by not having to do so, yet still make the pattern reversal needed by devoting their efforts and attention to their present and future effectiveness rather than staying mired in their past trauma. This all fits perfectly with the process paradigm. Many paths may lead to the same results, as we saw in the discussion in Chapter 4 of the open process system concept of equifinality.

THE PROCESS OF PTSD TREATMENT

With all of this in mind, it may help bring the discussion of PTSD treatments down to earth by returning to the several cases from the beginning of the chapter. Each case in turn will represent an alternative approach to resolution, yet all were effective resolutions to the client's PTSD.

Bobbie From World War I

Recall the multiple traumas experienced 40 years earlier in World War I by Bobbie, the boy's new stepfather. Despite the years passing and a wonderful life after immigrating to the United States, Bobbie often awoke yelling—reexperiencing the traumas of the gas attack, his own head injuries from the bomb exploding before him, and seeing so many comrades die in horrific ways. His view, however, was that all of that was in the past. For decades, he had neither really thought of that trauma nor ever recounted it. Yet his young stepson, admiring his new dad and fascinated with his experiences in World War I, would sit up late listening to his stepdad's stories, horrible as they were, yet mixed with wonderful and often funny experiences as well. The two of them bonded closely over that time. They developed what they affectionately called a "mutual admiration society." What the boy noticed was that his new dad eventually seemed to be sleeping through the night. It was only years later, long after Bobbie passed away, that the boy, now a young man, realized how therapeutic those stories had been in helping his beloved new father resolve so many long-standing traumatic memories. He healed those traumatic wounds through exposure, retelling all of those experiences in a newly created bond with his stepson. In some broad ways, this is similar to the therapeutic bonds of the working alliance so important in helping clients take those paradoxical steps of reexperiencing their trauma to put it to rest.[1]

Susan's Fight With Her Past Abuse

Now remember Susan, whose recent rape by a man she met through an Internet dating site triggered memories of sexual abuse at the hands of her older brother in her youth. Not only was she recalling images of her childhood abuse and the rape, she was also avoiding leaving her apartment. The worst experiences for her were nightly "voices," which tended to be popular male singers taunting her and putting her down. She fought back against the voices most nights, and yet she was losing sleep and was exhausted most days.

Susan eventually won those battles, but not by fighting harder. She won by moving forward and beginning again to live a life worth living. After she had discussed the nature of PTSD symptoms like hers with her therapist, they began to make more sense of them. Her therapist talked about how her

[1]I was that young boy, and Bobbie was my beloved stepdad. He was an officer in the Scottish Highland Division, Ninth Royal Scots, and he was awarded the Military Cross for bravery by King George. It was pinned on him by Princess Mary.

perpetrators had not only violated her trust but also taken power over her, and they would likely be pleased that they continued to do so. It seemed no mistake that the voices taunting her were all male. Susan agreed with her therapist: "The best revenge would be living well." The more she fought the voices, the more they won by engaging her. The same went for her reengaging with memories of her brother's abuse. Her actions would speak louder than words. In the course of treatment, Susan got a dog and began walking her. She volunteered for the local animal shelter, and later for a local civic organization. She also confronted her mother about not believing her or protecting her as a girl, and they came to some resolution. She joined a church and began attending their young singles group activities. At first the voices increased, as did the flashbacks, yet they gradually went away. Whenever they resurfaced, she took it as a cue to do more to move ahead in spite of them. As Susan attended to her current life, disengaging from her past traumas and investing in her future, she won. Her life was in the present and future, not in the past. She was living well.

Isaac's Traumatic Devotion to His Faith

It was important to Isaac for those dying at the hands of terrorists to have a proper burial in the traditions of his faith. That meant gathering their bodies, even if broken and separated, to be buried and honored by their families. Yet gathering the dismembered and decapitated remains of children and youth in their prime of life had become almost too much. The memories of those horrors were entering his dreams and his days even more after the trolley bombing when he feared his daughter had been killed as well.

Fortunately, Isaac consulted a psychiatrist in Tel Aviv who was a member of his temple and who was renowned for his knowledge of PTSD and his skill in treating it. After recounting his traumatic experiences, Isaac learned more about his trauma from the psychiatrist. He learned that his struggle with those traumatic images was preventing their resolution. He also shared his deep faith and his commitment to the families who had lost their loved ones. After listing the most intense images, including finding the head of that girl under the bench, he began the process of EMDR. Watching the waving fingers of his therapist while experiencing each set of images, he reexperienced the original emotions and thoughts, yet they began to fade. Revisiting them with his deep faith and commitment to his religion and those grieving families, new associations and feelings began to replace the old ones. He recalled and embraced the life of his daughter and rededicated himself to his work in the aftermath of terror attacks. He knew that new traumas were yet to come for himself and others, but he now had the rededication of his original faith to bring with him as he moved forward. He thanked God for bringing him to this psychiatrist and for the opportunity to reengage in his own life and that of his family.[2]

MANY PATHS TO THE TOP OF THE MOUNTAIN

The process-based views of many Eastern religions like Buddhism suggest that there are many ways to achieve enlightenment, or, as the metaphor goes, there are many paths to the top of the same mountain. Although we may not consider successful problem resolution of PTSD quite the same as enlightenment, the separate evidence-supported approaches resonate with that view. All of these cases represent the sequelae of PTSD in the lives of these people. Each resolved their traumatic responses, and yet each did so following their own separate paths. Bobbie put his nightmares of the horrors of the war to bed as he recounted the good and bad of his experiences while bonding with his new son. Susan's path was present centered. Giving up her fight with her past memories and the voices of her perpetrators, she took opposite actions to reclaim her life, embracing the motto "The best revenge is living well!" In the final case, Isaac's path was through exposure to EMDR. His faith in his practitioner and his courage to reexperience his traumatic experiences gathering the remains of the dead enabled him to renew his faith and resolve his PTSD symptoms: His mission was noble, as it would be in the future. Of these approaches, three involved exposure, and one focused on the present and future. However, they all achieved pattern reversals in each person's solution-generated traumas. As with all treatments that work, there are always many paths to the top of the mountain in the process of change.

CYCLING BACK

The vicious cycles of solution-generated problems with PTSD mirror those of anxiety and depression. Through varying attempts of mastery by avoidance and attempts to "remember to forget" their trauma, clients exacerbate their PTSD symptoms. The more they avoid assimilating or accommodating to the trauma, the more it remains fixed and unresolved. The more they try remembering to forget it, the more that paradox keeps it in their

[2]I had the privilege of reviewing video of Isaac's EMDR sessions with his psychiatrist in Tel Aviv. Although I was not a believer or advocate of EMDR, and I still question the eye movement component as crucial, there was no doubt of its success with Isaac. It was a touching, compelling, and successful experience.

memories, surfacing in flashbacks and dreams. As we have seen, problem resolution will always involve counterintuitive solution pattern reversals. These are evident in three approaches that engage clients in reversing their avoidance, instead resolving it through reexperiencing what they most fear. In present-centered approaches, clients reverse their struggles with their past traumas and engage in opposite new actions to reclaim their lives in the present and moving toward the future.

Clients achieve all these second-order changes by stepping to a metalevel and joining a working alliance with a trusted guide or therapist. From this metalevel, they can view the failed solution patterns surrounding the traumatic event, accept a new and fitting frame to make sense of their PTSD symptoms, and buy into a related treatment rationale that helps make sense of new and formerly counterintuitive solutions. The vicious solution-generated cycles of PTSD resolve as clients reverse their solutions and either go through their traumas to resolve them or reverse their struggles with their past trauma and take opposite and new actions to regain their lives.

9

COUPLE PROBLEMS

> *It seems to me that most couple problems amount to two people trying to reach accord through opposition.*
>
> —*John H. Weakland*

Maria and Lars had been happily married for 2 years. They were a middle-class couple in their 30s and living in a large city in the Midwest of the United States. Maria's family had emigrated from Central America, and Lars's parents were from Finland. Beyond her beauty, Lars had been attracted to Maria's vibrancy and her ability to express her feelings and her joy of life. Maria had always loved Lars for his stability and the way he loved his family. He always worked hard to make a good life for them. Last year, Maria gave birth to their first child, and that seemed to mark a turn in their relationship. The baby created more demands on the couple, but Lars's business was taking a downturn. They came to therapy with what they called "communication problems," resulting in constant quarrels. Each felt at his or her wit's end.

Maria complained that she felt overwhelmed with the baby and couldn't get Lars to help. He seemed to be spending more time at work, and when he came home, he retreated to his home office right after dinner, often not coming

---

Andrew Solovey was coauthor on this chapter.

http://dx.doi.org/10.1037/0000078-010
Unifying Effective Psychotherapies: Tracing the Process of Change, by J. S. Fraser

to bed until the middle of the night. Maria would often cry herself to sleep. The more she asked him for his help, the more he said he just couldn't afford the time if his business was to survive to keep a roof over their head and food on the table. Lars said that Maria simply would not understand, and lately she was nagging more and more, and seemed to explode at him. He had to stay calm and centered to keep the business and their family from coming apart. Maria saw Lars becoming so cold that she feared he would leave her. The more she tried to engage him, the more he seemed to shut down.

The partners each had their own family histories, which created differences. Maria's culture and family supported the rich expression of emotions. They showed their connections with each other by hugging, laughing, and, at times, quarreling to sort out their differences. It also seemed that Maria's family had a long history of husbands abandoning their wives. Lars, a product of culture and family, took pride in stoicism in the face of adversity. To show emotion was to admit you were out of control. He admired the strength of his father, yet always pushed back against his mother's attempts to guide his future.

Maria and Lars were afraid they might split up over their growing distance and distress. They were trapped in an escalating vicious cycle. Both seemed to have the best of goodwill for the other and for the future of their young family. Yet they were becoming polarized and discouraged about the future of their marriage. They came for couples therapy.

There is, perhaps, no other set of empirically supported treatments that more explicitly targets first- and second-order change than those for a couple's problems. Couple problems are clearly described as escalating vicious cycles of solution-generated problems, as we can classically see with Maria and Lars.

Recall once again that the process of change perspective, applied to psychotherapy, is *transdiagnostic and transtheoretical*. As a transdiagnostic perspective, the process of change view serves as a golden thread connecting the nature of problem patterns across most all diagnostic categories treated in psychotherapy. We saw this with anxiety problems (see Chapter 6, this volume), where all variations of anxiety problems and their related treatment converged on reversing vicious cycles of anxious avoidance through exposure. As a transtheoretical perspective, the process of change unites psychotherapeutic approaches by showing how each approach facilitates similar problem pattern changes across problems. This was evident as we saw how each of the four major theoretical perspectives offered different frames and rationales, yet converged on reversing downward spirals and self-fulfilling prophecies in depressed clients. As such, the process paradigm serves as a unifying perspective. It emphasizes the core role of change—how problems evolve through failed attempts at change—and how problems resolve by changing those failed attempts. From this view, problems are vicious cycles of repeating and escalating failed solutions. Resolutions involve pattern shifts and reversals, which redirect problem patterns, allowing further flow and evolution within our lives and those of our clients. Change occurs by creating working alliances that are catalysts to problem pattern shifts by flexibly fitting frames and rationales that explain the nature of problems, and then interdicting and redirecting interaction, creating new virtuous cycles.

Couples treatment is the paradigm case of this process view of problems and their resolution. With couples, and in couples therapy, it's all about changing these cycles. In all couples treatments, couples learn how to negotiate change with their partner, how to avoid escalating demands for change, and how to de-escalate a spiraling dance of change gone awry. They learn how to repair failed attempts at change, how to accept that there is no need for change, how to change their view of their partner and of their life together, and how to evolve through changes in their relationship over time. Therapists learn how to balance negotiating the need for change in their clients against the prospect that the couple might do best by accepting things the way they are. Interventions are designed to either block or redirect partners' solutions to challenges in their relationship. In all cases, second-order change is at the heart of it.

In this chapter, I look first at what the literature says about the classic vicious cycle patterns found in couples in dominant Western culture. I then turn to two evidence-supported approaches to couples treatment to see how each approach, based on very different assumptions on the nature of couples' problems, achieves the same successful ends. Finally, I return to Maria and Lars to apply these two approaches.

THE CONTEXT AND PROCESS OF COUPLE PROBLEMS

As Christensen, Wheeler, Doss, and Jacobson (2014) stated, "The term 'couple therapy' (as opposed to 'individual' or 'group' therapy) refers to clinical approaches for improving the functioning of two individuals within the context of their romantic relationship to one another" (p. 704). That people experience problems in their relationships is supported by divorce rate statistics in the United States that estimate 50% to 67% of first marriages and 60% to 67% of second marriages end in divorce (Gottman, 1999). It is no surprise, then, that, with the exceptions of anxiety and depression, people more often seek therapy for marital and partner difficulties than for any other type of problem (Gottman, 1999; Veroff, Kulka, & Douvan, 1981). Gottman (1999) cited a range of support for the consequences of such couple distress and dissolution, including increased physical illness and mortality from illness, decreased life span, and increased physical violence, suicide, and homicide, among other kinds of emotional and psychological distress. Therapists have been treating couples in distress using an array of approaches for a long time. However, researchers have only recently looked into the validity of our assumptions about what makes for strong vital relationships and into the effectiveness of most common couples therapies.

Couple Problems Defined

In the *Diagnostic and Statistical Manual of Mental Disorders* (*DSM–5*; American Psychiatric Association, 2013), couple problems fall in the category "Relationship Distress With Spouse or Intimate Partner." The *International Statistical Classification of Diseases* (10th rev.; World Health Organization, 1993) labels these as "Problems in Relationship With Spouse or Partner." The convergent *DSM–5* definition is as follows:

> This category should be used when the major focus of the clinical contact is to address the quality of the intimate (spouse or partner) relationship or when the quality of that relationship is affecting the course, prognosis, or treatment of a mental or other medical disorder. Partners can be of the same or different genders. Typically, relationship distress is associated with impaired functioning in behavioral, cognitive, or affective domains. Examples of behavioral problems include conflict resolution difficulty, withdrawal, and overinvolvement. Cognitive problems manifest as chronic negative attributions of the other's intentions or dismissals of the partner's positive behaviors. Affective problems would include chronic sadness, apathy, and/or anger about the other partner. (p. 715)

Relationship distress represents a condition that does not quite fit the medical model, and so it is relegated to a category referred to as "other conditions that may be a focus of clinical attention." For the most part, insurance companies do not reimburse "other conditions." The problem from the medical model perspective is that relationship distress is between people and so does not fit the model of individual psychopathology. At the same time, relationship distress is a significant concern for clients who present for psychotherapy and the clinicians who treat it.

Lebow (2014) indicated that couple distress remains among the most frequently encountered difficulties in psychotherapy practice. Beyond statistics about divorce (the current rate is approximately 50%), 20% of couples meet the criteria for couple distress at any time, with levels of satisfaction decreasing considerably over the first decade of marriage. A considerable amount of data suggests that couple and family distress has a strong association with individual, mental, and physical problems. Further, he cited mounting evidence that such distress in not only correlated with but has a causal role in the generation and maintenance of individual psychopathology. There are strong associations between marital distress and bipolar disorder, alcohol use disorders, and generalized anxiety disorders. Expressed emotion in families has been implicated as a powerful factor in determining the level of functioning of individuals with schizophrenia, bipolar disorder, borderline personality disorder, and several other diagnoses (Chambless, Bryan, Aiken, Steketee, & Hooley, 2001; Hooley, 2004, 2007). At the same time, the association between distress and specific diagnoses is viewed as circular. Each frequently leads to the other.

Vicious Cycles

All approaches to couple distress view couple problems as vicious cycles. Wile (2013) reflected on various authors who explain these cycles using the terms *pursuit and distance*, *demanding–withdrawn*, and *rejection-intrusion*, among other terms. He explained these classic patterns as follows:

> one partner seeks connection (time together, intimate talk, affection, romance, or sex) and the other seeks separation (time alone, independent activity). The result is a vicious cycle. Pursuing partners feel increasingly abandoned and intensify their connection-seeking whereas distancing partners feel increasingly invalidated and intensify their separation-seeking. Each partner's solution exacerbates the other's problem. (p. 19)

This is the paradigm case of the process view's solution-generated problem as a positive feedback loop in a dynamic self-organizing system like a couple. Similarly, regarding couple relationships, Jacobson and Christensen (1996) stated,

> there are times when efforts to change one's partner actually have the opposite effect. Direct attempts to change an intimate partner are often self-defeating, both because the particular efforts are misguided and because such attempts are likely to have the opposite effect. (p. 13)

They described couple problems in classic vicious cycle terms from an initial trigger, to a set of solutions that only serve to exacerbate the problem, to a full-fledged solution-generated problem, which takes on a self-fulfilling life of its own. As indicated earlier in this volume, all varying descriptions of problem patterns represent positive feedback loops and vicious cycles. In other words, whether distilled through the lens of the family therapy theories of Minuchin, Bowen, Johnson, or others, stuckness is accounted for by positive feedback loops. The more problem, the more solution, the more problem, the more solution, and so forth. This is the case whether a clinician is describing issues related to structure, cognition, emotions, triangulation, or any other formulation. Similarly, Davis and Piercy (2007a, 2007b) concluded that a common element of all couple and family therapies is helping clients interrupt or disrupt dysfunctional relational cycles.

Returning to Daniel Wile's (2013) overview of couples' pursuit-and-distance vicious cycle, he described a sequence of how these patterns develop and suggested what best pattern options might be. In his view, these pursuer–distancer patterns are not a reflection of one or another partner's personality; the pursuer in one instance may be the distancer in another. Nonetheless, according to Wile, many couple perspectives suggest that there may be particular sensitivities or vulnerabilities in one or another partner that trigger these escalating disputes. (This is similar to the idea of vulnerabilities in depression suggested by Barlow in his unified protocol for emotional disorders as, discussed in Chapters 6 and 7, this volume, on anxiety and depression; see, e.g., Barlow & Kennedy, 2016.) For example, in the case of Maria and Lars, Maria, given her history, may be sensitive to being abandoned; Lars, given his history and culture, which encourage rugged individuality and the downplaying of emotions, may be sensitive to emotional demands. Their combined sensitivities are the perfect platform for the escalating disputes noted in their case. For example, from the emotion-focused therapy (EFT) approach to couples, which emphasizes bonding issues, this couple's contrasting strategies might be a product of what EFT would term *insecure attachments*. In contrast, a behavioral approach, such as integrative behavioral couples therapy (IBCT), might view these complementary vulnerabilities as a product of each of their histories of avoidance of perceived negative consequences.

Either way, Wile (2013) described the evolution of the vicious cycle as a combination of what he termed *pursue–withdraw* and *attack–withdraw* cycles. Gottman and DeClaire (2001) referred to these positions of pursue, attack, and withdraw as a familiar triad of turning toward, against, and away. Wile proposed that, in most instances, the pursue–withdraw pattern typically changes into one of attack–withdraw. As one party gets more frustrated with the other's withdrawal, attacks increase out of anger and attempts to spur engagement. In our initial case, Maria resorted to attacking Lars for his refusal to commit and engage with her. This sequence may then evolve to attack–defend, and eventually withdraw–withdraw. According to Wile, "couples can go on for years circling through pursue–withdraw, attack–withdraw, attack–defend, and withdraw–withdraw" (p. 23).

Turning to resolution (or re-solution), Gottman and DeClaire (2001) suggested that the tipping point in redirecting these vicious cycles is helping partners make positive bids for connection with their partner and for their partner to notice and accept those bids. The trick for therapists is to help couples see their negative patterns, notice the positives between them, and orient toward repairing damages and offering connections and support for their partner. Wile (2013) likewise stated that "the result is engage–engage—

a very different kind of feedback loop, one that is relieving and empowering . . . Engage–engage is a virtuous rather than a vicious circle" (p. 24). This, of course, reflects the pattern shifts and reversals described in Part I to describe how the process paradigm views problems and resolutions. They are both positive feedback cycles. Whether they are described as vicious cycles or virtuous cycles is simply a value judgment made by observers. In the case of couples, the engage–engage cycle serves their values and goals of creating and sustaining a positive relationship, and therefore the couple and therapist view it as a virtuous cycle. As we shall see, these ideas are reflected in both the research on couples and in evidence-supported approaches such as EFT and IBCT that I describe and apply as the chapter proceeds. Therefore, it is helpful to turn our attention to some of the key insights gained by research on couples and couples therapy.

COUPLE RESEARCH

First, the answer to the question "Is couples therapy effective?" is a resounding yes. Studies show that most couples therapy is effective, with roughly 70% to 80% of cases showing positive change (Shadish & Baldwin, 2003, 2005). Couple problems have been found through meta-analysis to be consistent difficulties, which do not improve without treatment (Baucom, Hahlweg, & Kuschel, 2003). However, similar to individual therapy, few differences in effectiveness have been found among different approaches to couples therapy (Shadish & Baldwin, 2003; Wood, Crane, Schaalje, & Law, 2005). In effect, couple and family treatments are highly effective for treating relational concerns. Relational approaches have also been effective for helping persons with specific diagnoses, such as depression, conduct disorder, schizophrenia, and other diagnosis. However, Sprenkle, Davis, and Lebow (2009) argued that within the realm of couple and family therapy, certain classes of therapy are probably more effective for certain problems. (Note their use of the term *class*, which echoes our earlier distinction between group and class from the theory of logical types. In this case, they refer to several separate groups, representing approaches to family treatments, which work best for specific types of family problems.) For example, ecologically based therapies (those that include multiple systems in the community) are probably more effective for adolescents with conduct disorder. At the same time, they note that there is little evidence that any particular ecological approach is superior to the others. (Ecologically based family therapies are the subject of the next chapter.)

By far the most influential research clinician on couple relationships is John Gottman. His work and that of his colleagues on what makes for happy marriages and what factors lead to divorce has had more to say on what makes for success in couples and what key factors must exist in couples therapy to build more satisfaction in distressed couples than nearly any other current research group. Both evidence-supported approaches that I describe in this chapter explicitly refer to Gottman's work as at least a partial foundation of their approaches. Most all of Gottman's work describes the workings of solution-generated problems in distressed couples as they progress through repeated vicious cycles of trying to solve mostly unsolvable problems. What follows are some of his key findings.

Process Versus Content in Couple Problems

Gottman learned that it is the *process* of how couples interact that determines their satisfaction and success. Consequently, the process of how couples negotiate their differences, and not the content of their disagreements, should become the focus of treatment. (Note again the emphasis on process and pattern here, paralleling the process and flow premises of a process paradigm.)

Emotional Bank Accounts

There are many ways for couples to be successful. (Recall the premise, from the chapter on process-based systems explaining equifinality, that there are multiple paths to the same end in open dynamic systems.) According to Gottman (1999),

> There are three types of stable, happy couples, not just one. These three types—volatile, validating, and conflict avoiding—have very different attributes, yet they are similar in that they all have a 5 to 1 ratio of positive-to-negative exchanges. This ratio suggests that there is something like an "emotional bank account" that is operating to make these marriages very rich climates of positivity, yet very *different* rich climates. (p. 88, emphasis in original)

(In terms of groups and classes, they each appear different yet all belong to the same class of couples sharing a ratio of five positives to one negative—and thus are all members of the same class of successful marriages.) It was not so much that these different types of couples did not argue; in fact, they all frequently did argue, each in their own way, and this emotional engagement was vital to their success. They even exhibited many of the toxic elements of arguments that couples headed for divorce used. The difference tended to be how they argued, what they argued about, and how successful they allowed themselves to be in repairing the damage caused by these quarrels. The main element missing from how they argued was the use of contempt, which was most often present in couples headed for divorce. The couples seemed to accept a wide range of differences between themselves as tolerable and focused their disagreements on more solvable problems. Finally, they had enough of a reserve of positive regard for their partner to accept their partner's attempts to repair any potential damage done in their arguments. Gottman has used these key factors, among a few others, to define the desired target for successful couples therapy.

Dow Jones Averages

Returning to various cycles, his research group learned a great deal by studying couples arguing in their lab and then finding out what factors in their way of arguing predicted eventual divorce. (Once again, their emphasis was on the pattern of the arguments, rather than on their content or topics.) One prominent factor alluded to in the preceding quote on the 5:1 ratio of positives to negatives in happy stable couples is what Gottman (1999) termed the *Dow Jones ratios*. He calculated the sum of all positive things during one person's turn at speech minus all the negative things and found not only that the five positives to one negative ratio predicted stability and satisfaction but that couples whose ratios got closer and closer to one negative for each positive had greatly increased probability of divorce in the next 4 years. Therefore, the more baseline negativity in couples' interactions, the more likely they were to split. The greater the positive ratio was, the more positive was their prospect of satisfaction. It wasn't the fact that couples argued that predicted further distress and eventual divorce; it was *how* they argued that mattered. The pattern of arguing predicted the vicious cycles spiraling toward divorce. (Again, in terms of the language of groups and classes, these couples formed a class of couples with a one to one ratio of positives to negatives, resulting in the similar outcome of divorce.) There was much more that this research group learned from the way these arguments took place.

Harsh Start-Ups

The first factor, after the ratio of positives to negatives, that predicted divorce turned out to be what Gottman (1999) termed *harsh start-ups*. It turned out that the way partners introduce a topic of disagreement is critically important to predicting marital outcomes. Harsh start-ups (quick escalations from neutral to negative affect), particularly by the wife, were found to be highly associated with marital distress and divorce. In fact, in the graphs of the "Dow Jones averages" of couple positives to negatives in arguments, researchers needed only the first minute of the argument to predict divorce or stability for 96% of the couples (Gottman, 2000). Harsh starts predicted harsh endings.

The Four Horsemen

However, the group gained even more richness from studying how these couples argued. True to the process paradigm, the pattern of the process became the primary source of data. They found in counting negatives that not all negatives were equal. Four behaviors emerged, which Gottman (1999) eventually termed the *Four Horsemen of the Apocalypse*. These four, found to be the most corrosive, were criticism, contempt, defensiveness, and stonewalling. *Criticism* implies that there is something globally wrong with one's partner (e.g., "You always . . . ," "You never . . . ," "What's wrong with you?" "Why are you so . . ."). As can be seen, a healthy dose of toxic blame is imbedded within criticism, which can also include sarcasm. The second horseman is *defensiveness*, a common response to criticism. It usually includes denying responsibility for the problem, implying that the other partner is at fault, fueling further escalation. The third horseman, *contempt*, turns out to be one of the deadliest in that it appeared in most couples that eventually divorced. Gottman (1999) defined contempt as any statement or nonverbal behavior that puts oneself on a higher plane than one's partner. It includes a universal facial expression combining pulling the corner of the lip to the side, rolling the eyes, and looking up. Mockery, especially in public, is a particularly harmful example, as is correcting one's partner's grammar during a fight. Contempt is the single best predictor of divorce to the extent that arguments in a happy marriage included essentially no contempt. The final horseman is *stonewalling*. Gottman (1999) defined stonewalling as any way in which one partner withdraws from interaction with the other. It occurs most often in men (85% in several of the group's studies). In fact, when stonewalling was found in women, it became highly predictive of divorce. As Wile (2013) noted in his work on pursuit–distancing, and as the two evidence-supported treatments described subsequently show, stonewalling is intimately related to characteristic demand–withdraw or approach–avoidance patterns in married couples. It turns out to be a strong element of most vicious cycles in couple disputes. Interestingly, women are significantly more likely to initiate topics of disagreement than are men. Thus, men find themselves on the receiving end of complaints much more than women, resulting in the eventually greater stonewalling by men than by women. These demand–withdraw patterns occur in all marriages; however, and they are only exacerbated in distressed couples.

Gender Differences

Furthermore, lest we blame women only in this demand–withdraw pattern, Gottman (1999) found that the pattern is triggered by early cues of agitation and withdrawal in male partners, drawing approaches or demands from the woman. Causality is circular, not linear. Gottman's group also found distinct differences in physiological reactivity between men and women. Likely due to evolutionary differences, men's cardiovascular systems remain more reactive than women's and slower to recover from stress. Adrenaline will cause quicker responses to perceived danger, and blood pressure will be higher and stay elevated longer for men than women during and after a quarrel. In the face of danger, men are more likely to stay vigilant than women. Such heightened diffuse physiological arousal in men can lead to the phenomenon of *flooding* and related stonewalling and withdrawal in men. *Flooding* refers to the experience of being so overwhelmed with a sudden barrage of negativity from one's spouse that one shuts down and withdraws as a form of defense, leading to the phenomenon of stonewalling. In true vicious cycle form, however, one's partner may meet such withdrawal with frustration, and a new round of demands may then emerge for the other to engage. As Gottman (1999) described, he and his group also found that men were much less open to allowing themselves to be influenced by their wives than were women open to influence by their husbands. A man's willingness to accept influence from his wife was associated with greater marital satisfaction. Conversely, his unwillingness to accept such influence was correlated with greater marital distress. Thus, women are often drawn into a demand–withdraw pattern by the multiple characteristics of their male partners. The downward spiral continues.

Downward Spirals Toward Divorce

Emotional disengagement tends to be the eventual result of these cascading cycles on negative interactions. This is characterized as the absence of positive affect, partners leading parallel lives, little friendship, unacknowledged tension with little soothing by either partner for the other. Combining these and other related factors, Gottman and his colleagues have been able to predict divorce with 96% accuracy (Gottman, 2000). These successive factors include harsh start-ups to disagreements, presence of the Four Horsemen, flooding, body language and cues of physiological discomfort, failed repair attempts, and pervasive negativity (bad attributions and memories). He described the four final stages of failed relationships as seeing the marital problems as severe, attempting to solve things on one's own, beginning to lead parallel lives, and finally loneliness sets in as the couple turns away from each other more and more. This is a clear downward spiral.

Repair Attempts

Gottman (2000) suggested that the greatest savior of all marriages is the ability to successfully repair potential damage during and after arguments.

He defined a repair attempt as anything done by one or the other partner that attempts to prevent negativity from escalating out of control in their disagreements. Repairs may consist of a comment on the communication itself, deferring to the other's position, expressing appreciation for the partner, softening the complaint, laughing about the argument as an example of how silly they can get, and so on. As noted earlier, in the three different yet successful types of marriages, their greatest strength was not that they didn't argue; it was that the partners were readily willing and able to accept each other's attempts at repairing their relationship during and after these quarrels. However, it is not simply that attempts to repair do not occur in distressed couples and that this is the problem. Repair attempts occur even in the most distressed relationships. What makes a difference is whether the attempt to repair is successfully *allowed* and *received*. In fact, in highly distressed marriages, there are frequent repair attempts during arguments, yet this research has found that the higher the rate of repair attempts, the higher the rate of their failures in these highly distressed couples. The ability to receive a repair attempt appears to be related to the store of positives in a couple's "emotional bank account" and subsequently to their positive views of their partner and their relationship. This is a key element of being able to override negatives in successful stable marriages. Both current evidence-supported approaches reviewed in this chapter consider these findings as they shape their interventions with distressed couples. The remaining critical factor in distinguishing successful from distressed relationships is a couple's ability to distinguish between solvable and unsolvable problems. Perpetual arguments about unsolvable problems are, above all, one of the greatest core problems to be resolved in helping distressed marriages.

Perpetual Problems

Perpetual problems are long-standing, solution-generated problems, as described earlier. After studying the stability of marital interactions over 4-year or longer periods and turning to the content of the arguments, Gottman (1999) concluded,

> I contend that the current emphasis in marital therapy on problem-solving is greatly misplaced . . . we found that 69% of the time they were talking about a "perpetual problem" that they had had in their marriage for many, many years. (p. 56)

He went on to say the following:

> We discovered that, instead of *solving* these perpetual problems, what seems to be important is whether or not a couple can establish a *dialogue*

> with their perpetual problems. If they cannot establish such a dialogue, the conflict becomes *gridlocked*, and gridlocked conflict eventually leads to emotional disengagement. Hence, I think that *the goal of most of the therapy around problem-solving ought to be to help the couple move from gridlocked conflict with a perpetual problem to a dialogue with the perpetual problem*. (p. 56, emphasis in the original)

Perpetual problems tend to be based on incompatibilities, vulnerabilities, and both parties becoming polarized and entrenched in their position. Both approaches reviewed in this chapter attend to this. Couples show little give-and-take in their discussions around these issues, and there is considerable hurt and wish for vilification. The pattern of the problem thus becomes self-perpetuating and cause for hurt, mistrust, and alienation in itself. It becomes an example of what is wrong with the marriage. Gottman (1999) has offered example lists of such perpetual problems. What he has found important from his research is solving not the perpetual problem but the emotions that surround discussing the problem. Again, both the IBCT and the EFT approaches discussed in what follows attend to this factor, but with different emphases. If the Four Horsemen have taken over, there is little positive affect, and demoralization is setting in, then the couple is headed for further distress and potential divorce. Perception of the other becomes crucial in differentiating successful from unsuccessful relationships as they move through these negative interchanges. In happy marriages, partners tend to evaluate negative actions of the other as transient and situational, and positives as a result of enduring internal qualities of their partner. Conversely, distressed couples ascribe negative actions of the partner to personal character flaws, whereas positives are seen as unstable, fleeting, situational, or even cause for suspicion. (This is, in fact, quite similar to Martin Seligman's research [e.g., Seligman, 2011] on learned optimism, where he found that more resilient and optimistic people tended to see problems as transient and situational, while viewing successes as personal, positive, and pervasive). With these respective positive or negative overrides in place, arguments over perpetual problems become easier to categorize as either something harmless that just needs to be accepted, or else another example of the malevolence of their partner and the hopelessness of their relationship. Gottman (2000) noted that this pervasive negative perception has caused distressed couples to underestimate the occurrence of actual positives in their relationship by a factor of about 50%. The relevance of this to ongoing arguments about perpetual unsolvable problems is that the growing negativity makes it increasingly difficult for each partner to accept the repair attempts of the other, either during or after disagreements. Happy, stable couples tended to be able to accept the inevitability of the unsolvable problems between them, work on the solvable ones, and accept repair attempts from their partner no matter what problem.

The distressed couples' pervasive negativity prevented them from accepting influence or repairs form their partner, and they continued their destructive perpetual problem cycles.

Going Toward Disagreements in New Ways

Thus, Gottman's targets are: helping couples to disengage from perpetual arguments over unsolvable problems, developing a dialogue around them, identifying solvable problems, building more positive perceptions of each other to allow for more positive interchanges and ultimately accept repair attempts from each other as they move forward in their relationship. In other words, Gottman seeks to reduce the triggers for solution-generated problems while having couples *go toward* their inevitable arguments in new ways. This should by now be a hallmark for readers of the counterintuitive pattern reversals of second-order change. This comes down to interrupting first-order change and pursuing second-order solutions. Turning to how two evidence-supported treatments in couples therapy assess and intervene in these solution-generated couple problems will complete the picture.

MODELS AND THE PROCESS OF CHANGE

Turning to evidence-supported approaches in couples therapy, two have emerged in recent years. Interestingly, similar to what we found in Chapter 7 on depression, these two represent two very different, sometimes polar opposite, theories. One is based in behaviorism (IBCT) and the other in humanistic–existential theory (EFT). Although EFT methods of approaching vicious cycles have much in common with IBCT, the underlying theory is different. This makes for interesting comparisons from the process-of-change perspective.

Integrated Behavioral Couples Therapy

Gurman (2013) reflected with sadness that critics of behavioral couples therapy (BCT) have often presented a caricatured version of its contemporary principles, while leaving out its evolution over the years. He made clear that BCT has undergone significant changes as it evolved over four decades. (In its present form, BCT is referred to as integrative behavioral couples therapy—IBCT.)

Doss, Benson, Georgia, and Christensen (2013) provided a clear synopsis of IBCT in their article on translating their method to a web-based program. They noted the roots of IBCT are in traditional behavior exchange and in communication and problem-solving training. They then followed the evolution of the approach in the early 1990s as Andrew Christensen and Neil Jacobson integrated strategies for fostering emotional acceptance with the direct change interventions of BCT. They added emotional acceptance as a key mechanism and change strategy, recognizing that couples needed to be able to be collaborative and accommodate one another before being ready to change. Couples often enter therapy entrenched in anger and blame, making collaboration on conflict resolution difficult, as described earlier with regard to vicious cycles. Therefore, the idea was to improve emotional acceptance before offering direct change strategies.

The IBCT conceptual model holds that relationship distress develops primarily through couples' repeated unsuccessful attempts to deal with natural differences or initial localized disagreements that are often emotionally loaded because of partners' sensitivities and vulnerabilities. Once more, this reflects research from Gottman (1999), mentioned earlier, who described a viscous cycle in which mutual efforts to change each other meet with resistance, fueling greater efforts to change the other, which results in greater resistances and so on. John Weakland, a pioneer in relational therapies (Fisch, Weakland, & Segal, 1982), has referred to this bind as failed attempts to reach accord through opposition. The IBCT thinkers refer to this same process as *polarization*. They further mention that these polarities may have been common differences that the partners found attractive in each other early in the relationship. Although both parties may realize that their positions have escalated to extremes, acquiescing to their partner seems untenable. This creates a position of "stuckness" referred to as a trap.

Gurman (2013) indicated that IBCT does not conceptualize underlying dynamics such as attachment issues as necessarily driving problematic interactive cycles. Neither does it necessarily privilege feelings. Instead, IBCT explains vicious cycles as a function of behavior in context. Partners in a couple respond to cues, which become mutually triggering based on their past learning histories and relationship patterns.

The architects of IBCT (Jacobson, Christensen, Prince, Cordova, & Eldridge, 2000) described a predictable process of argumentation that follows along the line of cuing. In their diagram of the *anatomy of an argument*, these authors pictured the evolution of this cycle from an *initial problem* (the content of the argument, consisting of either provocations, incompatibilities/vulnerabilities, or anger/hurts), to the process of *unsuccessful coping* with the initial problem (through accusation/blame/coercion; avoidance/denial/minimization; overreaction; or forming alliances/coalitions), and finally to the *reactive problem* (or the vicious cycle of the solution-generated problem in the relationship). This evolution mirrors the findings of the Gottman group and of Wile discussed earlier.

The classic ABCs of intense arguments are referred to as a *toxic triad* or *toxic cures*. Christensen and Jacobson (1999) stated that "toxic cures are solutions that make the problem worse. They are treatments that aggravate the disease. Their intent is often to create change for the better: their result is to create change for the worse" (p. 198). These ABCs are accusation, blame, and coercion (a D can be added for *defensiveness*). *Accusation* is simply pointing out that your partner has either done or not done something implicitly or explicitly expected in the relationship. This may take the form of accusing our partner of insensitivity, neglect, lack of collaboration, or a range of other perceived violations embodied in the triggering event. This accusation itself may be met with defensiveness or a counteraccusation: It was her reaction to my action that was the problem. This can kick in the cycle right away. However, the addition of *blame* turns the cycle distinctly more negative. This is reminiscent of Gottman's Four Horsemen, and Wile's evolution through the vicious cycles of advance–retreat through attack–defend and so on. Here we start claiming that the cause of our partner's offense is their broadly defined negative personality characteristics. These may include one's moral character, mental or emotional instabilities, personal failings, or inadequacies, to name but a few. The point is that such statements become a personal indictment of our partner. Something deeply wrong with their character is at the root of the problem. All of this breeds defensive counterarguments from our partner. Finally, *coercion* goes beyond mere accusations and attacks. Coercion is intended to force our partner to do what we want through a barrage of demanding, nagging, criticizing, complaining and making our partner feel guilty until they finally give in. The inherent trap in this sort of coercion is that it most assuredly will escalate based upon how it works. One partner's coercion is reinforced because the other finally complied. The other's compliance is reinforced because the coercion stopped. However, future rounds of the same badgering are doomed by an intermittent ratio schedule of the partner's compliance, and their habituation to the other's demands. In other words, we never know when our partner will finally relent and comply, and our partner may simply get used to the coercion. Thus, coercion is described as an addictive drug where early immediate effects require increasing doses to achieve the same effect. Partners may eventually deliberately ignore or actively resist these barrages, and the positive feelings and loving atmosphere of the relationship eventually erodes.

Each successive vicious cycle is described as proceeding through the characteristic phases from escalation, to polarization, to alienation. *Escalation* between partners is not only the increase in tension, volume, or viciousness of the argument but also in the expansion of its focus to include other related or unrelated issues brought in to justify points or simply to retaliate. *Polarization* refers to the process of becoming rigidly fixed and extreme in our views by listening to our own reiterated arguments and using our partner's behaviors as proof for the truth of our position. *Alienation* is generally the result of escalated polarized arguments. It may be a product of frustration, hurt, or refusal to address a problem, but it is always a negative development with partners turning away from each other. This reflects Gottman's (1999) idea of turning away and Wile's (2013) withdraw–withdraw phases.

Polarization and the Mutual Trap

The result of failed mutual efforts to bring about change in partners' personality differences is alienation and polarization. As Jacobson and Christensen (1996) stated, "When two people engage in such change efforts simultaneously, the almost inevitable outcome is polarization or an exacerbation of the differences. When polarization occurs, the conflict increases rather than decreases" (p. 199). The mutual *trap* is the outcome of polarization. Although polarization does not necessarily stop, there comes a point when each partner feels trapped, stuck, helpless, and desperate. This is a separate, private, and rather implicit experience for each partner of a sense of entrapment in the very problem each is trying to resolve.

Assessment

Before working with couples on release from the trap, IBCT-trained clinicians conduct a thorough assessment with the couple. The assessment takes three sessions and starts with a conjoint session, followed by seeing each person for an individual session, before providing feedback.

Assessment has three overriding goals. The first is to come up with a formulation that will guide the treatment plan. The second is to assess where the couple is on the dimensions that will lead the therapist toward interventions targeting change strategies or acceptance strategies. *Change strategies* encompass the behavior exchange and communication problem strategies of traditional behavioral therapies. *Acceptance strategies*, in contrast, are designed to help the couple disengage from their escalating struggles around key differences and begin to accept aspects of their relationship as not amenable to or needing change. The third goal is to *build an alliance* with the therapist, providing some therapeutic relief and hope for the clients. Unlike EFT, a number of formal paper-and-pencil assessment scales are sent to the couple to fill out jointly and separately before the sessions. These surveys, filled out by the couple separately before the sessions begin, identify specific concerns of each partner.

The initial conjoint session focuses on getting information on the following questions: (a) How did they get together? (b) What was their courtship like, and what was the relationship like before the problems began? (c) How is the relationship different now on days when the partners are getting along? (d) How would the relationship be different if the problems that currently exist were no longer present? One of the purposes of these questions is to create more positive affect between the couple, while getting information on the nature of their relationship and their hopes and expectations for its future.

During the remainder of the assessment, the therapist tries to answer six questions, the answer to which will shape both the formulation of the couple's problem and the treatment plan. The resulting formulation also uses these six areas. The questions are as follows: (a) How distressed is this couple? (b) How committed is this couple to their relationship? (c) What are the issues that divide them? (d) Why are these issues such a problem for them? (e) What are the strengths holding them together? (f) What can treatment do to help them?

Trap Release

According to Doss and colleagues (2013), release from the trap entails the clinician empathically joining with the couple to increase emotional acceptance by creating greater intimacy between partners. Toward this end, the clinician asks couples to share fears and vulnerabilities that make the conflict so distressing. Fears and vulnerabilities are referred to as *soft emotions*. The couple is also asked to reveal emotional experiences during the pattern. The clinician urges partners to disclose soft emotions that underlie *hard emotions*, such as anger, irritation, and others. In addition, the cycle itself, not the partners in the couple, is explained as causing the problem. The clients and therapist may refer to the cycle as an "it" or perhaps even give it a name. (This directly reflects the second-order change step of creating a metalevel platform to look at the solution patterns of the couple.) Wile (2013) described this step as

> creating a metalevel, a permanent platform or perch above the fray [reflecting] Jacobson and Christensen's (1996) "unified detachment," Fishbane's (2011) "power with rather than power over," Gottman and Gottman's (2008) "dialogue regarding a perpetual problem," Johnson's (1996) "pattern," and White and Epston's (1990) "externalizing the problem." (p. 28)

An important caveat is that IBCT clinicians make strategic decisions related to acceptance and asking couples to reveal vulnerable feelings. For example, this is not done when there are concerns around domestic violence. In addition, some couples may agree that their polarized distance is a problem and that they are willing to seek compromises on issues that trigger conflict. Here, the IBCT clinician will move directly to problem-solving approaches. However, more than half of couples do not present in this way. They are highly distressed, relatively less committed to each other, and invested in polarized issues that divide them and draw them back into the gridlocked repeating vicious cycles of their problematic relationship. In this state, partners in a couple are unlikely to agree on many things, particularly that their problem does not need solving. Consequently, they are often equally reluctant to comply with therapists on how to change things. This is where the acceptance strategies of IBCT find their greatest value.

According to Doss et al. (2013), when partners become more accepting of one another, they extricate themselves from the trap. This may significantly improve the relationship and resolve the couple's concerns without needing to move on to problem-solving. If other issues remain, the couple is ready to work on them in a spirit of collaboration. Here, standard behavioral interventions such as problem-solving, as suggested earlier, can be employed. In a context of acceptance, problem-solving may be thought of as contingency-shaped, meaning that the couple is now willing to engage in give-and-take out of mutual caring. This is different from behavioral contracting that characterized earlier iterations of the method. Couples often find behavioral exchange without acceptance ungenuine, further triggering the vicious cycle.

IBCT further enhances the acceptance process by using tolerance-building techniques. Proponents of IBCT view tolerance as a stepping-off point on the way to acceptance. The couple moves from resignation to tolerance and then to acceptance. At the acceptance phase, partners are able to discuss differences from the perspective of seeking understanding versus seeking change in one another. This parallels Gottman's goal of having partner move toward disagreements and differences and dialogue around what may be differences that cannot be changed. Toward the goal of acceptance, the clinician may highlight the positive features of negative behavior. For example, Lars's avoidance of coming home from work might be framed as his dedication to making money to support his growing family. Maria's lectures about working too late might be framed as her concern for her husband's health.

The following is a set of explicitly acceptance and tolerance-based strategies used in the IBCT approach. They are not mutually exclusive, and in fact, they generally overlap in that they flow from the basic premises of the acceptance-based perspective. Acceptance strategies are generally described as both tools for turning problems into vehicles for intimacy and as processes for increasing tolerance for things that may not change.

- *Empathic joining around the problem* is one of the first acceptance steps. Therapists emphasize the pain and honest efforts of each partner without accusation. The formulation itself becomes a central vehicle for this joining by casting the couple's dilemma as flowing from an honest difference that naturally led to polarization and eventually alienation. Therapists emphasize using soft rather than hard emotion descriptions in their reflections, and they encourage the partners to do the same. Hard emotions such as anger and resentment, implying assertion, power, and control, are most often expressed in partners who are in defensive positions. Soft emotions such as hurt, fear, and disappointment convey doubt, uncertainty, and vulnerability and are more easily accepted by partners. The use of these may be taught, prompted, coached, or modeled by the therapist.

- *Encouraging unified detachment, or making the problem an "it,"* follows from empathic joining. Here the couple is encouraged to continually do more detached intellectual analyses of the problem using the formulation as a guide. Rather than blaming each other, the problem is externalized and often given a metaphorical name as an "it." "Two porcupines trying to dance," is an example. Couples are then asked to analyze their conflicts at home, putting the imaginary therapist or the problem in a chair to address as they track the common sequence of their conflict according to the formulization and polarizing process rather than directly and spontaneously engaging in it.
- *Highlighting the positive features of negative behavior* relates directly to the dialectical or polar nature of the couple's dilemma. As partners begin to acknowledge the positive qualities of negative actions (e.g., creative vs. flighty, decisive vs. bossy, deferring vs. uncommitted), they begin to merge these actions into a more unified whole. This continues the basic acceptance in the relationship by both affirming distress and confirming positives. It reduces polarization. Complementary differences usually create balance in relationships. These differences can even become a positive aspect of the couple's relationship and something for them to be proud of and feel close about.
- *Role-playing negative behavior during the therapy session* is a commonly used technique in IBCT. This entails having the couple act out the pattern via role-play in session. Gurman (2013) pointed out that this is done with paradoxical intent, meaning seeking an opposite reaction. The idea is to help the couple to do on purpose what they have been doing reflexively. The intent is for the partners to lower their arousal levels through desensitization to the pattern. Lowered arousal allows for problem-solving in the face of the problem. The purpose is fully explained to the

couple. Similar to practicing the vicious cycle in session, couples may be asked to fake negative behavior at home. Again, the purpose is desensitization and not paradoxical intent. (However, recall that all second-order change or pattern reversals appear paradoxical from the original level of the problem.)

- *Faked incidents of negative behavior at home, or "faking bad,"* is explained as a way to promote tolerance by desensitizing partners to negative behavior. Partners are asked to deliberately pick fights or deliberately do or not do something that creates conflict when they would not ordinarily do this. The faker is then asked to observe the process of the vicious cycle, polarization, and pain to better track and learn from it. Directions are given with both partners present, and they are told not to divulge when they are doing it. This is another symptom prescription that basically undercuts the couple's problem patterns. Neither partner is able to know whether this is a real conflict or one staged for therapeutic purposes. It has powerful effects in de-escalating fights and reinforcing the formulation of how the conflicts occur.
- *Preparation for backsliding* is an inoculation used as progress is made. It is basically relapse prevention that inoculates the partners against both assuming that the problem has started again and trying to fix it using the same old vicious-cycle, first-order solutions.
- *Emotional acceptance through greater self-care* has two elements. The first is to have each partner begin doing things for himself or herself to feel better and to learn self-soothing. The second is to learn to do self-care during arguments, polarization processes, and other instances of negative behavior.

Each of these interventions is part of the process view, which suggests that all change involves a step to a metalevel with clients (a second-order change, or shift from group to class in the language of logical type theory). From that new metalevel, the couple can detach from their problem, see the problems inherent in their vicious cycles, see overlooked positives, and consider new and formerly unthinkable solutions. What remains is for the new treatment alliance of the couple and therapist to keep the frames and rationales, support new patterns, reframe them as positives, reinforce them, and build tolerance and relapse prevention.

As sensible as this behaviorally based approach may be, an alternative and equally effective approach is available in EFT.

Emotion-Focused Couples Therapy

In her manual on EFT, Susan Johnson (2004), the force behind EFT for couples, said,

> Well, basically, it's a humanistic approach. And it's an approach that privileges emotion. I sort of think of it as kind of like, it's sort of like as if Carl Rogers sat down to tea with Salvador Minuchin, and they kind of agreed to sort of put an approach together. (p. 22)

A more technical definition states that EFT for couples is an experiential–humanistic, systemically oriented intervention for couples with substantial empirical support (Greenman & Johnson, 2013). It is based on several theoretical and philosophical principles (Johnson, 2016). EFT privileges emotions. Emotion organizes attachment behaviors, which orient and motivate communication of our needs and longings to them. It focuses on partners' here-and-now responses, tracking and expanding both internal experiences and interactional moves and countermoves. EFT views change as occurring in the session as partners experience themselves differently and interact in new ways, similar to the way we saw EFT applied to depressed clients in Chapter 7. Its goal is to reprocess experience and to reorganize interactions to create a secure bond between partners and a sense of secure connectedness. EFT takes couples as they are, in that partner's needs, desires, and primary emotional responses are seen as adaptive. It does not view people as deficient. Instead, couples evolve problems by how they express their needs and desires in times of vulnerability and periods of danger. Once the problem pattern is set, then both partners become absorbed in the pattern and lose sight of the repeating process. This, of course, is a direst restatement of the process perspective's description of problem-solvers caught in the process of their problem and needing to step to a metalevel, or second-order, change to begin resolution. Thus, EFT for couples reflects the humanistic-existential bases of EFT for depression discussed in Chapter 7 of this volume. Its goals and processes are identical.

EFT is delivered in three phases. Before Phase I, there is an assessment to ensure that the couple is suitable for treatment, involving eight tasks (Johnson, 2016). These include the inevitable steps of creating a collaborative therapeutic alliance, including bonds, goals, and tasks, and assessing the couple's response to the therapist. In this process, therapists also assess how open and receptive the couple is to the major EFT frame that the partners' problems rest in their history of bonding and emotional ways of defending against further vulnerability to wounds and loss. Therapists tell the couple that the sessions will focus on how they interact in the here-and-now process of the session. The therapist will also assess for the couple's strengths, their personal attachment history, and their relationship history and key events, including any violence and abuse, which is a contraindication to EFT treatment. As opposed to the paper-and-pencil, pretherapy assessment forms of IBCT, the EFT approach focuses on a here-and-now, in-session perspective of how the couple interacts to guide therapists' assessment, conceptualizations, and interventions. As Greenberg and Johnson (1988) stated in their original manual on EFT for couples, assessment

> begins by the therapist observing a behavioral sequence as the couple enact the sequence in the session or as they narrate recent episodes of conflict. The therapist begins to see how the partners attempt to make contact or maintain distance, influence the other, and/or protect themselves in the relationship. Distressed couples exhibit extremely rigid, repetitive patterns of interaction that can be easily identified most of the time. These patterns or "cycles," so called since the actions of each spouse are at once a stimulus for and a response to the actions of the other, are automatic, immediate, and self-perpetuating, with the couple taking habitual positions in each interaction. (p. 73)

The authors went on to say that the therapist then "attempts to enter each partner's phenomenological world in order to draw hypotheses as to the insecurities, vulnerabilities, and/or resentments underlying the position each client takes in the negative interactional cycle" (p. 78). This assessment of personal vulnerabilities is key to the intervention that follows.

Phase I

As in all treatments, the therapeutic alliance is partly contingent on the clients buying in to the frame and rationales for treatment. In the first stage, clinicians help couples to see that their problem is not one another but instead the problematic pattern of interaction, which is obscuring their true needs. That need is to feel connected with and closer to one another. This represents the classic step to a metalevel in which clients step outside their problem patterns and view them as something separate from themselves. The clinician uses reflection, repetition, and evocative questions to sensitize couples to myriad emotional experiences that drive their negative interaction pattern. Beyond anger, these emotions include sadness, loneliness, fear, and shame. These emotions are born out of desire to feel emotionally close and connected to one's partner. This is a core premise of the EFT approach: In accordance with attachment theory, EFT seeks to create more secure attachment bonds between partners, modify perceptions of threat, and create a functional safe haven and secure base for the partners to thrive. Again, fitting this frame to the couple is crucial to moving forward in treatment. If it is not accepted, then the therapist works to adjust the fit or shifts to some more pragmatic problem-solving work before returning to the original frame.

Greenman and Johnson (2013) published a crisp encapsulation of EFT that lays out the three phases of treatment. The primary objective of Phase I is working with the couple on *cycle de-escalation*. Issues couples bring to therapy are usually organized around a vicious cycle Greenman and Johnson referred to as *demand–withdraw*, similar to that of Wile (2013) noted earlier. Here, one partner (the demander) tends to blame or criticize the other to get him or her to engage, while the other partner (the withdrawer) attempts to disengage through emotional withdrawal. As has been described in earlier chapters, the pattern becomes a positive feedback loop in which both participants unwittingly bring on the responses opposite from what they are seeking from their partner. More demand brings on more withdrawal, and more withdrawal brings on more demand.

With one party expressing hard emotions such as anger or disgust, the other partner in turn expresses shame, fear, or defensive anger. This type of emotional expression fosters the push–retreat effect that characterizes the demand–withdraw cycle. Hard emotions activate distancing from one's partner, and emotions that attract closeness go unexpressed. This again parallels the findings of the Gottman group (Gottman, 1999) on "hard start-ups" fueling downward spirals in couples. Distancing, fueled by emotions that prompt retreat, is said to hide each partner's true desire for closeness (a core element of the EFT frame for couple problems). However, EFT sees both partners' reactions as adaptive to the specific emotions as described subsequently.

Phase II

Phase II involves restructuring the couple's interactions to achieve a secure attachment bond. This involves assisting the demander with softening his or her approach by expressing the soft side feelings that are underneath the complaining and anger. (Interestingly, this use of the term *soft emotions* is the same as in the IBCT approach discussed earlier.) To do this, emotions that lurk behind anger are identified and expressed—sadness, loneliness, and fears around loss of connection. On the other side, the therapist assists the withdrawer with engaging. This involves expressing one's own hurts, fears, and need to be comforted. Therapists assume that as both partners recognize their needs for security and ask their partner to meet those needs in a coherent, inviting way, it will lead to a secure attachment. When attachment is secure, partners can receive positive, soothing responses, while remaining open and responsive to one another's emotional needs. Through the process of expressing soft side emotions and making direct requests to one's partner to meet one's needs, a new way of responding unfolds and replaces the demand–withdrawal pattern.

Phase III

Finally, in Phase III, gains are consolidated, and long-standing conflicts are addressed using the newly learned interactive pattern. Former triggers of the demand–withdraw cycle are also discussed. The therapist then acts as a facilitator of effective problem-solving, and as a process consultant.

Clearly, there are numerous ways that the EFT approach parallels the IBCT approach in interdicting couples' vicious demand–withdraw cycles, yet the results are achieved on the basis of very different theoretical assumptions. Each approach of course emphasizes empathy and bonding to enhance the therapeutic alliance and helping couples buy in to the frames and rationales of the approach. Thus, a critical question for therapists becomes which approach to apply when working with a given couple. To address this concern, it is helpful to turn to issues of common factors, rationales, and creating fit with couples before we apply each of these two approaches to our couple, Maria and Lars.

CREATING AN ALLIANCE THAT FITS

As in individual treatment, much of the impact of psychotherapy, regardless of the therapist's orientation, depends on a client and therapist sharing an alliance as the foundation of treatment (Sprenkle et al., 2009). As noted earlier, the therapeutic alliance is critical for clients to help take a metalevel view outside their problem system, join with a therapist to reflect on the patterns of their problem, open themselves to a new frame for the problem, and adopt a related rationale to make sense of formerly counterintuitive solutions. As related to couples treatment, a study of EMT found a 22% posttreatment satisfaction rate, and at follow-up, 29% of that satisfaction was attributable to the couple's alliance with the therapist (Johnson & Talitman, 1997). A similar result was found in cognitive-behavioral couples therapy (Krupnick et al., 1994). Furthermore, the power of therapist warmth and the alliance has also been found to contribute significantly to success in the form of family therapy developed by the Mental Research Institute Brief Therapy Center (Palo Alto, California), where the alliance is downplayed (Green & Herget, 1991). Relating to the therapeutic alliance in couples therapy, Sprenkle and colleagues (2009) concluded that virtually all empirically supported knowledge from individual psychotherapy research about common factors (e.g., the importance of therapist competence regardless of the model employed) applies likewise to relational therapy approaches.

In addition, Friedlander and colleagues (Friedlander, Escudero, & Heatherington, 2006) indicated that the alliance assumes greater importance in couple and family therapy because of the multiple participants and accompanying struggles to build several simultaneous alliances and to keep the level of alliance in balance. In individual therapy the objective is to establish an alliance with one person; relational therapists are tasked with forming alliances with all participants even when those participants are vehemently at odds. This suggests that therapists who work with couples and families must be skillful at connecting with different viewpoints while remaining nonjudgmental. This applies not only to skills but to the person of the therapist as well. Clients react to who the person of the therapist is: gender, culture, way of speaking, and so on. To be effective, clinicians who work with couples and families need awareness of the impact of these factors on their clients so that they can adapt and find a good fit. Once again, therapists' sensitivity to their complex relationship with couples and their flexibility and attention to fitting their frames and rationales to what makes sense to couples are the first steps in second-order change. It helps clients step out of their relationship system and into a new metalevel alliance with therapists.

MODERATED COMMON FACTORS

The question remains as to how providing common factors important to the success of all therapy interacts with fitting a given effective treatment approach and its related interventions to a given couple. To this end, Sprenkle and colleagues (2009) proposed a moderate common factors approach as a metamodel of change in couples therapy. The approach is grounded in the notion that therapy models matter, in complement to the power of common factors. Sprenkle et al. suggested that, in effect, models and common factors work together to bring about change. Regarding how a therapist might usefully choose an approach to interrupt a given couple's vicious cycle patterns, Sprenkle et al. stated,

> Although the entry point into the cycle varies, all systemic models focus on altering an aspect of the cycle . . . contrary to conventional model-specific wisdom, we believe that the most effective point of entry into the cycle—be it cognitive, affective, or behavioral—is determined more by client preference than the objective superiority of one point over the other (e.g., emotions versus cognitions). We hypothesize that *a change in one aspect of the cycle will be associated with changes in the others*. Perhaps the most important element of systemic intervention is not *which* aspect of the cycle a therapist focuses on but rather that the therapist focuses on the one aspect that fits with the clients and that the therapist intervenes in a systemic way. (p. 136, emphasis in the original)

Also, relating to fit, they went on to say,

> For therapy to be effective, both the therapist and the client have to "buy into" the clinical approach that is offered. . . . The clients will likely "buy" the therapist's conceptualization if they view what is being said as relevant to their problems and they can see that the therapist believes what he or she is talking about. (p. 131)

This perspective captures the essence of the process of change paradigm. Yet, as we turn to the theory of groups and logical types and the concepts of first- and second-order change, there is something more to add. Creating a therapeutic alliance, along with its elements of empathy, validation, and trust, also moves clients to a metalevel outside of their problem patterns as they join with their therapists. Recall that major transformations of any group cannot be achieved from within the assumptions and rules of interaction of the group itself. Members must move to a metalevel where they are not only able to view and evaluate those assumptions and rules, but where they are open to adopting new frames for their problem and rationales for resolution. The key here is that these metalevel frames and related treatment rationales help clients to "make sense" of new solution patterns that were formerly not considered or, more importantly, that were considered *counterintuitive* or *paradoxical*.

Reflecting on this move to a metalevel, or second-order change from group to class, Wile (2013) resonated with this perspective:

> Improving partners' ability to shift from alienated to intimate states is the first of two therapeutic goals. Creating a metalevel, a permanent platform or perch above the fray, is the second. . . . The task in helping partners deal with such problems is to increase their ability at important moments to climb on a platform and commiserate about these problems. (p. 28)

From this metalevel, and from the new and best fitting frames and associated rationale for treatment, all clients—and in this case, couples—are able to reverse their vicious cycles by opting for pattern reversals that made no sense from within their former points of view and solution-generating problem patterns. Either the IBCT or EFT approach may fit the bill to achieve this, as the case of Maria and Lars explores next. In returning to their story, I use the perspectives of context, process, and change as described earlier in this volume.

FLEXIBILITY AND FIT WITH A DISTRESSED COUPLE

Context

As already noted, both of the couples therapy approaches described in this chapter have the ingredients necessary to bring about change. Moreover, there is strong evidence to support that alliance building and maintenance is critical to outcome. IBCT and EFT embed strong relationship-building skills and methods in their frameworks. IBCT focuses on empathic joining, whereas EFT clinicians do the same through Rogerian active listening and intense focusing. Each framework joins equally with both partners and treats each with respect. Both approaches are sensitive to clients' use of language, and clinicians are encouraged to adapt their language to fit with their couples. There is also joining between the couple and the clinician. This is done by taking blame off the couple. IBCT and EFT clinicians openly blame the demand–withdraw cycle and enlist the couple in doing the same. Taking blame away from the couple creates a nonjudgmental context for experimenting with different, more productive ways of addressing couple conflicts. Each approach stresses that engaging and bonding is a process that occurs throughout the course of therapy. Consequently, in theory, although there may be some differences in how it is done, each approach arrives at a similar place, and that place is a pattern shift in vicious cycle processes between partners.

At the same time, outside factors play an important role as to what type of therapist will best help Maria and Lars or whether a therapist will even get a chance to apply her or his framework. Sometimes couples have preferences as to whether the therapist is a male or female. How will the clinician respond if Maria or Lars confesses that she or he prefers a therapist of a different gender? Will the clinician address this defensively, offer to refer the couple to a colleague, or perhaps offer an experiment to see whether they can all work together? Maria is Latina. Lars is Scandinavian. Is it important to them that their therapist is Hispanic or is familiar with the Scandinavian culture? How about religion? Are they Roman Catholic? Protestant? Agnostic? Does it matter to the couple whether the clinician believes in God? Can the clinician work with differences in this area?

Therapist style can also matter with client fit. It may be assumed that all clients interpret the Rogerian style of reflective listening as empathic. Fraser and Solovey (2007) presented evidence that this is not the case. The client best interprets what is empathic, and clients vary. Not all clients resonate with nurturing-based approaches that focus on feelings. Some prefer a more businesslike approach. Although some clients appreciate a nondirective clinician who co-constructs dialogue, others may prefer a more direct style and ask for advice. The question here is whether the clinician is able to adjust her style to match with the couple.

We have identified that the cycle common to couples is demand–withdraw. The question then becomes one of fit for the couple. Does this formulation make sense to them? What does the clinician do when a couple presents with concerns around not talking, when both withdraw, or when the theme is attack–attack? What if the theme involves a third party or other parties, such as children or extended family? Is the clinician able to adjust?

From the perspective of context, client, and therapist, fit factors may be more important to Maria and Lars in selecting a clinician than the specific orientation of the therapist. These fit factors also play a significant role in whether they will achieve a positive outcome.

Process

There is little difference between the IBCT and EFT rationales about vicious cycles. Both perspectives detail the dynamics of demand–withdraw in a similar fashion. They both view the couple as trapped in a cycle of behavior that is mutually reinforcing. As stated earlier, Maria's demanding is brought on by Lars's withdrawal, and Lars's defensive withdrawal is brought on by Maria's demanding approach. Both perspectives place this behavior in a nonpathologizing context. The IBCT approach suggests that the development of the cycle is a matter of context and negative attributions ascribed to personality characteristics that were once attractors. For example, when they were courting, Maria may have been attracted to Lars because he was a hardworking man with an even temperament. She also liked how he went out of his way to please her. On the other hand, Lars really liked Maria's passion and willingness to speak her mind. He didn't have to worry whether he was pleasing her because she was quite clear on this. With the birth of their new baby came a perfect storm for threatening the couple's fit. Lars was trying to make money for his newly expanded family during a downturn in his business. The downturn brought on criticism from his customers and employees. This was difficult for him to bear, so he spent more hours at work. The extra hours at work displeased Maria, which was also difficult to bear. Given his aversion to conflict, Lars looked for more ways to hide. He became resentful that Maria was always speaking her mind and that she wouldn't cut him some slack. This drove him to hide from Maria as well as from confrontations at work. On the other side, Maria was wiped out and overwhelmed with the added responsibility of a new baby. She couldn't get things done around the house and needed Lars to be home more to help. She was growing increasingly frustrated that Lars kept covering for his supervisees at work. His even-mannered approach made her mad. She also couldn't understand why he didn't come to bed with her. This made no sense. She was worried for Lars's health and was scared he didn't love her anymore and might abandon her, as other men had done to women in her family.

An EFT therapist would see the content of Maria and Lars's demand–withdraw pattern in a similar way as an IBCT clinician, with one caveat: Rather than focusing on context as underlying the vicious cycle, the focus of EFT is insecure attachment. The current struggle would be conceptualized as playing out insecure attachment behaviors in their highly stressful situation. Their family backgrounds and the way Maria and Lars were raised might indicate that they had insecure attachments to their primary caregivers. The insecurity in their attachments may thus not have been resolved, making them vulnerable to the type of problem they were experiencing.

With respect to goals, each framework would work with the couple to establish specific treatment goals. The approaches agree on the overarching goal of replacing the demand–withdraw cycle with a virtuous positive feedback loop. However, there is some difference in how the goal is framed. The objective of IBCT is acceptance of personality differences, followed by conflict resolution, if needed. The goal of EFT is secure attachment, followed by conflict resolution, if needed.

From the process perspective, regardless how a vicious cycle is labeled, it follows the principle of positive feedback loops, as described over and again in this volume. At the end of the day, there is no extra benefit for Maria or Lars from the theory of vicious cycles espoused by either of these frameworks. They are both plausible and equally effective despite differences in some of their theoretical constructs. The key is that the rationales are coherent and fit the constructs of the clinician and the couple. This circles back to the arguments we made in the foregoing section on context. There is a value added when clinicians understand that all couple patterns operate on the positive feedback loop principle. Then, flexibly fitting a coherent and fitting rationale and related procedures to each couple follows more easily. Of course, this asks more of couples therapists by assuming that they will develop knowledge and skills in several approaches to couples treatment—likely not a simple task for most practitioners. Understanding the positive feedback principle in the process of change view may also make it easier to adapt therapy for couples that do not classically fit the demand–withdraw pattern.

Change

As we have seen, therapy is all about change. Competent therapists do not form relationships with couples for the sake of building relationships. Therapeutic relationships have a direction. The direction is change in the way couples are trying to change, or pattern shift. Caring, engaging, delivering rationales, developing collaborative goals, and assigning mutually agreed on tasks are all in the service of pattern shift. Each of these elements is part of a recursive pattern that feeds back into itself. For example, establishing mutual goals feeds back to empathy, because forming mutual goals enhances the sense that the clinician is on the client's side (Fraser & Solovey, 2007). Change can occur at any point in the treatment process. By showing empathic understanding for each partner in a couple, one or the other might feel heard for the first time and soften his or her approach. If Maria softens her approach, Lars might become more engaged with her. This can happen before any action by the therapist to facilitate softening of hard emotions. The act of simply attending therapy could convince Maria that Lars still loves her, beginning the pattern-shift process before they step foot in the door of the therapist's office. With that said, let's look more carefully at what is behind the direct efforts to bring about change by IBCT and EFT therapists.

The overall goal of pattern shift is the same for each of the frameworks under analysis. Each framework seeks to stop the current pattern and initiate a different and more satisfying way of interacting. An important step toward facilitating pattern shift is providing an overarching rationale that validates the couple for having a problem and makes sense of processes that will be used to bring about change. For example, as I previously stated, describing the vicious cycle as an "it," as is done with IBCT, accomplishes the task of validating the couple by taking the blame for the problem away from the couple as individuals: It is the pattern's fault. In addition, as I explained earlier, each treatment model has a way of doing this. Each model's argument is compelling. What the therapist will do follows from the rationale. IBCT clinicians will talk about desensitizing Maria and Lars from the intense feelings they have when they are in conflict, so they can soften their approach to one another. The EFT therapist will tell Maria and Lars that the pattern is constricting their emotional expression. The problem is really more about how their unique histories of relationships have played into how they relate to each other—a problem of their unique histories and not of them as a couple. Treatment will be about sensitizing them to a wider range of emotions that will better serve them as a couple and deepen their attachment.

From the process of change perspective, the rationale makes sense of, or implies the resulting patterns of the treatment. The dynamic of the demand–withdraw cycle is that Maria is over-pursuing change, as described in Chapter 3. Thus, the solution on her end will be the opposite: stopping or reversing her pursuit. Lars, in contrast, is going away from the problem by withdrawing. The solution for him, is also the opposite and will have something to do with going toward or engaging with Maria. The systemic aspect of the process view postulates that change will occur as Maria, Lars, or both alter their solution patterns. In this respect, IBCT and EFT are both in line with the process view.

CYCLING BACK

Couple problems revolve around escalating approach–withdrawal cycles. Couples research confirms how these patterns escalate and suggests pattern reversals for resolution. At least two evidence-supported treatments take on this pattern reversal. However, they do this from two alternative and very different theoretical assumptions. The process of change view easily accommodates this. Successful couples treatment will come down to the flexibility of therapists to fit their relationship and rationale with the couple to create the best working alliance. Once achieved, this alliance will help make sense of the pattern reversals needed to de-escalate the vicious cycles and move the couple toward a more flexible and fulfilling pattern.

10

FAMILY SYSTEM PROBLEMS

Joey is a 14-year-old Caucasian boy, living with his mother and her current live-in partner, Roger. Joey dresses to intimidate, wearing black and sporting tattoos. He is about 6 feet tall and likely weighs about 185 pounds. In this session, he wore a T-shirt emblazoned with the name of a heavy metal rock group, Megadeth, which seemed an appropriate metaphor for what he was trying to portray! The case had been seen for a while in the agency before this consult, and it had been giving everyone problems. Joey has an older brother who was kicked out of the home several years ago for using drugs.

A key past incident occurred about 2 years ago when Joey's abusive and neglectful father hung himself in the family garage. Joey was the one who found him and had to cut down his dead body. Since then, Joey has become

---

Select passages from this chapter first appeared in the following: *Integrative Families and Systems Treatment (I-FAST): A Strengths-Based Common Factors Approach*, by J. S. Fraser, D. Grove, M. Y. Lee, G. J. Greene, and A. D. Solovey, 2014, New York, NY, Oxford University Press. Adapted with permission; and adapted from *Second-Order Change in Psychotherapy: The Golden Thread That Unifies Effective Treatments*, by J. S. Fraser and A. D. Solovey, 2007, Washington, DC: American Psychological Association.

http://dx.doi.org/10.1037/0000078-011
Unifying Effective Psychotherapies: Tracing the Process of Change, by J. S. Fraser

more oppositional and defiant with his mother and teachers. He was expelled from school and is doing computer homeschooling but is not really complying with that either. This past year, Joey claimed he was an alcoholic and was put into a youth alcohol program; counselors there found that he in fact was not really drinking much and discharged him. Joey has shown much bravado with others, telling them that a scar on his shoulder was from being shot (which was not true), and often escalating disagreements with and threatening his mother. Joey's mother is now with a new man, who is actually rather kind and strong as a role model. However, he has stayed out of parenting Joey. Joey's mother has very real heart problems, likely requiring a pacemaker, but she tends to use this as an excuse not to set limits with Joey, stating that he might escalate, causing her to have a heart attack. Joey tends to intimidate and make a scene even in the waiting room at the agency when he can, and staff had asked for help with this. Joey's mom doesn't set limits partly because he is her youngest and partly because she feels sorry for the events around Joey finding his father hung, feeling that Joey must be handled gently due to his potential emotional state and the traumatic loss.

When therapists have tried to convince her to start setting limits, she has pushed back, claiming she might have a heart attack if things escalate and noting Joey's potentially fragile emotional state. Mom's language is rough in that she "curses like a sailor," as they say, and she is argumentative with Joey and others. Her position is that she is essentially a "tough broad" who will do what she thinks best despite what others say. She was reactive in that way, as was Joey.

THE CONTEXT AND PROCESS OF PARENT–CHILD PROBLEMS

The literature in dominant Western culture will likely define Joey's behavior as an example of a disruptive behavior disorder. The disruptive behavior disorders as described in the literature include attention-deficit/hyperactivity disorder (ADHD), oppositional defiant disorder (ODD), and conduct disorder (CD). These disorders have also been referred to as *externalizing* or *acting-out disorders*. In recent years, there has been a growing number of evidence-supported approaches targeting CD and ODD. This offers another chance to do comparative analysis from the process-of-change view. Toward this end, this chapter focuses on CD and ODD.

Kazdin (2002), reporting on treatments for CD, indicated that several treatments have been shown to be either promising or probably efficacious. As has been the case with psychotherapy in general, these treatments have theoretical underpinnings that are often at odds. Kazdin (2002) has said,

> Theory is needed to sort through an indefinite range of factors and to explain how these factors relate to the treatment process. In both

> research and clinical practice, we wish to maximize therapeutic change. This requires knowing what the critical factors are in treatment and how change occurs. (p. 77)

This chapter defines the disruptive behavior disorders, looks at the vicious cycle phenomenon from several well-known perspectives, and relates them to the process perspective. Two classes of approach are addressed. The first focuses on parent–child problems. The second addresses those youth and families who are involved with multiple agencies and other community or correctional systems.

Defiance Defined

Oppositional Defiant Disorder

According to the *Diagnostic and Statistical Manual of Mental Disorders* (*DSM–5*; American Psychiatric Association, 2013) and the *International Statistical Classification of Diseases* (10th revision [ICD–10]; World Health Organization [WHO], 1993), ODD refers to a recurrent childhood pattern of negativistic, defiant, disobedient, and hostile behavior toward adult authority figures that are developmentally inappropriate. There are specific behaviors associated with ODD. To qualify for the diagnosis, the child must exhibit four or more behaviors from the following list: often loses temper, often argues with adults, often actively defies or refuses to comply with adults' requests or rules, often deliberately annoys people, often blames others for his or her mistakes or misbehavior, is often touchy or easily annoyed by others, is often angry and resentful, and is often spiteful or vindictive. In addition, these behaviors tend to cause clinically significant impairment in social, academic, or occupational functioning.

Conduct Disorder

According to Kazdin (2002), antisocial behaviors refer to a variety of acts that reflect social rule violations and actions against others. Behaviors such as fighting, lying, and stealing occur in varying degrees in most children. CD refers to antisocial behavior that is clinically significant and clearly beyond the realm of "normal functioning." The extent to which antisocial behaviors are sufficiently severe to constitute CD depends on several characteristics of the behaviors, including their frequency, their chronicity, whether they are isolated acts or part of a larger syndrome with other deviant behaviors, and whether they lead to significant impairment of the child. The overriding feature is a persistent pattern of behavior in which the rights of others and age-appropriate social norms are violated. Isolated acts when severe enough, such as physical aggression, destruction of property, stealing, or fire-setting, are sufficient to warrant concern and attention in their own right. The ICD–10 (WHO, 1993) differentiates a range of conduct disorders, including CD confined to family context, childhood-onset type, and adolescent-onset type, but converges with the *DSM* descriptions.

Attention-Deficit/Hyperactivity Disorder

Many children who meet diagnostic criteria for disruptive behavior disorders have ADHD as a comorbid condition. Greene, Ablon, Goring, Raezer-Blakely, et al. (2004) indicated that ADHD is a diagnostic label used to describe children who exhibit developmentally extreme levels of inattention, hyperactivity–impulsivity, or both in the *DSM*. (The ICD–10 includes five subtypes, including ADHD predominantly inattentive type, predominantly hyperactive type, combined type, other, and unspecified [WHO, 1993].)

Children with ADHD often have deficits in neurological skills referred to as *executive functions* (Greene, 2014; Greene, Ablon, Goring, Fazio, & Morse, 2004). Although there is some disagreement as to the precise cognitive skills that constitute executive functioning, there is agreement that this is an important factor in ADHD and the development of ODD. Greene (2014) further suggested that delays in the development of any or all of the executive functioning skills place a child at risk for developing ODD. Executive functions include the ability to shift efficiently from one mind-set to another, the ability to organize a coherent plan in problem-solving, the ability to perform multiple thinking tasks simultaneously, and the ability to regulate emotional arousal in the service of a goal-directed action.

In general, children with executive functioning deficits often come across as demanding, self-centered, and lacking in empathy and social tact. Self-awareness and empathy require a continuous process of reflecting on and rethinking of experience and perspective taking, and this process is short-circuited by deficits in executive skills. From this perspective, Greene (2014) argued that children's defiant behaviors only appear to be willful disobedience, and behind the mask of willful defiance is a child who is inflexible and frustrated with his inability to meet the demands of adults.

Parent Discipline

Chamberlain and Patterson (1995) identified four subtypes of *parent inadequate discipline* that contribute to coercive parent–child interchanges: inconsistent discipline; irritable explosive discipline; low supervision and involvement; and inflexible rigid discipline. Greene, however, is critical of research that separates child and parent risk factors. On the basis of the characteristics of children who have disruptive disorders, it is difficult to determine whether the child's defiance provokes poor parenting or poor parenting provokes defiance. In other words, the reciprocal relationship between parent and child behaviors better fits a transactional model that integrates parent and child characteristics. Viewed in this way, the concept of goodness of fit emerges, addressing the degree to which the characteristics of the child are compatible with those of his or her parents. From this interactional view, if an impulsive, poorly emotionally regulated child has a parent who is patient and slow to anger, the child will be less likely to develop disruptive behaviors. However, if the same child has a parent who is also impulsive and quick to anger, then goodness of fit is incompatible and the child will be more likely to develop disruptive behaviors.

Russell A. Barkley (2014), a preeminent researcher and spokesperson for parent training (PT) in the behavioral tradition, indicated that larger contextual events such as stress, marital discord, parental isolation, or events affecting the family from the outside may serve to increase the probability of defiant child behavior. This occurs by virtue of the toll these events take on the consistency of parental management of the child, the positive reinforcement of compliant child behavior, and the general monitoring of child activities by parents.

The Vicious Cycle

Although described in different terms, a common theme among researchers and clinicians is that disruptive behavior disorders are triggered in multiple ways but are maintained by a vicious cycle. The child, parents, and others who become involved in the cycle share a strikingly similar characteristic: They are all unwitting participants. As unwitting participants, all parties develop premises and actions that direct their participation in a worsening situation. Participants are generally unaware that they are contributing to the problem. This is a repetition of the now-familiar process view seen across all previous chapters. Problems across domains of concern, and the effective psychotherapies for those problems, target vicious cycles of first-order change patterns and succeed by initiating second-order change. This is the golden thread connecting them in the class of effective treatments.

Barkley's Vicious Cycles

The following summarizes Barkley's (2014) perspective on how vicious cycles of disruptive behavior develop: (a) The sequence is usually initiated by a command, given by the parent, for the child to engage in a task that is not considered enjoyable or reinforcing by the child. (b) When the child does not comply, the parent will repeat the command. (c) When the repeated command is not followed, it is repeated again, and so on. (d) At some point, parental frustration increases, and the emotional intensity of the interaction escalates. The parent may warn or threaten the child that if he does not follow instructions, punishment will occur. (e) Here, the child may continue to be noncompliant because threats are frequently part of the sequence and most often do not actually occur, hence the parent does not have credibility. (f) Over time, both the child and parent escalate their emotional behavior toward each other, with voices rising in increasing volume and intensity, as well as displays of anger, defiance, and perhaps destructiveness. (g) This sequence may end in two ways: on rare occasions, the parent will perhaps send the child to his room and deny some privilege or the parent will acquiesce to the child, without the child completing the command.

In some situations, the parent may obtain full compliance from the child, and herein lies the rub. In these situations, parents may believe that they have won the battle with their child because they have finally made the child comply. However, from the child's point of view, he has, at a minimum, delayed following through on the command. This is doubly reinforcing because he is able to continue with the desired behavior for a little longer while delaying the unpleasant task. Therefore, to his parents' chagrin, he is highly unlikely to give up his defiant behavior because he does not understand that he has lost. To make matters worse, as the cycle of defiance unfolds over time, the parent may resort to coercive tactics in an effort to de-escalate the child's emotional outbursts. Parents may offer treats if he settles down. In other situations, the child may injure himself while acting out, and the parent may soothe or comfort the child. This additional reinforcement accelerates the defiant behavior. The child becomes locked into the cycle through unwitting parental reinforcement. Parents become locked in the cycle through partial success with the child. This is a classic vicious cycle.

Another outgrowth of the continuing cycle is that parents may tend to shy away from the child, perhaps to avoid confrontation. Consequently, the parents miss opportunities to provide reinforcement for prosocial or appropriate behaviors of the child. Even when they know that the child is behaving well, the parents may withhold comment or fail to notice. Failure to notice may also allow the defiant child to engage in additional deviant behaviors. As the process continues to unfold, parents may become so angry with the child that they inadvertently punish prosocial behavior. They may make sarcastic comments when he exhibits prosocial behavior, insinuating malevolent ulterior motives. Worse yet, the rapidly escalating episodes of mutual aggressive behavior of parents and children may become *self-reinforcing* with parents and children coming to believe that perhaps one more episode will settle the growing war in their favor. This leads to a never-ending cycle of final showdowns.

Greene's Vicious Cycles

Ross Greene (2014) also described a vicious cycle but viewed it from a different angle. As previously stated, Greene has argued that noncompliant behavior is fueled by the goodness of fit between parents and children depending on a variety of temperamental, developmental, neurological, and social traits found in both children and parents. Furthermore, he viewed these traits as skills that, when delayed, result in uneven development for the child. Skill deficiencies cluster in such a way as to form an *inflexible child*. An inflexible child is easily frustrated by demands requiring skills outside of his narrow repertoire. This feeds a vicious cycle as follows: (a) When children are noncompliant, they behave as if they are attempting to escape from parental commands; however, this is illusory. In effect, the child wishes to be compliant but is unable to do so because she cannot shift gears quickly enough to satisfy parental expectations. (b) This creates frustration, which then causes the child to shut down or go into what Greene (2014) referred to as a mental form of vapor lock. Vapor lock is a metaphor taken from automobiles in which, under certain conditions, a car stalls out and will not go. (c) In frustration, parents are prone to read vapor lock as defiance. When parents read the child's noncompliance as willful, they are compelled to impose their will on the child for fear of losing their authority. This then stimulates an emotional symmetrical escalation that is similar to that described by Barkley. However, the problem is given a biological basis as a more positive frame than willful defiance.

Such escalations are likely to be repeated because the child is unable to expand his flexibility skills in an environment where there is much pressure and either little teaching or teaching that is mistimed during the middle of an emotionally escalating situation. As long as the parents view the child as engaging in deliberate coercive behaviors, they are unlikely to change their style. Greene (2014) referred to the escalation sequence as a *meltdown*. His formula for a meltdown is inflexibility + inflexibility = meltdown.

The Connecting Pattern

In the vicious cycles just described, parents make two common strategic errors that contribute to disruptive behavior formation and maintenance. Both errors have a similar theme: They involve trying too hard to obtain compliance from the child, resulting in overpursuit. In essence, this is synonymous with the term *coercion*—to force someone to act or think in a given manner.

The first of these strategic errors involves parental strategies that are designed to reach accord with the child through opposition. Here the parent, preoccupied with authority issues, becomes involved in haranguing the child in an effort to obtain compliance with specific behaviors. The harangue overshoots the mark because it is really directed at forcing the child to treat the parent with the respect, care, or deference that the parent feels is due. In effect, to be in compliance, the child must not only perform the required task but also acknowledge the parent is "one-up." This is more than simply obeying a request. Consider the child directed to brush her teeth. If she obeys but appears disrespectful, she will not be in compliance. This will trigger a harangue about showing the proper respect for her parent. The Mental Research Institute Group wrote that "this form of problem solving provokes the very behavior the complainant wishes to eliminate, whether the demand for one-upness is phrased as being right or being in charge, and whether it is pursued by threats, force, or by logic" (Fisch, Weakland, & Segal, 1982, p. 140).

The second type of strategic error is another form of overpursuit that takes on a more manipulative quality. This involves attempts to obtain compliance through volunteerism. Here the parent is afraid of being seen as dictatorial. Consequently, she engages in endless attempts to get the child to agree with or want to follow directives that are necessary but perhaps unpleasant. This type of error is summed up in the statement "I would like him to do it, but even more, I want him to *want* to do it." Again, directives that come out of this mode go far beyond a simple request for compliance. To follow such a directive, the child must change his internal emotional state. Any sign, verbal or nonverbal, that he has not done so will bring on lectures and sermons that ultimately result in a meltdown or explosive episode.

As parents become frustrated with their inability to obtain compliance from the child, they initiate a pattern of overpursuit. In this pattern, the parent goes beyond efforts to obtain compliance with specific requests. Instead, each request represents an effort by the parent to obtain categorical compliance from the child. The parent is in essence trying to transform the child's nature. Greene (2014) referred to such categorical compliance as a developmental step toward self-control and emotion regulation. Hence, from this perspective, the parent is unwittingly attempting to *force* the achievement of a human developmental milestone. This is akin to trying to make a young child instantaneously acquire a full complement of language skills. Thus, the target for change is to reverse this coercive demand–pursue process. (This parallels the demand–withdraw and accuse–defend cycles discussed in Chapter 9 on couple problems.)

Sequentially, a two-step process is apparent. The first step involves the parent *attempting to coerce change in the child*. The second step is *withholding validation until change occurs*. In response, the child resists change and is deprived of validation. The child in turn invalidates the parent through noncompliant behavior. A vicious negative affect cycle ensues, characterized by mutual invalidation. This is a key first-order trap for parents and children.

THE PATTERN OF CHANGE SEQUENCE

After carefully reviewing empirically supported disruptive behavior treatment methods, we find that a number of common processes occur with effective treatment. The general order of this sequence is as follows:

1. Parents and other caregivers adopt a more charitable view of what motivates the child's defiant behaviors. (New *frames* for the child's behavior help parents "make sense" of shifting to a more validating relationship.)
2. Parents and other caregivers develop a proactive plan that narrows problem-solving efforts to a subset of specific target behaviors. (New *rationales* help parents reverse their demands to change everything and focus only on a small set.)
3. Parents and other caregivers decrease or eliminate arguments with the child by refusing to engage in argumentation. (Parents *reverse* their willingness to fight, de-escalating former escalating vicious cycles.)
4. There is a shift to rely on natural consequences as the primary mode of teaching the child. Natural consequences are consequences that occur as a direct result of nature, such as becoming hungry if one does not eat. (Parental *acceptance* stops the vicious cycle before it starts.)
5. Parents dramatically reduce the use of punishment or significant consequences. If used at all, they are reserved only for serious situations, are part of a larger proactive plan, and are enforceable. Instead, they attend to the presence of positives rather than negatives. (Parents initiate *virtuous cycles* of desired patterns through attention and reinforcement.)

This process occurs within the context of a new pattern of parent–child interaction. The new pattern reverses the "force change then validate" sequence by having the parent validate the child *before* requesting change. It also interdicts former vicious cycles and initiates virtuous ones. The central challenge in treatment is obtaining compliance from parents and other caregivers to follow this reversed pattern. Recall the critical role of common factors in helping parents to join in a therapeutic alliance with a therapist and stepping to a metalevel to observe the patterns of their family. The next step is for the parents to agree to a fitting problem frame with its associated treatment rationale. In Barkley's approach, the problem is framed in strictly behavioral terms, whereas Greene offers a biological and developmental frame. However, after adopting one or the other problem frame and seeing their vicious cycles through this new lens, both approaches shift the problem cycle in similar ways. More specifically, the steps are as follows:

1. The parent(s) shows interest in the child by noticing the child when he is playing or engaging in independent or problem-solving activities. (A new *rationale* initiates a new and *reversed* parent–child relationship. It helps make sense for parents to reverse their positions with their children.)
2. The parent(s) looks for ways to validate the child or take the child's perspective. (Validation *precedes* requests for compliance rather than the opposite. This soft response *reverses* previous hard, demanding positions that triggered escalations.)
3. The parent(s) establishes specific behavioral goals or expectations for the child. (Treatment rationales *reduce* opportunities for defiance.)
4. The parent(s) reduces or restrains expectations for *categorical* change in the child. (This *reverses* the demand pattern.)
5. The parents look for and validate incremental changes as they occur. (This *reverses* prior attention to noncompliance and defiance and replaces it with attention to compliance.)

These steps also tend to match Jerome Frank's (Frank & Frank, 1991) contextual model components. Those components, common to all effective treatments, include an emotionally charged validating relationship, a set of rationales or "myths" to describe the problem and set a direction for treatment, and a set of related procedures to produce that change. Again, this reverses the pattern of "force change then validate" to "validate then work toward gradual change." This is a new *change sequence*.

THE PROCESS OF CHANGE IN PARENT–CHILD DIFFICULTIES

I now review family-oriented methods of treating disruptive behaviors from the perspective of the process of change. The first two treatments are Russell Barkley's (2014) PT program and Ross Greene's (2014) collaborative problem solving (CPS) approaches. These are two leading empirically supported approaches that focus on parent–child interaction. Next, I turn to evidence-supported approaches for so-called conduct-disordered youth involved with multiple systems. However, it should be noted that a variety of other empirically supported approaches also merit close attention by anyone interested in working with this more severely disruptive range of children and adolescents.

For now, I compare the Barkley and Greene approaches to follow the thread of the process view. I begin by discussing assessment and its effects on change. I discuss how therapists enhance their relationship with parents and then replicate that relationship-building process in the parents' relationship with their children through new rationales and validating interactions. I then move to how narrowing the focus of behaviors needing change and the general procedures of both approaches enable multiple reversals or second-order shifts in the ways parents interact with their children. In the end, I reemphasize how the process of change in these two empirically supported treatments represents a second-order intervention producing impressive results with disturbed disruptive parent–child problems.

Assessment

The first step in the process of engaging families with disruptive children in treatment is assessment of the child and family. Although both Barkley's and Greene's treatment methods involve an elaborate assessment process, the precise focus of the assessment varies. For example, in addition to behavioral checklists, Greene (2014) stressed the importance of psychoeducational testing that is aimed at understanding difficulties that the child may be experiencing in a wide range of domains, including cognitive functioning, achievement skills, executive functioning, language processing, and developmental delays. Barkley (2014), while interested in similar domains, placed special emphasis on the parents filling out a variety of checklists specifically directed at assessing the child's disruptive behaviors at home and in school.

Enhancing the Parent–Child Relationship

Both of the family frameworks described here have within their method a procedure or set of procedures designed to assist the parent with developing a renewed interest in the child. As previously stated, the heart of disruptive behaviors is a "toxic negativity cycle" between parent and child (Sexton & Alexander, 2015). This cycle involves reciprocal attribution of negative motivation ascribed by parents toward the child and vice versa. Barkley's and Greene's approaches frame the need to reverse this pattern but with different premises—one behavioral, the other biological/developmental. Stepping out of the solution-generated system to a new metalevel, seeing the vicious cycles and adopting a new problem frame and rationale for solution is critical to success across all effective treatments. Without these steps, the pattern reversals of treatment will remain counterintuitive to parents. Taking positions that seem paradoxical to parents from their initial frames and positions makes parental acceptance of new problem frames and related treatment rationales crucial to successful treatment.

A Behavioral Frame and Rationale

Barkley's (2014) more behaviorally based PT frames the problem for parents as faulty reinforcement patterns. This is a critical step in softening parents' approach to their children and interdicting the repeated, escalating vicious cycles. From a behavioral view, parents slowly become reinforcers for their child while reversing the previous toxic cycle. Parents are taught to engage their child in nondirective play early in therapy, long before addressing the child's noncompliant behaviors. The parent spends 5 to 10 minutes daily joining the child while he or she plays. Parents show interest but do not attempt to direct or correct the child. If the child engages the parent in competitive play, parents are to let the child establish the rules and allow the child to win. Parents also go along with the child if he or she breaks the rules. This begins reestablishing a parent–child bond while allowing for increased positive interactions and validation. It also blocks and reverses the parents' responses to firmer triggers for the toxic vicious cycles.

A Biological/Developmental Frame and Rationale

Greene's (2014) biological/developmental method creates a new interest in the child by using information gleaned from the child's psychological tests to show that the noncompliant behavior is a function of difficulty with thinking clearly through frustration. In effect, Greene reframed willful noncompliance as a set of skills that the child is unable to perform. This is a central therapeutic rationale. Consequently, the focus of therapy for parents becomes helping their children learn new tasks rather than punishing them for defiant noncompliance. With this new frame for their child's problem, they become supportive rather than combative as they assist their child to learn new things. As in Barkley's (1997) behavioral frame, Greene's biological/developmental frame helps parents make sense of doing the opposite of their former disruptive style and de-escalates the core vicious cycles in the process.

Shifting Contexts and Setting Treatment Rationales

Clients often come for therapy when they are in a state of demoralization. However, with the disruptive disorders comes a twist: The parents of the child are usually in a demoralized state, but the child has little or no insight into the problem. For this reason, family-oriented approaches have evolved with therapists developing a partnership with parents around changing the child's behavior. This is a relatively new development in the field and runs counter to the tradition of attempting to treat the child in individual therapy. Referring to their multisystemic therapy (MST) approach, Henggeler, Schoenwald, Borduin, Rowland, and Cunningham (2009) wrote,

> Mental health services for children have traditionally placed parents on the periphery of treatment or viewed caregivers as the problem, not the solution. MST involves a shift from child-centered services to the family as the client. This shift is extremely difficult for many clinicians. (p. 8)

The shift to family-centered therapy is not isolated to MST but exists in all of the family-oriented approaches. In effect, the shift of reference from child to family represents a second-order change in the child therapy field from individual to group context.

Thus, in family-centered approaches to parent–child problems, the parents or caregivers are treated as the primary client. Given this, family-oriented therapists use validation as a tool for relationship building with parents first. To validate parents, the therapist makes a distinction between parental intent and actions. The child or adolescent is viewed as posing special challenges for parenting. Being unaware of the hidden complexities, parents engage in parenting practices that may seem to be reasonable but do not work. From this perspective, parents have good intentions. They are unfortunately operating on false premises that guide their parenting practices. In other words, therapists validate or justify the parents' dilemma on the basis that they are doing as well as they can, given their current understanding of the child's behavior. Again, as in all treatments, clients must first feel understood and affirmed by their therapists to take the step out of their solution-generated problem level into the metalevel of a therapeutic alliance. This is the first critical step in the process of initiating second-order change. (It is a step from the level of group to the metalevel of class in the language of groups and logical types discussed earlier in Chapter 3.) Although both approaches normalize and contextualize parental frustrations and prior solutions, they do so in different ways.

A Behavioral Rationale

In Barkley's (2014) PT, providing a problem frame and its related treatment rationale that validates parents is the primary focus of the first treatment session. The PT approach takes blame off parents by showing how complex the causes of misbehavior are. This starts with temperament contributions, physical characteristics of the child, and developmental abilities that can complicate problem-solving, as well as the child's ability to comprehend and follow commands. The objective is to show that the child's misbehavior is not entirely the parent's or child's fault. In many ways, this is similar to Greene's (2014) frames and rationales. Returning, however, to a behavioral frame and rationale, therapists next show how children misbehave to gain positive consequences or rewards or to escape from currently ongoing unpleasant, boring, or effortful activities. Therapists use the behavioral concept of intermittent reinforcement to show how children become noncompliant by avoiding unpleasant things when their noncompliant behavior works even some of the time. Therapists explain how stressful events may also cause parents to become inconsistent in their commands, supervision, and use of consequences with the child. Furthermore, sometimes characteristics of the parent or child are such that they will naturally prove irritating to the other. The objective of the treatment is to *change the fit* between parent and child where possible to lessen the behavioral problems of the child. Once again, setting a compelling behavioral frame and related rationale for treatment that the parents "buy" or can understand is the next key to successful therapy. It helps "makes sense" of the reversals to come.

A Biological Rationale

In contrast, Greene's (2014) CPS approach emphasizes the *child's characteristics*, rather than pure learning histories as the cause of current difficulties. This rationale places special emphasis on emotion regulation, frustration tolerance, adaptation, and problem-solving skills. A major objective is thus helping adults who interact with the child develop a clear understanding of her unique difficulties, including specific factors that fuel her inflexibility or explosiveness. Furthermore, it is important that the parents accept this frame and understanding before initiating interventions with the child's problem behaviors. This validates parents. Greene takes blame away by focusing on the child's problems, described as neurologically based. Furthermore, helping their child will require a special kind of care. The child will need a "user-friendly" environment. Offering a rationale implying that "special care" is needed for a neurologically based problem also justifies or validates why parents may not have known the proper way to raise the child in the first place. This also helps the parents reverse their formerly harsh and demanding patterns to soft and supportive approaches formerly unthinkable. Just as with other problems reviewed in previous chapters, shifting to a metalevel and adopting new frames for problems enables clients to reverse their solution patterns and begin what would have been paradoxical solutions from their former views.

Establishing and Validating Parent–Child Relationships

Following the process of validating parents, family-oriented clinicians then seek to initiate a process in which the parents validate the child. Barkley (2014) stated that the value of parental attention is quite low at the beginning of therapy. This makes efforts to motivate the child toward improved behavior useless in many cases. Therefore, PT designs early sessions to assist parents to increase attending to and appreciating the child's behavior. Barkley has stated that consequences, positive or negative, will not have much effect on the child until the parent–child relationship has been restored. This behavioral rationale is also a key step in softening the formerly hard, polarized positions of parents, similar to the softening of partners in their vicious cycles discussed in the last chapter on couple problems.

The work of Greene (2014) has a similar pattern. Treatment starts with the previously described no-fault framing and rationale used to validate the parents. Embedded in this frame is a no-fault frame for the child as well. The child is not responsible for his or her temperamental difficulties because these are inborn. He or she is not responsible for physical characteristics that make her prone to defiant behavior, nor is he responsible for developmental disabilities that may also contribute to the problem. Therefore, if the child's behavior is to improve, he will need a "user-friendly environment." In other words, the child's misbehavior is understandable given the context of his or her impairments. This rationale blocks formerly demanding and withholding patterns, initiating collaborative and affirming interactions in their place. Although the problem frames of these two effective approaches are different, they both reframe the child's problem from stubborn defiance to merely a product of their interactional or biological context. In this way, the parents are helped to make sense of taking an opposite and softer stance as they interact with their child. Once more, this is a key influence of treatment rationale because it helps parents reverse their solution patterns to the formerly paradoxical positions of taking a "one-down" rather than a "one-up" position with their "defiant" child. With less to defy, the child will find it challenging to escalate battles in the old ways.

Establishing Goals (Narrowing the Field of Change)

As previously noted, the core issue around the treatment of children with disruptive behaviors is that parents try too hard to obtain compliance from the child. Parents lose perspective as they attempt to coerce compliance on a wide range of issues ranging from trivial to major. They may treat all issues with the same intensity. For example, parents may assign the same importance to picking up toys as playing with knives.

Effective parent–child treatments counter these problems through the process of goal setting. Each framework has a method for placing parents in charge of developing a plan that establishes specific parenting priorities. Each also assists parents with ignoring issues that are of lesser importance. Parents shift from *reactive* to *proactive* parenting because they are now preplanning which behaviors they will seek to change and which behaviors they will let go. Notice that these shifts occur before any direct efforts to change the child's noncompliant behavior.

Solution-Reversing Rationales

Three Baskets

Greene (Greene, 2001, 2014; Greene, Ablon, Goring, Fazio, et al., 2004) has developed a method for assisting parents with establishing priorities that was initially referred to as a "basket framework," although its name and metaphor may be changed. Using the basket metaphor, parents are to imagine three baskets in a row, Basket A, Basket B, and Basket C. The baskets are then used to assist the parent in establishing priorities and goals for the child. These goals and priorities will also have powerful influence on reducing the number and frequency of escalating vicious cycles, while encouraging collaboration.

Basket A represents situations in which the parent needs to maintain authority. These situations involve safety, such as harm to self, others, animals, and property. A three-point litmus test helps determine whether a behavior should go into Basket A. First, the issue must be important enough to endure a meltdown. Second, the child must be capable of successfully exhibiting the behavior on a consistent basis. Third, the parent must be able to enforce his or her wishes.

Basket B involves a list of behaviors that are important but not worthy of a meltdown. Basket B is considered the most important basket because here is where the parent is going to do the work of teaching the child flexibility and frustration tolerance skills. This is the field of change. The work here is presented as shifting contingencies between the parents and child to achieve a win–win resolution. These represent compromises where both the parent and child "win" by negotiating and following agreed-on plans of reinforcement for compliance.

Basket C contains goals and behaviors that were once a high priority but will now be downgraded. This basket is considered the largest basket or the basket that overflows. When children engage in Basket C behaviors, parents are instructed not even to mention the behavior. A wide range of behaviors fall into this category, including decisions the child might make to go out in the cold without gloves or poor selections on what food to eat. Not responding to these behaviors and instead allowing natural consequences to take their course is a key second-order change for parents. Using this rationale, parents are coached not to respond to triggers that would formerly set off a new round of escalating battles.

Token Economies

Barkley (1997) described a different approach for assisting parents with establishing parenting priorities for the child. It is done sequentially. Here parents are given assistance establishing a token economy. Establishing a token economy requires that parents list specific desired social behaviors and place a value on each behavior. Colored tokens are used to symbolize the relative values of the desired behaviors. Here again we see a similar pattern to de-escalate the range of issues for attention. In addition, parents shift focus to the presence of positive behaviors for attention instead of giving negative attention for their absence. Parents are taught to change the environment so that there are fewer objects that the disruptive child can damage, engage the child in nondirective play, catch the child doing something good so that this can be validated, give simple commands once, redirect the child or ignore her when she does not follow commands, and engage the child in complementary activities. This process downplays noncompliance while celebrating and rewarding compliance. Once more, this reverses the former escalating battles.

Following the Process

Parent–child problems are widely viewed as the result of vicious cycles where parents try to force compliance with their demands and children and adolescents resist. Second-order interventions reverse the change sequence for parents by offering rationales for why the escalating battles happen, then having parents de-escalate their demands by connecting with and validating their children first before gradually shaping collaboration. The golden thread of second-order change finds its path through both of the approaches reviewed. Establishing a validating relationship for whatever rationale, coaching parents to refuse to fight except in extreme instances, and focusing on compliance rather than noncompliance de-escalates the vicious cycles and allows a new, more positive relationship to begin. Again, the inseparable foundation of first- and second-order change is at the center of another set of impressively effective treatments.

MULTISYSTEM PROBLEMS WITH AT-RISK YOUTH AND FAMILIES

Recall from Chapter 4 on process and systems, the concepts of *attractors* and *fractals* in dynamic self-organizing systems like human relationships.[1] The Celtic image on this book's cover represents this with its repeated and interlocking spirals. This may be viewed as the multiple family members involved in each case seen, the multiple systems involved with each family, or the multiple effective approaches to similar problems, or all of the above. Within the context of any given culture, there are premises, norms, and rules for what

[1]Portions of this section are from Fraser, Grove, Lee, Greene, and Solovey (2014).

constitutes problems and how to resolve them. At the start of this chapter, CD was defined as youth behavior in which the overriding feature is a persistent pattern of behavior that violates the rights of others and age-appropriate social norms. Isolated acts that are severe enough (e.g., physical aggression, destruction of property, stealing, fire-setting) warrant concern and attention in their own right and usually draw multiple community systems into play. Such systems usually include schools, police, courts, drug treatment agencies, and child protective service agencies, to name but a few. In such cases, from the process view of dynamic systems, all parties and groups are drawn into similar response patterns shaped by context. Recall from Chapter 4 that these similar patterns are referred to as *attractors*. Within that context, the youth and family's behaviors *attract* similar response patterns from all involved. They *repeat* themselves in similar patterns at different levels of scale and systems around the youth and their family. Recall once more from Chapter 4 that these repeated patterns are termed *fractals*. What this means for youth and families at the more extreme level of CD is that the classic vicious cycles of solution-generated problems tend to be reflected and repeated in the response patterns of those larger systems drawn into the case. With CDs, we are dealing with multiple involved systems. Thus, rather than addressing one vicious cycle pattern as in parent–child problems, we are dealing with patterns of similar cycles within cycles linked with similar cycles.

Fortunately, there are several well-established evidence-based approaches to working effectively with these high-risk youth and their families. These include such models as brief strategic family treatment (Szapocznik, Muir, Duff, Schwartz, & Brown, 2015), MST (Henggeler et al., 2009), multidimensional family treatment (Liddle, 2015), and functional family treatment (Sexton & Alexander, 2015). These approaches represent integrative models, meaning that numerous pure-form family treatment approaches and strategies are woven into each format. Each model is, in fact, a product of integrating numerous pure-form family treatment approaches and strategies into each respective format. Each of these approaches is also the result of admirable and sustained work by a number of dedicated clinical research teams. These approaches have shown such impressive results with youth involved in juvenile courts, with substance abuse, and with CD and other general mental health difficulties that they have come to be designated as evidence-based approaches.

That these approaches are considered evidence-based is both good and bad news for agencies wanting to use best practices. The good news is that there are several approaches available. The bad news is that they are all generally equally effective with the same kinds of client problems and populations. Thus, how does one choose among them? Additional good news is that most of these approaches have become "franchised" in that agencies may purchase treatment and training packages and consultation to implement each of these approaches. The bad news here is that these costs may be expensive for agencies and require a somewhat demanding adherence to an array of parameters, which agencies may or may not be able to easily support. In addition to initial and ongoing training time and expense, there is the common demand for strict fidelity to the treatment model, usually provided by practitioners with advanced degrees in one of the mental health professions, along with regular linkages for consultation and data collection and reporting. (Recalling our earlier discussion of so-called specific factors vs. common factors in Chapter 2, these approaches are specific factor approaches.) Although there are excellent arguments in support of each of these requirements, they frequently pose hurdles for agencies in adopting or sustaining the implementation of these established approaches to treating at-risk youth and families.

Aside from these very real practical dilemmas, a broader question remains as to what common elements, if any, these evidence-based approaches share that support their effectiveness. If these factors could be in some way synthesized, might there be an integrated approach that could be equally effective and offer greater flexibility and cost-effectiveness in adaptation? This question is in no way meant to diminish the outstanding work behind each of these current evidence-based approaches. The point is to see whether each approach needs to be adopted fully in the way it was developed in the "lab" of its clinical trials or whether a synthesis of common factors shared among these approaches might be equally effective.

DEVELOPING A METAMODEL

With all of these questions in mind and with great concern for the growing population of distressed youths and families in the state, a large Midwestern state in the United States set out to determine which evidence-supported approach to use for these problems. Yet rather than literally buying into one or another of the preceding evidence-supported, specific-factor approaches, the state looked into developing its own approach. This was quite an undertaking. However, if a "home-grown" approach could be developed and tested that was teachable; adaptable to multiple types of problems; adaptable to varying strengths, skills, and perspectives of therapists and agencies; and independently sustainable by those providers, then the state considered the investment in research and development a good one. Their effort would also be unique in that it involved creating a flexible treatment manual rather than a manual demanding rigid adherence or fidelity. This presented the paradox of devising a manual requiring flexibility and fit to all parties rather than rigid adherence to one set of premises, guidelines, procedures, and target population.

After discussion with a clinical practice and applied research team, the state initiated a multiyear research and development contract with that group. Because the team held the very process-of-change view we are tracking in this book, they took on the contract with enthusiasm as an opportunity to develop and test a working model of the process perspective with challenging, multiproblem and multiagency involved at-risk youth and families in community settings. The result of this work was an approach they called Integrative Family and Systems Treatment (I-FAST), a metamodel based on identified factors that established approaches to family treatment have in common. The result was a published treatment manual to teach and support such a new, flexible, integrative approach and test its effectiveness (Fraser, Grove, Lee, Greene, & Solovey, 2014).[2]

These shared common elements put forward in the manual included the levels of theoretical/philosophical constructs, evidence-based common factors, and specific practice techniques. At the level of evidence-based common factors, it drew on the work of Jerome Frank on the common factors in psychotherapy and healing (Frank & Frank, 1991) and the meta-analyses of psychotherapy conducted by Bruce Wampold (Wampold, 2001; Wampold & Imel, 2015a). The approach identifies the following treatment components as central to positive treatment outcomes in families: (a) Creating a therapeutic alliance with families that will facilitate the collaborative development of a common understanding of the problem, behaviorally specific treatment goals, and activities to achieve these goals with the family. (b) Working collaboratively with the family members to change vicious cycle patterns, resulting in solving presenting problems and achieving treatment goals, by using rationales and procedures consistent with the family's frame or view of the problem. (c) Developing and maintaining collaborative teamwork with community agencies by honoring their views, fitting problem frames and treatment rationales to their agency culture and thus reversing their vicious cycle patterns and addressing the needs of the family and the child (systems pattern shifts and collaboration). (d) On the basis of theory and evidence-based common factors, I-FAST provides metaframes on practice techniques at different phases in the treatment process. The theoretical elements include using process systems theory, social constructionism, and a strength-based perspective. Thus, the key common factors include building therapeutic working alliances, creating interactional vicious cycle pattern shifts in families, and initiating vicious cycle pattern shifts in the involved larger systems. The key practice phases and procedures include phases focusing on engaging, tracking

[2]At the risk of appearing self-serving, this manual and approach are reviewed in some detail here. The approach represents the application and effectiveness research of the process of change paradigm that is at the heart of this volume. Biased, as it will be, with me as author of this volume, and the first author of the I-FAST manual, it still deserves attention as a real-world application of the ideas of this book.

interaction patterns or solutions, goal development and consensus, fitting problem frames and rationales to the family and all involved systems, initiating and amplifying changes, and building resilience and stepping down.

The major assumptions of the I-FAST approach are as follows: (a) Engaging with and validating the positions of all involved parties and systems is the crucial first step to successful treatment. (b) Fitting problem frames and related treatment rationales to families and larger systems is critical to success. (c) The target of change is interdicting and reversing vicious cycles and initiating and supporting virtuous cycles in all involved systems. (d) Respect for all involved parties' strengths and perspectives is an integral factor. (e) Engaging parents as partners in a working alliance is essential to outcome. (f) Creating multisystemic working alliances with all involved larger systems (e.g., schools, courts) are also integral elements. (g) The approach must also be flexible and adaptable to fit the involved practitioners as well as their agencies. (h) The approach must be sustainable by the practitioners and agencies without ongoing supervision/consultation from outside trainers. The result is a flexible, adaptable, empowering, strength-based, and sustainable approach. As in all evidence-supported approaches to these "conduct disordered" at-risk families, in-home and agency outreach visits are core components of the approach.

The I-FAST approach directly fits the process views discussed in Part I of this volume. Therefore, it deserves close attention. It acknowledges that the family and multiple agencies will be drawn into the self-organizing system of the problem. It attends to the cultural and subcultural contexts represented by each system and seeks fitting frames and treatment rationales for each. It uses the same flexible approach for all levels of systems involved. The youth's and family's problems become attractors for similar variations on the same response or solution patterns not only for the family but also for all larger systems drawn into addressing the problems. (Recall the concepts of attractors and repeating fractal patterns in open, dynamic, self-organizing systems from Chapter 4 on process and systems.) The goal of intervention in such systems is linking with and redirecting the problem-generating solution patterns of those multiple systems. The essence of intervention in I-FAST is the interruption of vicious cycles or identification and amplification of exceptions to these cycles in all involved systems.

The question remains as to whether such a metamodel can be taught to front-line practitioners in the field and found effective. The preliminary answer is yes. The first caveat is that all studies conducted thus far have been done by the developers of the model and are strongly susceptible to confirmation bias. More studies by neutral parties are clearly needed. However, the I-FAST model has been developed, taught, implemented, and researched in a preliminary pilot study. Although the details of the study are available elsewhere (Lee et al., 2009), the results have been promising. The pilot used a one-group pretest–posttest design with a 6-month follow-up to explore the effectiveness of I-FAST in treating families with children at risk of out-of-home placement and receiving home-based treatment. Seventy-seven families with children who had *DSM* diagnoses and received services from two large community mental health centers participated. Multiple reporting sources were used, including parents, child clients aged 12 years or older, and I-FAST case managers. The outcomes indicated that I-FAST treatment led to significantly improved functioning, reduced problem severity in the child, reduction in out-of-home placement of the child, improved family functioning, increased parental competency in addressing the child's problems, and increased family participation in the treatment process.

An additional positive larger systems qualitative result of this several-year training and study pilot was that when the multiple agencies within the counties involved were offered additional state and federal funds to apply to any project they wished, they uniformly applied those funds to adding additional I-FAST therapists. Furthermore, the positive multisystem collaboration element of the I-FAST approach was confirmed in a follow-up study using focus groups with 26 agencies across 11 counties and confirmed key process, ingredients, and components of successful systems collaboration predicted by the model (Lee et al., 2012). A related study found that I-FAST systems collaboration with schools positively influenced parental competence with children, which positively predicted level of functioning in children and negatively predicted problem severity in children (Lee, Teater, et al., 2013). Regarding comparability of results with that of other evidence-supported approaches, another study compared 79 families who received I-FAST with 47 who received MST (Lee, Greene, et al., 2013). Using a nonrandomized noninferiority trial design, I-FAST was noninferior to MST in reducing problem severity and improving functioning based on youths', parents', and workers' assessments. Therefore, this process-based common-factors I-FAST approach has shown promise of comparable effectiveness to at least one of the already confirmed evidence-supported approaches noted earlier.

In the years since the end of the pilot, numerous other agencies have been trained in the model in both rural and urban settings, in small and medium-sized cities, and in one of the nation's largest metropolitan areas. Regarding sustainability, some of these groups are now functioning on their own with trained internal supervisors who maintain the general structure of the model while being empowered in the process of adapting it to their own agency, therapist, and client needs.

A study of the model comparing efficacy and sustainability of the approach in agencies with and without ongoing consultation after training (Lee et al., 2016) found no significant difference between the two groups of clients who had achieved reliable change on problem severity and functioning based on parents' assessments. In this study, the independent agency with 136 children and adolescents and their families received I-FAST services (68% males and 32% females). Again, multiple reporting sources were used, including parents, child clients aged 12 years and older, and I-FAST case managers. The results found significant decreases in children's level of problem severity from pretreatment to posttreatment and significant increases in children's level of functioning from pretreatment to posttreatment; in addition, approximately 60% of the clients achieved clinically significant and reliable changes or some improvement in their level of problem severity and level of functioning from pretreatment to termination. Thus, the goal of sustainability without external consultants appears promising.

As we have seen in the vicious cycles of parent–child problems, so now have we seen a model similar to the process view do the same with more severe problems in a multisystemic context. In all instances, the key elements are engendering trust in the related systems to join in an alliance with therapists. From this metalevel, or second-order, position, they may see the problem-generated solution patterns and adopt a fitting frame and related rationale to make sense of adopting new and often opposite patterns. Then, with the support and structure of the therapy alliance, new patterns, or "re-solutions" can evolve and be supported. As in previous chapters, we can bring this process to life by revisiting the case we introduced at the beginning of this chapter.

THE PROCESS OF CHANGE WITH JOEY

Recall Joey, his mother, and her live-in partner from the beginning of the chapter. They were involved not only in multiple escalating cycles among themselves but also with the multiple systems that came into play around Joey's problems. For the sake of organization, we will track the interventions in this case using the phases of the I-FAST model used by a consultant and team. Recall from earlier in the chapter that these phases include engaging with all parties and systems, tracking solution patterns of all involved, collaborating with all parties on goals, framing the problem and treatment rationale for all involved, initiating and supporting pattern change, and, finally, building resilience and terminating. Let's follow each stage in turn with Joey.

Engaging

The key members of Joey's family system were Joey, his mother, and her partner, Roger. Remember, however, that the agency staff had been involved with Joey, as had the schools. Because staff members had initiated the consultation, they were the first group to be engaged. Next, because Joey's mother had also made the request for help, she was seen on her own, then she and Roger, then Joey, and finally the school. All involved parties needed to be heard and to have their positions and frustrations validated.

Tracking Solution Patterns

A list of related problem patterns might be as follows: (a) The more staff pushes Joey, the more he rebels. (b) The more practitioners push Mom to set limits, the more she objects. (c) The more Joey shows frustration and anger, the more others escalate their concern. (d) The more Joey pushes for independence, the more restrictive Mom and others become. (e) The more practitioners and the school invalidate Joey's situation and exclude him, the more dramatic he gets. (f) The more others try to calm Joey down, the more he escalates. (g) The more Joey gets his way by escalating, the more he escalates.

Goal Consensus With All Parties

Agreed-on goals with all parties were as follows: (a) Agree with the staff that Joey needs to settle down in the waiting room and Mom needs to begin to comply with treatment. (b) Agree with staff on having Mom and Roger set limits. (c) Agree with Mom and Roger that Joey needs to do his jobs, homework, and show responsibility and respect. (d) Agree with Mom and Roger that they will form a team to set limits and reward. (e) Agree that if Joey complies, they will offer freedoms, and they will give him chances to show them responsibility. (f) Agree with Joey that he needs freedoms. (g) Agree with Joey to show compliance with rules to gain respect and freedom. (h) Agree with schools to let Joey back in class if he complies with school rules.

Framing and Treatment Rationales

With Staff

The consultant described the familiar escalating cycle Joey played out in the waiting area when he came in to the center. As with all others, when they tried to calm him down, and in some ways deny the reasons Joey had for not wanting to be there, Joey increasingly pushed back. He needed their support for his life situation. The next visit, they were to commend Joey on how good he was at getting his points across. They were to describe his waiting-room protests as "show time," and commiserate with him for needing to be there rather than doing whatever else he might want. They would love to see the day he didn't need to come and had more freedom and trust from everyone.

With Mom and Roger

The consultant agreed that Joey was "out of hand" and needed to be reined in. He agreed with Mom that Joey was still likely reeling from being confronted with his father's corpse after his suicide. He might even fear the loss of his mother from her severe heart problems and thus want to stay near her. Yet the consultant worried that if Mom started setting more limits, Joey would clearly act up more, and that might trigger her heart attack as she had told all others. She had to weigh this risk carefully. Roger had stayed on the sidelines of parenting, but Mom now wanted his help. Roger was a strong yet gentle guy who loved hunting, fishing, and worked rehabilitating apartment complexes. Maybe it was time for Roger and Joey to spend some more positive time together. Joey might appreciate a new male role model.

With the School

After commiserating with the school and validating their concerns over Joey's disruptive in-school behavior, the staff practitioner shared more on Joey's father's suicide and the tragedy that Joey had to cut down his father's dead body. The first cause of his behavior might be rage over that trauma. The other element might be some learning delays that made school hard for Joey. Compassion and educational support would likely help with both challenges. The practitioner was also willing to collaborate on a plan.

With Joey

The consultant began a session with Joey on his own (but accompanied by this therapists) by saying he heard Joey was good at putting on a show in the waiting room, and the consultant was surprised he hadn't heard any shouting out there that day. He commiserated with Joey over needing so many people in his life, and he was amazed at how restrictive his Mom and others were with him. "What did they think he was going to do, blow something up, or rob a store or something?" He shared sadness over Joey's dad's suicide, yet he agreed with Joey that he needed to go on, gain more freedom, trust, and grow up. He just needed a chance to prove himself. Warned that his mom and Roger were thinking of setting more limits, the consultant agreed with Joey that this was the time to bargain with them for more freedom to show what he could do.

Initiating Change

The Staff

After supporting Joey's reasons for being upset, and complimenting him on his waiting-room bravado, his therapist used the priming words "It's Show Time" to describe his bravado. The next time she greeted Joey in the waiting room, she said, "Hi, Joey. . . . Is it 'Show Time' today?" In response, Joey didn't act out. (If he had, however, he and the practitioner would have been in some ways not in conflict but on the same "Show Time" team.) Instead, he smirked and came back cooperatively from then on. The following sessions were spent sorting through Joey's father's death and supporting his plans to move forward and show his trustworthiness in trade for more freedom.

With Mom and Roger

Mom pushed back hard against our cautions about a potential heart attack, saying she simply had to set limits with Joey. She invited Roger into the session and asked for his help with Joey as a team together. They were cautioned that Joey would escalate his tantrums as they set firmer limits. When he did react, they were to take this as a sign that they had his attention, yet they needed to offer him a chance to gain more of what he wanted. They agreed to let him out more, set longer curfews, and see if they could "catch him doing good things." Roger agreed to take Joey fishing and hunting just to give them some good quality time to bond. He also suggested he might include Joey in his job a bit.

With the School

The school agreed to do some educational testing with Joey and link him with the school guidance counselor if he returned to school. They were grateful to learn more about his father's suicide and the circumstances of Joey's discovery of his body. They speculated that he might qualify for a special services class to help with his learning delays as they were found. The practitioner reached out to the high school's football coach, mentioning Joey's size and strength, and wondered whether Joey might try out for the team if he returned to school.

With Joey

Joey agreed to take any opportunity he could to get his mom's and Roger's attention by doing chores unprompted and adding extra things he might think of to see if they would notice. He also agreed to strike bargains to go out more on his own and then surprise them by coming in before his curfew. Learning of the prospect of trying out for the football team, Joey showed interest in returning to school with more support in a smaller, contained classroom.

Supporting Change and Building Resilience

The results of this work were gratifying for all, yet not without some bumps. Joey started doing more home chores and, to his surprise, got praise from both Mom and Roger. He gained more freedoms, and his folks were impressed by how he stayed out of trouble even when other friends did get into trouble.

Joey loved his time with Roger, hunting and fishing, but he said, "You don't mess around with Roger—when he asks you to do something, he means it." Joey enjoyed bashing down walls at construction sites with Roger, yet he learned that everyone needed to clean up afterward—including him. Joey also spent time discussing his dad's death with the in-home therapist, who was also kind of a "man's man."

Joey returned to a special class at school and made the freshman football team. He obeyed school rules forbidding tattoos by wearing a glove over a tattoo on his hand. However, after having difficulty reading aloud in front of others in class, he spitefully removed his glove, thus showing the tattoo and risking expulsion. To prevent Joey from being expelled, the therapist collaborated with the school to keep him in school by having him work for a week with individual help before returning to the class.

Joey's mom did go into the hospital that year to have a pacemaker implanted in her heart. She was concerned about what Joey would do without her supervision. When she got a call from him in the hospital, she feared the worst. To her amazement, he had done a wash, and he was calling her to find out how to set the dryer! She was proud of his turnaround, and so was Joey, as well as others.

All were warned that "life is a roller-coaster" and adolescence in itself always presents challenges. The staff, family, and schools were asked to "practice fire drills" by picking challenging triggers to confront to see what they could learn and how things would go. Two years later, Joey remained in school. He had a girlfriend and more tattoos. He was seen walking with her in town, dressed in black, with a long black coat, and his eyeteeth sharpened to look like fangs. Yet he continued to work with Roger, and overall, he was doing okay.

CYCLING BACK

Cases like Joey's are multiproblem and multisystem challenges. Yet viewed from a process-of-change perspective, they offer the chance to honor all parties' views, and feelings and collaborate on frames and rationales to make sense of the problem and imply new directions to reverse escalating cycles. Parent–child problems represent the same patterns escalated and repeated with more involved community systems as children and youth behaviors become more severe. The essence of effective parent–child and family interventions across all approaches is similar. They invite all parties into a trusting, validating working alliance with therapists at a metalevel from which to reflect on their current and former sensible solutions and consider their reasonable yet problematic results. From this metalevel platform, each party and system is better able to accept an alternative frame that makes sense of the problem and a rationale for doing what would have before seemed counterintuitive. As with all problems, there are "many paths to the top of the mountain." There are many strong, evidence-supported treatment approaches. The general premises and frames of each approach may differ, yet the processes of pattern reversals are the same, just as they were with depression, anxiety, posttraumatic stress, and couples therapy, reviewed in previous chapters. They all reflect the process view of problems and their resolution.

III

FROM PROCESS TO PRACTICE

11

THE PROCESS OF CHANGE IN CLINICAL CONTEXT

It may seem counterintuitive to offer a new clinical model that merely unifies other effective models. Might such an enterprise be no more than what we have termed a *first-order change*—might it be just one more "best practice"? Translating the process-of-change view into clinical practice needs to fit the rationales and related procedures of the growing array of effective psychotherapies. This process should entail a unifying perspective on how each of them approaches the same overriding processes leading to problem resolution. It should honor the growing evidence that effective treatments must fit with both clinicians and clients and support the powerful connections among positive relationships, working alliances, and effective treatment. It should allow for the enhancing effects of therapists' allegiance to a therapeutic perspective. It should acknowledge the hope-enhancing effects of working within a coherent perspective, invested in by all participants and directly related to agreed-on goals.

http://dx.doi.org/10.1037/0000078-012
Unifying Effective Psychotherapies: Tracing the Process of Change, by J. S. Fraser

Matching all of these and other requirements in a practical, teachable clinical metamodel is a big task. If the metamodel is too narrow and prescriptive, it runs the risk of being too rigid. If it is too broad, it runs the risk that it will not be useful to guide clinical practice. With these questions and cautions in mind, this chapter looks into one version from the process-of-change perspective. It may prove to be just another approach striving to translate this certain "something" into clinical practice. It might be too narrow to include all of what is emerging as linked with effective treatment. Maybe it will be too large a perspective, including everything yet guiding little. The jury is still out—and you, the reader, sit on this jury.

THE PROCESS OF CHANGE

As we have found, the literature includes many calls for paradigm shifts in understanding human social interaction along with laudable, ongoing efforts to achieve such a shift. Each of the approaches fit many of the trends in the psychotherapy literature, yet continued to fall short. Social constructionism addressed the relativity of realities while just beginning to embrace the process perspective on flow and change. The dynamic systems view embraced open systems and first- and second-order change, yet had not broadened its view to all psychotherapies. A moderate common factors approach affirmed social constructionist views, the central role of treatment rationales in delivering common factors, and the importance of pattern shift, yet limited its focus to couples and family therapy instead of broadening its scope to all psychotherapies. Others pursued a unified protocol for mood disorders with great effect, yet limited the protocol to mood disorders instead of extending it to a wider range of problems. Still another approach advocates principles of therapeutic change, along with flexibility and fit, yet lacks grounding in an underlying view of human social interaction, patterns of persistence, and the nature of change. Above all, they all lack a consistent paradigm from which they emerge. The process-of-change perspective is a potential solution that confirms the array of converging approaches while extending the model to embrace the core element of change in all psychotherapies.

However, how might such a general model translate into a broad set of steps for therapists to take as they negotiate psychotherapy from a process-of-change view? We might consider diagraming the general flow of practice from a process perspective. For now, let us consider the diagram in Figure 11.1. To apply the process model to a particular context, the acronym PROCESS offers a set of phases a practitioner might follow, as illustrated in the cyclical progression of Figure 11.1.

These phases may still appear rather static and cryptic. Therefore, I look at each phase with the literature reviewed in past chapters to add more detail to each step. I then turn to a more detailed review of the case done for the APA Psychotherapy Video Series (discussed briefly in a footnote to Chapter 6 of this volume). Between these two discussions, this PROCESS model may come to life in clinical practice. Although the case analysis is just

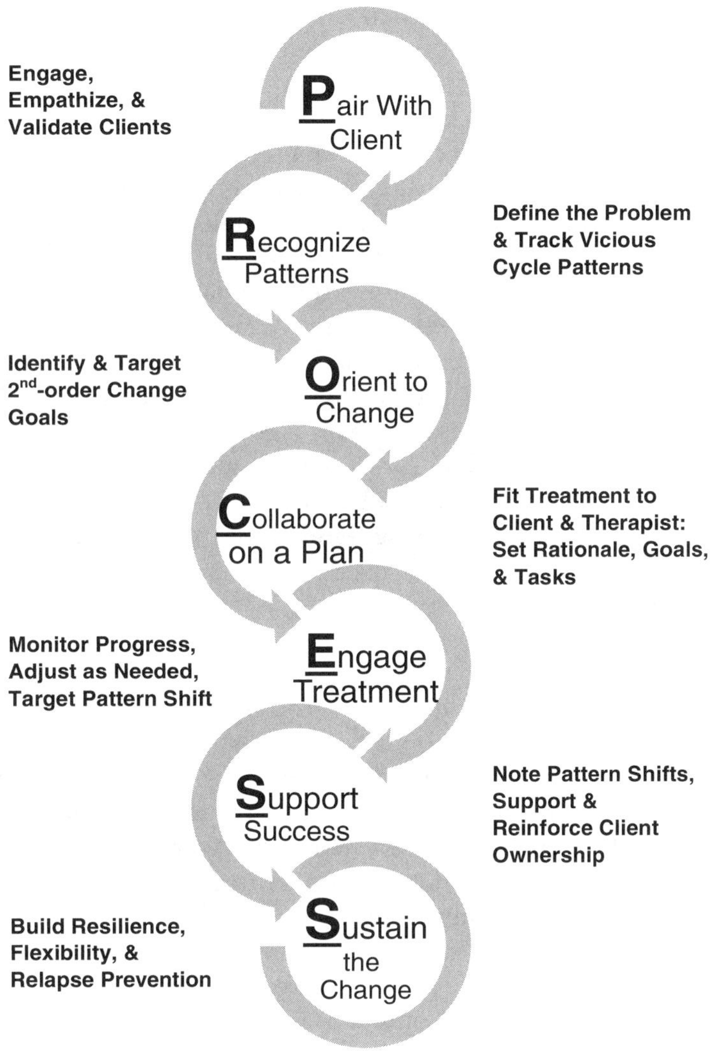

Figure 11.1. The PROCESS phases of effective therapy.

one example, it may offer a chance for some generalization to others. I turn first to providing more detail on each phase of the PROCESS model.

FOLLOWING THE PROCESS MODEL IN CLINICAL PRACTICE

Pair With the Client

The literature is abundantly clear that common factors are highly correlated with success in psychotherapy. Elements such as empathy, positive regard and affirmation, congruence and genuineness, goal consensus, and collaboration are crucial for practitioners to attend to—especially in the beginning of treatment but also to monitor throughout the therapeutic relationship. To reiterate, in the process view, these elements help clients to build enough trust in their therapist to take the step out of the level of their problem and into the metalevel of a therapeutic alliance. (Recall the theory of logical types, requiring a step up to a metalevel for true problem pattern change.) Personal stories, linked frames, and metaphors often help form these bonds and humanize the therapist, while validating clients' distress. Turning to the Venn diagram of the therapeutic contract in Figure 5.1, this is represented as the intersection of client and therapist spheres. Here we are looking for a close match or fit. It is up to the therapist to attend to how his or her own identity characteristics, such as age, gender, and race, are perceived and reacted to by the client. This is a dance of responsivity. The closer the therapist can attend to clients' values, language, metaphors used, and position on the problem, mirroring and using these in their dialogue, the better the fit.

Recognize Patterns

The process view looks for repetitive patterns in clients' lives. These include both positive and problematic patterns. It is just as important to learn about clients' strengths and build on them as it is to attend to the repetitive vicious cycle patterns around their identified problems. Here clinicians need to attend to the general problem patterns of the identified problem within the dominant culture and noted in the literature on that problem, as we have seen in the chapters on anxiety, depression, posttraumatic stress disorder (PTSD), couples therapy, and family problems in Part II of this volume. The typical vicious cycles of solution-generated problems noted generally in depression, for example, offer a starting point to learn the pattern of the problem for this client. This represents the Context Variable sphere from the Venn diagram. However, it is equally important for clinicians to learn how their clients' unique identity variables and personal history contribute to their problem patterns. It may be that clients' unique variables match closely with those found in the dominant culture, thus altering the general pattern little.

However, the client's personal history, culture or subculture, faith, able-body characteristics, and the like may exert such influence on their ways of identifying the problem and reacting to it that their problem patterns become unique. This represents the overlap between client and context spheres. The point in this phase is to ask clients to define their problem, ask what they have done about it, find out what they usually do about it, ask how that has typically worked, and learn what others (including other therapists) have tried to do or suggested that they do about it. As noted in the points about self-similarity and the concept of fractal patterns, it is good for therapists to ask for at least three examples of the pattern across different times, contexts, and levels of interaction. For practitioners, identifying the vicious cycle pattern is the ultimate target.

If clients have been to other therapists, it is best to learn what those therapists have done within what therapeutic rationales, how that worked, and how it was received. If interventions have not worked in the past, therapists are well advised to revisit them cautiously, if at all, even if the interventions are compelling. Therapists need to avoid initiating another vicious cycle repeated from the past. Here it is also important to gain some view of clients' position on their problem and their openness to influence from others. The stage-of-change literature comes in handy here. If clients do not really feel they have a problem or think that it is others who feel they have a problem, for example, it will be folly for the therapist to act as if they do. Cautioning clients against change or aligning with them that maybe they really don't have the problem others think they do is a second-order change for therapists and requires a rationale for therapists to help them understand the intervention and remain authentic. The stage-of-change and motivational interviewing literature offers just such a rationale. Noting and aligning with clients' position on change and their openness to intervention is another pattern that is crucial to building a useful alliance with clients.

Orient to Change

As noted in Figure 11.1 of the PROCESS flow, this phase has the therapist attending to and targeting the second-order changes and vicious cycle reversals needed in the client's problem cycles. Again, to know what is "a difference that makes a difference," the therapist needs to determine what has been the same over and again, or the pattern of the vicious cycle. As noted in the last phase, that pattern may resemble that found in the literature of the dominant culture, such as the mastery-by-avoidance variations of anxiety or PTSD diagnoses, for example. Yet these patterns may take on slight to major variations, given the unique characteristics of the clients' involved. The overlaps in the Venn diagram of the therapy contract between the client and the context sphere, as well as that overlap between the therapist and context spheres, represent the views of the client, and those of the therapist, respectively, on such vicious cycle patterns and what may need to be done to interdict them. Although the client is unlikely to have any perspective on this pattern, the therapist will. The therapist's theoretical position on problems and the rationale for resolution come in here as well. This is the point when therapists need to align with what will make sense to the client to fit problem explanations and therapy rationales to the client. This leads to the next phase of collaboration and building a therapeutic alliance.

Collaborate on a Plan

The collaboration phase is another way to refer to the therapeutic alliance. Some have blurred the distinction between therapeutic alliance and therapeutic relationship, and surely an alliance is built on a positive relationship. However, the alliance is one way of noting what has been achieved by building a strong relationship. The work of therapy is done through this alliance—this collaboration. Finding the best fit between client and therapist on an understandable, sensible, and workable frame and rationale for treatment is crucial to building a strong alliance. Frames and rationales may include theoretical explanations, research-based explanations, developmental explanations, frames fitting spiritual or cultural traditions, and many more. Of course, the closer the frame fits the client's worldviews, values, and beliefs, the better. Matching frames to some patterns or solutions already present in the client's repertoire and matching their values is often most helpful. From the process view, this is the linchpin between the common factors of relationship and the procedures of treatment. These frames and rationales will initiate and sustain problem pattern reversals as treatment moves forward. As noted in the process view, these second-order changes are most often counterintuitive or paradoxical to clients when viewed from the level of their initial struggles with the problem.

Thus, strong buy-in to an understandable explanation or frame for their problem and collaborating on a sensible, related therapy rationale are keys to the next phase of treatment: engaging the procedures, supporting pattern shifts as they begin, and sustaining those changes over the long run. The alliance must help clients make sense of solutions not considered or thought counterintuitive from their former ideas about and solutions to their problem. Frames, metaphors, and personal stories are often helpful, especially when the intervention will be particularly counterintuitive, such as mindfulness or other interventions in which clients must "fix a problem by not trying to fix it." In the working diagram of the therapy contract in Figure 11.1, this represents the intersection of the three spheres of context, therapist, and client in a collaborative therapeutic alliance. This forms the nexus of the therapy to follow. It sets the stage and sustains the frame for all further treatment.

Engage Treatment

Saying that treatments start at a set stage is not exactly true. In fact, treatment may begin even before the first session. Clients may have gotten a recommendation to a given practitioner based on his or her reputation for success, creating an expectancy halo of hope; based on their particular theoretical position, which may match clients' point of view; and so on. In many ways, the same can be said about the other preceding phases: Matching, fit, and treatment often start before a client meets the therapist.

Similarly, therapists' theoretical perspective shapes the type of questions they ask, what they attend to, follow up on, and even whom they may include in sessions. Assessment and intervention are essentially inseparable. They influence and shape the course of interaction and information in an evolving cocreated "truth" about the client's problem as well as about the therapist. The dance of intervention, so to speak, begins immediately. Therapist interests through the early part of any session may focus on history, interpersonal relationships, thoughts and beliefs, pure behavior sequences, social networks, the way the client reacts in the moment to the therapist, or combinations of all of these and more. So how is it that we designate a particular point to engage treatment?

As noted in the previous step of collaboration, the idea of building an alliance with a client or clients entails building a framework for treatment. As that alliance builds, so does the fit between client and therapist. Effective therapists make numerous midcourse adjustments in their questioning, their language, and interpersonal positions, eventually matching with clients, offering empathy and validation for their distress, and inviting them into a treatment alliance. As this evolves, so do the frames offered to explain the problem, along with the related treatment rationales that will guide future sessions, treatment interventions, and tasks. The subsequent "interventions" and "procedures" (as so-called specific factors) must make sense to both clients and therapists within the treatment alliance's frames and rationales as those interventions or new solutions often seem counterintuitive from the client's original perspectives on their problem.

Subsequent treatment techniques and procedures may include in-session enactments, two-chair dialogues, Socratic questioning, modeling, rehearsals, in-session bonding and affirmations, interpretations, homework assignments, and a range of other specific treatment techniques. Of course, many of these interventions will blend in any treatment. For example, succeeding sessions might include a series of prolonged exposure treatments for PTSD or eye-movement desensitization and reprocessing sessions for the same problem. They might include empty chair or other emotional enactments of emotion-focused therapy, or the Socratic questioning and planned experiments of cognitive behavioral therapy for depression. Most often, therapists will assimilate them into a given theoretical position on problems and their resolution. From the process view, what matters is that the interventions succeed in interdicting and reversing the problem-generating solutions of the client's presenting problems. As noted earlier, those vicious cycles may match the literature in the dominant culture, (e.g., classic mastery-by-avoidance or approach–withdrawal patterns), or they may be more idiographic patterns shaped by clients' unique histories and other identities. What matters is that the interventions create new "kick points" or shifts to initiate desired virtuous cycle patterns. In the Venn diagram of the process oriented treatment contract (Figure 11.1), all of this comes out of the nexus of the intersecting spheres of context, client, and therapist in their collaborative working alliance.

Support Success

All therapists note and support positive pattern shifts, as well as client ownership of those changes as clients engage in the process of change through treatment. Early and continued research has affirmed that even in considerably less directive forms of person-centered treatments, evidence of clients' authenticity, emotional engagement, and resilience is consistently and subtly reinforced by therapists' attention, questioning, and support. From a process view, the goal is to support an evolving virtuous cycle consistent with agreed-on goals. Client ownership of these changes is important across treatments. In many ways, most treatments contextualize problems as reasonable reactions to the course of historical and current stressors and events. This may take the form of dynamic, interpersonal, behavioral, cognitive, emotional, or other frames and explanations, depending on the treatment frames and rationales. However, they consistently affirm the client's distress as a product of context. Most treatments cast problem patterns, while distressing and understandably negative, as transient and situational. The movement is from clients viewing their problems as *personal*, *negative*, and *pervasive*, to owning their strengths, resilience, and successes in the face of such adversity as *personal*, *positive*, and *pervasive*. Shared affirmations and celebrations of successes are common and important, but so is a "pleasant surprise" and questions such as, "How were you able to do that?" in response to clients' successes as they overcome present and former challenges. As such support is offered, therapists reaffirm its significance within the problem frame and treatment rationales of their work together. All of this occurs within the ongoing collaborations and goal agreements of the working alliance. From the process view, clients have stepped out of their problem struggles to a metalevel relationship with their therapist. (Recall here the theory of logical types, in which group members must step up to a metalevel and out of the level of their current assumptions and solutions to be able to reflect on and re-solve their solution-generated problems.) The new frames, rationales, and treatment interventions help make sense of formerly counterintuitive solutions that interdict vicious cycles. Therapists support and amplify the new virtuous cycle through the treatment alliance. This sets the stage for sustaining those changes.

Sustain the Change

All evidence-supported treatments include some final phase in which they build resilience and engage in relapse prevention. All treatments acknowledge the potential for future life challenges and potential relapse into the original problem cycles. From the process view, there will always be triggers to former patterns. Prior patterns are likely embedded in numerous cultural and contextual definitions of problems, assumptions about norms and needed change, and the recommended remedies for straying outside those expectations. Family and social network histories and pressures to conform or feel shame and/or guilt over stepping outside old roles or expectations will likely offer ever-present signals to return to past assumptions and patterns. These represent the contextual and client spheres of the original diagram in Figure 11.1. Again, the goals of all treatments are to sustain changes once they occur and continue the virtuous cycles.

Most treatment interventions here resemble the notion of predicting and prescribing. Clinicians usually warn clients of the hurdles ahead. They discuss future challenges and even rehearse responses in sessions. Under the idea that "forewarned is forearmed," clients and therapists collaborate as they predict future obstacles. Anticipating that "life is a roller-coaster," they defuse from the idea that any future distress or challenges will spell a return to their old problems. Those points will always happen, requiring clients once again to engage the new assumptions, frames, and tools learned in treatment.

Turning to the idea of prescribing, the usual approach before ending treatment is, once clients have developed a new, sustained patterned resolution, to have them actively confront old situations, thoughts, and emotions. This presents a paradox in itself, particularly for clients who have formerly been in the mastery-by-avoidance cycle. It is a second-order change that reinforces their new patterns while achieving several more things. First, if clients find themselves relapsing into old patterns, they learn something they can discuss and address in later sessions. Second, deliberately trying to reengage in old responses, formerly viewed as coming on spontaneously, offers another paradox. It is directly contradictory to have a panic attack in a controlled and deliberate manner, for example. When a client forces herself to stay in bed and ruminate, it becomes more of a challenge to stay there and not get up. It just isn't the same as the old pattern. It is hard to "relapse spontaneously"! Most clients will find, to their satisfaction, that it is harder to return to those old patterns even if they try. This builds resilience and helps sustain the new virtuous cycles. In addition, for most contemporary treatments, therapists cast themselves in the same light as family practitioners. Clients never consider that they will not return to a trusted family doctor after recovering from a recent illness. This goes as well for psychotherapists. Most therapists now welcome clients back for booster sessions, a practice actively supported by the literature.

Although much more may be said about each of the phases of the PROCESS model of treatment, the general structure offers a well-supported and flexible format for integrating psychotherapies that work from a process point of view. Turning to a case example may bring this process more to life.

THE CASE OF SARAH

The following case, which was first introduced in Chapter 8, offers a nice example of the phases of a process view in a single session, with a given client, in a dominant Western cultural context, conducted by me as a unique practitioner. It will show the integration of a number of techniques and approaches found effective for this client's problems. Yet, these phases and those interventions will be adapted to fit this unique client, filtered through my own unique style and expertise in treatment. As Lao Tzu would have it, this approach will follow a *middle path*, integrating a generic process and generally effective techniques for this client's problems, with this client's *unique identities* and history interfacing with my own. This demonstration case will thus offer an example of practice from a process view, yet effective practice by other clinicians with other clients should look different than this, if it is done well. After recounting the specifics of this client's case, we will follow the session through the PROCESS phases discussed above applied to this single session.

Background Information

Sarah came to therapy "looking for more tools to defeat her anxiety and depression." She was a 40-year-old African American woman, living in a large southeastern city in the United States. It seemed that the basic problem was her anxiety, particularly her panic attacks. After these panic attacks and losing her temper with her children, the depression would set in, and it became hard to get out of bed. However, she had to get up. Sarah was a single parent of three children. She worked as a nurse's assistant in a hospital and was taking college courses to finish her degree. Sarah had previously been in therapy for a few years and gained some skills from a trusted therapist, yet some things, such as relaxation exercises and guided imagery, just didn't fit for her. She didn't like the idea of medication and wanted to look into more "holistic psychological" options. One strength, however, was her newly renewed Christian faith.[1]

Pairing With Sarah

As mentioned earlier, the session with Sarah began before we met. First, Sarah had a problem she wanted to address. She was likely in an action phase of a stage-of-change perspective and thus likely to be open and willing to engage in treatment. Second, she was aware that she would be seeing some acknowledged "expert," offering a positive expectation of success even before treatment began. Turning to client and therapist variables, however, there was not an immediate match based on demographics. Sarah was an African American woman with a high school education, enrolled in college while working full time, living as a single parent of three in economically distressed conditions. As her therapist, I am an older, White, married man with children, with a doctoral degree, having been a university professor, and coming from an economically and culturally privileged position within the dominant culture. These differences need attention as the session proceeds.

Sarah and I met briefly before the session and spent about 10 minutes chatting. After asking what brought her to come in for this demonstration session, Sarah replied that she didn't have much money, and the money she would receive for this session would pay for a nice gift for her son's birthday that day. Responding to my comment of how she had managed with three kids, a job, and college courses, she shared that she had a deep faith she had recently renewed.

Moving into the session, my aim in the first phase of the session was to engage with Sarah and learn her goals for the session. Because goal consensus

[1]This case is available in video format through the APA Psychotherapy Video Series. The DVD of a consultation session with the author, along with discussion of the case and key video clip examples, titled *The Process of Change in Integrative Psychotherapy*, may be helpful to the interested reader. This case is presented with permission from the APA Psychotherapy Video Series.

and collaboration are strongly associated with positive change in effective treatments, it was important to note and address Sarah's goals as best as I could in this session. After a brief introduction, the session moved to this as follows:

Therapist: Thanks for coming in, um, I know a little bit about your situation. We met briefly, um . . . I'll also say that our time is going to be short today, it's going to go even faster than we imagine. So, one of the things I would want to know from you is, what is it that you, if we're successful today, what is it that you hope to get?

Sarah: Well, I hope to gain more knowledge on how to deal with the depression, and when I feel like a panic attack or something is coming upon me, some ways to cope with it . . . deal with it . . . maybe talk about some different . . . if I had to take medication . . . some natural approaches, rather than taking the pills.

Therapist: Okay. Great. So if we could come up with some . . . um . . . some ideas on how you could handle being depressed, and . . . ah . . . wrestling with panic attacks coming on for you . . . um . . . If we could get a little perspective on pills . . . an alternative to that . . . that would be great.

Sarah: Okay.

Therapist: Okay. Got it.

After learning these goals, I turned quickly to a thumbnail sketch of Sarah's life situation as a single parent to see if I could gain some trust by recalling her situation, then beginning to joke a bit on our shared situation as parents. This was an attempt to bond, contextualize, and normalize the challenges and joys of being a parent. (Brief client or therapist comments are placed in brackets for ease of interpretation and flow.)

Therapist: So, another thing that I know is that, um, you're a single parent . . . [Correct] . . . you have three kids . . . [Yes] . . . We were just chatting about that before we started . . . so let me see if I remember . . . one 13 [Um hum] . . . one 11 . . . [Yes] . . . and, the most special one [laughs] . . . is gonna be 5 today . . . [Yes] . . . Congratulations on the 5-year-old, and as I said before, I'm sorry about the 13-year-old. [Both chuckle] [Thank you] They are all going to get to be teenagers sooner or later . . . [Right] . . . I said that I am proud of both of my kids . . . and, uh . . . There was a time . . . I tell this story over and again . . . I think my son does too, where he wasn't going to get on the bus . . . he bolted out the back door, and I tackled him in the backyard . . . [Both laugh together] . . . and the neighbors are saying, "There's that psychologist next door. I guess we're okay." [Both laugh together again]. So kids can be a handful, but they can also be a joy . . . [Right] . . . Okay.

This sequence flowed well, and the bonding as parents seemed to move things forward. I then proceeded to confirm that she was employed as a nurse's aide, as well as going to college to get her degree. We agreed, "That's a bundle!" I then turned toward learning more about her past counseling and learned the last session was about a year ago, and that counseling lasted for about 3 years. Wanting to know more about what others had advised her to do, I asked,

Therapist: What did you do in that kind of counseling?

Sarah: She would give me, like breathing techniques, um, just talking was therapeutic . . . [Was it? Just sharing.] . . . Yes. She would just give me different ideas. She actually helped me, 'cause I was looking for new jobs, she helped me with the search for that . . . [Really!] . . . Yes.

Therapist: So, very practical stuff . . . [Yes] . . . and you were pretty anxious . . . [Right] . . . and, how did that go?

Sarah: Not well at all. I even suffer from migraines too . . . [Oh?] . . . Yeah.

Therapist: So you are still pretty anxious . . . [Um hum] . . . and you suffer from migraines [Yes] . . . Ah, what do you understand about the migraines?

Sarah: It's brought on by stress. When I'm really stressed out, they come . . . [They come, and then just have to be in a dark room and all that.] . . . Right.

Therapist: So things got better with that counseling . . . [Yes] . . . and there were some pretty practical things, some breathing techniques [Yes] . . . even shifting jobs [Right] . . . getting things off your chest . . . [Right]

Sarah: She had me have a journal as well . . . [Ah, you journaled, and how was that?] . . . I loved it . . . [Still do that?] . . . Still do . . . [And is it still helpful?] . . . Yes . . . [Great. And yet, you still feel pretty stressed.] . . . Yes, because the situation has improved but at times it is still overwhelming. And so, I just wanted another approach from another professional just to see what they could do with the panic attacks when they come on, or the anxiety and with the depression.

I had gotten some sense of what has helped Sarah in counseling. She trusted her therapist; she gained some good ideas and breathing techniques and some effective advocacy in finding a new job. She also gained perspective by journaling. Not all clients can do this. The fact that she had complied with journaling boded well for her willingness to comply with other ideas and suggestions in therapy. Nevertheless, she still felt the same stress, anxiety, and depression, and wanted more tools to defeat them. I then wanted to know more about what she meant by anxiety and how she connected it with being depressed. All of this started to overlap with the next phase of recognizing and tracking patterns.

Recognizing Patterns

This marks a transition to tracking and recognizing what Sarah defined as her problem and the patterns of what she did about it. Some of these patterns were likely to be generic patterns around anxiety and depression, and some might be unique and personal. It was important to learn what she knew about her problems, what she had done, what she had been told to do, and what had worked and not worked. If there was a way to begin to offer some explanations for her symptoms, this was a place to try some of those on to see if they made sense. In addition, it was important to see how Sarah linked her anxiety with depression, which co-occur in a great number of clients. Did one lead to another, and if so, how?

Therapist: So how do you think the anxiety and depression are related? Are they?

Sarah: Yes, they are definitely related . . . [How so?] . . . Stress!

Therapist: So you get so stressed [Yes] then you just get down [yes] and low [yes], and what's that like when you're that low?

Sarah: Not good at all . . . [What's it look like?] . . . I'm just probably laying around, I isolate myself [So you isolate] . . . um hum . . . not get up . . . [Not get up . . . Appetite?] . . . It depends . . . because I stress eat, overeat . . . [yeah]

Therapist: And so, stressing out seems to lead to that . . . feeling low. [Yes] . . . Now, your last therapist taught you some breathing techniques [Um hum] . . . do you use them?

Sarah: Um, yes, um, a little bit. Like when I get really stressed . . . like, wait, like sometimes I get numb, and so I just have to tell myself to calm down . . . you're okay, and I just breath . . . [And how do you understand getting numb?] . . . I just know when I get stressed, it's always on my right side [A little tingling too?] . . . Yes, tingling sensations as well . . . [Your therapist tell you what that was about?] . . . My doctor did . . . [And what did they say?] . . . that it was stress . . . I thought I was having a stroke one time . . . [Yeah, Yeah, right] . . .

Therapist: So it sounds like, when you're that stressed . . . [I like what you are doing, by the way.] When you are that stressed . . . people just do that . . . it's like you are holding yourself, holding your breath . . . and the more you are holding your breath, the more you are not getting any oxygen out into these [gestures with his hands] . . . and you really are getting numb . . . so when you start breathing, it gets the oxygen back in there [Um hum] and your hands are saying, I'm alive again. [Both chuckle] [Right]. So did you ever do some relaxation types of things with her?

Sarah: Um, not with her. With someone else I seen before her, uh, he had a CD he gave me, but I didn't like that [didn't like it, so it just didn't work?] . . . No.

Therapist: Yeah. There are different paths for different people, it's real clear. Sometimes those types of things work [Um hum]. So what else have you been doing lately to kind of "master this"?

Sarah: Just the same things that she had taught me. That's what I said, I wanted to see a different approach that's different from the same things that we had went over in prior sessions. [Did she explain at all where the anxiety comes from?] . . . Yeah, we definitely talked about it, and we had came up with the situation, as far as dealing with the kids by myself, and work, and school [Yea, makes good sense to you, but you still got all of that.] . . . Right.

Therapist: And so, when you are in the midst of all of that and it starts overwhelming you, can you tell me what do you notice about yourself? One of them is like, I'm probably holding my breath, so breath. [Um hum]

Sarah: Well, another thing I used to notice is that I would get real angry . . . unapproachable like . . . it was like a rage . . . I noted that a lot . . . I definitely still deal with that, and that's why I'm trying to cope with that. [Got it!]

Therapist: So, it just builds [Right], and it's like "If, Mama ain't happy, ain't nobody gonna be happy!" [Right . . . Exactly]

Orienting Toward Change

At this point, it was becoming clear that Sarah was moving through two related patterns in the literature on anxiety and depression. She was cycling through the mastery-by-avoidance patterns of anxiety, attending to the cues of anxiety and holding back, and finally either having a panic attack or exploding in anger. Similarly, with depression, she was becoming so overwhelmed and discouraged with her situation that she would enter the "downward spiral" of depression, including becoming listless, not getting up, and withdrawing from others. It was also clear that some things, such as breathing, had helped somewhat, but others that are often found useful, such as relaxation exercises, didn't fit for her. It was also becoming clear that Sarah was so locked into a determined battle to get over these problems that she felt that she just needed one more tool to "defeat" her anxiety and depression—a vicious cycle in itself.

Orienting toward change in this case meant looking toward the second-order pattern reversals that needed to happen in Sarah's solution-generated problems. The first step seemed to have already happened in that Sarah appeared to have begun bonding and joining with me at a metalevel outside her problem. She was tracking well with my comments, and our dialogue was flowing, with easy and affirming interchanges. I had already affirmed with her what has worked to some degree, such as breathing. I had also stated that not everything fits for everyone, like relaxation CDs. She had to find things that fit for her.

Clearly, the second-order changes for her panic and anxiety needed to be exposure in some way. Similarly, for her depression, she needed to reverse her inertia and withdrawal and continue taking action on her bills and related tasks. However, Sarah's overriding solution patterns seemed to be over-engaging with active solutions to defeat her problems. Her initial request, for example, was to learn new techniques to defeat her problems. In this case, the pattern reversal was for Sarah to fight with her anxiety and depression by not fighting with them. The major intervention was likely to involve some form of acceptance. In some ways, this combined the pattern reversals of moving toward, or exposing herself to the anxiety- and depression-inducing triggers while resisting the temptation to react to them with anxious or depressive ruminations. Clearly, both second-order shifts were likely to appear counterintuitive or paradoxical to her. They wouldn't make sense without clear frames, rationales, examples, stories, and metaphors to make these changes make sense. This marks the move to the next phase of Collaborating.

Collaborating on a Plan

As mentioned earlier, pairing, bonding, and building a working alliance (key elements of what are called *common factors*) form the linchpin that connects common and the specific factors of pattern reversing techniques together. Sarah needed a set of explanations, frames, and rationales to help her make sense of the pattern reversals she would need to make. Furthermore, I needed to be mindful of Sarah's initial goals and begin to address them. In addition to gaining new tools to defeat her anxiety and depression, she wanted to know more about medications and ways to solve her situation without them.

This was a phase when I could bring in information on the nature of anxiety and panic from the literature, but the more down to earth my explanations were, the better. It was a time to offer stories and metaphors to help make sense of the second-order reversals ahead. Certainly, theoretical explanations and rationales come in here, whether cognitive, behavioral, interpersonal, or emotional. The most effective rationales would be those that fit best for Sarah (and several might) and also for me, her therapist. Finally, the alliance needed to take into consideration Sarah's strengths and her values. She was a good mother and a hard worker. She was open and engaged in trying to overcome her problem. She was in the action phase of a stage-of-change perspective and therefore likely to be open to new information and suggestions. She also had a deep faith she could build on, which is similar to some of the acceptance-based mindfulness she might need to learn and employ. The following segments of dialogue from the session represent this phase of frames, explanations, and metaphors. They all lead to a plan of action that we agreed to try in the session itself. The first step was to address her goal of learning about medication versus therapy to address her problem.

Therapist: So nobody has said whether medication or therapy is better for anxiety or depression? [No] Okay, so let me tell you about that. What we know about medication, with depression particularly, in most psychotherapy research for approaches, and there are several different ones . . . those psychotherapies are just as effective as medication . . . and in some sense, more so, because they are longer lasting because they empower you. It's not the chemical that's doing it, it's you, and you have learned some new things [Um hum], and you're going in new ways. So in partial answer to that—and sometimes, by the way on the anxiety thing—some anxiety medications, as you saw, can get in your way [Um hum]. And, um, they may not be as good to take if you are doing some therapy or counseling to learn to master it. Okay? [All right] Because sometimes, um, there are some of those medications that also can be habit-forming. I don't know if anybody ever told you that. [I have family members that had got hooked to those drugs] Yeah, I'll bet, I'll bet. And, um, once you do . . . [It's hard to get off] . . . It's hard to get off. Yeah. You haven't experienced that? [Um um] And so, maybe that's another reason you wouldn't quite want to go that way. [Right] Well, good for you.

Another thing I wanted to let Sarah know, particularly given that she was looking for new tools, is that anxiety and depression are problems for which psychotherapy is very successful. This was a direct effort to continue to instill hope. I also wanted to let her know that there are a number of effective ways to proceed, and the best path is the one that makes the most sense to her. Furthermore, I wanted to reinforce the positive relationship she had with her former therapist and encourage her to reconnect. I would only be with her for this hour, whereas that therapist could sustain their relationship.

Therapist: A couple of other things are that . . . being anxious and depressed are things we are good at . . . we're good at helping people get over. Um, there's, a lot of paths towards it, though. And, as you say, it's got to fit right for you [Hum] . . . medication doesn't quite feel right for you [No], and, um, you know, those relaxation tapes, they didn't, they just, it wasn't you [No . . . No]. Now, they are to some folks and not for you. And that's another thing we've come to know, come to understand, is that, um . . . those of us who are therapists, we got to be flexible, and, um, make sure things fit well for you as somebody who's seeking help. [Right]. And, you got to make sure that there's a fit . . . and that you trust the people that you're working with . . . and that you have faith in how they have explained your situation and where you are going to go with it. Um, sounds like you felt pretty good with that . . . she was a woman right? [Yes] . . . You spent about 3 years, and it really felt good. [Client nods yes] Good for you. I'm glad you found her. Is she still around? [Yeah] Would you go back? [Yeah] Aright . . . well . . . do so! [Okay]

Next, I wanted to offer something the literature is clear on with anxiety, and that is the vicious cycle of trying to keep a lid on anxiety escalates the very thing we wanted to control. Here I wanted to get into the idea of being anxious about being anxious. This was a frame or explanation from the literature about her problem that needed to make sense to her.

Therapist: As you say, you get into stressing, and um you just do, and . . . don't let me put words in your mouth . . . but it seems that the more you're in it, the more you just try to keep a lid on it [Yes, nodding] and keep a lid on it again, and like I'm fighting this down, and by God, that's my route, and I'm not giving it up! [Right]. Until, man you're angry, and man you blow [I blow!]. Or else, it's just like, oh man, I don't want to get anxious [Um hum, nodding] and the more you get there, it's like "I'm anxious about being anxious!" [Client nods and laughs out loud] Right? And that's pretty much of a vicious cycle, and the more you're on it, it's like . . . oh God, there goes the breathing . . . [Yes] . . . and then oh man here goes the tingling fingers. [Um hum, nodding] . . . And, uh, "Welcome to the club" . . . but that's just one you don't want to belong to! [Client laughs and agrees] But, you now, it's a natural thing for folks who are in your situation, and you're still going to be . . . those kids are going to hit their teens . . . you got one now and there are two more coming. [Right] So, enjoy the 5-year-old now!

Having gained agreement of that frame for her anxiety, I wanted to link it with her depression.

Therapist: And it sounds to me like, when you get that anxious, it's almost like you get sad about it, cause it's like . . . here I am again. [Right] . . . "Can't win for losing." [Right, nodding] . . . Again, don't let me put words in your mouth. [No, no. That's correct.] . . . Okay . . . I'm talking a lot right now, is this okay? [No, your fine . . . nodding. I'm listening.]

So once Sarah had agreed to the frames, or explanations of her anxiety and depression cycles, it was time to turn to a rationale for doing something about them. However, this new tool would likely not make sense to Sarah. She wanted to fight these feelings, not give in to them. Therefore, there would need to be multiple metaphors and related stories laid out for her to get with this new path. I inoculated her by saying that this likely won't make sense (because most second-order shifts don't make sense at first).

Therapist: So there's another way to fight with this. And, in some ways I don't know if I can get this across to you because it's, it's . . . different. Some folks hear it and say, well, that isn't right. I don't get it. It just doesn't make sense. So I'll try to help it make sense to you.

Now, I turned to one of her strengths and values as the first step to making sense of this new path: We build on her faith.

Therapist: You know you said, in some ways, just as we first met, you said that you had a faith [Client nods] and that helps [Yes] and there's certain points, I'm sure for you that you just say, "I've got to give it up." [Yes, nodding] Got to give it up to God. [Yes, yes] And as you do . . . how is that for you?

Sarah: Therapeutic, um, that's why I've come a long, long way [Good, nodding] by, you know, getting more into God. [How long ago is that . . .] I've always been saved, but it isn't where you just go to church, but you give your life over to God, and make changes [Yeah. When was that? Can you mark that? Do you know that?] Well, it's been the last couple of years. [Wow, and so you said, "I'm giving it over"] Yes. [And that's been a great help] Great help. [And I can just see it. I can just see it in you.] [Client smiles and laughs gently]

Therapist: And that's a little of what I'm talking about here. And it's something you got to practice. You got to practice it like, as you say, you can just go to church, or you can get saved. [Right] This is different. This is an experience for me. It's who I am. [Right]

This link with Sarah's faith resonated strongly with her, and it would form a fine path toward helping her learn and understand the mindfulness practice and exercise I was going toward. Yet, given the strong paradox of giving up her struggle and going toward her distress, I felt I still needed to offer a few more frames and rationales for her. The next was the cognitive triad translated into words she might understand for her depression. I felt it would be helpful to explain her depressive rumination.

Therapist: I think you are probably in the same situation that most everybody is . . . it's like . . . Oh man, here's this thing coming down on me again [Yes, nodding], it's like, that's awful, it's going to be awful, I'm awful, and I'm not going to go through it [client nodding] . . . and then I got to keep a lid on it [Um, client nodding], and it makes sense to battle it, you know, it makes sense to try to push it down [client nodding] . . . and yet . . . I'm fond of saying sometimes to people who are grieving the loss of something . . . it's like you got to remember to forget that, you know . . . you got your hands against the door and, you don't have any more efforts to live your life [Right] Even if you take one hand away, you're still, pushing on it. And so, you got to kind of let some of that go [Client nodding] . . . and what would that be like? I know that some of the words, the terms . . . I know your words would be, giving it up . . . I got to accept this . . . [Right] it's acceptance. Other people would say, I'm being mindful of this, and . . . there is a way you can get with that. [Client nodding, Okay]

Having set the stage, with the cycle and the metaphor, it was time to turn toward engaging in the treatment. This represented the time when our treatment alliance had been formed and she understood the frames and rationale for the treatment. However, I continued to offer more metaphors and stories to continue to confirm the frame and drive home its power. The treatment alliance continued to offer the frame for treatment throughout the techniques and procedures. This set the stage for engaging in treatment, even though, as noted earlier, treatment runs throughout all sessions, from beginning to end.

Engaging Treatment With Sarah

Therapist: Now, I know that you don't want to think about those things . . . the bills, or whether you can buy your 5-year-old a birthday present today [Right] . . . it will be a matter of having some times where you let some of those things come into you and yet . . . I'm happy that you have that kind of faith, the experience of that faith, because, as you do . . . do you feel a certain sense of peace? [Yes, nodding] It's bringing some of that peace to yourself. So you might want to do that, and, as you do . . . let some of that junk come up for you [client nods] . . . there are those bills . . . sometimes people do this with their eyes open, other times they will do it with their eyes closed . . . it's entirely up to you . . . and as you do, you let that kind of thought come [therapist moving his hand in front of him slowly across his front]. Like "those bills are due" . . . don't judge it . . . just say "There it is" . . . it's just like a cloud that's there in the sky. And it moves . . . and then let the other things go in . . . like "Yes, but, I don't have the money for them" . . . and as that comes up, let that go, let that be there, don't judge it don't embrace it necessarily, cause, that's just a thought, it's just an idea [client continually nodding] and let it go, let it go . . . and as you do, come back to that sense of, "I'm giving those things up" . . . and for you, maybe "I'm giving it up to you, Lord." [Client smiles and nods]

This segment gave instructions for mindfulness practice, and the client continued to track with these descriptions. I offered a few more metaphors, including the children's finger trap discussed in previous chapters, into which you need to push your fingers to get them out. Similarly, it would be counterintuitive to go toward anxiety and not fight it. I also talked about children fearing monsters in their closet and mentioned a children's book where the child scares the monster and then brings it to bed with him. We talked about this as a different kind of tool—it's a different way of battling. We then reviewed all the cycles of her depression, rage, and panic, and Sarah agreed by repeating them aloud to me. I probed her twice, asking whether this made sense, or if it was just another CD I was giving to her, or if she just wanted to make me look good on the recording. She said no, she would have told me if it didn't make sense. We then proceeded to try a mindfulness exercise. She agreed to try, and we moved through bringing the Lord into herself and gaining peace while imaging the bills and not having money for them pass through her. After that, I asked her to return to our dialogue.

Therapist: And, as you are ready then, come back here. Yeah [client nodding]. How was that for you?

Sarah: It was helpful. It was peace. Serenity. [Laughs] [It is, isn't it?] Yes. I just feel like a burden has lifted. [Yeah, yeah, yeah]

Therapist: Those bills will still need to be paid. There will be a way. And, at the same time that . . . do you feel it . . . you got the power. [Right, nodding] And you got the power by . . . you gave up the struggle. [Client nodding . . . Yes]

I decided to use one more metaphor at this point to further capture her process. This was one of my favorites from the first *Star Wars* series in which Luke Skywalker, battling his father, Darth Vader, puts away his weapon and refuses to fight. His father, moved, does the same and then tosses the Dark Lord over an abyss. Sarah resonated by saying, "And that dark lord was the devil." We then returned to the force of being drawn back into the cycle and needing to practice this new tool to resist.

Supporting Success

Therapist: You'll get drawn into it. It's only logical. People will say, you know, fight that! Put a lid on it. Pull my fingers out of that finger trap! [Client continuing to nod . . . Right] but you have to push them back . . . now, just like praying, going to church, that would be something you would need to do, and practice on a little more regular basis. [Yes] You seemed to be able to do it pretty well today. [Client laughs, and lights up with a big smile] . . . You got a good smile. [Thank you] . . . It came pretty easy, didn't it? [Yes] Were the thoughts there? Were they real? [Client nods . . . Yes] [Therapist, laughs, leans forward and shakes Sarah's hand and they both laugh] Congratulations. [Thank you] Way to go. [Thank you.] And, what we know is that works. There's a lot of things that work, and there are a lot of paths to the top of that mountain, you know [Um hum], breathing can work, muscle relaxing could have worked, but it has to fit for you, you know, it has to be right for you. [Right] The more you do this, you're not fused with those things any more, they are just thoughts, just things that used to spook you . . . and they can go . . . and as they do . . . there goes that anxiety. [Right] You're not anxious about being anxious anymore because you just stopped it before it started [client continuing to nod] . . . and you're not going to be sad afterword, because you've still got energy . . . you've got both of those hands to do what needs to be done [Client nods] now you are free to live it, engage in it. [Yes, client nodding, Yes] Cool! [Both laugh and shake hands again] How was this? [I loved it] Really, great. I did too. That seems to be right for you. [Client nods . . . Right] We should be giving you things to help you go live your life. You don't need to be in therapy to be in your life. I think you get it. I think that's a fit. [Client quietly nods . . . Yeah] Cool! [Both laugh again]

Sustaining Success and Closing

Wrapping up the session, it was important to check in with Sarah to find out how it was for her. Did she get what she wanted? Moreover, I wanted to review what we did and what she could do next.

Therapist: So, this was good. [Yes] What did you get?

Sarah: To just let it go . . . the bills, the kids getting on my nerves, whatever else life throws at me, I got to let it go . . . can't keep holding it down [client pushes her hands down] until you blow up

Therapist: Yeah, you can't battle it. It's a different way to battle it. It's like Luke Skywalker, you got to just put away that light saber. [Right] You got to push in on the finger trap. [Right]

Sarah: And also just talking to you. This was just wonderful. [She laughs] [Oh good! I'm so glad.] [Both laughing]

Therapist: Well, you are really good at sharing your life, and I'm always privileged to step into people's lives with them and see where we can go.

Sarah: And, also, seeing this is being recorded, then someone can see this and maybe it can help them if they are feeling like me. [Oh, that's it, that's it, that's it]

Therapist: If there is some way that this can help someone else, that will be so good. [Right] Great. Good job today. [Thank you] All right, I guess we're wrapped up!

After the recorded session, I had a brief time with Sarah to say goodbye and wish her well. At this time, I also reinforced the idea that she would need to practice the mindfulness exercise we did, like praying and attending church as she did regularly. I asked her if there was a significant word she might choose to use during her mindful sessions. She immediately said she would choose the word *peace*. I reinforced this and said that eventually the word *peace* would help her quickly recover her mindful, acceptance position when the kids acted up or bills were due (echoing the classical conditioning principle of association from the literature). She agreed. We agreed that life is a roller-coaster, and there would be more challenges, yet using these new skills would give her new energy to actively engage in living her life with both hands. Finally, she agreed to reconnect with her trusted therapist, and we parted.

CYCLING BACK

This session followed the PROCESS phases in Figure 11.1, integrating a range of effective treatment approaches to interdict and reverse this particular client's vicious cycles. Her problem patterns around her anxiety and depression fit the major descriptions from the literature, yet her dogged attempts to defeat her problems became the overriding target for change. The specific mindfulness intervention fit the literature on what works for anxious and depressive ruminations and offered a good fit for Sarah by linking them with her strong faith and practices. Problem resolution would entail reversing her attempts to master her anxiety and depression by avoidance and withdrawal. Instead, she would interdict these cycles before they began by going toward their triggers yet not attempting to judge or solve them. This offered a perfect fit for the second-order change of problem pattern reversal and resolution for her. However, true to the process view, there might have been a number of equally effective intervention variations within this same set of PROCESS phases, depending on the identity and expertise of the therapist and the fit with this client. For other clients, other problems, and other therapists in other contexts, the content, contract, and design of treatment will clearly be different. However, the process will be the same: pattern reversal in solution-generated vicious cycles. This all flows from following the process of change—a shift in paradigm that unifies psychotherapies that work.

REFERENCES

Addis, M. E., & Cardemil, E. V. (2006). Psychotherapy manuals can improve outcome. In J. Norcross, L. Beutler, & R. Levant (Eds.), *Evidence-based practices in mental health* (pp. 131–139). Washington, DC: American Psychological Association.

Addis, M. E., & Carpenter, K. M. (2000). The treatment rationale in cognitive behavioral therapy: Psychological mechanisms and clinical guidelines. *Cognitive and Behavioral Practice, 7*, 147–156. http://dx.doi.org/10.1016/S1077-7229(00)80025-5

American Psychiatric Association. (1980). *Diagnostic and statistical manual of mental disorders* (3rd ed.). Arlington, VA: Author.

American Psychiatric Association. (2013). *Diagnostic and statistical manual of mental disorders* (5th ed.). Arlington, VA: Author.

American Psychological Association. (2006). *APA Presidential Task Force on Evidence-Based Practice*. Washington, DC: Author.

American Psychological Association, Society of Clinical Psychology. (2016a). *Research-supported psychological treatments for depression*. Retrieved from http://www.div12.org/psychological-treatments/disorders/depression

American Psychological Association, Society of Clinical Psychology. (2016b). *Research-supported psychological treatments for PTSD*. Retrieved from http://www.div12.org/psychological-treatments/disorders/post-traumatic-stress-disorder

Azalea Health. (2017). *Behavioral health ICD–10 crosswalk—top 20 codes*. Retrieved from http://www.azaleahealth.com/wp-content/uploads/Psychiatry-ICD10-Crosswalk.pdf

Baldwin, S. A., & Imel, Z. (2013). Therapist effects: Findings and methods. *Bergin and Garfield's handbook of psychotherapy and behavior change* (6th ed., pp. 258–297). Hoboken, NJ: Wiley.

Barkley, R. A. (1997). *Defiant children: A clinician's manual for assessment and parent training* (2nd ed.). New York, NY: Guilford Press.

Barkley, R. A. (2014). *Attention-deficit hyperactivity disorder: A handbook for diagnosis and treatment*. New York, NY: Guilford Press.

Barlow, D. H. (2002). *Anxiety and its disorders: The nature and treatment of anxiety and panic* (2nd ed.). New York, NY: Guilford Press.

Barlow, D. H. (2014). *Clinical handbook of psychological disorders: A step-by-step treatment manual* (5th ed.). New York, NY: Guilford Press.

Barlow, D. H., Allen, L. B., & Choate, M. L. (2016). Toward a unified treatment for emotional disorders [Republished article]. *Behavior Therapy, 47*, 838–853.

Barlow, D. H., Conklin, L. R., & Bentley, K. H. (2015). Psychological treatments for panic disorders, phobias, and social and generalized anxiety disorders. In P. Nathan & J. M. Gorman (Eds.), *A guide to treatments that work* (4th ed., pp. 409–463). New York, NY: Oxford University Press.

Barlow, D. H., Farchione, T. J., Fairholme, C. P., Ellard, K. K., Boisseau, C. L., Allen, L. B., & Ehrenreich May, J. T. (2010). *Unified protocol for transdiagnostic treatment of emotional disorders: Therapist guide*. New York, NY: Oxford University Press. http://dx.doi.org/10.1093/med:psych/9780199772667.001.0001

Barlow, D. H., & Kennedy, K. A. (2016). New approaches to diagnosis and treatment in anxiety and related emotional disorders: A focus on temperament. *Canadian Psychology, 57*, 8–20. http://dx.doi.org/10.1037/cap0000039

Bateson, G. (1955). A theory of play and fantasy. *Psychiatric Research Reports, 2*(12), 39–51.

Bateson, G. (1972). *Steps to an ecology of mind: Collected essays in anthropology, psychiatry, evolution, and epistemology*. Chicago, IL: University of Chicago Press.

Bateson, G. (1979). *Mind and nature: A necessary unity*. New York, NY: Dutton.

Baucom, D. H., Hahlweg, K., & Kuschel, A. (2003). Are waiting-list control groups needed in future marital therapy outcome research? *Behavior Therapy, 34*, 179–188. http://dx.doi.org/10.1016/S0005-7894(03)80012-6

Beck, A. T., Rush, A. J., Shaw, B. F., & Emery, G. (1979). *Cognitive therapy of depression*. New York, NY: Guilford Press.

Benish, S. G., Imel, Z. E., & Wampold, B. E. (2008). The relative efficacy of bona fide psychotherapies for treating post-traumatic stress disorder: A meta-analysis of direct comparisons. *Clinical Psychology Review, 28*, 746–758.

Benish, S. G., Quintana, S., & Wampold, B. E. (2011). Culturally adapted psychotherapy and the legitimacy of myth: A direct-comparison meta-analysis. *Journal of Counseling Psychology, 58*, 279–289. http://dx.doi.org/10.1037/a0023626

Berger, P. L., & Luckmann, T. (1966). *The social construction of reality: A treatise on the sociology of knowledge*. New York, NY: Anchor Books.

Beutler, L. E., & Clarkin, J. F. (1990). *Systematic treatment selection*. New York, NY: Brunner/Mazel.

Beutler, L. E., & Clarkin, J. F. (2014). *Systematic treatment selection: Toward targeted therapeutic interventions*. New York, NY: Routledge.

Beutler, L. E., & Harwood, T. M. (2000). *Prescriptive psychotherapy: A practical guide to systematic treatment selection*. New York, NY: Oxford Press. http://dx.doi.org/10.1093/med:psych/9780195136692.001.0001

Beutler, L. E., Harwood, T. M., Kimpara, S., Verdirame, D., & Blau, K. (2011). Coping style. *Journal of Clinical Psychology, 67*, 176–183. http://dx.doi.org/10.1002/jclp.20752

Beutler, L. E., Harwood, T. M., Michelson, A., Song, X., & Holman, J. (2011a). Reactance/resistance level. In J. C. Norcross (Ed.), *Psychotherapy relationships that work: Evidence based responsiveness* (2nd ed., pp. 261–278). New York, NY: Oxford Press.

Beutler, L. E., Harwood, T. M., Michelson, A., Song, X., & Holman, J. (2011b). Resistance/reactance level. *Journal of Clinical Psychology, 67*, 133–142. http://dx.doi.org/10.1002/jclp.20753

Bohart, A., & Wade, A. G. (2013). The client in psychotherapy. In M. J. Lambert (Ed.), *Bergin and Garfield's handbook of psychotherapy and behavior change* (pp. 219–257). New York, NY: Wiley.

Borah, P. (2011). Conceptual issues in framing theory: A systematic examination of a decade's literature. *Journal of Communication, 61*, 246–263. http://dx.doi.org/10.1111/j.1460-2466.2011.01539.x

Borkovec, T. (1994). The nature, functions, and origins of worry. In G. C. L. Davey & F. Takkis (Eds.), *Worrying: Perspectives on theory, assessment, and treatment* (pp. 5–33). New York, NY: Wiley.

Bowlby, J. (1969). *Attachment and loss*. New York, NY: Random House.

Bowlby, J. (1977). The making and breaking of affectional bonds. II. Some principles of psychotherapy. The fiftieth Maudsley Lecture. *The British Journal of Psychiatry, 130*, 421–431. http://dx.doi.org/10.1192/bjp.130.5.421

Bradley, R., Greene, J., Russ, E., Dutra, L., & Westen, D. (2005). A multidimensional meta-analysis of psychotherapy for PTSD. *The American Journal of Psychiatry, 162*, 214–227. http://dx.doi.org/10.1176/appi.ajp.162.2.214

Branson, A., Shafran, R., & Myles, P. (2015). Investigating the relationship between competence and patient outcome with CBT. *Behaviour Research and Therapy*, 68, 19–26. http://dx.doi.org/10.1016/j.brat.2015.03.002

Brewin, C. R., Dalgleish, T., & Joseph, S. (1996). A dual representation theory of post-traumatic stress disorder. *Psychological Review, 103*, 670–686. http://dx.doi.org/10.1037/0033-295X.103.4.670

Briggs, J., & Peat, F. D. (1989). *Turbulent mirror: An illustrated guide to chaos theory and the science of wholeness*. New York, NY: HarperCollins.

Buckley, W. (1967). *Sociology and modern systems theory*. New York, NY: Prentice Hall.

Castonguay, L. G., & Beutler, L. E. (2006a). Common and unique principles of therapeutic change: What do we know and what do we need to know. In L. G. Castonguay & L. E. Beutler (Eds.), *Principles of therapeutic change that work* (pp. 353–369). New York, NY: Oxford Press.

Castonguay, L. G., & Beutler, L. E. (Eds.). (2006b). *Principles of therapeutic change that work*. New York, NY: Oxford Press.

Castonguay, L. G., & Hill, C. E. (Eds.). (2017). *How and why are some therapists better than others? Understanding therapist effects*. Washington, DC: American Psychological Association. http://dx.doi.org/10.1037/0000034-000

Chamberlain, P., & Patterson, G. R. (1995). Discipline and child compliance in parenting. In M. H. Bornstein (Ed.), *Applied and practical parenting* (4th ed., pp. 204–255). *Handbook of parenting* Mahwah, NJ: Erlbaum.

Chambless, D. L., Bryan, A. D., Aiken, L. S., Steketee, G., & Hooley, J. M. (2001). Predicting expressed emotion: A study with families of obsessive-compulsive and agoraphobic outpatients. *Journal of Family Psychology, 15*, 225–240. http://dx.doi.org/10.1037/0893-3200.15.2.225

Chambless, D. L., & Hollon, S. D. (1998). Defining empirically supported therapies. *Journal of Consulting and Clinical Psychology*, 66, 7–18.

Chambless, D. L., & Ollendick, T. H. (2001). Empirically supported psychological interventions: Controversies and evidence. *Annual Review of Psychology, 52*, 685–716. http://dx.doi.org/10.1146/annurev.psych.52.1.685

Christensen, A., & Jacobson, N. S. (1999). *Reconcilable differences*. New York, NY: Guilford Press.

Christensen, A., Wheeler, J. G., Doss, B. D., & Jacobson, N. S. (2014). Couple distress. In D. H. Barlow (Ed.), *Clinical handbook of psychological disorders: A step-by-step treatment manual* (5th ed., pp. 703–731). New York, NY: Guilford Press.

Clark, D. A. (2009). Cognitive behavioral therapy for anxiety and depression: Possibilities and limitations of a transdiagnostic perspective. *Cognitive Behaviour Therapy*, *38*(Suppl. 1), 29–34. http://dx.doi.org/10.1080/16506070902980745

Clark, D. A., & Taylor, S. (2009). The transdiagnostic perspective on cognitive-behavioral therapy for anxiety and depression: New wine for old wineskins? *Journal of Cognitive Psychotherapy*, *23*, 60–66. http://dx.doi.org/10.1891/0889-8391.23.1.60

Classen, C. C., Palesh, O. G., Cavanaugh, C. E., Koopman, C., Kaupp, J. W., Kraemer, H. C., . . . Spiegel, D. (2011). A comparison of trauma-focused and present-focused group therapy for survivors of childhood sexual abuse: A randomized controlled trial. *Psychological Trauma: Theory, Research, Practice, and Policy*, *3*, 84–93. http://dx.doi.org/10.1037/a0020096

Constantino, M. J., & Bernecker, S. L. (2014). Bridging the common factors and empirically supported treatment camps: Comment on Laska, Gurman, and Wampold. *Psychotherapy*, *51*, 505–509. http://dx.doi.org/10.1037/a0036604

Constantino, M. J., Boswell, J. F., Bernecker, S. L., & Castonguay, L. G. (2013). Context-responsive psychotherapy integration as a framework for a unified clinical science: Conceptual and empirical considerations. *Journal of Unified Psychotherapy and Clinical Science*, *2*, 1–20.

Constantino, M., Overtree, C. E., & Bernecker, S. L. (2014). Emerging technologies and innovations in professional psychology training. In N. J. Kaslow & W. B. Johnson (Eds.), *The Oxford handbook on education and training in professional psychology* (pp. 23–34). New York, NY: Oxford University Press.

Coyne, J. C. (1976). Depression and the response of others. *Journal of Abnormal Psychology*, *85*, 186–193. http://dx.doi.org/10.1037/0021-843X.85.2.186

Craske, M. G., & Barlow, D. H. (2014). Panic disorder and agoraphobia. In D. H. Barlow (Ed.), *Clinical handbook of psychological disorders: A step-by-step treatment manual* (5th ed., pp. 1–61). New York, NY: Oxford University Press.

Craske, M. G., Treanor, M., Conway, C. C., Zbozinek, T., & Vervliet, B. (2014). Maximizing exposure therapy: An inhibitory learning approach. *Behaviour Research and Therapy*, *58*, 10–23. http://dx.doi.org/10.1016/j.brat.2014.04.006

Davis, S. D., & Piercy, F. P. (2007a). What clients of couple therapy model developers and their former students say about change, part I: Model-dependent common factors across three models. *Journal of Marital and Family Therapy, 33*, 318–343. http://dx.doi.org/10.1111/j.1752-0606.2007.00030.x

Davis, S. D., & Piercy, F. P. (2007b). What clients of couple therapy model developers and their former students say about change, part II: Model-independent common factors and an integrative framework. *Journal of Marital and Family Therapy, 33*, 344–363. http://dx.doi.org/10.1111/j.1752-0606.2007.00031.x

Dimidjian, S., Martell, C. R., Addis, M. E., Herman-Dunn, R., & Hubley, S. (2014). Behavioral activation for depression. In D. H. Barlow (Ed.), *Clinical handbook of psychological disorders: A step-by-step guide* (5th ed., pp. 353–393). New York, NY: Oxford Press.

Doss, B. D., Benson, L. A., Georgia, E. J., & Christensen, A. (2013). Translation of integrative behavioral couple therapy to a Web-based intervention. *Family Process, 52*, 139–153. http://dx.doi.org/10.1111/famp.12020

Dougherty, D. D., Rauch, S. L., & Jenike, M. A. (2015). Treatments for obsessive-compulsive disorder. In P. Nathan & J. M. Gorman (Eds.), *A guide to treatments that work* (4th ed., pp. 545–570). New York, NY: Oxford University Press.

Duncan, B. L., & Miller, S. D. (2006). Treatment manuals do not improve outcome. In J. Norcross, L. Beutler, & R. Levant (Eds.), *Evidence-based practices in mental health* (pp. 140–148). Washington, DC: American Psychological Association.

Duncan, B. L., Miller, S. D., Wampold, B. E., & Hubble, M. A. (Eds.). (2010). *The heart and soul of change: Delivering what works in therapy*. Washington, DC: American Psychological Association. http://dx.doi.org/10.1037/12075-000

Ehlers, A., & Clark, D. M. (2000). A cognitive model of posttraumatic stress disorder. *Behaviour Research and Therapy, 38*, 319–345. http://dx.doi.org/10.1016/S0005-7967(99)00123-0

Elkin, I. (1994). The NIMH treatment of depression collaborative research program: Where we began and where we are. In A. E. Bergin & S. L. Garfield (Eds.), *Handbook of psychotherapy and behavior change* (4th ed., pp. 114–139). Oxford, England: Wiley.

Elkin, I., Shea, M. T., Watkins, J. T., Imber, S. D., Sotsky, S. M., Collins, J. F., . . . Parloff, M. B. (1989). National Institute of Mental Health Treatment of Depression Collaborative Research Program: General effectiveness of treatments. *Archives of General Psychiatry, 46*, 971–982. http://dx.doi.org/10.1001/archpsyc.1989.01810110013002

Farmer, C. C., Mitchell, K. S., Parker-Guilbert, K., & Galovski, T. E. (2017). Fidelity to the cognitive processing therapy protocol: Evaluation of critical elements. *Behavior Therapy, 48*, 195–206.

Ferster, C. B. (1973). A functional analysis of depression. *American Psychologist, 28*, 857–870. http://dx.doi.org/10.1037/h0035605

Fisch, R., Weakland, J. H., & Segal, L. (1982). *The tactics of change: Doing therapy briefly*. San Francisco, CA: Jossey-Bass.

Fishbane, M. D. (2011). Facilitating relational empowerment in couple therapy. *Family Process, 50*, 337–352. http://dx.doi.org/10.1111/j.1545-5300.2011.01364.x

Foa, E. B., & McLean, C. P. (2016). The efficacy of exposure therapy for anxiety-related disorders and its underlying mechanisms: The case of OCD and PTSD. *Annual Review of Clinical Psychology, 12,* 1–28. http://dx.doi.org/10.1146/annurev-clinpsy-021815-093533

Frank, J. D., & Frank, J. B. (1991). *Persuasion and healing: A comparison study of psychotherapy.* Baltimore, MD: Johns Hopkins University Press.

Franklin, M. E., & Foa, E. B. (2014). Obsessive-compulsive disorder. In D. H. Barlow (Ed.), *Clinical handbook of psychological disorders: A step-by-step treatment manual* (5th ed., pp. 155–205). New York, NY: Oxford University Press.

Fraser, J. S. (1984). Paradox and orthodox: Folie à deux? *Journal of Marital and Family Therapy, 10,* 361–372. http://dx.doi.org/10.1111/j.1752-0606.1984.tb00577.x

Fraser, J. S., Grove, D., Lee, M. Y., Greene, G. J., & Solovey, A. D. (2014). *Integrative family and systems treatment (I-FAST): A strengths-based common factors approach.* New York, NY: Oxford University Press.

Fraser, J. S., & Solovey, A. D. (2004). A catalytic approach to brief sex therapy. In S. Green & D. Flemons (Eds.), *Quickies: The handbook of brief sex therapy* (pp. 189–213). New York, NY: Norton.

Fraser, J. S., & Solovey, A. D. (2007). *Second-order change in psychotherapy: The golden thread that unifies effective treatments.* Washington, DC: American Psychological Association. http://dx.doi.org/10.1037/11499-000

Fraser, J. S., Solovey, A. D., Grove, D., Lee, M. Y., & Greene, G. J. (2012). Integrative families and systems treatment: A middle path toward integrating common and specific factors in evidence-based family therapy. *Journal of Marital and Family Therapy, 38,* 515–528. http://dx.doi.org/10.1111/j.1752-0606.2011.00228.x

Friedlander, M. L., Escudero, V., & Heatherington, L. (2006). *Therapeutic alliances in couple and family therapy: An empirically informed guide to practice.* Washington, DC: American Psychological Association. http://dx.doi.org/10.1037/11410-000

Friedlander, M. L., Escudero, V., Horvath, A. O., Heatherington, L., Cabero, A., & Martens, M. P. (2006). System for observing family therapy alliances: A tool for research and practice. *Journal of Counseling Psychology, 53,* 214–225. http://dx.doi.org/10.1037/0022-0167.53.2.214

Frost, N. D., Laska, K. M., & Wampold, B. E. (2014). The evidence for present-centered therapy as a treatment for posttraumatic stress disorder. *Journal of Traumatic Stress, 27,* 1–8. http://dx.doi.org/10.1002/jts.21881

Gelo, O. C., & Salvatore, S. (2016). A dynamic systems approach to psychotherapy: A meta-theoretical framework for explaining psychotherapy change processes. *Journal of Counseling Psychology, 63,* 379–395. http://dx.doi.org/10.1037/cou0000150

Gendlin, E. T. (1962). *Experiencing and the creation of meaning.* New York, NY: Free Press.

Gergen, K. J. (1985). The social constructionist movement in modern psychology. *American Psychologist, 40,* 266–275. http://dx.doi.org/10.1037/0003-066X.40.3.266

Gergen, K. J. (2014). Pursuing excellence in qualitative inquiry. *Qualitative Psychology, 1*, 49–60. http://dx.doi.org/10.1037/qup0000002

Gergen, K. J. (2015a). *An invitation to social construction* (3rd ed.). Los Angeles, CA: Sage.

Gergen, K. J. (2015b). The quantitative/qualitative distinction: Blessed are the impure. *Qualitative Psychology, 2*, 210–213. http://dx.doi.org/10.1037/qup0000034

Gergen, K. J., Josselson, R., & Freeman, M. (2015). The promises of qualitative inquiry. *American Psychologist, 70*, 1–9. http://dx.doi.org/10.1037/a0038597

Gleick, J. (1987). *Chaos: The making of a new science*. New York, NY: Viking.

Goffman, E. (1974). *Frame analysis: An essay on the organization of experience*. Cambridge, MA: Harvard University Press.

Goldenberg, H., & Goldenberg, I. (2012). *Family therapy: An overview*. Belmont, CA: Brooks/Cole.

Goodheart, C. (2004). Evidence-based practice and the endeavor of psychotherapy. *The Independent Practitioner, 24*, 1–9.

Gortner, E. T., Gollan, J. K., Dobson, K. S., & Jacobson, N. S. (1998). Cognitive-behavioral treatment for depression: Relapse prevention. *Journal of Consulting and Clinical Psychology, 66*, 377–384. http://dx.doi.org/10.1037/0022-006X.66.2.377

Gottman, J. M. (1999). *The marriage clinic: A scientifically-based marital therapy*. New York, NY: Norton.

Gottman, J. M. (2000). *Clinical manual for marital therapy*. Seattle, WA: Gottman Institute.

Gottman, J. M., & DeClaire, J. (2001). *The relationship cure: A five-step guide for building better connections with family, friends, and lovers*. New York, NY: Three Rivers Press.

Gottman, J. M., & Gottman, J. S. (2008). *And baby makes three: The six-step plan for preserving marital intimacy and rekindling romance after baby arrives*. New York, NY: Three Rivers Press.

Gould, S. J. (1977). *Ever since Darwin: Reflection in natural history* (N. York, Trans.). New York, NY: Norton.

Gould, S. J. (1990). *Wonderful life: The burgess shale and the nature of history*. New York, NY: Norton.

Green, R. J., & Herget, M. (1991). Outcomes of systemic/strategic team consultation: III. The importance of therapist warmth and active structuring. *Family Process, 30*, 321–336. http://dx.doi.org/10.1111/j.1545-5300.1991.00321.x

Greenberg, L. S. (2002). *Emotion-focused therapy: Coaching clients to work through their feelings*. Washington, DC: American Psychological Association.

Greenberg, L. S. (2010). Emotion-focused therapy: A clinical synthesis. *Focus, 8*, 32–42.

Greenberg, L. S. (2015). *Emotion-focused therapy: Coaching clients to work through their feelings* (2nd ed.). Washington, DC: American Psychological Association.

Greenberg, L. S., & Johnson, S. M. (1988). *Emotionally focused therapy for couples*. New York, NY: Guilford Press.

Greenberg, L. S., Rice, L., & Elliott, R. (1993). *Process-experiential therapy: Facilitating emotional change*. New York, NY: Guilford Press.

Greenberg, L. S., & Watson, J. C. (2006). *Emotion-focused therapy for depression*. Washington, DC: American Psychological Association. http://dx.doi.org/10.1037/11286-000

Greene, R. W. (2001). *The explosive child*. New York, NY: HarperCollins.

Greene, R. W. (2014). *The explosive child: A new approach for understanding and parenting easily frustrated, chronically inflexible children*. New York, NY: Harper Collins.

Greene, R. W., Ablon, J. S., Goring, J. C., Fazio, V., & Morse, L. R. (2004). Treatment of oppositional defiant disorder in children and adolescents. In P. Barrett & T. H. Ollendick (Eds.), *Handbook of interventions that work with children and adolescents: Prevention and treatment* (pp. 369–393). Chichester, England: Wiley. http://dx.doi.org/10.1002/9780470753385.ch16

Greene, R. W., Ablon, J. S., Goring, J. C., Raezer-Blakely, L., Markey, J., Monuteaux, M. C., . . . Rabbitt, S. (2004). Effectiveness of collaborative problem solving in affectively dysregulated children with oppositional-defiant disorder: Initial findings. *Journal of Consulting and Clinical Psychology, 72*, 1157–1164. http://dx.doi.org/10.1037/0022-006X.72.6.1157

Greenman, P. S., & Johnson, S. M. (2013). Process research on emotionally focused therapy (EFT) for couples: Linking theory to practice. *Family Process, 52*, 46–61. http://dx.doi.org/10.1111/famp.12015

Gurman, A. S. (2013). Functions and factions: A reflection on possibilities for couple therapy integration. *Journal of Marital and Family Therapy, 39*, 424–426. http://dx.doi.org/10.1111/jmft.12037

Hayes, S. C. (2016). *The most crucial thing for our modern world*. Retrieved from https://www.praxiscet.com/blog/most-crucial-thing-our-modern-world

Hayes, S. C., Pistorello, J., & Levin, M. E. (2012). Acceptance and commitment therapy as a unified model of behavior change. *The Counseling Psychologist, 40*, 976–1002. http://dx.doi.org/10.1177/0011000012460836

Hayes, S. C., Strosahl, K. D., & Wilson, K. G. (2012). *Acceptance and commitment therapy: The process and practice of mindful change*. New York, NY: Guilford Press.

Heimberg, R. G., & Magee, L. (2014). Social anxiety disorder. In D. H. Barlow (Ed.), *Handbook of psychological disorders: A step-by-step treatment manual* (5th ed., pp. 114–154). New York, NY: Guilford Press.

Hembree, E. A., Foa, E. B., Dorfan, N. M., Street, G. P., Kowalski, J., & Tu, X. (2003). Do patients drop out prematurely from exposure therapy for PTSD? *Journal of Traumatic Stress, 16*, 555–562. http://dx.doi.org/10.1023/B:JOTS.0000004078.93012.7d

Henggeler, S. W., Schoenwald, S. K., Borduin, C. M., Rowland, M. D., & Cunningham, P. B. (2009). *Multisystemic therapy for antisocial behavior in children and adolescents*. New York, NY: Guilford Press.

Henriques, G. R. (2003). The tree of knowledge system and the theoretical unification of psychology. *Review of General Psychology, 7*, 150–182. http://dx.doi.org/10.1037/1089-2680.7.2.150

Henriques, G. R. (2008). Special Section: The problem of psychology and the integration of human knowledge: Contrasting Wilson's consilience with the tree of knowledge system. *Theory & Psychology, 18*, 731–756. http://dx.doi.org/10.1177/0959354308097255

Henriques, G. R. (2017). Achieving a unified clinical science requires a metatheoretical solution: Comment on Melchert (2016). *American Psychologist, 72*, 393–394. http://dx.doi.org/10.1037/amp0000143

Hooley, J. M. (2004). Do psychiatric patients do better clinically if they live with certain kinds of families? *Current Directions in Psychological Science, 13*, 202–205. http://dx.doi.org/10.1111/j.0963-7214.2004.00308.x

Hooley, J. M. (2007). Expressed emotion and relapse of psychopathology. *Annual Review of Clinical Psychology, 3*, 329–352. http://dx.doi.org/10.1146/annurev.clinpsy.2.022305.095236

Hubble, M. A., Duncan, B. L., & Miller, S. D. (Eds.). (1999). *The heart and soul of change: What works in therapy*. Washington, DC: American Psychological Association. http://dx.doi.org/10.1037/11132-000

Huey, S. J., Jr., Tilley, J. L., Jones, E. O., & Smith, C. A. (2014). The contribution of cultural competence to evidence-based care for ethnically diverse populations. *Annual Review of Clinical Psychology, 10*, 305–338. http://dx.doi.org/10.1146/annurev-clinpsy-032813-153729

Imel, Z. E., Laska, K., Jakupcak, M., & Simpson, T. L. (2013). Meta-analysis of dropout in treatments for posttraumatic stress disorder. *Journal of Consulting and Clinical Psychology, 81*, 394–404.

Institute of Medicine. (2001). *Crossing the quality chasm: A new health system for the 21st century*. New York, NY: National Academy Press.

Jackson, M. R. (2015a). The purity and impurity of paradigms: Response to Gergen (2015) and Madill (2015). *Qualitative Psychology, 2*, 221–225. http://dx.doi.org/10.1037/qup0000027

Jackson, M. R. (2015b). Resistance to qual/quant parity: Why the "paradigm" discussion can't be avoided. *Qualitative Psychology, 2*, 181–198. http://dx.doi.org/10.1037/qup0000031

Jackson, M. R. (2017). Unified clinical science, or paradigm diversity? Comment on Melchert (2016). *American Psychologist, 72*, 395–396. http://dx.doi.org/10.1037/amp0000125

Jacobson, N. S., & Christensen, A. (1996). *Integrative couple therapy: Promoting acceptance and change*. New York, NY: Norton.

Jacobson, N. S., Christensen, A., Prince, S. E., Cordova, J., & Eldridge, K. (2000). Integrative behavioral couple therapy: An acceptance-based, promising new treatment for couple discord. *Journal of Consulting and Clinical Psychology, 68*, 351–355. http://dx.doi.org/10.1037/0022-006X.68.2.351

Jacobson, N. S., Dobson, K. S., Truax, P. A., Addis, M. E., Koerner, K., Gollan, J. K., . . . Prince, S. E. (1996). A component analysis of cognitive-behavioral treatment for depression. *Journal of Consulting and Clinical Psychology*, *64*, 295–304. http://dx.doi.org/10.1037/0022-006X.64.2.295

Johnson, M. (2008). Philosophy's debt to metaphor. In R. W. Gibbs, Jr. (Ed.), *The Cambridge handbook of metaphor and thought* (pp. 39–52). New York, NY: Cambridge University Press. http://dx.doi.org/10.1017/CBO9780511816802.004

Johnson, S. M. (1996). *The practice of emotionally focused marital therapy: Creating connection*. New York, NY: Brunner/Mazel.

Johnson, S. M. (2004). *The practice of emotionally focused marital therapy: Creating connection* (2nd ed.). New York, NY: Brunner-Routledge.

Johnson, S. M. (2016). *Emotionally focused therapy for couples: Key concepts*. Retrieved from http://www.holdmetight.com and http://www.iceeft.com

Johnson, S. M., & Talitman, E. (1997). Predictors of success in emotionally focused therapy. *Journal of Marital and Family Therapy*, *23*, 135–152.

Joseph, S. (2017). The problem of choosing between irreconcilable theoretical orientations: Comment on Melchert (2016). *American Psychologist*, *72*, 397–398. http://dx.doi.org/10.1037/amp0000134

Karlin, B. E., Ruzek, J. I., Chard, K. M., Eftekhari, A., Monson, C. M., Hembree, E. A., . . . Foa, E. B. (2010). Dissemination of evidence-based psychological treatments for posttraumatic stress disorder in the Veterans Health Administration. *Journal of Traumatic Stress*, *23*, 663–673.

Kazdin, A. D. (2002). Psychosocial treatments for conduct disorder in children and adolescents. In P. Nathan & M. Gorman (Eds.), *A guide to treatments that work* (2nd ed., pp. 57–86). New York, NY: Oxford University Press.

Keller, M. B., McCullough, J. P., Klein, D. N., Arnow, B., Dunner, D. L., Gelenberg, A. J., . . . Zajecka, J. (2000). A comparison of nefazodone, the cognitive behavioral-analysis system of psychotherapy, and their combination for the treatment of chronic depression. *The New England Journal of Medicine*, *342*, 1462–1470. http://dx.doi.org/10.1056/NEJM200005183422001

Kelly, G. A. (1955). *The psychology of personal constructs: Vol. 1. A theory of personality*. New York, NY: Norton.

Kessler, R. C., Chiu, W. T., Demler, O., Merikangas, K. R., & Walters, E. E. (2005). Prevalence, severity, and comorbidity of 12-month *DSM–IV* disorders in the National Comorbidity Survey Replication [correction appears in *Archives of General Psychiatry* (2005), 62, 709]. *Archives of General Psychiatry*, *62*, 617–627. http://dx.doi.org/10.1001/archpsyc.62.6.617

Kessler, R. C., McGonagle, K. A., Zhao, S., Nelson, C. B., Hughes, M., Eshleman, S., . . . Kendler, K. S. (1994). Lifetime and 12-month prevalence of *DSM–III–R* psychiatric disorders in the United States. Results from the National Comorbidity Survey. *Archives of General Psychiatry*, *51*, 8–19. http://dx.doi.org/10.1001/archpsyc.1994.03950010008002

Kihlstrom, J. F. (2006). Scientific research. In J. C. Norcross, L. E. Beutler, & R. F. Levant (Eds.), *Evidence-based practices in mental health: Debate and dialogue on the fundamental questions* (pp. 23–30). Washington, DC: American Psychological Association.

Kim, Y. W., Lee, S. H., Choi, T. K., Suh, S. Y., Kim, B., Kim, C. M., . . . Yook, K. H. (2009). Effectiveness of mindfulness-based cognitive therapy as an adjuvant to pharmacotherapy in patients with panic disorder or generalized anxiety disorder. *Depression and Anxiety, 26,* 601–606. http://dx.doi.org/10.1002/da.20552

Klein, D. F., & Ross, D. C. (1993). Reanalysis of the national institute of mental health treatment of depression collaborative research program general effectiveness report. *Neuropsychopharmacology, 8,* 241–251. http://dx.doi.org/10.1038/npp.1993.27

Klerman, G., Weissman, M., Rounsaville, B., & Chevron, E. (1984). *Interpersonal psychotherapy of depression.* New York, NY: Basic Books.

Kramer, U., & Stiles, W. B. (2015). The responsiveness problem in psychotherapy: A review of proposed solutions. *Clinical Psychology: Science and Practice, 22,* 277–295. http://dx.doi.org/10.1111/cpsp.12107

Krupnick, J. L., Elkin, I., Collins, J., Simmens, S., Sotsky, S. M., Pilkonis, P. A., & Watkins, J. T. (1994). Therapeutic alliance and clinical outcome in the NIMH treatment of depression collaborative research program: Preliminary findings. *Psychotherapy: Theory, Research, & Practice, 31,* 28–35. http://dx.doi.org/10.1037/0033-3204.31.1.28

Kuhn, T. S. (1976). *The structure of scientific revolutions* (2nd ed.). Chicago, IL: University of Chicago Press.

Kupfer, D. J., First, M. B., & Regier, D. A. (Eds.). (2008). *A research agenda for* DSM–V. Arlington, VA: American Psychiatric Publishing.

Lakoff, G. (1993). *The contemporary theory of metaphor.* New York, NY: Cambridge University Press. http://dx.doi.org/10.1017/CBO9781139173865.013

Lakoff, G. (2014). *The all new don't think of an elephant!: Know your values and frame the debate.* White River Junction, VT: Chelsea Green.

Lakoff, G., & Johnson, M. (2008). *Metaphors we live by.* Chicago, IL: University of Chicago Press.

Lambert, M. J. (1992). Psychotherapy outcome research: Implications for integrative and eclectical therapists. In J. C. Norcross & S. L. Garfield (Eds.), *Handbook of psychotherapy integration* (pp. 94–129). New York, NY: Basic Books.

Lambert, M. J. (2013). *Bergin and Garfield's handbook of psychotherapy and behavior change.* New York, NY: Wiley.

Landrum, B., & Garza, G. (2015a). Mending fences: Defining the domains and approaches of quantitative and qualitative research. *Qualitative Psychology, 2,* 199–209. http://dx.doi.org/10.1037/qup0000030

Landrum, B., & Garza, G. (2015b). A reply to Gergen (2015) and Madill (2015). *Qualitative Psychology, 2*, 226–228. http://dx.doi.org/10.1037/qup0000029

Lang, P. J. (1977). Imagery in therapy: An information processing analysis of fear. *Behavior Therapy, 8*, 862–886. http://dx.doi.org/10.1016/S0005-7894(77)80157-3

Laska, K. M., Gurman, A. S., & Wampold, B. E. (2014). Expanding the lens of evidence-based practice in psychotherapy: A common factors perspective. *Psychotherapy, 51*, 467–481. http://dx.doi.org/10.1037/a0034332

Laska, K. M., & Wampold, B. E. (2014). Ten things to remember about common factor theory. *Psychotherapy, 51*, 519–524. http://dx.doi.org/10.1037/a0038245

Lebow, J. (2014). *Couple and family therapy: An integrative map of the territory*. Washington, DC: American Psychological Association. http://dx.doi.org/10.1037/14255-000

Lee, M. Y., Greene, G. J., Fraser, J. S., Edwards, S. G., Grove, D., Solovey, A. D., & Scott, P. (2013). Common and specific factors approaches to home-based treatment: I-FAST and MST. *Research on Social Work Practice, 23*, 407–418. http://dx.doi.org/10.1177/1049731513483181

Lee, M. Y., Greene, G. J., Hsu, K. S., Solovey, A., Grove, D., Fraser, J. S., . . . Teater, B. (2009). Utilizing family strengths and resilience: Integrative family and systems treatment with children and adolescents with severe emotional and behavioral problems. *Family Process, 48*, 395–416. http://dx.doi.org/10.1111/j.1545-5300.2009.01291.x

Lee, M. Y., Hsu, K., Liu, C., Greene, G. J., Fraser, J. S., Grove, D., . . . Scott, P. (2016). Treatment efficacy of integrative family and systems treatment (I-FAST) with and without consultation: The role of model training in the sustainability of evidence-based family treatments. *Administration and Policy in Mental Health, 43*, 579–591.

Lee, M. Y., Teater, B., Greene, G. J., Solovey, A. D., Grove, D., Fraser, J. S., . . . Hsu, K. S. (2012). Key processes, ingredients and components of successful systems collaboration: Working with severely emotionally or behaviorally disturbed children and their families. *Administration and Policy in Mental Health Services Research, 39*, 394–405. http://dx.doi.org/10.1007/s10488-011-0358-8

Lee, M. Y., Teater, B., Hsu, K. S., Greene, G. J., Fraser, J. S., Solovey, A. D., & Grove, D. (2013). Systems collaboration with schools and treatment of severely emotionally disturbed children or adolescents. *Children & Schools, 35*, 155–168. http://dx.doi.org/10.1093/cs/cdt013

Lewinsohn, P. M. (1974). Clinical and theoretical aspects of depression. *Innovative Treatment Methods in Psychopathology* (pp. 63–120). New York, NY: Wiley.

Lewinsohn, P. M., & Gotlib, I. H. (1995). Behavioral theory and treatment of depression. In E. E. Beckham & W. R. Leber (Eds.), *Handbook of depression* (2nd ed., pp. 352–375). New York, NY: Guilford Press.

Liddle, H. (2015). Multidimensional family therapy. In T. L. Sexton & J. L. Lebow (Eds.), *Handbook of family therapy* (pp. 231–249). New York, NY: Routledge.

Linehan, M. (1993). *Cognitive-behavioral treatment of borderline personality disorder.* New York, NY: Guilford Press.

Madill, A. (2015). Qualitative research is not a paradigm: Commentary on Jackson (2015) and Landrum and Garza (2015). *Qualitative Psychology, 2,* 214–220.

Mandelbrot, B. (1982). *The fractal geometry of nature.* San Francisco, CA: W. H. Freeman.

Markowitz, J. C. (2004). *Interpersonal psychotherapy for dysthymic disorder.* New York, NY: American Psychiatric Publishing.

Martell, C. R., Dimidjian, S., & Herman-Dunn, R. (2013). *Behavioral activation for depression: A clinician's guide.* New York, NY: Guilford Press.

Masters, W. H., & Johnson, V. E. (1970). *Human sexual inadequacy.* New York, NY: Little, Brown.

Masters, W. H., & Johnson, V. E. (1976). Principles of the new sex therapy. *The American Journal of Psychiatry, 133,* 548–554. http://dx.doi.org/10.1176/ajp.133.5.548

May, R. (1967). *Existential psychotherapy: Six talks for CBC radio.* Ontario, Canada: Canadian Broadcasting Corporation.

McCullough, J. P. (2000). *Treatment for chronic depression: Cognitive behavioral analysis system of psychotherapy.* New York, NY: Guilford Press.

McDonagh, A., Friedman, M., McHugo, G., Ford, J., Sengupta, A., Mueser, K., . . . Descamps, M. (2005). Randomized trial of cognitive-behavioral therapy for chronic posttraumatic stress disorder in adult female survivors of childhood sexual abuse. *Journal of Consulting and Clinical Psychology, 73,* 515–524. http://dx.doi.org/10.1037/0022-006X.73.3.515

Melchert, T. P. (2016). Leaving behind our preparadigmatic past: Professional psychology as a unified clinical science. *American Psychologist, 71,* 486–496.

Mesle, C. R. (2008). *Process-relational philosophy: An introduction to Alfred North Whitehead.* West Conshohocken, PA: Templeton Foundation Press.

Messer, S. B. (2006). Patient values and preferences. In J. Norcross, L. Beutler, & R. Levant (Eds.), *Evidence-based practices in mental health* (pp. 31–39). Washington, DC: American Psychological Association.

Miller, W. R., & Rollnick, S. (2012). *Motivational interviewing: Helping people change.* New York, NY: Guilford Press.

Milrod, B. (1997). *Manual of panic-focused psychodynamic psychotherapy.* Arlington, VA: American Psychiatric Publishing.

Monson, C. M., Resick, P. A., & Rizvi, S. L. (2014). Posttraumatic stress disorder. In D. H. Barlow (Ed.), *Handbook of psychological disorders: A step-by-step treatment manual* (5th ed., pp. 62–113). New York, NY: Oxford Press.

Moses, E. B., & Barlow, D. H. (2006). A new unified treatment approach for emotional disorders based on emotion science. *Current Directions in Psychological Science, 15,* 146–150. http://dx.doi.org/10.1111/j.0963-7214.2006.00425.x

Mowrer, O. (1950). *Learning theory and personality dynamics: Selected papers*. New York, NY: Ronald Press.

Mowrer, O. (1960). *Learning theory and behavior*. New York, NY: John Wiley & Sons Inc.

Nathan, P. E., & Gorman, J. M. (Eds.). (2002). *A guide to treatments that work* (2nd ed.). New York, NY: Oxford University Press.

Nathan, P. E., & Gorman, J. M. (Eds.). (2015). *A guide to treatments that work* (3rd ed.). New York, NY: Oxford University Press. http://dx.doi.org/10.1093/med:psych/9780199342211.001.0001

National Institute of Mental Health. (2015). *Major depression among adults*. Retrieved from https://www.nimh.nih.gov/health/statistics/prevalence/major-depression-among-adults.shtml

Norcross, J. C. (2002). *Psychotherapy relationships that work: Therapist contributions and responsiveness to patients*. New York, NY: Oxford University Press.

Norcross, J. C. (Ed.). (2011). *Psychotherapy relationships that work: Evidence-based responsiveness*. New York, NY: Oxford University Press. http://dx.doi.org/10.1093/acprof:oso/9780199737208.001.0001

Norcross, J. C., & Beutler, L. E. (2014). Evidence-based relationships and responsiveness for depression and substance abuse. In D. H. Barlow (Ed.), *Clinical handbook of psychological disorders: A step-by-step treatment manual* (5th ed., pp. 617–639). New York, NY: Guilford Press.

Norcross, J. C., Beutler, L. E., & Levant, R. F. (Eds.). (2006). *Evidence-based practices in mental health: Debate and dialogue on the fundamental questions*. Washington, DC: American Psychological Association. http://dx.doi.org/10.1037/11265-000

Owen, J., & Hilsenroth, M. J. (2014). Treatment adherence: The importance of therapist flexibility in relation to therapy outcomes. *Journal of Counseling Psychology*, *61*, 280–288. http://dx.doi.org/10.1037/a0035753

Payne, L., Ellard, K., Farchione, T., Fairholme, C., & Barlow, D. (2014). Emotional disorders: A unified transdiagnostic protocol. In D. H. Barlow (Ed.), *Clinical handbook of psychological disorders: A step-by-step treatment manual* (pp. 237–274). New York, NY: Guilford Press.

Perls, F., Hefferline, G., & Goodman, P. (1951). *Gestalt therapy: Excitement and growth in human personality*. New York, NY: Delta.

Piaget, J. (1950). *The psychology of intelligence*. New York, NY: Routledge.

Piaget, J. (1997). *The moral judgement of the child*. New York, NY: Simon & Schuster.

Progress monitoring and feedback [special issue]. (2015, December). *Psychotherapy*, *52*.

Pukay-Martin, N. D., Torbit, L., Landy, M. S. H., Macdonald, A., & Monson, C. M. (2017). Present- and trauma-focused cognitive-behavioral conjoint therapy for posttraumatic stress disorder: A case study. *Couple & Family Psychology: Research and Practice*, 6, 61–78. http://dx.doi.org/10.1037/cfp0000071

Reed, G. M. (2006). Clinical expertise. In J. C. Norcross, L. E. Beutler, & R. F. Levant (Eds.), *Evidence-based practice in mental health: Debate and dialogue on the fundamental questions* (pp. 13–55). Washington, DC: American Psychological Association. http://dx.doi.org/10.1037/11265-001

Rehm, L. P. (1977). A self-control model of depression. *Behavior Therapy*, 8, 787–804. http://dx.doi.org/10.1016/S0005-7894(77)80150-0

Rescher, N. (1996). *Process metaphysics: An introduction to process philosophy*. Albany, NY: SUNY Press.

Resick, P. A., Monson, C. M., & Chard, K. M. (2007). *Cognitive processing therapy: Veteran/military version*. Washington, DC: Department of Veterans Affairs.

Roemer, L., & Orsillo, S. M. (2014). An acceptance-based behavioral therapy for generalized anxiety disorder. In D. H. Barlow (Ed.), *Clinical handbook of psychological disorders: A step-by-step treatment manual* (5th ed., pp. 206–236). New York, NY: Oxford University Press.

Rogers, C. (1961). *On becoming a person: A therapist's view of psychotherapy*. New York, NY: Houghton Mifflin Harcourt.

Rosenzweig, S. (1936). Some implicit common factors in diverse methods of psychotherapy. *American Journal of Orthopsychiatry*, 6, 412–415. http://dx.doi.org/10.1111/j.1939-0025.1936.tb05248.x

Schnurr, P. P., Friedman, M. J., Engel, C. C., Foa, E. B., Shea, M. T., Chow, B. K., . . . Bernardy, N. (2007). Cognitive behavioral therapy for posttraumatic stress disorder in women: A randomized controlled trial. *JAMA*, *297*, 820–830. http://dx.doi.org/10.1001/jama.297.8.820

Schnurr, P. P., Friedman, M. J., Foy, D. W., Shea, M. T., Hsieh, F. Y., Lavori, P. W., . . . Bernardy, N. C. (2003). Randomized trial of trauma-focused group therapy for posttraumatic stress disorder: Results from a department of Veterans Affairs cooperative study. *Archives of General Psychiatry*, 60, 481–489. http://dx.doi.org/10.1001/archpsyc.60.5.481

Segal, Z., Williams, J., & Teasdale, J. (2002). *Mindfulness-based cognitive therapy for depression: A new approach to relapse prevention*. New York, NY: Guilford Press.

Seligman, M. E. (2011). *Learned optimism: How to change your mind and your life*. New York, NY: Vintage Books.

Sexton, T. L., & Alexander, J. F. (2015). Functional family therapy. In T. L. Sexton & J. L. Lebow (Eds.), *Handbook of family therapy* (pp. 250–270). New York, NY: Routledge.

Shadish, W. R., & Baldwin, S. A. (2003). Meta-analysis of MFT interventions. *Journal of Marital and Family Therapy*, *29*, 547–570. http://dx.doi.org/10.1111/j.1752-0606.2003.tb01694.x

Shadish, W. R., & Baldwin, S. A. (2005). Effects of behavioral marital therapy: A meta-analysis of randomized controlled trials. *Journal of Consulting and Clinical Psychology*, *73*, 6–14. http://dx.doi.org/10.1037/0022-006X.73.1.6

Shapiro, F. (1989). Eye movement desensitization: A new treatment for post-traumatic stress disorder. *Journal of Behavior Therapy and Experimental Psychiatry*, *20*, 211–217. http://dx.doi.org/10.1016/0005-7916(89)90025-6

Shapiro, F., & Forrest, M. (2001). *EMDR: Eye movement desensitization and reprocessing*. New York, NY: Guilford Press.

Shapiro, F., & Maxfield, L. (2002). Eye movement desensitization and reprocessing (EMDR): Information processing in the treatment of trauma. *Journal of Clinical Psychology*, *58*, 933–946. http://dx.doi.org/10.1002/jclp.10068

Simon, H. A. (1985). Human nature in politics: The dialogue of psychology with political science. *The American Political Science Review*, *79*, 293–304. http://dx.doi.org/10.2307/1956650

Skinner, B. F. (1953). *Science and human behavior*. New York, NY: Simon & Schuster.

Snyder, C. R., Michael, S. T., & Cheavens, J. S. (1999). Hope as a psychotherapeutic foundation of common factors, placebos, and expectancies. In M. A. Hubble, B. L. Duncan, & S. D. Miller (Eds.), *The heart and soul of change: What works in therapy* (pp. 179–200). Washington, DC: American Psychological Association. http://dx.doi.org/10.1037/11132-005

Snyder, M., & Thomsen, C. J. (1988). Interactions between therapists and clients: Hypothesis testing and behavioral confirmation. In D. C. Turk & P. Salovey (Eds.), *Reasoning, inference, and judgment in clinical psychology* (pp. 124–152). New York, NY: Free Press.

Sprenkle, D. H., Davis, S. D., & Lebow, J. L. (2009). *Common factors in couple and family therapy: The overlooked foundation for effective practice*. New York, NY: Guilford Press.

Stiles, W. B., Honos-Webb, L., & Surko, M. (1998). Responsiveness in psychotherapy. *Clinical Psychology: Science and Practice*, *5*, 439–458. http://dx.doi.org/10.1111/j.1468-2850.1998.tb00166.x

Substance Abuse and Mental Health Administration. (2016). SAMHSA's national registry of evidence-based programs and practices. Retrieved from http://www.nrepp.samhsa.gov

Sullivan, H. S. (1953). *The collected works*. New York, NY: Norton.

Swift, J. K., Callahan, J. L., & Vollmer, B. M. (2011). Preferences. *Journal of Clinical Psychology*, *67*, 155–165. http://dx.doi.org/10.1002/jclp.20759

Szapocznik, J., Muir, J. A., Duff, J. H., Schwartz, S. J., & Brown, C. H. (2015). Brief Strategic Family Therapy: Implementing evidence-based models in community settings. *Psychotherapy Research*, *25*, 121–133. http://dx.doi.org/10.1080/10503307.2013.856044

Tryon, W. W. (2016). Psychotherapy integration via theoretical unification. *International Journal of Integrative Psychotherapy*, *7*, 1–26.

Tryon, W. W. (2017). Basing clinical practice on unified psychological science: Comment on Melchert (2016). *American Psychologist*, *72*, 399–400. http://dx.doi.org/10.1037/amp0000133

Turk, C. L., Heimberg, R. G., & Hope, D. A. (2001). Social anxiety disorder. In D. H. Barlow (Ed.), *Clinical handbook of psychological disorders: A step-by-step treatment manual* (pp. 114–153). New York, NY: Guilford Press.

Veroff, J., Kulka, R. W., & Douvan, W. (1981). *Mental health in America: Patterns of help-seeking from 1957–1976*. New York, NY: Basic Books.

Wampold, B. E. (2001). *The great psychotherapy debate: Models, methods, and findings*. Mahwah, NJ: Erlbaum.

Wampold, B. E. (2006). Not a scintilla of evidence to support empirically supported treatments a more effective than other treatments. In J. Norcross, L. Beutler, & R. Levant (Eds.), *Evidence-based practices in mental health* (pp. 299–307). Washington, DC: American Psychological Association.

Wampold, B. E., & Imel, Z. E. (2015a). *The great psychotherapy debate: The evidence for what makes psychotherapy work* (2nd ed.). New York, NY: Routledge/Taylor & Francis.

Wampold, B. E., & Imel, Z. E. (2015b, March). *What do we know about psychotherapy?—and what is there left to debate?* Retrieved from the Society for Advancement of Psychotherapy website: http://www.societyforpsychotherapy.org/what-do-we-know-about-psychotherapy-and-what-is-there-left-to-debate

Wampold, B. E., Imel, Z. E., Laska, K. M., Benish, S., Miller, S. D., Flückiger, C., . . . Budge, S. (2010). Determining what works in the treatment of PTSD. *Clinical Psychology Review, 30*, 923–933. http://dx.doi.org/10.1016/j.cpr.2010.06.005

Wampold, B. E., Mondin, G. W., Moody, M., Stich, F., Benson, K., & Ahn, H. (1997). A meta-analysis of outcome studies comparing bona fide psychotherapies: Empirically, "all must have prizes." *Psychological Bulletin, 122*, 203–215. http://dx.doi.org/10.1037/0033-2909.122.3.203

Watters, E. (2010). *Crazy like us: The globalization of the American psyche*. New York, NY: Simon & Schuster.

Watzlawick, P., Beavin, J. H., & Jackson, D. D. (1967). *Pragmatics of human communication: A study of interactional patterns, pathologies, and paradoxes*. New York, NY: Norton.

Watzlawick, P., Weakland, J. H., & Fisch, R. (1974). *Change: Principles of problem formation and problem resolution*. New York, NY: Norton.

Webb, C. A., DeRubeis, R. J., & Barber, J. P. (2010). Therapist adherence/competence and treatment outcome: A meta-analytic review. *Journal of Consulting and Clinical Psychology, 78*, 200–211. http://dx.doi.org/10.1037/a0018912

White, M., & Epston, D. (1990). *Narrative means to therapeutic ends*. New York, NY: Norton.

Whitehead, A. N. (1978). *Process and reality: An essay in cosmology*. New York, NY: Free Press.

Whitehead, A. N., & Russell, B. (1912). *Principia mathematica* (2nd ed., Vols. 1–3). Cambridge, England: Cambridge University Press.

Wile, D. B. (2013). Opening the circle of pursuit and distance. *Family Process, 52*, 19–32. http://dx.doi.org/10.1111/famp.12004

Wittgenstein, L. (1951). *Tractus logico-philosophicus*. New York, NY: Humanities Press.

Wood, N. D., Crane, D. R., Schaalje, G. B., & Law, D. D. (2005). What works for whom: A meta-analytic review of marital and couples therapy in reference to marital distress. *American Journal of Family Therapy*, *33*, 273–287. http://dx.doi.org/10.1080/01926180590962147

World Health Organization. (1993). *International statistical classification of diseases and related health problems* (10th rev.; *ICD–10)*. Geneva, Switzerland: Author.

Yalom, I. D. (1980). *Existential psychotherapy*. New York, NY: Basic Books.

Young, J. E., Weinberger, A. D., & Beck, A. T. (2001). Cognitive therapy for depression. In D. H. Barlow (Ed.), *Clinical handbook of psychological disorders: A step-by-step treatment manual* (3rd ed., pp. 264–308). New York, NY: Oxford University Press.

INDEX

ABOUT THE AUTHOR

J. Scott Fraser, PhD, is a clinical psychologist with nearly 40 years of clinical practice, supervision, training, and academic teaching. He has served as director of internship training, associate dean, and director of clinical training and as professor of clinical psychology in the nationally ranked and pioneering doctoral program in the School of Professional Psychology at Wright State University in Dayton, Ohio. Before that, he was director of a crisis/brief therapy center in a large general hospital setting for 14 years. He is a Diplomate in Family Therapy through the American Board of Professional Psychology and an approved supervisor in the founders' track of the American Association for Marital and Family Therapy. Dr. Fraser has presented and trained therapists in the United States, Europe, and Asia, and his recent writing focuses on integrating evidence-based approaches to psychotherapy. A companion DVD titled *The Process of Change in Integrative Psychotherapy*, which uses the process model described in this book, is available from APA in the Systems of Psychotherapy Video Series. Dr. Fraser coauthored *Integrative Families and Systems Treatment (I-FAST): A Strengths-Based Common Factors Approach* (2014), which represents the first research-based manual for teaching and practicing a moderated common factors approach to at-risk youth and families in community settings. His related book, coauthored with Andrew D. Solovey, *Second-Order Change in Psychotherapy: The Golden Thread That Unifies Effective Treatments* (2007), applies this integrative model across all evidence-supported approaches to psychotherapy. Now serving as emeritus professor, Dr. Fraser continues to write, train, and supervise through these models.